Teach...
Inspire...
Lead...

**With REA's MTEL
English test prep, you'll
be in a class all your own.**

We'd like to hear from you!
*Visit **www.rea.com** to send us your comments*
*or e-mail us at **info@rea.com**.*

Research & Education Association

The Best Teachers' Test Preparation for the

MTEL™
English (07)

 TestWare® Edition

Audrey A. Friedman, Ph.D.
Boston College
Chestnut Hill, MA

For updates to the test or this book visit:
www.REA.com/MTEL/mteleng.htm

Research & Education Association
61 Ethel Road West
Piscataway, New Jersey 08854
E-mail: info@rea.com

The Best Teachers' Test Preparation for the
Massachusetts MTEL™ English (07) Test
with TestWare® on CD-ROM

Printed in the United States of America

Library of Congress Control Number 2009930332

ISBN-13: 978-0-7386-0540-1
ISBN-10: 0-7386-0540-9

The competencies presented in this book were created and implemented by the Massachusetts Department of Education and Pearson Education, Inc., or its affiliate(s).

REA® and TestWare® are registered trademarks of
Research & Education Association, Inc.

About Research & Education Association

Founded in 1959, Research & Education Association is dedicated to publishing the finest and most effective educational materials—including software, study guides, and test preps—for students in middle school, high school, college, graduate school, and beyond.

REA's Test Preparation series includes books and software for all academic levels in almost all disciplines. Research & Education Association publishes test preps for students who have not yet entered high school, as well as for high school students preparing to enter college. Students from countries around the world seeking to attend college in the United States will find the assistance they need in REA's publications. For college students seeking advanced degrees, REA publishes test preps for many major graduate school admission examinations in a wide variety of disciplines, including engineering, law, and medicine. Students at every level, in every field, with every ambition can find what they are looking for among REA's publications.

REA's practice tests are always based upon the most recently administered exams and include every type of question that you can expect on the actual exams.

REA's publications and educational materials are highly regarded and continually receive an unprecedented amount of praise from professionals, instructors, librarians, parents, and students. Our authors are as diverse as the fields represented in the books we publish. They are well-known in their respective disciplines and serve on the faculties of prestigious high schools, colleges, and universities throughout the United States and Canada.

Today, REA's wide-ranging catalog is a leading resource for teachers, students, and professionals.

We invite you to visit us at *www.rea.com* to find out how REA is making the world smarter.

Acknowledgments

We would like to thank Larry Kling, Vice President, Editorial, for his editorial direction; Pam Weston, Vice President, Publishing, for setting the quality standards for production integrity and managing the publication to completion; John Cording, Vice President, Technology, for coordinating the design, development, and testing of REA's TestWare® software; Alice Leonard, Senior Editor, for project management and preflight editorial review; Diane Goldschmidt, Senior Editor, for post-production quality assurance; Amy Jamison and Heena Patel, Technology Project Managers, for their software testing efforts; Christine Saul, Senior Graphic Artist, for cover design; Rachel DiMatteo, Graphic Artist, for text design.

We also gratefully acknowledge Caroline Duffy for copyediting, Kathy Caratozzolo of Caragraphics for typesetting, Ellen Gong for proofreading, and Stephanie Reymann for indexing the manuscript.

From the Author

Teaching was *never* an option. I wanted to be a biological researcher. I enrolled in every science course and participated in every science fair. A quirky Latin teacher (I was sure she had slept with Caesar.) who recounted vivid tales about "*little* Julius" sealed the deal: I would major in Zoology/Classics at the University of Massachusetts, Amherst. During orientation, however, my advisor, a disgruntled Ph.D. student nixed the idea; the "Classics were not hot," so I pursued literature instead. Enrolling in "Romantic Poets" offered only to "declared" English majors, I needed an "override." I could remain in the class only if I received an "A" on the first assignment due the following week. I thought my dissection of Coleridge's poem was brilliant and thankfully, so did he. At the end of junior year, I applied to a Ph.D. program in endocrinology, received a scholarship to Marquette University, but was blindsided by a marriage proposal. Senior year brought the "ED BLOCK." I would become a biology teacher (something I vowed I would *never* do), an ironically auspicious twist! I loved teaching, learning with students, acting out protein synthesis, and creating chemical magic. I graduated in May 1972 with licenses in biology, general science, and English, passed a grueling, 3-hr., audio taped interview, and landed a job in a South Philadelphia middle school. On contract-signing day, Principal Julius Caesar Bennett (another Caesar!) ambushed me. "Come to the Parkway Program, an experimental Philadelphia public high school, where you can teach biology, chemistry, physics, and English, create curriculum, and use the city as your classroom!" I did! This "last chance" high school for diverse students, ranging from special needs to gifted, indigent to wealthy, and criminal to upstanding, was an extraordinary context for a novice teacher!

Reality smacked! Most of my students could not read or solve equations; I needed help. I studied literacy at Penn, taught my students to read and write, and earned an M.S. in Reading and Language Arts in 1975. Three years later, I taught English to reluctant learners in hometown Attleboro, Massachusetts, earned an M.A. in Critical Thinking in 1989, and wrote curriculum materials. I enrolled in the Ph.D. in Curriculum and Instruction at Boston College in 1990, where I taught English, Reading, and Curriculum Methods, Children's Literature, and Inquiry to undergraduates and graduates, received the Donald J. White Distinguished Teaching Award, given to the top graduate student instructor at the university, and served as a teaching supervisor and literacy coach at two urban schools. After earning my doctorate (1995) at the age of 45, I was appointed Adjunct and later Assistant Professor of Education at Boston College in 1998.

"Do what you love!" my mentor counseled. "If you get tenure, wonderful! And if you don't you will have done what you love." I took her advice. Teaching, adult cognitive development, and collaboration intersected in outreach scholarship. Journal articles "Using Literature-based Inquiry to Nurture Reflective Judgment" (2000), "Writing and Evaluating Assessments in the Content Area" (2000), "The Relationship between Personality Traits and Reflective Judgment among Female Students" (2004), "Beyond Mediocrity: Transformational Leadership within a Transactional Framework" (2004) and book chapters "Agents of literacy change: Working with Somali Students in an Urban Middle School (2002), "What we would have Liked to Know: Preservice Teachers' Perspectives on Effective Teacher Preparation" (2002), and "The Power of Professionalism" (in press) explore teacher dilemmas, effective instruction, reflective practice, collaborative inquiry, and teacher education. Authored with undergraduates, graduates, and colleagues, articles "Characters at Crossroads: Reflective Decision Makers in Contemporary Newbery Books" (2004), "Telementoring as a Collaborative Agent for Change" (2004), "Crossing Borders: Developing an Innovative Collaboration to Improve the Preparation of High School English Teachers" (2006), "Reflective Practice Interventions: Raising Levels of Reflective Judgment (2009), "Perceived Changes in Student Learning and Teacher Practice Using Science Portfolios (in press), and "Teacher Subcultures of Democratic Practice despite the Oppression of Educational Reform (in press)" address reflective practice and leadership. In 2001, I received the university's Distinguished Faculty Teaching Award, in 2004 promotion to Associate Professor and election to Department Chair, and the Boston Higher Education Partnership Award (2005), but my most coveted award (2003) is the Mary Kaye Waldron Award, an honor awarded by undergraduates to faculty or an administrator "who has worked to enhance student life at Boston College." An elegant, crystal eagle, this symbol reminds me of just how fortunate I am that teaching is *indeed* an option.

—Audrey Friedman, Ph.D.

Contents

CONTENTS

Introduction

ABOUT THIS BOOK AND TESTWARE®

REA's *The Best Teachers' Test Preparation for the Massachusetts MTEL English (07) Test with TestWare®* on CD-ROM is a comprehensive guide designed to assist you in preparing to take this exam, which is a requirement to teach English in Massachusetts. To help you succeed in this important step toward your career in teaching English in Massachusetts schools, this test prep features the following:

- An accurate and complete overview of the Massachusetts MTEL English (07) test

- The information you need to know about the exam

- A targeted review of each subarea

- Tips and strategies for successfully completing standardized tests

- Diagnostic tools to identify areas of strength and weakness

- Two full-length, true-to-format practice tests based on the most recently administered Massachusetts MTEL English (07) test

- Detailed explanations for each practice test answer. These allow you to identify correct answers and understand not only why they are correct but also why the other answer choices are incorrect.

When creating this test prep, the author and editors considered the most recent test administrations and professional standards. They also researched information from the Massachusetts Department of Education, professional journals, textbooks, and educators.

The result is the best MTEL test preparation materials based on the latest information available.

ABOUT THE MTEL ENGLISH (07) TEST

The purpose of the MTEL English (07) test is to assess prospective teachers' knowledge and skills as applicable to being awarded a license to teach English in Massachusetts.

About Test Selection

The MTEL English test is given during the afternoon test session. Test sessions are four hours in length. To obtain the most current dates for the test, visit the MTEL Web site: *http://www.mtel.nesinc.com/MA12_testdates.asp.*

What Does the Test Cover?

The Massachusetts Tests for Educator License Test Information Booklet states, "The English test is designed to assess the candidate's proficiency and depth of understanding of the subject at the level required for a baccalaureate major, according to Massachusetts standards." The following table lists the objectives used as the basis for the MTEL English (07) test and the approximate number of questions in each subarea. A thorough review of all the specific objectives is the focus of this book.

Test Overview

Subareas	Objectives	Approximate Number of Multiple-choice Questions	Number of Open-response Questions	Approximate Weight in Test
I. Literature and Language	01–09	63–65		51%
II. Rhetoric and Composition	10–12	20–22		17%
III. Reading Theory, Research, and Instruction	13–14	14–16		12%
IV. Integration of Knowledge and Understanding	15	—	2	20%

What Types of Questions Are on the Test?

The MTEL English (07) test has multiple-choice questions that cover the subareas listed in the table. It also has open-response questions. These can relate to any of the topics covered in any of the subareas. They will require a wide knowledge of English and the ability to relate concepts from different aspects of the field. Your responses need to be appropriate and accurate in the application of subject matter to knowledge. You will need to support your opinions or conclusions with strong and accurate evidence.

How Is the MTEL English (07) Test Scored?

The MTEL English (07) test is composed of 100 multiple-choice items and two open-response items. The multiple-choice section counts toward 80 percent of the available points, and the constructed-response section counts toward 20 percent of the available points.

Raw scores (the number of items answered correctly) are converted to scaled scores. The scaled score has a number of points achieved in a range of 100 to 300, with a scaled score of 240 being the passing score. You do not "lose" any points for wrong answers, and each multiple-choice answer is equal in value when your score is totaled.

The scaled score for the open-response questions is taken from the scores earned by your written responses. A scale is used to score each open-response question. This scale judges the level of your performance on that question from weak to thorough. The open-response section of the MTEL English (07) test counts for 20 percent of your total test score.

When Will I Receive My Score Report, and What Will It Look Like?

Your test scores will be mailed to you on the score report day listed in the test registration booklet. (This is approximately five weeks from the test date.)

Unofficial test scores are posted on the Internet at 5 p.m. eastern standard time on the score report dates listed on *http://www.mtel.nesinc.com/MA12_testdates.asp*.

To learn more about receiving your scores online, visit *http://www.mtel.nesinc.com/MA12_releaseofscores.asp*.

Your score report will indicate whether you met the qualifying score. It will give you your total test score if you did not meet the qualifying score, and your general performance on each subarea or section of the test.

Reporting of Scores

Your test scores will be sent to the Massachusetts Department of Elementary and Secondary Education and to any institution that you listed at test registration. Be sure to keep your scores for your personal records.

Can I Retake the Test?

If you wish to retake a test, you may do so at any subsequent test administration. Please consult the MTEL Web site at *www.mtel.nesinc.com* for information about test registration. The MTEL Web site also includes information regarding test retakes and score reports.

Who Administers the Test?

The Massachusetts Tests for Educator Licensure (MTEL) program was initiated by the Massachusetts Department of Elementary and Secondary Education, which has contracted with the Evaluation Systems Group of Pearson to assist in the development and administration of the MTEL.

For additional information you can contact

Massachusetts Tests for Educator Licensure
Evaluation Systems
Pearson
P.O. Box 660
Amherst, MA 01004-9013
Web site: *www.mtel.nesinc.com*
Telephone: (413) 256-2892
(866) 565-4894 (toll free)

Operators are available from 9 a.m. to 5 p.m. eastern standard time, Monday through Friday, excluding holidays. Automated Information System is available 24 hours daily.

Fax: (413) 256-7077

Note: Registration forms may not be transmitted by fax.

When Should I Take the Test?

To receive information on upcoming administrations of the MTEL English (07) test, consult the MTEL Web site at *www.mtel.nesinc.com.*

Do I Pay a Registration Fee?

Yes, to take the MTEL, you must pay a registration fee. For information about the fees and payment options, log on to *http://www.mtel.nesinc.com/MA12_testfees.asp.*

HOW TO USE THIS BOOK AND TESTWARE®

When Should I Start Studying?

It is never too early to start studying for the MTEL English (07) test. The earlier you begin, the more time you will have to sharpen your skills. Do not procrastinate! Cramming is not an effective way to study because it does not allow you the time you need to think about the content, review the subareas, and take the practice tests.

What Do the Review Sections Cover?

The targeted review in this book is designed to help you sharpen the basic skills you need to approach the MTEL English (07) test, as well as provide strategies for attacking the questions.

Each teaching area included in the MTEL English (07) test is examined in a separate chapter. The skills required for all subareas are extensively discussed to optimize your understanding of what the examination covers.

Your schooling has taught you most of the information you need to answer the questions on the test. The English classes you took should have provided you with the knowledge needed to pass the MTEL English (07) test. The review sections in this book are designed to help you fit the information you have acquired into the competencies specified on the MTEL. Going over your class notes and textbooks together with the reviews provided here will give you an excellent springboard for passing the examination.

STUDYING FOR THE MTEL ENGLISH (07)

Choose the time and place for studying that works best for you. Some people set aside a certain number of hours every morning to study, while others prefer to study at night before going to sleep. Other people study off and on during the day—for instance, while waiting for a bus or during a lunch break. Only you can determine when and where your study time will be most effective. Be consistent and use your time efficiently. Work out a study routine and stick to it.

When you take the practice tests, simulate the conditions of the actual test as closely as possible. Turn off your television and radio, and sit down at a table in a quiet room, free from distraction. On completing a practice test, score it and thoroughly review the explanations to the questions you answered incorrectly; however, do not review too much at one time. Concentrate on one problem area at a time by reviewing the question and explanation, and by studying the review in this guide until you are confident that you have mastered the material.

Keep track of your scores so you can gauge your progress and discover general weaknesses in particular sections. Give extra attention to the reviews that cover your areas of difficulty, so you can build your skills in those areas. Many have found the use of study or note cards very helpful for this review.

How Can I Use My Study Time Efficiently?

The following study schedule allows for thorough preparation for the MTEL English (07) test. The course of study presented here is seven weeks, but you can condense or expand the time line to suit your personal schedule. It is vital that you adhere to a structured plan and set aside ample time each day to study. The more time you devote to studying, the more prepared and confident you will be on the day of the test.

STUDY SCHEDULE

Week	Activity
1	After having read this first chapter to understand the format and content of this exam, take the first practice test on CD-ROM. The scores will indicate your strengths and weaknesses. Make sure you simulate real exam conditions when you take the test. Afterward, score it and review the explanations, especially for questions you answered incorrectly.
2	Review the explanations for the questions you missed, and review the appropriate material in each chapter. Chapter 2 will serve as a very comprehensive reference tool for your literature review. Useful study techniques include highlighting key terms and information, taking notes as you review each section, and putting new terms and information on note cards to help retain the information.
3 & 4	Reread all your note cards, refresh your understanding of the competencies and skills included in the exam, review your college textbooks, and read over notes you took in your college classes. This is also the time to consider any other supplementary materials that your counselor or the Massachusetts Department of Education suggests. Review the MTEL Web site at http://www.mtel.nesinc.com.
5	Begin to condense your notes and findings. A structured list of important facts and concepts, based on your note cards and the MTEL English (07) test objectives, will help you thoroughly review for the test. Review the answers and explanations for any questions you missed.
6	Have someone quiz you using the note cards you created. Take the second set of practice tests on CD-ROM, adhering to the time limits and simulated test-day conditions.
7	Using all your study materials, review areas of weakness revealed by your score on the second practice test. Then retake sections of the practice test printed in this book, as needed.

TEST-TAKING TIPS

Although you may not be familiar with tests like the MTEL, this book will acquaint you with this type of exam and help alleviate your test-taking anxieties. By following the seven suggestions listed here, you can become more relaxed about taking the MTEL, as well as other tests.

Tip 1. Become comfortable with the format of the MTEL. When you are practicing, stay calm and pace yourself. After simulating the test only once, you will boost your chances of doing well, and you will be able to sit down for the actual MTEL with much more confidence.

Tip 2. Read all the possible answers. Just because you think you have found the correct response, do not automatically assume that it is the best answer. Read through each choice to be sure that you are not making a mistake by jumping to conclusions.

Tip 3. Use the process of elimination. Go through each answer to a question and eliminate as many of the answer choices as possible. If you can eliminate two answer choices, you have given yourself a better chance of getting the item correct, because only two choices are left from which to make your guess. **Do not** leave an answer blank; it is better to guess than not to answer a question on the MTEL test because you are not penalized for wrong answers.

Tip 4. Place a question mark in your answer booklet next to the answers you guessed, and then recheck them later if you have time.

Tip 5. Work quickly and steadily. You will have four hours to complete the test. Taking the practice tests in this book will help you learn to budget your precious time.

Tip 6. Learn the directions and format of the test. This not only will save you time on test day but also will help you avoid anxiety (and the mistakes caused by being anxious).

Tip 7. When taking the multiple-choice portion of the test, be sure that the answer oval you fill in corresponds to the number of the question in the test booklet. The multiple-choice test is graded by machine, and marking one answer in the wrong place can throw off your answer key and your score. Be extremely careful.

THE DAY OF THE TEST

Before the Test

On the morning of the test, be sure to dress comfortably so you are not distracted by being too hot or too cold while taking the exam. Plan to arrive at the test center early. This will allow you to collect your thoughts and relax before the test and will also spare you the anguish that comes with being late. You should check your MTEL Registration Bulletin (or the MTEL Web site) to find out what time to arrive at the center.

What to Bring

Before you leave for the test center, make sure that you have your admission ticket. Your admission ticket lists your test selection, test site, test date, and reporting time.

You must also bring personal identification that includes one piece of current, government-issued identification in the name in which you registered, bearing your photograph and signature, and one additional piece of identification (with or without a photograph). If the name on your identification differs from the name in which you are registered, you must bring official verification of the change (e.g., marriage certificate, court order). If you don't have the specified identification with you, you will lose valuable test time filling out additional paperwork and having your photograph taken.

You must bring several sharpened No. 2 pencils with erasers, because none will be provided at the test center. If you like, you can wear a watch to the test center. However, you cannot wear one that makes noise, because it might disturb the other test takers. Dictionaries, textbooks, notebooks, calculators, cell phones, beepers, PDAs, scratch paper, listening and recording devices, briefcases, or packages are not permitted. Drinking, smoking, or eating during the test are prohibited. You may bring a water bottle into the testing room as long as it is clear and without a label but with a tight lid. During testing, you will have to store your water bottle under your seat.

Security Measures

Your thumbprint will be taken at the test site as part of the identification process. Your thumbprints will be used only for identity verification. If you refuse to have a thumbprint taken, you will not be allowed to take the test and no refund or credit will be given.

Additional security screening may be required at your test site. If it is conducted, you will be admitted to the test site only if you proceed through the security screening. If you refuse to do so, you will not be allowed to test and you will not receive a refund or credit of any kind.

Late Arrival Policy

If you arrive late for your test session, you may not be admitted into the test site. If you are permitted to enter, you will not be given any additional time for your test session. You will be required to sign a statement to this effect. If you are late and are not permitted to enter, you will be considered absent and will not be given any refund or credit of any kind. You will have to register again and pay to take the test at a future date.

Absentee Policy

If you are absent, you will not be given a refund or any kind of credit. You will have to re-register and pay to take the test on another date. For more information on test-day policies, visit *http://www.mtel.nesinc.com/MA12_reporttotest.asp*.

During the Test

The MTEL English (07) test is given in one sitting, with no breaks. However, during testing, you may take restroom breaks. Any time that you take for restroom breaks is considered part of the available testing time. Procedures will be followed to maintain test security. Once you enter the test center, follow all the rules and instructions given by the test supervisor. If you do not, you risk being dismissed from the test and having your score canceled.

When all the materials have been distributed, the test instructor will give you directions for completing the informational portion of your answer sheet. Fill out the sheet carefully, because the information you provide will be printed on your score report.

Once the test begins, mark only one answer per question, completely erase unwanted answers and marks, and fill in answers darkly and neatly.

After the Test

When you finish your test, hand in your materials and you will be dismissed. Then, go home and relax—you deserve it!

Literature and Language

Chapter 2, "Literature and Language," first presents a detailed overview of six major bodies of literature:

- American literature from the precolonial period through the end of the nineteenth century

- American literature from the twentieth century to the present

- The literature of Great Britain from the Anglo-Saxon period to the Romantic period

- The literature of Great Britain from the Victorian period to the present

- The literature of the ancient world to the fifteenth century

- World literature from the fifteenth century to the present

Each major body of literature is further organized into specific literary periods. In most cases, a brief historical background is provided in order to contextualize the period and provide the reader with a sense of the political, social, economic, religious, and cultural elements that influenced literary movements and particular works of the period. Following the historical background is a description of the literary elements pervasive in the literature of the period. In some instances, specific literary devices truly unique to the period are described and illustrated. Finally, a list of the major writers and works of the period are presented in alphabetical order. At the end of all sections is a series of time lines that not only help the reader visualize relationships between and among the various bodies of literature, but also the immensity of the category of literature and language itself.

Chapter 2 also presents three additional sections:

- The characteristics of various genres and types of literature, differentiating among the four major genres of literature, and defining specific forms within each genre, also identifying literary terms unique to each genre and form. Included in this section is a fairly thorough and inclusive list of literary devices and terms with which all English educators should be familiar

- Literary theory and criticism, the emergence of literary criticism as a form, and theories of literary criticism, describing elements that differentiate the various forms of criticism, authors aligned or identified with a particular theory of criticism, and illustrative examples of application of a particular form of critique

- The structure and development of the English language and chronicles the structure and development of the English language, identifying and elaborating on major areas of study such as phonology, morphology, syntax, and semantics

AMERICAN LITERATURE PRECOLONIAL TO THE END OF THE NINETEENTH CENTURY

Precolonial and Early Native American Literature

Historical Background

Approximately a century before the first permanent settlement in Jamestown, Virginia (1607), Native Americans had already encountered European explorers such as Christopher Columbus in the West Indies, Vasco Núñez de Balboa on the Pacific Coast of North America, Francisco Vasquez de Coronado in the Southwest, and later, Pedro Menendez de Aviles in St. Augustine, Florida. While no authentic, fixed or continuous written record of Native American literature exists, artifacts such as pictures painted on wood or stone have provided researchers with songs, myths, and legends derived from the Native American oral language tradition.

Literary Elements

Poetic and symbolic, this literature, viewed primarily as **folklore**, describes the beauty, power, and awe of nature. Most prevalent in this literature are **myths**, stories passed down from generation to generation that explain natural phenomena and significant cultural and religious rituals. Examples of these myths include *The Walum Olum* of the Delaware tribe and *The Navajo Origin Legend* and the "Night Chant" of the Navajo tribe, which detail tribal origins and are recounted during special ceremonies and religious celebrations.

Colonial Literature (1607–1763)

Historical Background

The colonial period in American Literature began with the first permanent settlement in Jamestown, Virginia, in 1607. Settlement in America began after a group of London merchants received a license from England to colonize "Virginia," a name, which referred to the entire eastern seaboard claimed by England. The Royal Council for Virginia was granted authority over two joint-stock, commercial companies: the London Company, which colonized the southern regions; and the Plymouth Company, which was given the north. Although the first charter addressed the obligation of the settlers to civilize the native inhabitants, whom they called savages and infidels, their primary motive was to dig, mine, and search for gold, silver, and copper. Maryland was settled under a charter granted to Lord Baltimore in 1634. The British took New Amsterdam from the Dutch and renamed it New York in 1664. By the mid-seventeenth century, the English dominated the entire coast, from Newfoundland to Florida.

Puritan settlers of New England came to North America primarily to establish a Puritan or Calvinistic brand of Protestantism, which remained the chief influence in that area until 1800. Puritans believed they were "chosen people" enacting New World Zion in the chapters of human history. Both the Puritans and Plymouth Pilgrims were dissatisfied with the English church under the Stuart monarchy and were persecuted ecclesiastically. The Puritans, however, insisted that their movement was nonseparatist (one of reform), while the Pilgrims broke from the Church of England. A critical event in colonial history is the Salem witch trials, where twenty women and men were executed by hanging or pressing for witchcraft. Cotton Mather, son of Increase Mather and grandson of Richard Mather, campaigned tirelessly to convince New England that witchcraft was a real and present danger affecting the well-being of the community. Cotton wrote *Memorable Providences, Relating to Witchcraft and Possessions.*

Literary Elements

The English Puritans, being the most literate, most well educated, and most committed to intellectualism, had the greatest impact on colonial literature. In 1636 the leaders of Massachusetts Bay Colony founded Harvard College (modeled after Cambridge University in England) and set up the first printing press at Harvard in 1639. Two themes dominated the literature: religion and politics. Puritan literature focused primarily on the defense or explanation of religious beliefs. The Puritan version of Protestantism emphasized the exclusive authority of the Bible in matters of faith and on the contractual nature of God's election of saints. Puritans committed themselves to the Bible and believed the Bible was the revealed word of God, a repository of literal truth. Puritan preachers' sermons comprised the first substantial literary genre in the English-speaking New World. The rhetoric was plain, emphasizing logic and clarity. Preachers such as Thomas Hooker, John Cotton, and Thomas Shepard combined biblical imagery and facts about living in America; their sermons exerted an influence on secular tales as well as on America's later writers. Puritans used allegories; for example, each Indian attack or natural event had a spiritual significance. This symbolic nature of the world would continue to influence the American literary tradition long after the Puritans died.

Every Puritan wrote a diary, often didactic, to be handed down to sons and daughters. Although Puritan dogma was based in determinism, the Puritan community demanded righteous behavior. Good deeds apparently were not the instrument of achieving justification, but were a sign of justification. Puritan diaries told personal stories and shared with their Renaissance contemporaries an enthusiasm for moral stories of Livy, Tacitus, and Plutarch. Puritan elegies lamented the loss of a deceased loved one. Puritans also composed meditations about the end of events, and because they felt they knew history's destination, they expressed apocalyptic expectations using biblical imagery.

Major Writers and Works

William Bradford (1590–1657), governor of his settlement, became the best source of information about the Pilgrims and early colonization of New England. In the *History of Plymouth Plantation*, he describes the separatist movement in England, exile in Holland, and the voyage of the *Mayflower*. He also authored *The Mayflower Compact*.

Anne Bradstreet (1612–1672) is noted for *The Tenth Muse, Lately Sprung Up in America*, a collection of poems written on philosophical subjects and strongly influenced by Elizabethan poets. She also composed journals about colonial New England life.

William Byrd (1540–1623), in *A History of the Dividing Line*, wrote about his journey into the swamps separating the Carolinian territories from Virginia and Maryland. A Cavalier poet, Byrd came to the New World on orders from King George.

Jonathan Edwards (1703–1758), the last of the great Calvinistic clergymen and an American theologian, studied at Yale. In his "Personal Narrative," he describes spiritual development and the idea that God in his infinite power permeates every part of the universe. He fought against liberalism in the church and was responsible for "Great Awakening," a series of religious revivals, which spread throughout the northern colonies. He is well known for his sermon "Sinners in Hands of an Angry God," an influential text that describes man's corruption and God's justice.

Richard Mather (1596–1669), an English clergymen, who was suspended from the Anglican Church because of Puritan tendencies, became the leader of the Separatist Church at Massachusetts Bay. His most remembered work is the *Bay Psalm Book*, rhymed versions of psalms.

Samuel Sewall (1652–1730) stands out among the Puritans as humane and lovable and was one of the first colonists to write pamphlets against slavery and mistreatment of Indians. He was also the *only* one of the Salem witchcraft judges to confess publicly that he had been wrong in condemning witches.

John Smith (1580–1631), condemned to death by Chesapeake King Powhatan, was rescued by Powhatan's daughter Pocahontas. The story is a romantic parable characterizing the inevitability of white triumph over Indian opposition. Smith's account of Virginia in 1608 was the first book written in English in America; his *Description of New England* followed.

John Winthrop (1588–1649) served as deputy governor of Massachusetts Bay Colony. He believed that God had sent his people to the New World and that all Europe had their eyes on them to see if they would succeed or fail. He is most well-known for his sermon "A Model of Christian Charity."

Revolutionary Literature (1764–1789)

Historical Background

From 1760 on, literary and cultural aspirations were linked to revolutionary politics. The British had spent a lot of money defending the colonies against attacks by the French and Native Americans (French and Indian War, 1754–1763) as their mission was religious conversion and territorial expansion. Both New England and New France wanted to expand their colonies and trading outposts. The Protestant colonists in New England also feared the French Catholic and papal influence. To fund the war, the British decided to shift the financial burden of high taxes to the colonists. The Stamp Act, in 1765, taxed all legal documents and newspapers, and was met with great uproar in colonies. It was repealed a year later in 1766. The Boston Tea Party in 1773 was an act of revolt against the British and their tax on tea.

The American Revolution began a year after the writing of the **Declaration of Independence**, in 1777, and the British eventually surrendered in 1781. In 1787, the members of the Constitutional Convention ratified the **Constitution of the United States of America**. The First Ten Amendments of the Constitution are the **Bill of Rights**. Important literature (both fiction and poetry) was slow to emerge in the New World, because residual Puritanism disapproved of storytelling. Also, the cultures of the western frontier, southern plantation, and northern commerce did not offer a rich environment for fictional art. Because of the primitive state of copyright laws, many American publishers pirated and reprinted the novels of Samuel Richardson, Henry Fielding, and Dickens. Also, Americans were skeptical of working within the literary conventions of a country from which they had separated themselves. The newly forged American Republic was often compared to the Roman Republic, and George Washington was compared to Cincinnatus, the farmer who left his plow to take up the sword, and Fabiu, who defeated Hannibal in the Second Punic War. The newly independent country had to define a culture commensurate with its sovereign political status.

Literary Elements

Benjamin Franklin was considered the colonies' first citizen, the man who personified the peculiar genius of America. Franklin wrote the "Dogood Papers" with common sense, humor, and freethinking irreverence. He dismantled the Puritan elegy, reducing it to formulas and hackneyed similes. Franklin's rise to international prominence signaled the end of the dominance of Puritan ideology. Franklin's *Autobiography*, similar to the Puritan diaries in its design and structure, offers his life as a representative model of trial, pilgrimage, and success intended to teach and instruct others. The difference, however, is that Franklin's journey is purely secular, in which *reason* is the primary guide, and heaven has become a vague metaphor for the unknowable and peripheral beyond. Franklin's self-portrait shows beginnings of the American myth/story: a poor boy finds his way to wealth, the chartered servant earns his freedom, the colonial subject takes up the cause of national independence.

Poetry was pressed into the service of nationalism. Hugh Henry Brackenrige and classmate Philip Freneau wrote a poem called "The Rising Glory of America." Freneau was a propagandist in democracy's cause and a poet of the Revolution. Freneau said that Thomas Paine enthroned Reason in politics and pulled down kings.

Major Writers and Works

John (1735–1826) and Abigail Adams's (1744–1818) letters in correspondence between Boston and Philadelphia serve as primary sources that document the dangerous period in history during the Revolution.

Benjamin Franklin (1706–1790) bought the unprofitable *Pennsylvania Gazette* and made it a widely read weekly periodical in America. He also authored *Poor Richard's Almanack*, which contained rash weather predictions and brief sayings that urged virtue and good business practices. He invented the Franklin stove and lightening rod and established the identity of electricity and lightening. He founded the debate club, which later turned into the University of Pennsylvania, and the first lending library. He affected the repeal of the Stamp Act, helped draft the Declaration of Independence, and negotiated an alliance with France during the Revolution. He signed the peace treaty in 1783 that ended the American Revolution and helped write and then signed the Constitution in 1787. His last public act was to petition Congress for the abolishment of slavery.

Alexander Hamilton (1757–1804) wrote the bulk of the series of eighty-five essays collected as *The Federalist*, in order to secure the ratification of the Constitution. James Madison and John Jay also contributed to the series.

Patrick Henry (1736–1799), a great orator of the Revolution, is remembered for two speeches: one to the Virginia Legislature about the Stamp Act, saying "Tarquin and Caesar each had his Brutus; Charles the First, his Cromwell; and George the Third may profit by their example! . . . If this be treason, make the most of it!" and the other to the Virginia House of Burgesses, in which he said, "Give me liberty or give me death."

Thomas Jefferson (1743–1826), the first American champion of the people, authored almost all of the Declaration of American Independence and the Statute of Virginia for

Religious Freedom and is father of the University of Virginia. *Notes on the State of Virginia* is a historic source of information on the region of Virginia.

Thomas Paine (1737–1809), author of *Common Sense*, appealed for complete political independence. His rhetorical power was his mastery of plain style. At Franklin's suggestion he came to America before the Revolution and began his writing career in Philadelphia. He served in the American army and published sixteen issues of his paper, *The American Crisis.*

Gustavus Vassa (1745–1797), or Olaudah Equiano, was taken from Africa and enslaved as a child. He later earned his freedom and became a leading figure in the eighteenth-century abolition movement. *The Interesting Narrative of the Life of Olaudah Equiano, or Gustavus Vassa the African* (1789), is an abolitionist autobiography.

George Washington (1732–1799) wrote letters, diaries, and other pieces, which have been collected in thirty-seven volumes. "Farewell to the Army of the Potomac," his best work, written with the help of Hamilton and James Madison, explains his reasons for leaving the presidency. It established the traditions of strong central government, isolation from European politics (isolationism), and two-term limits for presidents.

Phillis Wheatley (1753–1784), an African-born black woman, was captured at the age of eight and sold to John Wheatley, a Boston merchant. Attractive and intelligent, she was encouraged to learn by her owner. She began writing poetry at the age of thirteen and wrote her *Poems on Various Subjects* when she was twenty, written in English neoclassical style, imitative of Alexander Pope and Thomas Gray.

Hartford wits, men who shared a Yale connection, as they were clustered around Hartford, Conn., were led by John Trumbull (1750–1831), Timothy Dwight (1752–1817), and Joel Barlow (1754–1812). The Hartford wits produced satires, mock epics, and hymns to the New World. Conservative and Federalist, they intended to announce America's arrival on the national literary stage, relying on imitations of English models.

Romantic Literature (1790–1865)
(Also known as the American Renaissance)

Historical Background

America expanded its boundaries significantly in the time between independence and the Civil War. Jefferson purchased the Louisiana Territory from France in 1803 and doubled the nation's size. War and effective diplomacy added the areas of Texas, California, and Oregon. By 1860, twenty new states had entered the Union, adding to the thirteen original states. America began moving westward (Manifest Destiny).

Flatboats, keelboats, and packet boats sailed the rivers of the East, South, and Midwest. Steamboats, which permitted upstream travel, allowed for inland navigation canals (like the Erie Canal). The railroad guided and shaped much of economic development, and allowed the nation to meet the needs of its vast expansion. Cycles of economic boom and bust occurred as debates over currency continued. Financial panic swept through the nation's banks, wiping out many large and small investors. John Adams and Thomas Jefferson both died on July 4, 1826, the fiftieth anniversary of the Declaration of the Independence.

The War of 1812 with Britain, fought on land and sea, inspired the writing of the "Star-Spangled Banner" by Francis Scott Key. There were also three major orators whose speeches dominated the political climate between War of 1812 and the Civil War. Henry Clay (1777–1852), lawyer and statesman, advocated conciliatory measures such as the Missouri Compromise regulating slavery in Western territories, and made public attacks on abolitionism. John C. Calhoun (1782–1850) was an ardent supporter of slavery and states' rights. Daniel Webster (1782–1852), a supporter of nationalism, advocated conciliatory leaders like Clay, in opposition to Calhoun.

Literary Elements

This period saw the emergence of early American folktales and a distinctly American writing, not just the copying of English forms. The South revered learning and aspired to a literary culture. William and Mary, the nation's second oldest college, established Virginia's and the nation's intellectual leadership in the eighteenth and early nineteenth century. However, the South became increasingly dependent upon slavery, especially after the introduction of the cotton gin, and southern writers were driven to propagandize in defense of slavery or to write escapist fantasies. William Gilmore Simms wrote *The Yemasse*, one of the best works of southern fiction. The South produced a lot of romance fictions and chivalric melodramas, similar to Sir Walter Scott's *Waverly and Ivanhoe*. An indigenous southern genre was the plantation novel, which pictured slavery as white benevolence and black loyalty. Despite major works of southern literature, New England was still the center of American literature, as represented by major writers of this period: Henry David Thoreau, Ralph Waldo Emerson, Nathaniel Hawthorne, and Herman Melville.

During this period, a belief in transcendentalism emerged. Finding philosophical support in the writings of Immanuel Kant, transcendental thinkers and writers of Concord, Massachusetts, believed in a single God that manifests in all parts of the universe. Another movement, romanticism, encompassed reaction against the Age of Reason, observing a large-scale shift in sensibility that began in late eighteenth century and stormed across the first half of the nineteenth century. Romanticism involved subordination of rationality to emotion and intuition, found value and interest in the individual, and considered nature, which offered harmony, joy, and spiritual refreshment, the dwelling place of divinity. During the first few decades of this period, the best American writers imitated British authors: William Cullen Bryant imitated William Wordsworth, and James Fenimore Cooper imitated Sir Walter Scott's historical romanticism. A theme of literary independence emerged as Emerson wanted a complete break with Old World literary traditions, and Edgar Allan Poe and Hawthorne developed the short story into a distinctive American genre. Walt Whitman finally wrote entirely on American topics, from an entirely American point of view, and in a manner that deviated from the British traditionalism.

MTEL Tip

Romanticism considered nature to be the dwelling place of divinity.

The fireside poets, so called because American families read their works during the harsh and enduring New England winters, included writers such as James Russell Lowell, Oliver Wendell Holmes, Henry Wadsworth Longfellow, and John Greenleaf Whittier.

Major Writers and Works

William Cullen Bryant (1794–1878), born in a family of Puritan tradition in a small Massachusetts village, produced austere and intellectual poems. Most of his poems dealt with nature, the woods, or death. His most famous work is "Thanatopsis," a meditation on death.

James Fenimore Cooper (1789–1851), born in his father's frontier town in Cooperstown, New York, wrote *The Last of the Mohicans*, which depicts Natty (called Hawkeye), a young scout during the French and Indian War, and many chases and battles between white men and two Indians, Chingachgook and Uncas, who are the last of the Mohicans. He also wrote *The Pioneers*, part of the Leatherstocking Series, which features Natty Bumppo, a middle-aged frontiersman. Cooper owes the style of his romantic and historic fiction to Sir Walter Scott.

Ralph Waldo Emerson (1803–1882) wrote about hard work, the intellectual spirit of Americans, and the importance of learning about nature firsthand rather than through books. He encouraged readers to trust themselves and not the opinions of others. Considered the spiritual descendent of Jonathan Edwards, he observed that conscience should compel life. Like Edwards, he left the church because for personal reasons he could not administer the Lord's Supper. *Nature* (1836), his first and one of his best books, is considered a central piece on transcendentalism. Emerson also wrote volumes of poetry, including *Poems* (1847), *Representative Men*, *The Conduct of Life* (1860), and *English Traits* (1865). Also a master of oratory, Emerson is best known for his addresses "The American Scholar" (1837) and "The Divinity School Address."

Nathaniel Hawthorne (1804–1864) wrote *The Scarlet Letter*, a book about Puritan New England society whose members left England to establish religious freedom. The society's puritanical ways ruin the life of Hester Prynne, who has a child out of wedlock with a minister. Her child, Pearl, is condemned as she is considered the child of Satan. He also wrote *The House of the Seven Gables*.

Oliver Wendell Holmes (1809–1894), a New England poet, wrote "The Deacon's Masterpiece: or, The Wonderful One-Hoss Shay," a reduction of the logic of Calvinism and a parable of its breakdown.

Herman Melville (1819–1891) left Nantucket on the whaler *Acushnet* in 1841 and deserted ship in the Marquesas Islands. Hawthorne and Melville were neighbors in Lenox, Massachusetts, and were both interested in combining symbolism and romance. Hawthorne's obsession with the power of sin affected Melville's work *Moby Dick*, in which Captain Ahab tries to capture a great white whale that has taken his leg. At last the whale triumphs and crashes into the ship and sinks it, and Ahab is killed in the act of harpooning the whale. Melville's commentary on the gruesome and harsh life of a whaler in Nantucket is also depicted in *Billy Budd*, an allegory of how forces of evil triumph over innocence and beauty.

Edgar Allan Poe (1809–1849), a poet, wrote works that include "The Raven," "To Helen," "Annabelle Lee," "The Tell-Tale Heart," "The Cask of Amontillado," and "The Fall of the House of Usher." Poe was unyielding in his aesthetic commitment and was idolized for his poverty and early death. Known for his gothic, psychologically thrilling tales, he believed that beauty was akin to truth and considered writing a religious and moral obligation. Many of his poems venerated the death of women and dead female bodies, observing that there were always elements of strangeness in beauty.

William Gilmore Simms (1806–1870), sometimes called a Southern Cooper, wrote novels that featured two settings: the frontier and the Revolution. In *The Yemasee*, the son of a Yemasee chief gives aid to the English against his own tribe, and his Indian mother kills him to prevent his dishonorable banishment from the tribe.

Henry David Thoreau (1817–1862) wrote about nature in *On Walden Pond* and civil disobedience in "On the Duty of Civil Disobedience." The second greatest of the transcendentalists, Thoreau lived a hermetic life on Walden Pond to test his transcendental philosophy of individualism, self-reliance, and spiritual growth.

Walt Whitman (1819–1892) wrote *Leaves of Grass*. Whitman was an original writer and rejected the traditional elements of verse, meter, rhyme, and conventional poetic diction. His subject matter centered on democracy and the individual common man. Heavily influenced by Emerson and the transcendentalists, his work was sensual, displaying frank admiration for body, and was considered pansexual. He is also famous for writing the famous elegy for Abraham Lincoln, "O Captain! My Captain!"

Civil War Literature (1861–1865)

Historical Background

During this time, Thoreau wrote vicious abolitionist polemics like "Slavery in Massachusetts," in which he protested the return of two escaped slaves to their southern masters under the Fugitive Slave Law, passed as part of the Compromise of 1850. Later Thoreau met John Brown, concluding that he had found a man whose righteousness lifted him above the debased dead level of antebellum politics. Brown later attacked a federal arsenal at Harper's Ferry, Virginia, trying to provoke slave insurrection across the South. Although later hanged, Brown was a hero in the eyes of Thoreau and Emerson, who enrolled Brown in the ranks of the transcendental movement. Thus transcendentalism became connected with the abolitionist movement.

Territorial expansion repeatedly raised the question of slavery's extension beyond the borders of the original slaveholding South, resulting in the Missouri Compromise, and a variety of differences between North and South heightened sectional tensions and were exacerbated by newspapers, books, and pamphlets expressing antislavery sentiment (e.g., *Uncle Tom's Cabin*). A number of black abolitionists began working in groups and individually: Harriet Tubman made many dangerous trips to the South to help slaves escape; and Sojourner Truth, an orator and organizer, led campaigns for abolition and women's rights. Lincoln's election in 1860 caused eleven states to secede from the Union by 1861, forming the Confederacy led by Jefferson Davis. Hostilities mounted in April 1861 when the Union attempted to replenish Fort Sumter in Charleston Harbor. Confederate forces bombarded the fort, leading to its surrender and the eventual commencement of the Civil War.

Literary Elements

Significant literary themes during this period focused on abolition and polemics between advocates of slavery and abolitionists. Much of Whitman's writing was influenced by his experience in the Civil War as a field medic. The writing of this period precipitated, rather than reflected, tensions in the country as observed by Lincoln, who legendarily (and perhaps falsely) said that Harriet Beecher Stowe was the "little lady who made this big war." Writing in this period is obviously looked at in the context of new (or old) historicism rather than formalism. The transcendentalist tradition represented by Thoreau merged with John Brown's ideology; thus certain literary (and life) principles of the transcendentalists carried over to the abolitionist movement

Major Writers and Works

Frederick Douglass (1818–1895), in his *Narrative of the Life of Frederick Douglass*, wrote about slavery and masters' desires to keep their slaves ignorant. Knowledge was denied to slaves, as it would only bring discontent. Douglass's desire for freedom heightened as he learned to read. He noted that democracy and Christianity, although deformed by slavery, were worthy of allegiance.

Abraham Lincoln (1809–1865), a great statesman in spite of his lack of formal education, was a master of direct and tactful expression. An accomplished lawyer in Illinois, Lincoln persevered to become a Republican president in 1860, and his election triggered the Civil War. Lincoln is most famous for the Gettysburg Address, a classic of oratory. His less famous second inaugural address was a blueprint for the reconciliation of the nation ("With malice toward none, with charity for all . . ."), and his letter to Mrs. Bixby consoling her for the loss of her five sons in the war was a masterpiece of sympathy and compassion. Earlier speeches contained rough frontier humor and idioms of the common man, but his oratory style became known as directly to the point and appropriate for the occasion.

Harriet Beecher Stowe (1811–1896) wrote *Uncle Tom's Cabin*, a story of slave life written by a New England woman whose knowledge of the subject was limited to observations during her brief visit in Kentucky. She wrote the book to arouse antislavery sentiment and was so successful that Lincoln called her "the little woman who caused the great war." Its notable characters include honest, black Uncle Tom, the mischievous slave girl Topsy, little angelic Eva, and the cruel slave driver Simon Legree. The novel introduced a new era by presenting a realistic picture of contemporary life, rather than romantic adventures of past.

David Walker (1785–1830) wrote a landmark pamphlet titled *Appeal to the Colored Citizens of the World*, which united history, classical rhetoric, and the Bible on behalf of a sustained and bitter denunciation of the inhumanity of slavery.

Other abolitionist writers include William Lloyd Garrison (1805–1879), one of the founders of the American Anti-Slavery Society and the editor of the abolitionist newspaper *The Liberator;* Benjamin Lay (1681–1760), a Quaker and abolitionist; and Susan B. Anthony (1820–1906), who became an agent for William Lloyd Garrison's American Anti-Slavery Society of New York State, promoted women's rights, and although originally friends with Frederick Douglass, disagreed with his contention that only males should have the right to vote

Sectional Independence and Local Color Literature (1865–1930)

Historical Background

During this period, the population surged as millions of immigrants moved westward. From the Mississippi River to the Pacific Ocean, new states were admitted; territories were annexed and subdued in expansion of white settlement. The first transcontinental railroad system was established. Reconstruction after the Civil War was distinctly different in the North and the South. The South was impoverished for years afterwards, while the North remained virtually untouched. By 1900, America had become a leading economic power because of northern industry. Names like Rockefeller, Morgan, Gould, Carnegie, and Hill represented the achievement of a culture obsessed with success and the American dream.

Literary Elements

This literary era marked the transition between the nineteenth and twentieth century. This period included the Guilded Age (1873), which eradicated institutions that were centuries old, changed the social life in the country, and influenced literature and life in general. New England lost its monopoly on America's literary output. Themes included conformity, self-discipline, and dreams of material comfort as reflected in the work of Horatio Alger. There were moral tales and tales of rags to riches. The voice of the common people was heard from across the country initially in folk stories like "Johnny Appleseed," the "Hatfields and McCoys," "Paul Bunyan," and "Pecos Bill," then in the writing and speeches of humorists like Mark Twain. Readers became conscious of regional differences: romance of the Far West, rusticity of the Middle West, and glamour of the deep South. Literary works included poetry, elegy, puns, allegory, and satire.

Major Writers and Works

George Washington Cable (1844–1925) was one of the first to write about the rich color of New Orleans. *Old Creole Days* is a collection of short stories about a variety of ethnic groups mingled in New Orleans. *The Grandissimes* recounts a feud between two aristocratic families.

Willa Cather (1873–1947) wrote about life on the Nebraska prairie and the immigrant farmers of the West, with whom she lived from the age nine until she graduated from University of Nebraska. *O Pioneers!* describes the life of a Swedish immigrant who keeps her family together after the death of their father, building a prosperous farm on the "unfriendly" Nebraska prairie and finding happiness and love. *My Antonia* recounts how Antonia Shimerda, a Bohemian immigrant, becomes a loving and wonderful farmwife in spite of poverty, disgrace, and hardship. "Paul's Case," one of Cather's most moving short stories, is about a troubled, bright, young, gay man who eventually kills himself by being hit by a train. *One of Ours* won the 1923 Pulitzer Prize.

Kate Chopin (1851–1904), raised in St. Louis, moved to New Orleans with her Creole husband. After he died she moved back to St. Louis to support herself and her children. *Bayou Folk* and *A Night in Acadia*, her most successful work, are a series of sketches based on the Creole people and customs, which she observed during her marriage. This society was more European than American, civility was more relaxed, and cautious sensuality was regarded as the norm. *The Awakening*, an erotic and sympathetic exploration of female desire, takes her theme of passion dominating civility to extreme. Edna Pontellier, the wife of an affluent Creole husband and whose outwardly comfortable circumstances conceal a discontent, experiments with art, a separate residence, and adultery; however, her campaign of self-definition leads to her death.

Samuel Langhorne Clemens, "Mark Twain" (1835–1910), wrote about local color and the particularities of the region in which he lived, along the Mississippi. Twain preserved important elements of speech, like the dialect of the region. Considered a "great American humorist," he used vernacular language, exaggeration, and deadpan narration to create humor. Self-educated, he wanted to become a Mississippi steamboat pilot, which shows just how entrenched he was in southern culture. Inspired by the tall tales and frontier humor that came out of the old Southwest, for example "Paul Bunyan" and "Babe the Blue Ox," Twain based his literature on his early experiences along the Mississippi. Such works include "The Celebrated Jumping Frog of Calaveras County," a short story that relates the accomplishments of a frog named Dan'l Webster. The story brought Mark Twain immediate fame. *The Adventures of Tom Sawyer* depicts the carefree, primitive life Clemens had lived before his father died and he was forced to work at age twelve. Notable characters are Aunt Polly and Huck Finn. Tom is boyishly imaginative but more civilized than Huck. *The Adventures of Huckleberry Finn*, a sequel to *Tom Sawyer*, tells how a "half-civilized" Huck drifts down the river on a raft with a runaway slave named Jim, who is eventually freed by Tom. The text is very controversial and has been considered racist by some critics. Other works include *Life on the Mississippi* (a memoir), *The Prince and the Pauper*, and *A Connecticut Yankee in King Arthur's Court*.

Emily Dickinson (1830–1886), obviously out of place in this era, wrote minimally about the Civil War (if at all), traveled out of the state of Massachusetts *once*, never married, and spent most of her life in her home in Amherst. Dickinson left over 1,700 poems upon her death, which her sister Lavinia collected and published: "I heard a Fly buzz—when I died," "I felt a Funeral, in my Brain," "My Life had stood—a Loaded Gun," and "What Soft—Cherubic Creatures." Her poetry displayed an extremely effective use of slant rhyme, and the tones of her poetry ranged from mild whimsy to impassioned delight to paralyzed despair and terror. Her poetry also included satire, celebration, elegies, riddle poems, puns, and allegory. Dickinson wrote about abstractions as if they were familiar physical objects.

Bret Harte (1836–1902) is remembered as the man who made the West a favorite realm of fiction. As a young man he went to California and had a brief experience as a miner; he then became a San Francisco journalist. Harte wrote about what he called "the old West." "The Luck of Roaring Camp" appeared in the *Overland Monthly*, the first literary presentation of a colorful section of the country (the West). A rough mining camp was transformed into a model community by the presence of an orphaned, illegitimate half-breed baby. *The Outcasts of Poker Flat* followed the same formula of nobility coming out in desperate characters who possess hearts of gold.

The Age of Realism and Realist Literature (1890–1920)

Literary Elements

Several factors stimulated the rise of realist literature. Scientific interest instigated by Charles Darwin, T. H. Huxley, and Herbert Spencer and the emergence of a strong social consciousness stimulated by Karl Marx and Russian novelists influenced the writing of this period. There was widespread reaction to Victorianism and the estheticism of late Victorians. Realism avoided the false beauty of former writing, often going to the extreme to point out the cruel and ugly side of real life.

Other philosophies to emerge at this time were humanism and new humanism. Humanism transcended the scientific method and drew upon classical and early Christian philosophers. Humanism advised self-restraint as the highest ethical principle and the highest freedom, eliminating the need for external compulsion. New humanism, a movement brought about by P. E. More's *Shelburne Essays*, was a reaction against romanticism, realism, and naturalism. Naturalism focused on man's subjection to natural law, while humanism distinguished between man and nature, emphasizing ethical concepts and freedom of the will as being peculiar to man.

MTEL Tip

Humanism emphasized man's freedom of will.

Major Writers and Works

William Dean Howells (1837–1920), considered the father of American realism, succeeded in making his characters appear very real, but he placed too much emphasis on the commonplace, avoiding the real drama that does exist in real life. A writer for *Harper's New Monthly Magazine*, Howells showcased the work of Dickinson, Paul Lawrence Dunbar, and Stephen Crane. He is also known for stories about social issues, such as "Editha" (1905), and novels about race (*An Imperative Duty*, 1892) and female professions (*The Coast of Bohemia*, 1893).

Henry James (1843–1916) spent long residence abroad where he was influenced by Flaubert, Zola, Balzac, Goethe, and George Eliot. His "Americanism" was apparent in his study of conscience and ethics derived from Hawthorne and realism from Howells. He was most noted for contrasting American and European cultures. *Daisy Miller*, his most popular novel, tells how a charming American girl offends her European friends and an American gentleman of European training by her innocent familiarity with a young Italian. The style is simple and direct, unlike his later works. In *The Portrait of a Lady*, Isabel Archer, James's prototypical heroine (young, beautiful, and intelligent), is courted by an English nobleman, a wealthy English invalid, and an earnest Yankee. She marries the Yankee because of his intellect and shallow estheticism, but he only wants her money. She "bravely" faces an unhappy future with him because of her conscience.

William James (1842–1910), developer of American philosophy and Henry's brother, studied physiology and psychology. William had a clear and forceful style of writing, in complete opposition to his brother. Distinguished by pragmatic thinking, James rejected what was traditionally American and emphasized practicality as a criterion of truth. His *The Varieties of Religious Experience* is an interesting inquiry into the various forms of faith and topics such as conversion, the sick soul, and blind faith. He quotes a plethora of authors throughout history who have described religious experience, such as Leo Tolstoy.

Edith Wharton (1862–1937), friends with fiction writer Henry James, was born in New York and educated in the United States and abroad. She always lived in cosmopolitan circles, which supplied the setting for most of her work. Her major theme, the destructive effects of social conventions, is observed in *The House of Mirth*. *Ethan Frome* recounts the struggle of an individual against convention. While nursing his whining, invalid wife, Frome falls in love with her young cousin, Mattie Silver. Realizing that complete happiness is unattainable, they try to commit suicide by driving a sled into a tree. They do not die, become cripples, and are eventually nursed by Mrs. Frome.

Naturalist Literature

Literary Elements

During the late eighteenth century, American literature borrowed from French and Russian novelists, resulting in intense realism. Emphasizing man's subjection to the laws of nature, particularly natural selection, man is represented as lacking in free will and controlled by his passions and environment. With its depiction of man as an animal struggling against nature in an impersonal, amoral universe, the literature omits moral considerations and stresses unpleasant phases of life.

Major Writers and Works

Stephen Crane (1871–1900) is considered the first naturalist. *The Red Badge of Courage* is a realistic psychological novel of a Civil War soldier. Obviously not in the Civil War himself, Crane drew from Tolstoy and stories of Civil War veterans to create a very convincing depiction of a young soldier's first experiences in battle. Crane's poetry was notably similar to Emily Dickinson's work.

Charlotte Perkins Gilman (1860–1935) incorporated a Darwinist perspective to different ends. In *Women and Economics*, she conducts a wide-ranging inquiry into what she called the sexual-economic revolution. She demanded complete emancipation of women, not only in particular reforms in education, voting laws, and wages but also in the redefinition of institutions of marriage and motherhood, which she believed led to oppression. *The Yellow Wallpaper*, a popular work in today's literary canon, is the study of a woman driven out of her mind by the isolation imposed by her husband. Gilman herself endured treatment known as "rest cure" for women with psychological illness.

Jack London (1876–1916), essentially self-educated, read many adventure stories as a child. He became a tramp at eighteen and traveled around the United States and Canada. The experience taught him that wealth is important, and intellectual and physical strength are needed to acquire it. He sought gold in the Klondike, where he did not find gold but rather material for his stories. London pushed naturalism to its limits. *Call of the Wild* describes a tame dog, Buck, who is forced to revert to his original primitive state. His short story "To Build a Fire" reflects survival of the fittest. London's protagonists often reflect Nietzsche's concept of a superman.

Historical Background

This period was a time of overwhelming technological changes as well as two devastating world wars. There was immense grief over the loss of the past and fear of eroding traditions. This became evident in the work of the muckrakers, a term coined by Theodore Roosevelt to describe writers whose mission focused on exposing of corruption in politics and business. Several leading periodicals of the time lent their pages to the muckrakers, among them *McClure's*, *Collier's*, and *Cosmopolitan*.

Literary Elements

Literature reflected the dominant mood of this period, which was alienation and disconnection. Writing was highly experimental as authors made extensive use of fragments, stream of consciousness, and interior dialogue in efforts to create a unique style. A kind of regionalism reemerged emphasizing the belief that history is socially constructed, paving the way for multicultural literature. Literature moved beyond the notion that a writer writes for everyone. Instead, certain writers wrote from a particular social, cultural, and ethnic perspective, about social, cultural, and ethnic interests for a particular social, cultural, and ethnic audience.

Major Writers and Works

William Faulkner (1897–1962) wrote novels and short stories that dealt with the steady decline of aristocratic families in the fictional southern town of Jefferson, modeled after his own town of Oxford, Mississippi. Faulkner is noted for his convincing portrayal of abnormal minds and for his richly descriptive style with its affected and puzzling adjectives and metaphors. He was the most original writer of his time in terms of the subject of his literature: heritage, southern memory, reality, and myth. His works include *As I Lay Dying* and *The Sound and the Fury* (his masterpiece), which examines the Compson family as demonstrated in the thoughts of three of its members: the mentally retarded Benjy, the mean, dishonest Jason, and the intelligent Quentin who commits suicide after the marriage of his sister Caddy, whom he loved.

F. Scott Fitzgerald (1896–1940) chronicled the manners, moods, and culture of his time, the "Roaring Twenties." *The Great Gatsby* is an ironic and tragic treatment of the American success myth.

Ernest Hemingway (1899–1961) joined a volunteer ambulance unit in France, then transferred to the Italian infantry until the close of World War I, finally settling in Paris as a member of the expatriate group. Influenced by Ezra Pound and Gertrude Stein, he became a leading spokesman for the lost generation, expressing feelings of war-wounded people disillusioned by the loss of faith and hope. Demonstrating a stoic writing style, Hemingway did not emphasize emotions, only bare happenings reported with understatement and dialogue. His style was concise, direct, spare, objective, precise, and rhythmic. His works include *The Sun Also Rises*, which tells of the moral collapse of a group of expatriated Americans and Englishmen, broken by the war, who turn toward escape through all possible violent diversions; *A Farewell to Arms*, a love story of an English nurse and an American ambulance lieutenant during the war; *For Whom the Bell Tolls*, which is based on an incident in the Spanish Civil War and whose thesis is that the loss of liberty in one place means loss of liberty everywhere; and *The Old Man and the Sea*, a parable of man against nature, for which he won the Pulitzer Prize. He won the Nobel Prize for Literature in 1954.

John Steinbeck (1902–1968) combined naturalism and symbolism to express outrage and compassion for the plight of the farmers displaced by the Depression and the Dust Bowl. His writing reflected a belief in the need for social justice and the hope that people can learn from the suffering of others. *Grapes of Wrath* describes the Joads, a good-hearted family of sharecroppers, their eviction from their Dust Bowl farm, and their journey to California in a ramshackle car. *Of Mice and Men*, which reads like a play, is the objective description of six distinct episodes, with thoughts revealed only through dialogue. The gigantic but feeble-minded Lennie Small is cared for by his pal, George Milton. Lennie loves animals, like mice and puppies, but kills them accidentally with his strength. When he inadvertently breaks the neck of the wife of their boss's son, George shoots Lennie to prevent his lynching.

Upton Sinclair (1878–1968) is most famous for his work *The Jungle*, written about the corrupt and disgusting meatpacking industry in the early twentieth century. Sinclair's work depicts poverty, horrendous living conditions, and hopelessness.

Major Twentieth-Century Poets

T. S. Eliot and Ezra Pound were the two most influential poets and critics of their era. Their work dictated the tone, direction, and subject matter for a generation of poets. T. S. Eliot (1888–1965) wrote about questions that addressed our place in the universe and humankind's ability to love and communicate with others as reflected in the *Love Song of J. Alfred Prufrock*. His longest work, *The Waste Land*, critiqued the failure of Western civilization as illustrated by World War I. Ezra Pound (1885–1972) used ordinary language, free verse, and concentrated word pictures, a technique used by Japanese and Chinese poets, to create extraordinary imagery. This movement, called imagism, emphasized clarity, precision, and concise word choice. His later work, for nearly fifty years, focused on the encyclopedic epic poem he titled *The Cantos*. Accused in 1945 of treason for spreading fascist propaganda on the radio, Pound was acquitted but spent a decade in a mental institution.

e. e. cummings (Edward Estlin Cummings; 1894–1962) played around with form, punctuation, spelling, font, grammar, imagery, rhythm, and syntax. His works include *The Enormous Room* (1922), *Tulips and Chimneys* (1923), and *XLI Poems* (1925).

Robert Frost (1874–1963) is considered America's best-known and loved poet. He wrote in traditional verse forms and the plain speech of rural New Englanders. His poetry often explored the conflict between nature and industrialization. Among his works are "Death of the Hired Man," "Birches," "Stopping by Woods on a Snowy Evening," "The Road Not Taken," "Out! Out!," and "Mending Wall."

Carl Sandburg (1878–1967), one of Chicago's poets, described everyday Americans in a positive tone, with simple, easy-to-understand words and free verse. He is most well known for his *Chicago Poems*.

William Carlos Williams (1883–1963) wrote poetry and prose that drew on his experience as a physician and his observations of working class women whose babies he delivered. Although friends with Ezra Pound, Williams detested fascism and represented women realistically and responsively. Like Whitman, Williams incorporated American speech, expression, local culture and ethnicity, and rhythm into his poetry. His most often studied works include "The Young Housewife," "The Red Wheelbarrow," and "This Is Just to Say."

Harlem Renaissance Literature (1915–1929)

Literary Elements

The dominant mood of this period was alienation and disconnection. Writing was highly experimental with the use of fragments, stream of consciousness, and interior dialogue. African American writers sought to create a unique style, and the Harlem Renaissance was a catalyst. The Harlem Renaissance was a black cultural movement that emerged in Harlem during the 1920s, a time when literature, music, and art flourished. There was an outpouring of black prose and poetry. A pivotal event in literature was the publication of *The New Negro* in 1925. Conceived and edited by Alain Locke (1886–1954), *The New Negro* was a special issue of the *Survey Graphic* devoted to the district of Harlem in Manhattan. The publication was a springboard for a growing sense of confidence that black America was on the verge of a second emancipation: an emancipation of the will and the achievements of the people, and in particular the artists and intellectuals. During this literary period, African American writers asked questions like, Is there, in fact or theory, "Afro-American art"? Are black literary norms the same as white literary norms? What is different and what should be held in common?

Major Writers and Works

Countee Cullen (1903–1946) was considered the "black Keats" for his youth, skill as a poet, and use of traditional forms.

Langston Hughes (1902–1967) is considered the most successful black writer in America; he wrote poetry, drama, novels, songs, movie scripts, and so on. He is most famous for his poetry, which is marked by a powerful commitment to a separate and distinctive black identity, and a sense of the shared presence of African Americans. His poetry aims at imaginatively empathizing with the black "low-down folks." Some of his most popular works include the poem "Harlem," and the collections *Montage of a*

Dream Deferred and *Ask Your Mama*; the idea of a "dream deferred" continues to resonate today.

Zora Neale Hurston (1891–1960) observed through her research that women were denied access to the pulpit and the porch, the privileged sites of storytelling, and the chance of self-definition. Her aim was to revise and adapt vernacular forms to give a voice to women, creating a democratic oral culture. Her masterpiece, *Their Eyes Were Watching God*, follows Janie Crawford, an African American woman trying to win the right to see and speak about living for herself. She resists the demeaning definitions of society that encompass her first two failed marriages, and finally she marries Tea Cake, who gives her the chance to speak herself into being. Hurston was rediscovered by the women's movement in the 1970s.

Claude McKay (1889–1948) wrote poetry that evoked the heritage of his native Jamaica. McKay's "If We Must Die" won critical acclaim, as he was the first black poet to write in the form of an Elizabethan sonnet; it also established him as a militant. His poem, which conforms to the "white/English" sonnet structure is a statement of irony. McKay uses the poetic form of his oppressors as a call to war. He advocated violent resistance to violence.

Jean Toomer (1894–1967) wrote to establish his identity as a light-skinned black man in a rigid and racist society. *Cane*, a book of prose poetry based on his personal journey back to his southern roots, described the Georgian people and landscape. Toomer depicts the South as a dreamscape and a very real place of racial prejudice and violence, a romantic night world characterized by vibrant folk culture. *Cane* ends when a black man and a white man fight over a woman they love. The white man is stabbed and as a result, a lynch mob burns the black man to death.

AMERICAN LITERATURE FROM THE TWENTIETH CENTURY TO THE PRESENT

Historical Background

During this period, a media-saturated culture has emerged where people observe life as media presents it rather than experiencing life directly. This influence insists that values are not permanent but only "local" or "historical" and media culture interprets these values. This period is marked by post World War II prosperity, social protest against the Vietnam conflict, the civil rights movement, the rise of black militancy, and the beginning of a new century and new millennium. Inspired by the work of Michel Foucault and Jacques Derrida, writers of this period introduced postmodernism, displacing the notion that literature reflected an absolute "truth" with a belief that assumed that language is unstable and ambiguous and therefore contradictory, that the author is not in full control of what he or she writes, and that literature means nothing because language means nothing and therefore, there is no way of knowing what the "meaning" of a story is.

Literary Elements

The literature of this period represents a blurring of the lines of reality with a mix of fantasy and nonfiction. Heroes and antiheroes are generally absent from the literature, and writing is concerned with the individual in isolation, and is detached, unemotional, and generally humorless. This period marks the emergence of "Beat writers" whose work was highly intellectual, antitradition, and pre-hippie, and "confessional poets" who used the anguish of their own lives to explore America's hidden despair. Ethnic and women writers also emerge during this period.

Major Writers and Works

Beat Poets

William S. Burroughs (1914–1997), a major author of experimental novels, wrote *Naked Lunch* (1959), an extremely frank and candid autobiographical account of his life as a drug addict. The text, a collection of twenty-one satirical pieces about characters in Burroughs's life, includes characters like a mad scientist who researches automatic obedience processing and a kid who manufactures "All American Males" who are merely blobs of jelly.

Allen Ginsberg (1926–1997) wrote about people who countered the hidden despair of the 1950s. His work *Howl* used wildly exuberant language and depicted theatrical behavior. He is also famous for his poem, "A Supermarket in California."

Jack Kerouac (1922–1969) is considered a writer most representative of the Beat generation. Supposedly, Kerouac wrote *On the Road* without paragraphs or page breaks on a roll of translucent paper in three weeks. The characters are modeled after friends and Beat writers Burroughs and Ginsberg. Autobiographical, *On the Road* depicts the lives of two young men who travel across America in search of a Bohemian lifestyle and wild times, which include drugs and promiscuity. Some critics panned the work, observing that it represented the increasing lack of morality of youth, but others viewed it as original.

Confessional Poets

Robert Lowell (1917–1977) wrote *Land of Unlikeness* (1944) and *Lord Weary's Castle*, for which he received a Pulitzer Prize in 1947. Full of intense anguish, Lowell's work, written in a rigidly formal style, explored the dark side of America's Puritan legacy.

Sylvia Plath (1932–1963), probably the most famous confessional poet and novelist, wrote about suicide. *The Bell Jar* is a novel about a young woman named Esther who works for a fashion magazine in New York. She begins to feel trapped by society (hence the metaphor of the bell jar) and attempts suicide several times. In the end, she regains sanity.

Anne Sexton (1928–1974), a former model and a victim of serious depression, battled with suicide most of her life. She won a Pulitzer Prize for her work *Live or Die* (1967), which addresses the reality of serious depression that results in suicide. Sexton committed suicide.

Prose and Theater (1950–Present)

Major Writers and Works

Conrad Aiken (1889–1973), poet, essayist, novelist, and critic, was one of America's major figures in American literary modernism. His most powerful story, "Silent Snow, Secret Snow," depicts a young man who falls deeper and deeper into an almost autistic world, as if cut off from society by silence and snow. Somewhat autobiographical, Aiken feared that he would go insane as his father had.

Ray Bradbury (1920) is a prolific science fiction writer best known for novels such as *Fahrenheit 451*, set in a world ruled by a totalitarian government, in which a man whose job is to burn books begins to pilfer them and when discovered, must run for his life; and *The Martian Chronicles*, a futuristic story about colonizing Mars.

Shirley Jackson (1916–1965) received critical acclaim for her short stories, especially "The Lottery," which presented the disconcerting side of a small Midwestern farming town. Her intent was to shock a nation that was becoming desensitized to brutality and violence.

Arthur Miller (1915–2005) is regarded as one of the most famous contemporary playwrights. *Death of a Salesman* relates the story of typical and ordinary American Willy Loman, whose choices and their consequences lead to the destruction of the American dream. He treats himself as an economic unit/social commodity and kills himself so his family can have the insurance money. Another of Miller's best-known plays, *The Crucible*, is based on the actual events of the Salem witch trials (1692–1693) but was also written in response to the McCarthy hearings in the early 1950s, during which Miller refused to appear before the House of Representatives' Committee on Un-American Activities spearheaded by Senator Joseph McCarthy.

Flannery O'Connor (1925–1964), considered a writer in the genre of southern Gothic, wrote stories that critique the weaknesses of humankind. A highly unorthodox Roman Catholic in a predominantly Protestant region in the South, she interpreted readings of Christian eschatology to be tough, uncompromising, and without any of the compassion of excuses of human weakness. She saw humankind as not worthy of being redeemed. "A Good Man is Hard to Find," a short story, shows a world infested with evil, corrosion, decay, and superficiality.

Dorothy Parker (1893–1967), poet and critic, was best known for her sardonic wit and quotable one-liners like "Men seldom make passes at girls who wear glasses." Parker wrote for magazines in New York, starting with *Vanity Fair*, *The New Yorker*, *Life*, and others, contributing book and play reviews and earning a reputation as a sharp-tongued critic. She also wrote scripts for films including *A Star is Born* (1937).

J. D. Salinger (1919) fought in World War II, and as a result, his experiences affected him emotionally, ultimately leaving him with a serious nervous condition. He has not been interviewed since 1980 and has never allowed his famous novel *The Catcher in the Rye* to be made into a movie. *The Catcher in the Rye* became the symbol for a generation of disaffected youth; its protagonist, Holden Caulfield, much like Salinger, is a disturbed young man who thinks that all adults are phonies.

Gertrude Stein (1874–1946) believed that the traditional narrative was the enemy of language and reality because it relied on habit and continuity rather than spontaneity and memory. She wrote *Composition as Explanation*.

James Thurber (1894–1961) is most well known for witty short stories and lumpy cartoons, which appeared in *The New Yorker*. *The Secret Life of Walter Mitty*, the tale of a henpecked husband who escapes into heroic daydreams, is one of his best stories. Thurber's absurdist cartoons featured men, women, dogs, and other strange animals.

Kurt Vonnegut (1922–2007), satirical novelist, was a soldier and prisoner during World War II. This experience influenced his novel *Slaughterhouse Five* (1969), which depicts a soldier during World War II who experiences time travel. Although Vonnegut's work is often considered science fiction, Vonnegut used this genre to write black comedy. A humanist, Vonnegut believed in the value and dignity of all humans.

Eudora Welty (1909–2001), a native of Mississippi, set most of her prose around Mississippi life. *The Robber Bridegroom* occurs in eighteenth-century Mississippi and is based loosely on a Brothers Grimm fairy tale. In this text, Welty combines actual and extraordinary events so that they become indistinguishable. The book explores the ways in which we try to understand the past and assimilate it into the present, attaching memory to locality. The story also illustrates how landscape and history are both fictions, spun out of facts of space and time.

Contemporary Multicultural Literature

African American Literature

Maya Angelou (1928), a poet who writes novels that are part autobiography, part picaresque fiction, and part social history. The central characters in her texts are strong black women. *I Know Why the Caged Bird Sings* tells of her grandmother's religious influences and her mother's blues tradition. She meets other exemplary women, including one who teaches her to speak again after a rape has struck her dumb.

James Baldwin (1924) wrote autobiographical novels about his experiences growing up in Harlem. Baldwin became a preacher like his father but felt that writing would better detail the struggles of growing up poor in a racist society. *Go Tell It on the Mountain* (1953) is an autobiographical work about growing up in Harlem. Baldwin was a critical force in the civil rights movement, writing about black identity and racial struggle in *The Fire Next Time* (1963).

Gwendolyn Brooks (1917) was the first black female poet to win the Pulitzer Prize for her poem "We Real Cool" (1959). Her work in the 1970s, *Riot* and *Family Pictures*, focused on racial harmony, but her later work *Beckonings* (1975) and *To Disembark* (1980) demonstrated disappointment due to conflict between members of the civil rights and black militant groups.

Ralph Ellison (1913–1994) is most well known for the *Invisible Man* (1953), whose theme demonstrates that society willfully ignores blacks, and his collection of poems about critical social and political essays, *Shadow and Act* (1964).

Toni Morrison (1931) is the first black woman to receive the Nobel Prize for Literature (1993). Morrison's novels, which include *Sula*, *Beloved*, *The Bluest Eye*, and *Song of Solomon*, combine fantasy, ghosts, and what she calls "rememory" or the recurrence of past events to elaborate the horrors of slavery and the struggles of African Americans after being freed.

Alice Walker (1944) wrote *The Color Purple* (1982), which won her the Pulitzer Prize. Her novels focus on poor, oppressed black women in the early 1900s. One of her most widely read short stories, "Everyday Use," which appears in the short-story collection *In Love and Trouble: Stories of Black Women* (1973), tells the story of two daughters' conflicting ideas about identity and heritage.

Richard Wright (1908–1960) was one of the first black writers to attain both fame and fortune. *Black Boy* (1945), an autobiography, recounts his childhood growing up poor in racist Mississippi and his struggle for individualism. *American Hunger* (published posthumously in 1977) tells of his disillusionment with the Communist Party. Wright also wrote more than 4,000 haikus.

Asian American Literature

Maxine Hong Kingston (1940) grew up surrounded by other immigrants from her father's village hearing stories that influenced her later writing. Her first book, *The Woman Warrior: Memoirs of a Girlhood among Ghosts*, tells of a shy girl protagonist who finds resolution as she breaks her female silence and inherits an oral tradition that she carries on as a written tradition. *China Men* details male influences in her life and celebrates the strengths and achievements of the first Chinese men in America and the exploitation and prejudice they faced.

Amy Tan (1952) wrote *The Kitchen God's Wife* to chronicle the harrowing early life of her mother, Daisy, who escaped the turmoil of the Chinese civil war and the 1949 communist takeover to come to America. Her most famous book, *The Joy Luck Club*, depicts the lives of four Chinese American immigrant families who start the "Joy Luck Club," playing the Chinese game of mahjong for money.

Jewish American Literature

Saul Bellow (1915–2005), a Canadian-born novelist, received the Nobel Prize for Literature for his works *Herzog* (1965) and *Seize the Day* (1956). Bellow primarily wrote about urban Jews struggling to find spirituality and comfort in a racist and alienating society.

Bernard Malamud (1914–1986) was a master of parables and myths. His best work, *The Natural*, is based on the life of ballplayer Eddie Waitkus, who tries to make a comeback after being shot by a mad serial killer.

Elie Wiesel (1928), a Holocaust survivor, has authored almost forty works that address Judaism, the Holocaust, racism, hatred, and genocide. He was awarded the Nobel Peace Prize and the Congressional Gold Medal. *Night*, read widely in high schools across the nation, is a memoir that depicts Wiesel's struggle and guilt at having been the only one in his family to survive the Holocaust.

Latino American Literature

Julia Alvarez (1950) was born in New York City but spent her early childhood in the Dominican Republic, her parents' native country, during the Trujillo dictatorship. She returned to the United States in 1960. *How the Garcia Girls Lost Their Accents* describes the difficulties of learning American (conversational) English and being called a "spic" at school. The text is told in reverse chronological order and narrated from shifting perspectives, beginning with her four sisters' adult lives and moving to their childhood.

Sandra Cisneros (1954) is a Mexican American (Chicano) writer born in Chicago. During her childhood, her family constantly moved between Mexico and the United States, giving her the sense that she never belonged to either culture. Her stories reveal the misogyny present in both these cultures. *The House on Mango Street* (1984), told in a series of vignettes, is a novel about a young girl, Esperanza, growing up in the Latino section of Chicago and coming into her own.

Native American Literature

Louise Erdrich (1954)[1], a member of the Turtle Mountain Band of Chippewa, was very close with her extended family, who had a tradition of storytelling. Her collection of short stories, *Love Medicine*, features characters and speakers from four Anishinaabe families, each of which is represented in nonhierarchical terms by employing speakers of various ages and stations within the community. Furthermore, the fifty-year span of the novel is told cyclically rather than chronologically, weaving back and forth between 1980 and 1930.

---

[1] http://voices.cla.umn.edu/vg/Bios/entries/erdrich_louise.html

N. Scott Momaday[2] (1934), a Kiowa Native American, grew up on the reservations and pueblos of the Southwest, far from centers of learning and letters. In 1969, he won the Pulitzer Prize for Fiction for *House Made of Dawn*, a semiautobiographical account of his life at Jemez Pueblo. His main character, Abel, returns to his New Mexico reservation after fighting in World War II and struggles to re-adapt to what was once his home.

THE LITERATURE OF GREAT BRITAIN FROM THE ANGLO-SAXON PERIOD THROUGH THE ROMANTIC PERIOD

Old English or Anglo-Saxon Literature (450–1066)

Historical Background

In 55 BC, Julius Caesar and the Roman Army made their way to Ancient Britain, which at the time was inhabited by Celtic tribes. During the next 400 years, the Roman Empire colonized Britain and introduced Christianity. When Roman legions were withdrawn to protect Rome in AD 407, however, Germanic pagan tribes such as the Jutes, the Angles, and the Saxons invaded Britain as a result. The presence of the Angles and the Saxons thus gave rise to the literary period called the Old English or the Anglo-Saxon period.

Literary Elements

Old English literature is often described as the heroic age of English literature because it represented epic battles, heroic feats, and almost supernatural characters.

Beowulf and its Legacy

Beowulf is a major example of Old English literature. Although Christian monks transcribed the anonymous poem from an oral tradition, sometime between the years AD 700 and 900, its substance harkens back four or five centuries prior. Based on the pre-Christianity, Norse legend of Sigmund the dragon slayer, the epic tells the story of Beowulf, a warrior prince from Sweden who ventures to Denmark to kill Grendel, a vicious monster that has been attacking Heorot Hall, built by the Danish king Hrothgar. Although Beowulf slays Grendel, Grendel's mother retaliates, killing the hero.

---

[2] http://www.achievement.org/autodoc/page/mom0pro-1

An epic poem told in narrative verse, *Beowulf* addresses themes of order versus disorder and man versus nature. Heorot Hall symbolizes man-made order, security, and confidence, while the monsters symbolize nature and the unknown. Beowulf also embodies the Old English belief in fate, as Beowulf must die in his final confrontation in order to be a hero. Although the story reflects a compromise between the highly ordered agricultural society and the tale of a wandering warrior, Beowulf's society is bound by loyalty to one's lord as King Hrothgar offers protection (Heorot Hall) and food in return for defending the lord.

Beowulf makes use of a variety of literary devices:

Alliterative meter: *Beowulf*, like Old English verse in general, is told in alliterative meter. There are two or three alliterating stressed syllables in each line, reflecting Germanic prosody (pattern of speech), making the poem suitable for oral performance. "Now <u>B</u>eowulf <u>b</u>ode in the <u>b</u>urg of the Scyldings" (I, *l*.1).

Kenning: Common to Old English and Old Norse poetry, kenning is a complex phrase that replaces a simpler word to add color to a poem or to evoke imagery. For example, *sea wood* is used in place of *ship* or *mail armor* in place of *helmet*.

Stock epithet: Predominant in an oral tradition, this is a descriptive word or phrase used repeatedly in place of a name. For example, God is "the Ruler of Glory."

Caesura: A break in a line or poetry or a grammatical pause, caesura emerged from the oral tradition of poetry, in which the speaker pauses to break up a line of verse. There is a pause or break in every line of *Beowulf*. "LO, praise of the prowess of people-kings of spear-armed Danes, (*caesura*) in days long sped, (*caesura*) we have heard, (*caesura*) and what honor the athelings won!"(Prelude, *l*. 1).

Other Major Writers and Works

The Ecclesiastical History of the English People (Historia Ecclesiastica Gentis Anglorum), was written in 731 by Bede, the first English historian. His text recounts that St. Augustine's mission was to bring literary materials from Rome to England to support worship and service of the church. He explained how Latin was integrated into English cathedral and monastic schooling and how Christianity spread literacy. He also introduced the Roman alphabet to Britain.

The *Junius* manuscript, the *Vercelli Book*, and the *Exeter Book* are three other significant collections of English verse, all produced in monastic *scriptoria* or "writing rooms."

The Seafarer, an anonymous lyric poem, reflects on the hardships of living at sea, in contrast to the comforts of a settled life on land, like the insularity of the castle in *Beowulf* against the monsters on the outside. An **elegy**, which in Old English literature is a complaint about the struggles of isolation and separation told in the first person, *The Seafarer* describes the speaker's nostalgia for his past life on shore but a deep love of the sea, despite its loneliness. A metaphor for the Christian path of self-denial, the sea symbolizes a life on earth of struggle and difficulty, which is brief, however, compared to an everlasting life of happiness in heaven. In later periods, the term *elegy* came to describe a poem lamenting the loss of someone who has died.

Medieval English or Middle English Literature (1066–1510)

Historical Background

In 1066, William the Conqueror and the French Normans conquered Britain's lowlands (the Norman Conquest), where William replaced the English ruling class with the Norman French ruling class. During this time, Norman French became the language of the court and government, and Latin remained the language of learning and religion. Forcing the English church into the Norman view of piety, efficiency, and scholarship, William invited full participation in the church, and Christian discipline became a dominant part of life. The Normans also introduced ideals of chivalry linked to feudal obligations.

Literary Elements

Literary forms during this time emerged from the oral tradition. These forms were venues that enabled the church to instruct and guide its parishioners and permitted illiterate peoples to hear and see literature. **Morality plays** dramatized the abstract themes of vice versus virtue or mankind's struggle with his soul. The characters in such plays personified virtues, vices, or mental attributes. Set in allegory, a symbolic story that has a moral, political, or spiritual meaning, morality plays imparted lessons to guide a moral life. **Mystery and miracle plays** dramatized biblical events and stories in the lives of saints or martyrs that once truly existed. The

MTEL Tip

Characters in morality plays personify virtues, vices, or mental attributes.

major theme pervading such plays was inevitable punishment for those that revolted against divine guidance. **Folk ballads**, short, traditional, narratives told in song and transmitted orally from generation to generation, also emerged during this time. These generally adhered to the culture's own peculiar rhetoric and structure, unimpacted by literary conventions. **Frame stories**, or a story within a story, used fictive narrative or a series of smaller stories. Geoffrey Chaucer used this device in many of his stories, in particular *The Canterbury Tales*.

Major Writers and Works

The *Domesday Book*, a survey of English land ownership commissioned by the king in 1086, recorded the church's wealth and catalogued the material and territorial possessions of the newly imported secular aristocracy.

Geoffrey Chaucer (1340–1400), the "father of English literature," wrote in English vernacular instead of Latin. Chaucer wrote *The Canterbury Tales* during the latter part of his life. *The Canterbury Tales*, most likely the greatest work produced in Middle English, chronicles tales told by twenty-nine people representing various classes of society, during their four-day pilgrimage to the shrine of Thomas à Becket at Canterbury. Each pilgrim tells two tales on the sixty-mile ride to Canterbury and two on the way back. The significance of *The Canterbury Tales* is that it offers a cross section of British life, including saints' biographies; a sermon; animal fables; romantic escapades; religious allegories; fabliaux (cynical, humorous, or crass stories); pious, moralistic tales; and lewd and vulgar tales told by different members of English society: a knight, a miller, a monk, a shipman, a parson, and so on.

Sir Gawayne and the Grene Knight (also spelled *Sir Gawain and the Green Knight*) was written by the Gawain poet, a fourteenth-century contemporary of Chaucer. *Sir Gawayne and the Grene Knight* was the first great love story, a sophisticated tale of chivalry and emotion. Its 2,530 lines unite two Celtic legends: the Beheading and the Wooing. Alliterative verse varies from twenty to more than forty lines per stanza, with each being concluded by a **bob**, five short lines rhyming *ababa*.

Sir Thomas Malory (1450–1470) wrote *Le Morte d'Arthur*, actually written *Le Morte Darthur* ("the Death of Arthur"), which compiled French, English, and Malory's own stories about King Arthur, Merlin, Guenevere, and the Knights of the Round Table. The tales are a literary reflection of the political feudalism and chivalric code of the time.

Renaissance Literature (1510–1660)

Historical Background

The Renaissance (1450–1600) was the intellectual and cultural movement that embraced the reemergence of scholarship, ancient learning, religious and scientific inquiry, and the liberation of the individual from intellectual tyranny, feudalism, and secular matters of the church. Influences that led to the Renaissance included humanism, which revived the Greek and Roman emphasis on the "here and now" rather than "the hereafter"; geographic exploration and discovery; the invention of the printing press and the art of moveable type, which helped disseminate learning throughout Europe; and the Copernican system, which demonstrated that the earth and other planets revolved around the sun, upsetting traditional theology and science.

The Reformation, which began in 1517, marked a time of challenge to the dogma and practices of the Roman Catholic Church. King Henry VIII, desiring a male heir, petitioned Pope Clement VII to annul his marriage to Catherine of Aragon because she had only given him a daughter. When Clement refused, Henry made himself head of the Church of England and married Anne Boleyn. Their daughter Elizabeth I eventually became queen of England. Supported by Martin Luther's Ninety-five Theses published in 1517, which challenged the pope, the Roman Catholic Church's practice of selling indulgences, and the church's position on purgatory, the English Reformation represented England's turn to Protestantism.

The Elizabethan Age (1558–1603), the reign of Elizabeth I, signified the end of the medieval age. Although her predecessor, Queen Mary attempted to convert England back to Catholicism, she died, and Elizabeth firmly established Protestantism as the country's faith. Elizabeth identified with her country like no other ruler, which led to a growth of nationalism. The English defeat of Catholic Spain in 1588 further unified and identified England with Protestantism.

Elizabethan Literature (1558–1603)

Historical Background

Elizabeth's reign (1558–1603) was one of unprecedented literary growth. Forty-five years of peace allowed the arts to flourish. James Burbage leased land on which he built the first theater in London in 1576. The Globe Theatre, or just "the Theatre" as it was called, gave rise to drama troops such as the Earl of Leicester's Men and other theater "companies." Other London theaters such as the Rose Theatre and the Hope Theatre also emerged, but none was as popular and famous as the Globe Theatre. When Burbage's lease expired, the landlord, Giles Allen, refused to release the land because he wanted to dismantle the building in order to use the building materials. Burbage found a loophole in the lease, however, and with the help of the Acting Troupe dismantled the theatre and moved it to Bankside in Southwark. The new theater was called the Globe.

William Shakespeare and His Works

A prolific playwright and poet, William Shakespeare (1564–1616) is credited as the author of thirty-seven plays, including ten history, ten tragedy, and seventeen comedy plays; numerous sonnets; and several other poems. He also developed a new form of the sonnet, which is characterized by an octave (a set of eight lines) that presents some form of conflict, and a sestet (a set of six lines) that typically resolves the conflict.

During Shakespeare's time, all plays needed to be registered before they could be published. This provided censorship of critique of the Crown, public matters, and freedom of thought. Most of Shakespeare's work was not published until seven years after his death. Shakespeare wrote five types of plays: histories, tragedies, comedies, tragicomedies often referred to as romances or pastorals, and problem plays.

The history plays dramatized power struggles over five generations of monarchs beginning with King John in the Hundred Years' War with France, to Joan of Arc in *Henry V*, and the struggle between the House of York and the House of Lancaster, more commonly called the War of the Roses.

Shakespeare's tragedies always include a tragic hero (occasionally accompanied by a tragic heroine), a prominent and conspicuous man of rank who suffers profound calamity, which eventually leads to his death. Most often as in *Macbeth*, *Hamlet*, *King Lear*, or *Othello*, the hero plunges from a place of glory and honor to catastrophic depths. Shakespeare's tragic heroes are always responsible for their downfalls, in which one action leads to a series of complex consequences that create woefully encompassing situations. These characters always possess a tragic human flaw of frailty or perception whose realization comes too late to prevent inevitable catastrophe. The most popular tragedies include *Macbeth*, *Hamlet*, *King Lear*, *Othello*, *Julius Caesar*, and *Romeo and Juliet*.

Elizabethan comedy was defined differently than contemporary comedy. Shakespeare's comedies, more lighthearted than his other works, always have a happy ending, which usually involves marriage, and typically include disguises and mistaken identities; struggling lovers, jesters, and fools; and tensions and conflicts created by the elders in the family. The comedies incorporate intricate plots, puns, wordplay, humor, satire, irony, insults, and elaborately contrived endings. The hero is usually strong and virtuous, but possesses a character flaw. All Shakespearean comedies have five acts, in which the third contains the climax. Unlike the tragedies, there is no foreboding or foreshadowing; instead, Shakespeare jumps right into the plot. The most popular comedies include *Much Ado About Nothing*, *A Midsummer Night's Dream*, *As You Like It*, *The Merchant of Venice*, and *Twelfth Night*.

MTEL Tip

All of Shakespeare's comedies have five acts.

Tragicomedies, romances, or pastorals capitalize on medieval tales, focus on nature, and depict the struggles of a hero on a quest. Although these plays mix elements of tragedy and comedy, they always end happily. The characters do suffer loss, and they journey from unhappiness riddled with serious obstacles such as deceit, hurt, and disloyalty, but they overcome and essentially reverse these challenges through sacrifice and penance, ultimately gaining forgiveness. Furthermore, by the end of the play, all characters celebrate in the hero's triumph. Such plays include *The Winter's Tale*, *The Tempest*, *Pericles*, and *Troilus and Cressida*.

Problem plays, a term coined by critic F. S. Boas, describes those plays where the hero must negotiate a contemporary social problem or moral dilemma. In these plays, the usually ambiguous tone oscillates between dark and comedic, and the complex ending often seems abrupt, artificial, or even hokey as justice is rarely served. *All's Well That Ends Well*, *Measure for Measure*, and *Troilus and Cressida* are considered problem plays.

Other Major Writers and Works

Thomas More (1478–1535) offered a different literary focus when he described an imaginary commonwealth that incorporated the ideals of political and social order, education, and religion. More's *Utopia* advocates religious toleration and opposes organized war. All things are physically perfect, streets are twenty feet wide, and every house has a garden. More's life, however, was not as utopian as his work. Refusing to disavow the pope's authority and affirm King Henry VIII's divorce, More was beheaded for high treason.

Edmund Spenser (1552–1599) created *The Faerie Queene* to fashion the virtues and discipline of a gentleman or nobleman. Each of the twelve books features a knight that represents one of Aristotle's twelve virtues. This allegory represents the struggle of the English Reformed Church with atheism and paganism and glorifies the state. Queen Elizabeth, along with other contemporary Elizabethans, is represented in the text. In this work, Spenser created the nine-line Spenserian stanza, with eight lines written in iambic pentameter followed by a single alexandrine line in iambic hexameter.

Sir Thomas Wyatt (1503–1542), a contemporary of More, introduced the sonnet into English literature. Revising the Petrarchan sonnet (also known as the Italian Sonnet), Wyatt changed the rhyme scheme from *abba abba cdcdcd* or *abba abba cdecde* to *abba abba cddc ee*, thus ending his poems with a rhyming couplet. This later became the English sonnet.

John Lyly (1554–1606) was a dramatist and court poet. He became immensely popular around 1580 after writing *Euphues, or the Anatomy of Wit*. The father of euphuism, an elaborate style of prose that has complex sentence structure using much parallelism and including proverbs, similes from pseudoscience, and incidents from history, Lyly devoted his writing to the ladies. Lyly's romantic hero Euphues, whose name means "well-endowed by nature," and his style impacted Shakespeare's writing, especially in the characters of Moth in *Love's Labours Lost* and Polonius in *Hamlet*. Lyly also contributed writing to Martin Marprelate, a literary movement that critiqued Archbishop Whitgift and the Star Chamber for decreeing that the archbishop and the bishop of London had to approve all publications.

Christopher Marlowe (1564–1593), considered Shakespeare's greatest predecessor and popular for his tragedies, wrote *The Tragical History of Doctor Faustus* and *The Jew of Malta*. Marlowe was the first playwright to use blank verse in drama. He is also known for his poetry, especially "The Passionate Shepherd," which begins "Come live with me and be my love . . ." to which Sir Walter Raleigh responded with "The Nymph's Reply to the Shepherd."

Thomas Nashe (1567–1601), a satirist, poet, pamphleteer, playwright, and early progenitor of the novel, was one of many writers educated at Cambridge who wrote to earn money. His work critiqued contemporaries that plagiarized the works of classical authors and praised innovative writers like Spenser. Under the pen name Pasquil, Nashe, like Lyly, authored pamphlets in support of Martin Marprelate.

George Peele (1556–1593), a dramatist and lyricist known for his flowery diction and poetic beauty, wrote blank verse in a way that was musical and sweet, different from Marlowe or Shakespeare.

Sir Walter Raleigh (1552–1618), a navigator, explorer, historian, poet, courtier, and a member of parliament and one of Queen Elizabeth's favorites, wrote *The History of the World* and a series of romantic poems, one which is a response to Christopher Marlowe's "The Passionate Shepherd." Known for an extensive wardrobe, Sir Walter may very well have thrown his coat over a puddle so that a lady could walk across.

Sir Philip Sidney (1554–1586), an Elizabethan courtier and poet, romanticized the pastoral and rustic way of life. Considered the flower of chivalry, he wrote numerous sonnets and *The Defense of Poetry*.

Jacobean Literature (1603–1625)

Historical Background

King James Stuart assumed the English throne in 1603 after Elizabeth I. English Puritans thought James would be sympathetic because he had been raised by Presbyterian tutors, but when Puritans submitted "Millenary," a petition requesting that each district's clergy meet to discuss doctrine, James became enraged and told them to conform or leave. First, Puritans left for Holland, then for New England, where they became the Pilgrim fathers of American history. At the same time, King James ordered a new translation of the Bible, making the King James Bible one of the most influential texts ever published in English. He also raised taxes to support his profligate lifestyle.

Literary Elements

Literature of the Jacobean Age was marked by sophistication and literary rivalry. This was the age of metaphysical poetry. This poetry was abstruse, employing powerful metaphors as a means of structure rather than description, striking phrases, and witty colloquialisms. Expressing anxiety about the crisis between church and court, this poetry was intentionally cerebral and difficult to understand.

Major Writers and Works

Francis Bacon (1561–1626), a philosopher, lawyer, and essayist, challenged medieval beliefs about science and approached scientific inquiry inductively. Bacon championed the scientific method of inquiry, which focused on using data gathered via the senses to discover knowledge about the natural world. Unlike his contemporary, John Donne,

Bacon wrote objective essays that described the pros and cons of abstract phenomena using common objects and everyday facts and sensory images.

John Donne (1572–1631), a metaphysical poet, wrote about worldly experiences in opposition to the Petrarchan love sonnets of his time. Born into a Roman Catholic family during a time of anti-Catholic sentiment, Donne eventually grappled with Catholic doctrine, writing two anti-Catholic arguments, which won him favor with King James I, who later appointed him royal chaplain. Donne is known as one of the greatest preachers of his time. Among his works are *"The Flea,"* *An Anatomy of the World*, "Death Be Not Proud," and *Holy Sonnets*.

Ben Jonson (1572–1637), poet and playwright, was best known for his satiric comedies. His first major play, *Every Man in His Humour*, was performed in the Globe Theater by an acting troupe called Lord Chamberlain's Men, in which William Shakespeare played the lead. The play, a series of comedies, poked fun at human actions based on impulse and affectation. Johnson's work addressed a wide audience because he wrote both in a scholarly fashion and in the vernacular of the common people.

Thomas Middleton (1580–1627) was a playwright, poet, and city chronologer whose work reflected a humorous cynicism about the human race. No person or rank was sacred; his characters represented every social rank and every sin, from greed to lust. There are no heroes in his works. A Calvinist, Middleton believed that salvation was reserved for a select few and that most would be damned, which is strongly reflected in his dramas. His works include *A Chaste Maid in Cheapside*, *Women Beware Women*, and *The Changeling*.

Carolinean Literature (1629–1649)

Historical Background

Succeeding King James in 1625, Charles Stuart I, sympathizing with the Catholics and eager to involve England in European affairs, sent troops to help the French and petitioned Parliament to support participation in the Thirty Years' War. This maddened the English, who did not want to spend tax money or become involved. Believing in High Anglicanism, a ceremonial and sacramental version of the Church of England, he further aggravated religious dissenters. Angry, Charles ruled England without Parliament, beginning "Eleven Years of Tyranny." When he introduced the High Anglican version of the English Book of Common Prayer, Scotland rebelled, forcing Charles to summon Parliament to get funds for the war. Vehement disagreements between Charles and Parliament caused the English to take sides—the Cavaliers loyal to Charles and the Roundheads loyal to Parliament—and civil war broke out. Charles I was beheaded in 1649, and Charles II was exiled.

Literary Elements

Literature of the Carolinean Age was marked by Cavalier poetry. These poets wrote mostly of love and sex and the ideal of being careless. All the Cavalier poets were aligned with Charles I and professed a libertine lifestyle. The Cavaliers were noted for their *carpe diem* or "seize the day" poems, erotic, libidinous, and candidly sexual poetry that reflected a philosophy of "life is too short, so live it to the fullest." This rhetorical device has pervaded literature since the Bible as it suggests both the enormous possibility and futility of life. The Stuart courts encouraged the circulation of literature and masques. Masques are static, superficial, spectacular pageants, rich in costume, scenery, and song with a casual and usually simple storyline.

Major Writers and Works

Robert Herrick (1591–1674) wrote *carpe diem* poetry. The often quoted "Gather ye rosebuds while ye may" comes from his famous poem "To the Virgins, to Make Much of Time," which implores readers to live life to the fullest because of the ephemeral nature of life itself.

Richard Lovelace (1618–1758), a Cavalier poet and Royalist, presented a petition to Parliament favoring the restoration of the Anglican bishops who had been excluded from the Long Parliament. As a result, Lovelace was imprisoned in Westminster Gatehouse where he wrote "To Althea, From Prison," which includes the famous words: "Stone walls do not a prison make, nor iron bars a cage." He is also noted for "To Lucasta, Going to the Wars."

Andrew Marvell (1621–1678), John Milton's assistant and protege, wrote *carpe diem* poetry and satire. "To His Coy Mistress" is a famous *carpe diem* poem in which the speaker tries to convince his mistress to have sex.

John Milton (1608–1674), a Puritan and countercultural poet, wrote sonnets and complex poetry that were solemn, religious, and puritanical. Famous for *Paradise Lost*, based on the Book of Genesis, Milton's religious work was written in blank verse and defied the clear, simple, and sensual *carpe diem* poetry of the period; it was haled as an epic poem comparable in scale to Homer's *Iliad* and *Odyssey* and Virgil's *Aeneid*. Milton also wrote the elegy "Lycidas," a moving poem that laments the demise of a dear school friend.

Sir John Suckling (1609–1642), also a Cavalier poet, wrote light, melodious lyrical poetry such as "Ballad Upon a Wedding." Sir John also added the elements of masques to his drama.

The Commonwealth Age (1649–1660)

Historical Background

During this time, the army, led by Oliver Cromwell, assumed leadership, making Britain a military dictatorship. Lord and protector of England, Cromwell, a Roundhead, presided in lieu of the traditional monarchy during a time of extreme civil war and costly foreign wars. Using force and intolerance, Cromwell closed the theaters and ruled like a dictator. After his death in 1660, his son Richard Cromwell assumed rule but did not have the confidence of the army and accumulated immense debt. Consequently, Richard abdicated his throne, leading to the Restoration.

The Restoration (1660–1689) of Charles II as King of Ireland, England, and Scotland was a reaction against extreme Puritanism. After Charles II died, however, James II, a Catholic, assumed the throne. King James II prohibited clergy from preaching against Catholicism, enlarged the army and stationed it outside London as a threat to Protestant dissidents. James was eventually deposed and fled the country. William of Orange and Mary (James's eldest daughter), both Protestants, took the throne, concluding the Glorious Revolution of 1688, ending the house of Stuart in England, and ensuring Parliament's dominance and the rule of law. The agrarian economy moved toward international trade, leading to increased colonization and trade in India, America, and the East Indies; the creation of a mercantile class; and the emergence of the stock market. Concomitant growth in sea power resulted in the development of general foreign policy.

Literary Elements

During this time, theaters, which had been closed under Cromwell's rule, reopened, giving rise to Restoration comedies. These comedies were sexually explicit, addressing topics of the day, busy plots, and the emergence of celebrity actors and actresses. The most popular dramas entertained murder, incest, and madness set in Italy or Spain, both

Catholic countries. Macabre in nature, these plays included villains and other characters that went to their deaths. Printing and publishing also grew during this time.

Major Writers and Works

John Bunyan (1628–1688), a preacher and student of scripture, is most well-known for his Christian allegory, *The Pilgrim's Progress*. He used simple and plain language to preach and write about theology. A diehard nonconformist and renegade Baptist, he was imprisoned for twelve years for preaching without a license. During this time, he wrote sermons, poems, books, and essays. Upon release from prison, he published the first of several editions of *The Pilgrim's Progress* (1678), an allegory in which a character named Christian encounters various perils on his way to Heaven and where vices and virtues are personified. This text became a standard of English literature and a Protestant catechism.

John Dryden (1631–1700), considered one of the chief founders of modern English prose, the first great English critic, and the most representative writer of the Restoration, dominated during this literary period. Although not particularly known as theatrical, he brought drama to the world and was known for his heroic dramas. Eventually his writing abandoned the heroic couplet and reverted to the Greeks' unities of action, time, and space. Juxtaposing absurd imagery with genuine beauty, Dryden had no sense of what was ridiculous or ghastly. His best-known plays are *All for Love*, *The Hind and the Panther*, and *The Rehearsal*. Dryden's major contribution to English literature was a direct and simple style of literary criticism. Elaborating on the ideas of Ben Jonson, Dryden integrated authority, weighed and considered numerous perspectives, and offered theses supported by textual evidence, essentially applying genuine standards of criticism.

Thomas Hobbes (1588–1679), an exiled philosopher who returned to England during the Restoration, wrote *Leviathan*. Believing in man's corruptible, materialistic, and egoistic nature, Hobbes encouraged humankind to surrender its power to the authority of an absolute sovereign; otherwise, consistent struggle over power would lead to an endless state of war.

Lucy Hutchinson (1620–1681), a well-educated Puritan author and biographer, is considered one of the progenitors of modern prose. The wife of one of Cromwell's most trusted officers, Colonel John Hutchinson who was imprisoned after the Restoration, she decided to write *Memoirs of the Life of Colonel Hutchinson*, which emerged as a short history of the political and religious struggles that ensued during the reign of the Stuart kings. Written from a dissenting Puritan perspective, *Memoirs* describes the lust and intemperance James I wrought on the throne as opposed to the honor, glory, and wealth his predecessor Queen Elizabeth I established during her reign.

Eighteenth Century Literature (1690–1780)

Historical Background

During this time, England began to take pride in being set apart from European norms, especially from the cultural and religious politics of Louis XIV of France. Although England and Scotland still remained hostile to each other, resulting in two Jacobite rebellions, a new morality, which reacted against the extravagance of the Restoration period, just as the Restoration had been a reaction against extreme Puritanism, emerged. This new morality was one of order, measure, and propriety, and gentility became fashionable in English society. With the introduction of coffee to England, coffeehouses became popular settings for literary and political discussions.

New thinking in science and philosophy also pervaded this period. Sir Isaac Newton published *Principia* in 1687 and *Opticks* in 1704, suggesting that there were intelligible laws in nature that could be demonstrated by math and physics. The ideal of universal law and order had widespread ramifications, especially in the context of

MTEL Tip

Newton suggested that there were laws in nature that could be demonstrated by math and physics.

contemporary philosophy. In the eighteenth century, rationalism, formalism, and reason prevailed over emotions and creativity. Descartes's *cogito ergo sum* ("I think, therefore I am") in his *Meditations* helped to usher in this kind of thinking. John Locke, a political philosopher who returned to England during the reign of William and Mary, believed that our understanding of reality derives from what we experience through the senses. The political implications of his theories supported the belief that people are born equal and that education can free people from the subjugation of tyranny. Locke also believed that government has a moral obligation to guarantee that individuals always retain sovereignty over their own rights, including ownership of property that results from their own labor. His *Essay Concerning Human Understanding*, an epistemological account rejecting innate ideas, observed that external sensations and internal reflection make up a person's body of knowledge (i.e., tabula rasa, or "blank slate").

Literary Elements

Marked by reasoned argument, good humor, and common sense in the Francis Bacon tradition as opposed to the discord between superstition and enthusiasm observed in

Bernard de Mandeville's (1670–1733) *Fable*, literature returned to neoclassicism as writers tried to imitate characteristics of Virgil, Horace, Cicero, and Lucretius, and others of the Augustan Age in Rome. This age marked the beginning of the newspaper, the periodical, and journalism. There was a return to satire and comedic banter. This period is sometimes called the Age of the Novel.

Major Writers and Works

Joseph Addison (1672–1719), essayist, playwright, poet, and statesman, and his dearest friend, essayist, pamphleteer, playwright, and politician Richard Steele (1672–1729) are most famous for publishing *The Tatler*, which eventually became *The Spectator*, a magazine whose purpose was to provide English readers with topics suitable for educated conversations and social interactions. These topics often promoted marriage, family, and courtesy. Addison and Steele desired to bring philosophy out of the libraries and colleges to the coffeehouses.

James Boswell (1740–1795) earned major recognition for immortalizing Dr. Samuel Johnson in *The Life of Samuel Johnson*. Although considered a celebrity chaser, Boswell developed a mutually gratifying relationship with Johnson.

William Congreve (1670–1729), a contemporary of Irish satirist Jonathan Swift and a student of John Dryden, is considered the greatest master of the English comedy of "repartee" (banter). Known for his highbrow, sexual comedy of manners, a type of comedy that satirizes the peculiar affectations of high society, Congreve used stock characters such as the fop or the rake (someone old trying to be young), plots that depicted illicit and scandalous love affairs, and bawdy and spirited dialogue. His works include *The Way of the World*, *The Mourning Bride*, and *Love for Love*.

Daniel Defoe (1659–1731), a pioneering novelist, journalist, and secret agent, was the first great realistic writer, spanning the interval between the old adventure novel and the modern realistic novel of character. His work *Robinson Crusoe* fixed the form of the historical novel, which led to Sir Walter Scott's *Waverly* and *Ivanhoe*.

Henry Fielding (1707–1754), a comedic satirist, is considered the founder of the English prose epic. In 1730, he produced *Tom Thumb*, which is his most famous and popular drama. It supposedly made Jonathan Swift laugh for the second time in his life. Fielding wrote twenty-five plays, but his novels gained critical acclaim, such as *The History of Tom Jones, a Foundling* and *The History of the Adventures of Joseph Andrews*, a parody of Samuel Richardson's *Pamela*. His witty burlesques, which critiqued government, eventually became his undoing. Sir Robert Walpole, prime minister at the time and focus of Fielding's satire, issued the Theatrical Licensing Act, ending Fielding's career in the theater.

Oliver Goldsmith (1728–1774), incredibly versatile, humorous, and gifted, gained fame for publishing a collection of essays, *The Citizen of the World*, a hugely successful play, *She Stoops to Conquer*, and a novel about English country life, *The Vicar of Wakefield*. His style commingled formal and colloquial speech with grace, finesse, and compassion.

Thomas Gray (1716–1771), most noted for "Elegy Written in a Country Churchyard," is considered one of the most important poets of the eighteenth century. His poetry was elegant, melancholic, and somewhat artificial, but reflected the literary elements of the period. His other works include "Ode to Spring," "Hymn to Adversity," and "Ode on the Favourite Cat Drowned in a Tub of Gold Fishes."

Although a Scotsman, James Hogg (1770–1835), a poet and novelist, wrote in Scots and English. Noted for *The Private Memoirs and Confessions of a Justified Sinner*, Hogg wrote about persecution, torture, delusion, and despair.

Dr. Samuel Johnson (1709–1784), a poet, critic, biographer, and political essayist, became a national sensation after writing *The Dictionary of the English Language*. The first writer to include quotations from other noteworthy authors to illustrate definitions, he took nine years to write his famous dictionary, which became the foundation of all subsequent dictionaries. One of his most famous quips is "Patriotism is the last refuge of a scoundrel." Johnson also wrote *The Lives of the Poets* and *The Rambler*.

Alexander Pope (1688–1744), a master of Augustan (neoclassicist) poetry, wrote a mock, heroic epic poem, *The Rape of the Lock*. This five-cantos work, echoing the *Iliad*, humorously details the story of young woman who flirts, drinks coffee, wears makeup, plays cards, and suddenly has a lock of hair stolen by an ardent suitor. A satire, *Rape* critiques high society and its penchant for glamour. An accomplished essayist, Pope wrote *Essay on Man* and *Moral Essays*. His first major essay, *An Essay on Criticism*, contains the famous line: "A little learning is a dangerous thing."

Samuel Richardson (1689–1761), a great English novelist and strong rival of Henry Fielding, was the first psychological novelist. An incredible letter writer, Richardson did not write his first novel until he was fifty-one years old. His first novel, *Pamela; or, Virtue Rewarded*, presented a heroine who resists the advances of a lascivious master until he marries her. Readers enjoyed the story because it offered a realistic and humble setting and a story that could happen to anyone as opposed to previous romances replete with larger-than-life heroes accomplishing larger-than-life feats. This and his other novels had a moral purpose: resisting temptation is virtuous and results in reward.

Richard Sheridan (1751–1816), a skilled Irish playwright, reestablished the prominence of English comedies. His works *The Rivals*, *The School for Scandal*, and *The Critic* won acclaim for their ingenious plots, playfulness of language, and social satire.

Jonathan Swift (1667–1745), one of the most distinguished satirists of all time, believed that humankind destroyed and ruined everything it touched and that humans were generally odious beasts. His loathing of mankind is particularly evident in *Gulliver's Travels*, a political and social satire that relegates humans to filthy horses called Yahoos, who are ruled by intelligent and noble horses called Houyhnhnms. He considered being born in Ireland one of his misfortunes, yet he wrote extensively about Irish affairs during the Irish potato famine, best reflected in *A Modest Proposal*, wherein he suggests that the Irish landlords eat the children. Swift spent significant time in a mental institution.

With the emergence of periodicals and newspapers, this period was also marked by essays and editorials, which appeared in both venues.

Horace Walpole (1717–1797), a printer, author, and friend of Thomas Gray, began his own printing press at Strawberry Hill, a forty-acre estate including a structure that was redesigned in the style of Georgian Gothic architecture. Inspired by the reconstruction and a nightmare, Walpole wrote the first Gothic novel, *Castle of Otranto*. In this tale of curses, romance, terror, and fantasy, Walpole blended ancient and modern romance.

Romantic Literature (1780–1830)

Historical Background

The romantic period endured the Industrial Revolution with the invention of the spinning jenny, the power loom, and the steam engine. The discovery of large pockets of iron ore encouraged the growth of industrial towns and a powerful banking system. Inspired by the French, the movement broke with political conformity, finally recognizing the rights of women and children. Laborers began to organize and child labor laws were instituted to protect child laborers from exploitation. This period saw a decline in nobility and the emergence of a middle class. Wives stayed home and attended to the domestic needs of the family while the husband went off to *work*.

Literary Elements

The romantic period also marked a rebellion against neoclassicism. Emphasizing passion, imagination, and a deep sense of wonder and mystery, writing moved from the objective view of the Enlightenment to a stronger focus on subjective feelings. As most of the romantics had read Jean-Jacques Rousseau, who denounced almost everything about the eighteenth century, the romantic period was essentially a European movement. The romantic poets revived the Spenserian stanza and ode. Strongly influenced by the French Revolution, poetry recounted the triumph of the human spirit. A reaction to increasing industrialization, this literary movement elevated art in contrast to filthy factories and championed humanitarianism and democracy. Introduced earlier, Gothic romance, replete with sliding panels, secret chambers, rattling chains, eerie groans, shrouded figures, and bizarre torture also became popular. In light of the French Revolution, there was also a break in political conformity, as seen through the works of married couple William Godwin and Mary Wollstonecraft: *Caleb Williams*, written by the former, and *Maria, or, The Wrongs of Women* and *A Vindication of the Rights of Woman* by the latter.

Major Writers and Works

Robert Burns (1759–1796), a Scottish poet noted for his almost musical poetry, sense of humor, and ability to give dignity to the common man through his use of only Scottish dialect, was considered one of the great songwriters of his time. Hailed the national poet of Scotland, Burns authored hundreds of works including songs "Auld Lang Syne" and "Comin' thro the Rye" and poems such as "To a Mouse," "To a Louse," and "Highland Mary."

Poet of the Pre-Romantic Period

William Blake (1757–1827), a pre-romantic poet, painter, and engraver, anticipated Samuel Taylor Coleridge's simple diction and style, romanticism, and communion with nature. Written from a child's perspective of wonder, *Songs of Innocence*, which includes "Little Boy Lost," "Little Boy Found," and "Little Lamb," describes the natural world of spontaneity, innocence, and beauty. *Songs of Experience* assumes an ironic and darker tone where the beauty and innocence of childhood is met with the ugliness, truth, and fear often associated with adulthood. Blake's pervasive themes of heaven and hell, innocence and experience, and good and evil heavily influenced the romantic poets.

First-Generation Romantic Poets

Samuel Taylor Coleridge (1772–1834), a poet, collaborated with William Wordsworth on *Lyrical Ballads*. Far darker than Wordsworth and an opium addict, Coleridge preferred the weird and supernatural, unusual romantic themes, and creating hallucinatory realities. *The Rime of the Ancient*, a supernatural tale of sin, penance, and salvation, opened the collaborative work *Lyrical Ballads*. Among his other works are "Kubla Khan" and *Christabel*.

William Wordsworth (1770–1850), perhaps the most renowned romantic poet, is attributed, along with friend Samuel Taylor Coleridge, with launching the romantic poetry movement with his first major work, *Lyrical Ballads*. His immense love of nature and the landscape of the Lake District, where he spent most of his time, inspired his work. His magnum opus, *The Prelude*, is considered to be semiautobiographical. Wordsworth also wrote "A Slumber Did My Spirit Seal," one of the Lucy poems; as well as "An Ode to Duty," "I Wandered Lonely as a Cloud," "To a Skylark," "Tintern Abbey," and "Ode: Intimations of Immortality from Recollections of Early Childhood," among others.

Second-Generation Romantic Poets

Lord George Byron (1788–1824), a libertine, spent time with the Shelleys in Switzerland and wrote *The Giaour*, a romantic, Oriental tale (the theme of the "Oriental" was a popular infusion to the romantic tale), "She Walks in Beauty," and the successful, satirical epic *Don Juan*.

John Keats (1795–1821), a doctor at a time when being so was considered a working profession, was somewhat out of his element as a poet. Like his contemporaries, Keats revered a return to nature and beauty as observed in works such as "Ode on a Grecian Urn," "Ode to a Nightingale," "Endymion," and "Hyperion."

Percy Bysshe Shelley (1792–1822), a poet against despotism, was expelled from Oxford for writing and distributing *The Necessity of Atheism*. His other works include "Ozymandias," "Ode to the West Wind," "A Dirge," and the longer piece *Prometheus Unbound*. His sister Mary Shelley would eventually write *Frankenstein*, a true tale of horror and man's inhumanity to man, which won literary acclaim and financial reward.

Prose Writers of the Romantic Period

Jane Austen (1775–1817), considered a great novelist and one of the few with manner, offered intensely perceptive psychology in her novels even though her plots are fairly placid romantic comedies (everyone marries at the end.). Known for her unhampered, indirect discourse, Austen's work includes *Pride and Prejudice*, *Emma*, and *Sense and Sensibility*, among others.

Charles Lamb (1775–1834), English essayist, was noted for his charm and conversational style. Although he wrote poetry, he is most noted for his collection of essays, *Essays of Elia*, a mixture of fact and fiction about his grandmother.

Sir Walter Scott (1771–1832), a novelist noted as the author who popularized the genre of historical fiction, is particularly noted for *Ivanhoe*, in which he recounts the last important Jacobite movement of 1745 to place a Stuart on the throne.

LITERATURE OF GREAT BRITAIN FROM THE VICTORIAN PERIOD UNTIL THE PRESENT

Early Victorian Literature (1837–1857)

Historical Background

The first half of the 1800s was marked by social, industrial, and political unrest. This period saw the legislation of mechanisms of social regulation in order to control an increasingly complex society. Although the Chartist movement advocated for the political rights of the working class, such rights were excluded from the Reform Bill of 1832. The New Poor Law of 1834 confined paupers to workhouses, and there was a new sense of being an individual, fending for oneself in an urban world. An aggressive movement from an agrarian economy to a markedly industrial one seeded the once pristine countryside with railroads, changing how people related to each other. This period also saw the death of William IV (1837), Queen Victoria's accession to the throne, and Britain's withdrawal from India (1847), its last imperialist colony.

A period of unprecedented economic and social change began in 1848, climaxing in Chartist demonstrations in London and the New Public Health Act. More people lived in towns instead of the countryside, and the shift from people living in small towns, running family businesses, and knowing precisely who they were, to living as strangers in large cities and industrial centers like Manchester forced many to question their identity. Simultaneously, revolutions were occurring in France, Germany, Poland, Hungary, and Italy. Change and upheaval marked the century.

Despite this sense of darkening identity there was a spirit of burgeoning confidence and a belief that solutions to emerging problems could be found in increasing affluence. In 1851, the Great Exhibition was held at the Crystal Palace, the first of many international World's Fair exhibitions of culture and industry, which suggested that the world's products could be collected, catalogued, and controlled under a British-constructed roof. Such exhibitions became a popular feature of the nineteenth century.

Literary Elements

Victorian literature embraced a sense of nation's identity. The word *Victorian* implied a concern with British society, an emerging middle class, and a more regulated and disciplined society. Rapid social growth led to increased social control and affected the way people saw themselves and their relationship to the world at a very fundamental level. The old discourse and way of thinking about the world lost relevance, and a sense of the lonely and complex individual gained prominence. Government found itself having to address factors such as the disintegration of marriage and often anarchic forces of sexuality, which tended to disrupt a once smooth-running society, Government's answer was to institute so-called domestic order acts. And although Victorian England managed a large empire, it did not see itself as part of a broader European culture, as was the case during the seventeenth century.

The period from 1847 to 1848 was regarded as the most significant in the entire history of the English novel. During the nineteenth century, the novel was the most dominant form of literature, occupying the middle ground as it helped people make sense of their lives and guided people on how they could construct themselves in a changing world. Readers looked to the novel as a genre that could provide understanding and the vocabulary for articulating what it meant to be an individual in nineteenth-century Britain. The novel also portrayed a new sense of social order (increasingly middle-class white simultaneously/paradoxically developing a sense of psychological complexity) by presenting characters that faced the difficult dilemmas that were inherent in such a society or that withdrew into themselves, unable to deal with the distress of the times.

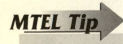

MTEL Tip

The novel was the most dominant form of literature in the 19th century.

This period also marked the presence of realistic novels that reflected a middle-class tone of voice, an imposed moral framework, and the inveterate contradictions, complexities, and frustrations that lay below the surface of respectable middle-class life. The Newgate novel, a form of fiction that dealt with lives of criminals also emerged during this period. Examples include *Paul Clifford* by Edward Bulwer-Lytton (1830) and *Rookwood* by Harrison Ainsworth (1834).

Poetry of this period engaged the more marginal, extreme, and unnerving dimensions of Victorian life, delving into the strange and dark depths of the mind, exploring strange and submerged feelings, and unearthing the tension between the mind of the speaker and world he or she occupies. Poetry provided a medium for dealing with the more awkward aspects of life that mainstream novelists preferred to neglect.

Major Writers and Works

Charlotte Brontë's (1816–1855) *Jane Eyre* (1847) examined the position of women in Victorian Britain. Demonstrating a consistent awareness of economic life in early Victorian Britain, Brontë portrayed individuals who remained outside of this new middle-class discourse as early Victorian Britain reconstructed and reconceptualized itself as an ordered and morally respectable society. The setting of Lowood School imposed conformity and discipline, illustrating the kind of regimentation that was a major feature of Victorian life. Brontë explored the complex depths of a female character whose way of thinking differs from dominant ways of thinking in patriarchal society, reflecting how Victorians were rethinking their world.

Emily Brontë's (1818–1845) *Wuthering Heights* (1847) depicts characters caught between an old way of life and the new world of Victorians and whose passion is so intense it transcends individualism. Architectural changes in the setting of this novel suggest how Victorians increasingly demanded their own private space and psychologically withdrew into themselves and detached themselves from others.

Elizabeth Barrett Browning (1806–1861), wife of Robert Browning, was better known as a poet than her husband. *Sonnets from the Portuguese*, written during her courtship, represents the most accurate representation of sonnets since the time of Shakespeare. Sonnet 43 from *Sonnets* begins with one of the most often quoted lines: "How do I love thee? Let me count the ways." Her epic poem/novel *Aurora Leigh* played a central role in debate about women and confronted fundamental questions about gendered identity.

Robert Browning (1812–1889), most famous for "My Last Duchess," also explored more bizarre states of mind, such as murderous jealousy and deepening insanity. Browning's dramatic monologues end with collapse, evil, and despair, as observed in *The Ring and the Book* and *Dramatis Personnae*.

Thomas Carlyle (1795–1881), a harsh and angry man, is most renowned for his spiritual autobiography *Sartor Resartus*, and detailed expositions on history, philosophy, and social problems in *Heroes and Hero-Worship* and *Past and Present*.

Charles Dickens (1812–1870) wrote novels that reflected stories of social reconciliation and reconstitution. Replete with working-class characters, his novels depict the lower class against a carnival-like backdrop and a middle class of morally advanced heroes and heroines. Success is represented in bourgeois virtues of industriousness, honesty, and charity. He used the novel to develop and strengthen individual identity by presenting role models of the idea of self and to provide reassurance for readers that they held the answers and solutions for social class issues that emerged from a complicated and mechanized world. His work elaborated the complexity of the age and prompted new narratives of the self, as he portrayed the crucial middle-class nature of nineteenth-century Britain. His *Oliver Twist* (1838) challenged the inhumane aspects of new social legislation, represented the fear of criminality and the mob (threatening herd of working-class people), questioned how to control an increasingly complex society, and endorsed emerging middle-class values. This text documents Oliver's progress as a hero who comes to terms with the world and embraces middle-class values, but who is simultaneously aware of the vulnerability and desires buried beneath the superficiality of polite manners. In *David Copperfield* (1849–1850) and *Great Expectations* (1860–1861), protagonists are at odds with and at the same time crave middle-class respectability. *Bleak House* (1852–1853) and *Dombey and Son* (1848), darker novels, recount death, murder, madness, despair, and suicide, negative but accurate consequences of a complicated, mechanized world.

Elizabeth Gaskell (1810–1865), in contrast to her contemporaries, portrayed the positive spirit encountered in fiction of the 1850s. *North and South* (1854–1855) depicts social reconciliation of hostility and division and engaging the new reality of industrial Britain. Her text presents two distinct versions of middle-class ideology: a liberal vision of moral responsibility for the general well-being of society and obligation to the less fortunate, and a conservative vision of business and profit. Her works such as *Wives and Daughters* (1864–1866), *Sylvia's Lovers* (1863), and *Mary Barton* (1848) suggest a personal answer to a political problem, but also present the conflict between creating and endorsing middle-class values that are flawed.

Thomas Macaulay (1800–1859), like Carlyle, had strong opinions about government and democracy, but unlike his contemporary, he exuded a quiet confidence and wrote against slavery in the colonies and for establishing a national education system in India. His most acclaimed work is the *History of England*, a work of detail, diligence, and competence, and although he died before its completion, the text was considered a bestseller.

Dante Gabriel Rossetti (1828–1882), a painter and poet, was significantly influenced by the writing of Robert Browning and Edgar Allan Poe. His final work, *Ballads and Sonnets*, reflects the sadness, despair, grief, love, and mysticism he experienced during his nine-year engagement and two-year marriage to Elizabeth Siddal.

William Makepeace Thackeray (1811–1863), characterized by his refusal to become enthusiastic about or accept the new values of Victorian era, rejected the new Victorian narratives, instead castigating the middle-class hero as selfish and offering little sympathy for heroine Becky Sharp (*Vanity Fair*, 1847–1848). Adhering to this rhythm of disrupting the new rhythm of Victorian life, *The History of Pendennis* (1849–1850) critiques the hero's loss of a role and direction in his life. In *The History of Esmond* (1852), Thackeray not only critiqued materialism but also portrayed the shortcomings of the Victorian emphasis on the self.

Middle Victorian Literature (1857–1876)

Historical Background

The 1860s marked a widespread sense of failure and awareness that material prosperity had not actually improved people's lives. Government enacted social legislation as it attempted to regulate a society that had been transformed by economic changes. The Victorians built sewage systems, hospitals, lunatic asylums, prisons, and schools as part of huge physical infrastructure designed to service and maintain society. This period ushered in the introduction of a police force and the emergence of the lawyer and doctor as central figures in society. The day-to-day functioning of life had to be policed, legislated, and nursed even more than before. Karl Marx published *Das Kapital* (1867), bringing a new understanding of the organization of working society, which had a major impact on twentieth-century political and philosophical thinking. The Reform Bill extended the right to vote to working-class men in towns.

By the 1870s, people understood that there were no simple remedies to social problems, and this kind of disillusionment began to fade. There was a contradiction between the loss of religious faith and a strong sense of religious conviction, and people desired the security of sound beliefs, rules, and fixed codes as an anchor in a rapidly changing world. As the old narratives of religion no longer provided people with a way to make sense of life, Victorians needed intellectual explanations to make sense of a world that was changing so fast. Colonialism tried to command, control, and explain everything while ignoring awkward local differences that challenged dominant authority. Charles Darwin, Karl Marx, and Sigmund Freud influenced literature by introducing three new types of narratives: evolution, international communism, and psychoanalysis, providing ways for people to explain things and make sense of their fast-changing world and lives. The middle class scorned vulgarity and approved moderation and economy. Mid-Victorian Britain presented a morally respectable atmosphere where people preferred not to talk directly about various aspects of life and demonstrated superior confidence that the British way of doing things was resilient. During this time, Britain continued the tradition of admitting foreign political exiles and politically subversive figures, admitting Karl Marx in 1848.

Literary Elements

The literature of these decades attempted to construct new narratives as a substitute for old narratives. Unlike former decades when critics came from the outside, mainstream authors now offered critical and dissenting voices. Literature described the tension between questioning middle-class values and committing and embracing commitment to such values. Novelists favored stories about middle-class life and ordinary domestic experiences, but narrated them in a tone that identified with the social and moral principles of such a society. Readers turned to fiction for written confirmation of the existence of middle-class values. Victorian realism shared a way of looking at the world, naming and labeling everyone and everything that made the world tangible and understandable. Novels assumed the narrative form and also included a new type, the sensation novel, a form of fiction that focused on ordinary middle-class life but included extravagant, horrible, and sensational events that affected the reader's senses. These novels looked at respectable society but simultaneously exposed convictions as hypocritical, fragile, and damaging.

Major Writers and Works

Matthew Arnold (1822–1888), a poet until the 1860s, wrote "Dover Beach," which identified the loss of religious faith as a central source of worry in Victorian life. His later novel, *Culture and Anarchy* (1869), saw culture as the vehicle for helping the Victorians out of their difficulties and observed no central authority to control the drift of civilization toward anarchy. Arnold was considered one of the Victorian sages, historians of their own time who helped others make sense of their lives.

Mary Elizabeth Braddon (1837–1915), in her novel *Lady Audley's Secret* (1862), looked skeptically and critically at roles imposed upon women in Victorian society, revealing the complicated truths behind façade of marriage and respectability.

Lewis Carroll (1832–1898) called on alternative logic in *Alice's Adventures in Wonderland* (1865), offering a different voice and constructing a different narrative in the midst of realistic fiction writing.

Wilkie Collins (1824–1889) wrote a sensation novel, *The Woman in White* (1860). Narrated like a legal enquiry, this novel reflected an age when people relied upon processes of law and questions, and undermined institutions and things of value that mid-Victorians relied upon. *The Moonstone* (1868) questioned British imperialism, specifically the British presence in India, portraying imperialism as exploitative instead of beneficial.

Charles Darwin's (1809–1882) *The Origin of Species*, which proposed and documented natural selection and survival of the fittest, moved people toward an evolutionary stance with little moral or spiritual purpose.

George Eliot (1819–1880), the pen name for Mary Anne Evans, wrote novels that reflected an era of tremendous prosperity, portraying a central theme of egoism and the duties and obligations of the individual as seen in *Adam Bede* 1859 and *Daniel Deronda* 1874–1876. *The Mill on the Floss* 1860 posed a middle-class perspective, evoking rural and domestic life and an awareness of the limitations and unyielding spirit of such view of life. *Middlemarch* (1871), considered the finest English realistic novel, concerns itself with ordinary dilemmas of life such as marriage, work, and relationships, depicting less self-absorbed characters whose egoism is curbed by social obligation and representing moral codes and values of polite middle-class English society, but also displaying the narrowness of the society.

Gerard Manley Hopkins (1844–1889), a Jesuit poet, did not become well-known until decades after his death. He believed that the purpose of his work was to glorify God and to display the significant nature of every creature. He called this focus "inscape," which is observed in "Pied Beauty," "Thou Art Indeed Just, Lord," and "God's Grandeur."

John Stuart Mill (1806–1873) profoundly influenced British thought and politics with his writing on logic, epistemology, economics, social and political philosophy, ethics, metaphysics, religion, and current affairs. His most well-known and significant works include *A System of Logic*, *Principles of Political Economy*, *On Liberty*, *Utilitarianism*, *The Subjection of Women*, *Three Essays on Religion*, and his *Autobiography*.

John Ruskin (1819–1900), a Victorian sage, published *Traffic* in 1859, in which he condemned laissez-faire economics, commended the dignity of labor and the moral and aesthetic value of craftsmanship, and attempted to reintroduce the human dimension into the factory-based economy.

Alfred Lord Tennyson (1809–1892), considered the greatest English poet of nostalgia and the leading poet of the time, identified individual identity as more haunted and lonely. Incorporating a sensuous and musical quality in his work, Tennyson created *In Memoriam*, an elegy dedicated to his friend who died at the young age of twenty-two. This sequence of 130 poems addresses the flux of changing Victorian life while exploring the almost disabling and confusing nature of loss and grief, and confronts issues that caused so much anxiety at the time: expressions of doubt felt in reconciling religion and science and God and nature. It is said that Queen Victoria valued this text second only to the Bible. His other works, "Mariana" (1830) and "The Lady of Shallott" (1832), simultaneously describe energy and guilt. *Idylls of the King* elaborates the stories of King Arthur and the Roundtable.

Anthony Trollope (1815–1882) documented the story of Phineas Finn's rise to parliamentary power through series of romantic attachments in *Phineas Finn* (1869). In *Phineas*, Trollope analyzed parliamentary society, seemingly celebrating the British political system but at the same time suggesting that the parliamentary system is a pretence that is irrelevant to the true state of nation and with few real connections to those it claims to represent. He portrays a system that excludes and wastes the talent of women, examines the political foundations of nineteenth-century British life, and evaluates the strengths and weaknesses of British way of doing things. In *The Way We Live Now* (1873–1874), Trollope creates a satiric picture of decadent society corrupted by greed and gambling and living on borrowed time, a society in which everything is beginning to fall apart. This text illustrates the beginning of the disintegration of discourse of realism.

Late Victorian Literature (1876–1901)

Historical Background

In 1877, Queen Victoria was declared Empress of India, reflecting the high point of British imperial self-confidence, but by 1879 William Ewart Gladstone, the former prime minister, denounced the imperial policy of Conservative government. This period saw the politics of empire, race, and nation as signs of weakness and a reflection of desire for simple answers and forceful action in a changing world. Between 1880–1900, Britain's economic lead over all other nations began to fade, and there were growing political and military tensions between European countries and increasing awareness of social problems and class hostility at home. As a result, it was difficult to focus narrowly on domestic concerns in a secure environment. The Boer War (1899–1902) erupted, a colonial conflict in which the British were fighting people of European origin (Dutch settlers in South Africa), an enemy extremely difficult to defeat. In society, there was the realization that the conventions and institutions established to promote well-being were at odds with the reality of what people were like; consequently, there was an increasing fear of the working-class mob. In response to a perceived sense of external threat (from competing nations and colonial subjects) and internal threat (the expanding working class), there was a resurgent spirit of conservatism. Imperialism continued to demonstrate abuse of power where the conqueror silenced all dissenting voices.

Literary Elements

The novel continued to be the most significant genre during this period. This period also saw new forms of social analysis, resurgent socialism, new feminist voices, and a fresh expression of liberal values. Sexuality was not as repressed and not seen as dangerous as in previous years, and the late nineteenth century reflected the first presence of a homosexual subculture. Literature reflected protagonists not as heroes or heroines but as real people, replete with human foibles, who are entrapped and impacted by social conventions that only exacerbate their conditions. Literature reflected a sense of disintegration, with the center steadily falling apart, crumbling social institutions such as family and marriage, and increasing skepticism toward conventional morality. Characters collided with society, and themes expressed the widespread feeling that society could not hold together. Irrational forces just below the surface become evident with texts exploring dark places of the mind. More sustaining fictions were replaced with troubling and disconcerting texts. Naturalist Emile Zola, whose style reflected an intense, research-like investigation of humankind, a strong presence of contemporary ideas of the environment and genetics, and the inevitable decline and downward spiral of the human condition due to disease, alcoholism, and madness, proved a significant influence in literature. Interests in evolution and social Darwinism coexisted with fears about regression, atavism, and decline, reflecting a loss of faith in goals traditionally pursed by middle-class hero and heroines, the denunciation of Victorian values with a move from solid moral convictions to mere emptiness, and the prevailing idea that something dangerous and irrational would destabilize society. This period also saw the emergence of aestheticism, portrayed as early as 1873 in Walter Pater's *Studies in the History of Renaissance*, a principle where art has no reference to life and therefore nothing to do with morality and represents a refusal or inability to engage with reality. Romance novels embraced the idea of escape and drama of the absurd and revived the belief that life is ridiculous, without substance or depth.

Major Writers and Works

Walter Besant (1836–1901), a slum novelist, wrote about class, education, and the unprivileged in *All Sorts and Conditions of Men* (1882).

George Gissing (1857–1903) represented late Victorian social pessimism and the despair of London's working-class life, presenting people as little better than savages. His works include *Workers in the Dawn* (1880), *The Unclassed* (1884), *Demos* (1886), *Thyrza* (1887), and *The Nether World* (1889). *The Odd Women* (1893) is the most substantial novel about single women, noting that the least fortunate character is the one who marries.

Thomas Hardy (1840–1928) was the most significant novelist in last quarter of the nineteenth century, writing from a perspective situated outside in the margins and questioning established values and distancing himself from the traditional or conventional social order. His novels, set almost exclusively in Southwest England (Wessex), depicted romantic, impractical, and disorganized characters that could not manage their lives. Hardy tended not to name his characters until later in the text, rather identifying them as males or females engaged in some form of activity, suggesting that there is something elemental about people that is more fundamental than social identity. His characters are powerless and defeated individuals in a huge universe who move aimlessly from place to place, a plot device that works effectively to convey sense of alienation. *Far from the Madding Crowd* (1874) and *The Return of the Native* (1878) emphasize the failure of relationships, breakdown of marriages, divorce, and sexuality, marking a distinct difference from earlier Victorian novels, where sexuality was considered a dark and guilty secret. *The Mayor of Casterbridge* (1886), about a vandal who steals sheep and is eventually executed, portrays the nature of indiscipline and a society that has instituted a system of laws and order to regulate people. *Tess of the D'Urbervilles* (1891) presents an indignant portrayal of the ways social regulations and conventions ruin people's lives and reflects the aggressive nature of patriarchal society, harshness of law, and lack of tolerance and understanding. *Jude the Obscure* (1895) critiques how education, class barriers, religious and moral conventions, and divorce laws conspire against the protagonist Jude.

Rudyard Kipling (1865–1936) transcended the uncertainty and ambiguity of the time, presenting a more coherent and positive vision of the world. Speaking for the nation for a short period of time, Kipling reinvented the aristocratic military code for a democratic change and attempted to calm fears that were rampant during this time, noting that stories were nothing more than illusions. In *Many Inventions* (1893), he proposed that social differences disappear when men agree to abide by the same set of rules; there is a set of values that is relevant to all ranks.

George Bernard Shaw (1856–1950), one of the few playwrights of the time, exposed social hypocrisy and presented a new kind of social analysis that reflected a commitment to socialism. His works include *The Philanderer, Heartbreak House, Widowers' Houses.*

Robert Louis Stevenson (1850–1894) focused on the romance of leaving Britain to embark on new adventures in *Treasure Island* (1883). The dark and sinister *Doctor Jekyll and Mr. Hyde* (1886) represents the continual conflict between the irrational factors in mind and rational identity.

Oscar Wilde (1854–1900), both playwright and novelist, expressed a radical, disconcerting vision of society, where characters use style and lack substance, drawing attention to themselves with no meaningful purpose. His plays included *Lady Windermere's Fan* (1892), *A Woman of No Importance* (1893), and *The Importance of Being Earnest* (1895). Wilde's novels include characters that play a role in society, raising the question of whether or not there is any substance behind the mask. His work probably reflects the most complete expression of the sense of disintegration of values at the end of nineteenth century. *The Picture of Dorian Gray* (1890), an example of aestheticism, demonstrates this disintegration as the portrait of Dorian Gray fades while the hero himself retains youthful beauty.

The Twentieth Century

Historical Background

This period in history brought not only advances in science, technology, and social welfare, but also upheaval, war, and poverty. Britain suffered World War I and its aftermath, losing thousands to fighting in the trenches. Furthermore, London, whose resources and investments had been depleted by war, was forced to relinquish its distinction as the financial capital of the world. Britain also lost its dominance in the political arena to the United States and the Soviet Union. Like the United States, however, Britain also saw the extensive and powerful emergence of mass media, with increased circulation of newspapers, magazines, films, and radio.

World War II, lasting from 1939 to 1945, was even more devastating as Britain, for most of the war, faced Adolf Hitler alone. Suffering significant bombings and air raids in London and other English cities, Britain lost fewer soldiers but far more civilians than during World War I. Winston Churchill, prime minister during World War II, is given much credit for his inspiring leadership, which seemed to lift spirits during a time of profound devastation. After World War II, the British Empire transformed into the Commonwealth of Nations.

Literary Elements

Continuing in the same vein as the late nineteenth century, British writers of the twentieth century used literature to discuss and portray the anxiety of their changing society. A technological revolution began to take place, and culture shifted into modern gear. Populations grew more used to new forms of media such as photography and film, granting new aesthetic ways of looking at the world, while previous political and ethical hegemonies were torn down.

Writers began to experiment with different styles that reflected the age: modernism played with shifting perspectives and "potentialities," to quote James Joyce, of the first half of the twentieth century and the unreliable narration this shifting perspective implied. Throughout this century of global wars, existentialism asked what an individual was to do in such a topsy-turvy, absurd world where meaning seemed no longer relevant or reliable, and finally explained that meaning could only be found in the self. Existential nihilism pushed against this and argued that life was intrinsically meaningless.

The dissolution of the British Empire—beginning in the mid-twentieth century after World War II with the "release" of India in 1947, and finally ending in 1997 with the "handover" of Hong Kong to China—inspired writers to question colonial policies and the idea of colonization itself. By the mid-twentieth century, following India's independence in 1947, a postcolonial literature was beginning to take shape and form a new genre around the world and in the very locus of the world's largest empire holder, Britain. As much of the world was colonized by Britain, many writers of Irish, Indian, African, or Caribbean descent were also British subjects for all or some period of their lives—their writing is thus classified perhaps tenuously as British.

Postmodernism, in the 1970s, finally began to suggest a total lack of social unity, regarding social and political ideals as ultimately unreal. Throughout the century, ideas about gender, sexuality, race, nationality, class, and power continue to be questioned and challenged to a stronger and stronger degree. Postmodernism marks the point where such deconstruction becomes the norm.

Major Writers and Works

Kingsley Amis (1922–1995) wrote *Lucky Jim*, an influential novel capturing the "angry young man" perspective in literature. His son, Martin Amis, has continued his controversial legacy.

W. H. Auden (1907–1973), one of the strongest voices of his generation, was "found" by T. S. Eliot, who published his first book, *Poems*, in 1930. He went on to write more collections, including *The Orators*, and *Look Stranger!*

Samuel Beckett (1906–1989), an Irish novelist and playwright, wrote *Waiting for Godot*, an existential play, and most of his other work while living in France. This play put him in the vanguard of the theater of the absurd. He is also known for his plays *Endgame*, *Krapp's Last Tape*, *Breath*, and *Not I*. His various novels include the trilogy *Molloy*, *Malone Dies*, and *The Unnamable*.

The Bloomsbury Group (1905) was an intellectual group headed by Virginia Woolf and her sister Vanessa Bell, a painter. The group welcomed the likes of E. M. Forster,

Roger Fry, and Lytton Strachey, as well as the economist John Maynard Keynes. It was an influential and innovative group that fostered the rise of the avant-garde and modern thinking about sexuality, pacifism, and feminism in English literature.

Anthony Burgess (1917–1994) wrote the disturbing and nightmarish *A Clockwork Orange*, a depiction of violent authoritarianism. He also authored of a wide array of other less-known works, including criticism on language, music, and politics, and a biography of Shakespeare.

A. S. Byatt (1936) wrote *The Virgin in the Garden*, the first book in a quartet about twentieth-century family life in Yorkshire, England. *Still Life*, *Babel Tower*, and *A Whistling Woman* followed. These stories chronicle the life of a young female intellectual growing up in a still largely male-dominated intellectual world. They follow this woman through the 1960s and its utopian impulses, and through her divorce. Byatt's best-known novel, *Possession*, won the Booker Prize.

Arthur C. Clarke (1917–2008) was one of the most prolific and influential science fiction writers of the twentieth century. He based his writing in real science. His short story "The Sentinel" formed the basis for Stanley Kubrick's film *2001: A Space Odyssey*.

E. M. Forster (1879–1970) questioned individuals' compliance with social conventions, and the consequences of leading an unquestioned life as such. A liberal realist, his major works include *Howard's End*, *A Room with a View*, and *A Passage to India*. His last novel, published posthumously, *Maurice*, was based on a strong homosexual theme.

William Golding (1911–1993) wrote the classic *Lord of the Flies*, a pessimistic and violence-ridden view of humanity that echoes the feelings of the Western world after World War II. Golding, a biologist, believed in the evolutionary premise of survival of the fittest.

Graham Greene (1904–1991) had an interest in the collected social angst of the twentieth century. He was also influenced by his deep but thoughtful Catholicism. His works include *The Power and the Glory*, *Our Man in Havana*, *The Quiet American*, and *The End of the Affair*.

Seamus Heaney (1939) is the Pulitzer Prize–winning author of several collections of poetry, plays, and essays. A Catholic from Northern Ireland, his poems such as "North," "Field Work," and "Casualty" exalt the raw political power of words.

Aldous Huxley (1894–1963) is the author of the famous novel *Brave New World*, a science fiction story that warned against the overwhelming powers of technology. Some of his other works include *Point Counter Point*, *Ape and Essence*, and *Brave New World Revisited*.

James Joyce (1882–1941), an Irish expatriate who lived most of his life in France (as did Beckett), modernized and revolutionized literature and writing with his novel *Ulysses*. The book's narrative, taking place on one day in Dublin, uses various narrative styles, techniques, and viewpoints, including a stream-of-consciousness style. The novel explicitly calls upon his other writings, including *A Portrait of the Artist as a Young Man*, as much as it alludes to a compendium of world literature and classics, requiring a sense of inter- and intratextual knowledge, as well as an ability on the reader's part to go with the flow of the often strikingly sensual and poetic prose in the stream-of-consciousness passages. Joyce's work was extremely influential, especially to Irish modern writers who came after, including Flan O'Brien and Samuel Beckett.

D. H. Lawrence (1885–1930) battled obscenity charges for his sexually explicit work, including *The Rainbow* and *Lady Chatterley's Lover*. Like Joyce, and coming before Joyce, Lawrence is considered a great force in the modernist movement in literature. He wrote daringly about personal and social hypocrisies, and he believed human nature was at its best when its consciousness was in harmony with its natural spontaneity. He was also an imagist poet.

V. S. Naipaul (1932) is an Indian-Trinidadian British writer, and the first Indian to win the Booker Prize (1971). He was later awarded the Nobel Prize for Literature for "having united perceptive narrative and incorruptible scrutiny in works that compel us to see the presence of suppressed histories." However, he has also been criticized for making unsympathetic portrayals of the underdeveloped nations he writes about. His novels include *In a Free State* and *A House for Mr. Biswas*.

George Orwell (1903–1950) spent time in Burma in the Indian Imperial Police and from this experience wrote his first novel, *Burmese Days*. From this experience, he drew inspiration for much of his social criticism, evident in his most popular novels, *1984* and *Animal Farm*.

Sir Ahmed Salman Rushdie (1947) is a British Indian novelist and essayist. Most of his work combines magical realism with historical fiction in which he describes the connections and relationships between the Eastern and Western worlds. Muslims protested his fourth novel, *The Satanic Verses* (1988), and he faced violent death threats and a fatwa (religious edict) issued by Ayatollah Ruhollah Khomeini, then supreme leader of Iran, in February 1989. Rushdie spent almost ten years underground but eventually was appointed a knight bachelor (2007) for his services to literature.

William Butler Yeats (1865–1939) was one of the most influential poets of the 20th century. The driving force behind the Irish Literary Revival, Yeats was not only a writer but also a politician. His most influential and cited poem is "The Second Coming," which depicts the profound moral consequences for humankind when rapid technology collides with critical human and social values. In 1923, he was awarded the Nobel Prize in Literature for work the Nobel Committee described as inspired, artistic, and influential. Other works include *The Tower* (1928) and *The Winding Stair and Other Poems* (1929), written after he received the Nobel Prize. Toward the end of career, Yeats became more radical in his work and was labeled somewhat of a nihilist.

LITERATURE FROM THE ANCIENT WORLD TO THE FIFTEENTH CENTURY

Ancient Greece and the Formation of the Western Mind (Beginnings–AD 100)

Historical Background

From 2000 to 1000 BC, the Minoan civilization flourished in Crete, and the Myceneans developed a wealthy and powerful civilization on mainland Greece. By 1000 BC, however, fires had destroyed the great palaces, and the arts, skills, and language of the Myceneans had vanished. This period was considered the dark age of Greece. Between 800 and 600 BC, the Greeks established city-states or colonies along the Mediterranean coast. The Greco-Persian wars followed (499–448 BC), and Athens and Sparta emerged as the two most prominent city-states after defeating the Persians (499–400 BC). Athens developed democratic institutions and became an empire, establishing league of subject cities. A great rivalry emerged between Athens and Sparta, resulting in the defeat of Athens during the Peloponnesian War (431–404 BC). In 385 BC, Plato established the Academy.

During this period, Greeks conceived their gods as an expression of the disorder of the world and its uncontrollable forces, morality as a human invention, and life as an implicit struggle with both destructive and creative impulses. Greek city-states varied in customs, political constitutions, and dialects, becoming rivals and competitors. Sophists or professional teachers educated affluent males of Athens in techniques of public speaking, government, ethics, literary criticism, and astronomy suggesting that "Man is the measure of all things" Protagoras. The year 753 BC is considered the traditional date of the founding of Rome. With military victories in North Africa, Spain, Greece, and Asia Minor, Rome changed the social, cultural, and economic makeup of life. From approximately 47 BC to the birth of Jesus Christ, Rome was ruled by dictators such as Julius Caesar (murdered in 44 BC) and Octavian (Augustus), who established an imperial regime from 27 to 23 BC. Rome continued to be ruled by dictators or emperors such as Tiberius (AD 14–37), Caligula (AD 37–41), and Nero (AD 54–68), who persecuted Christians by making them human torches.

Literary Elements

Greek comedy and tragedy developed from choral performances, and singing influenced the style of writing. Having established colonies in Asia, the Greeks adapted language to the Phoenician writing system, adding signs for vowels to transform it from a consonantal to an alphabetical system. This kind of writing was first used in commercial documents and later for treaties, political decrees, and literature. Homer was the first major poet who developed an intricate system of metrical formulas, standard scenes, and a known outline of the story. Lyric poems designed to evoke the joys and sorrows of a lover were performed with the accompaniment of a lyre (hence the word *lyric*). These poems employed Sapphic meter (developed by the lyrical poet Sappho), made up of any number of four-line stanzas, determined by quantitative meter based on the nature of the ancient Greek language in which syllables were either long or short, depending on vowel length and ending sounds. In Sapphic meter, the first three lines contain two trochees (metrical foot with one stressed syllable followed by an unstressed one), a dactyl (stressed syllable followed by two unstressed ones), and two more trochees. The shorter fourth and final line of stanza is called an adonic, which is composed of one dactyl followed by a trochee.

Greek drama, primarily tragedy, emerged from choral performances, with Thespis's initiating the use of dialogue between himself and a masked actor and Aeschylus creating the prototype of later drama marked by conflict. Poetry was often comic in the sense that it reflected obscenity, farce, wit, satire, and parody with serious undertones, as in the works of Aristophanes. In addition, literature incorporated dialectic, which is critical inquiry used to undermine the plausibility of widely held doctrines; Socrates and Plato developed and championed this technique or critical inquiry.

Majors Writers and Works

Aeschylus (ca. 525–456 BC) wrote *The Persians, Seven against Thebes, The Suppliants, The Oresteia* (*Agamemnon, The Libation Bearers*, and *The Eumenides*), and *Prometheus Bound*.

Aristophanes (ca. 448–380 BC) wrote *The Acharnians, The Knights, The Clouds, The Wasps Peace, The Birds, Lysistrata, Thesmophoriazusae* (*The Women Celebrating the Thesmophoria*), *The Frogs, Ecclesiazusae* (*The Assemblywomen*), and *Plutus* (*Wealth*).

Aristotle (384–322 BC) wrote *Poetics*, which was the first systematic work of Western literary criticism.

Euripides (ca. 480–406 BC) wrote *Alcestis, Medea, Trojan Women, The Bacchae*, and *Cyclops*.

Homer (eighth century BC) wrote *The Iliad* and *The Odyssey*.

Plato (ca. 424–347 BC) wrote *Menwn* (*Meno*), *Faidwn* (*Phaedo*), *Politeia* (*Republic*), *FaidroV* (*Phaedrus*), *Sumposion* (*Symposium*), *ParmenidhV* (*Parmenides*), *QeaithtoV* (*Theaetetus*), *TimaioV* (*Timaeus*), and *LegeiV* (*Laws*).

Sappho (630/612–570 BC), a lyrist, was the first author to write in the first person.

Socrates (ca. 469–399 BC) a Greek philosopher pondered what "self" truly was, while his contemporaries were more interested in themselves. As a result of his search for truth, which led him to interrogate the beliefs and assumptions of those considered "wise," Socrates was convicted of corrupting youth and executed by poisoning.

Sophocles (ca. 496–406 BC) wrote *Oedipus the King*.

Ancient Roman Literature

Historical Background

From AD 100 on, the Roman Empire engaged in a systematic but ultimately futile effort to destroy Christianity; 313 marked the last persecution of Christians, when Constantine became emperor and issued the Edict of Milan, declaring toleration of all religions. In the 380s, Christianity became the official religion of the Roman Empire, and in 391, pagan religions were outlawed. By 395 the Roman Empire had been permanently divided into the eastern empire based in Constantinople and the western empire, based in Rome. In 455 Rome was invaded by the Vandals, and the last emperor of the western empire was deposed by Odoacer, king of Heruli.

This period was marked by strong divisions of social class with increased importation of slaves creating a large class of poor urbanites, the rise of trade and crafts, and the increase of wealthy businessmen, who formed the senatorial class. This division laid the groundwork for political conflicts and the eventual demise of Roman Republic. Until the birth of Jesus, Roman religion was outward and visible, marked by public displays of human and animal sacrifices to the gods. The teachings of Jesus were considered revolutionary, and the Hebrew conception of God was inward, spiritual, and relational. During this time in Greek and Roman history, four languages were spoken: classical Hebrew by priests and other educated people, Aramaic by the general population, and Greek and Latin by Jews who had entered the administrative or commercial milieu under the Hellenistic and Roman empires.

Literary Elements

The Romans openly and proudly borrowed Greek sources and themes of heroism, imitating the Greek epics. In the *Aeneid*, Aeneas is the perfect prototype for the ideal Roman. Themes associated with sophisticated and high-edge life of the Roman elite also pervaded the literature. As the Hebrew conception of God broadened from personal, non-anthropomorphic, omnipotent, omniscient, infinitely just to infinitely merciful in justice, Hebrew literature addressed the personal, inner, and relational God.

Major Writers and Works

Virgil (30–19 BC) is most noted for the *Aeneid*. Inspired by Homer, Virgil sought to create a national epic for the emerging Roman Empire under the rule of Augustus Caesar and to link the dynasty of ancient Troy in the person of its surviving prince, Aeneas.

Ovid (AD 8) wrote the *Metamorphoses*, considered his masterpiece. Known for subtlety and psychological depth, unrelated characters, and dactylic hexameter, Ovid's work did not represent the values of Virgil's work. This anti-*Aeneid* epic poem of fifteen books influenced all other epic poems thereafter.

The Four Gospels of the Life and Sayings of Jesus and the Acts of the Apostles was written in Greek about sixty years after the death of Jesus. Each Gospel addresses a different audience: Matthew, the Jewish public; Mark, the Gentile audience; and Luke, the cultured Greek readers. John's writing differs from his peers in that his work consistently refers to Jesus as Christ and Lord, representing Jesus as the Omnipotent.

The final canon of the New Testament of the Christian Bible was established in 367.

The Middle Ages

Historical Background

The classical civilization of Greece and Rome radically transformed after contact with Germanic tribes from the north, Christians from Palestine, and Muslims from the Arabian peninsula and northern Africa. During the 500s, medieval Europe was hardly unified, politically or culturally. Within the next thousand years, common ideas and values emerged such as consensual government, recognition of religious difference, and individualism. The eighth to tenth centuries were marked by invasions of western Europe by Arabs, Norsemen, and Magyars. The eleventh century marked the consolidation of the feudal social structure and the Norman invasion of England. In 1099, knights of the First Crusade captured Jerusalem. The twelfth century saw the establishment of the universities of Paris, Oxford, and Bologna and the permanent recovery of Jerusalem by the Arabs.

Literary Elements

National literatures in the vernacular appeared. This period, sometimes called the busy millennium, produced literature concerned with religious faith and the appropriate use of physical force. Literature and culture in medieval Europe were very diverse: literate and oral, Germanic and Latin, secular and religious, tolerant and repressive, vernacular and learned, rural and urban, skeptical and pious, and popular and aristocratic, reflecting Arabs, Jews, and Christians. Many works during this time incorporated archetypal individuals that sought to seek to better understand themselves and their destinies. Works often borrowed from culturally specific non-Western traditions and thus offered universal appeal, with characters being imported back from non-Western parts of the world. Literary forms included a range of styles from the humblest, signified by colloquial humor, to the highest. Poetic tones varied with changes in intensity achieved by differing degrees of concentration and repetitions.

Major Writers and Works

Dante Alighieri (1265–1321) wrote *The Divine Comedy*, a poem that represents the supreme expression of the medieval mind in European imaginative literature. A comedy because it begins in misery and ends in happiness, *The Divine Comedy* is considered the greatest poem of the Middles Ages. Highly visual and symmetric, the work contains three divisions of identical length: *Hell* (*Inferno*), *Purgatory* (*Purgatorio*), and *Paradise* (*Paradiso*). The poem recounts Dante's descent through nine circles of hell and seven divisions of Purgatory proper, ante-Purgatory, and Earthly Paradise (Garden of Eden). Unlike the writing of Homer, Virgil, or Milton, this work is quiet, factual, and economical, rendering an air of simplicity.

Note: Other major works of the Middle Ages are addressed in this chapter's section on the literature of Great Britain.

African Literature

Historical Background and Literary Elements

The years spanning 200 to 350 saw the introduction and spread of Christianity in North Africa, while 600 to 1000 marked the introduction and spread of Islam into East and West Africa. The centuries between 500 and 1495 marked the rise of the West African savanna empires: Ghana in the northwest (ca. 500), Kanem around Lake Chad (ca. 900), Mali (ca. 1200), and Songhay in the Middle Niger (ca. 1495). The oral tradition was an integral part of African life and comprised various expressive forms such as folktale, legend, myth, and poetry, distinguishing it from ordinary speech. The rise of ancient Mali in the thirteenth century is closely associated with the spread of Islam into the region. Islam enabled an elite educated class to emerge and served early rulers of the three best-known medieval empires in western Africa: Songhay, Ghana, and Mali.

Major Writers and Works

The *Epic of Son-Jara* (thirteenth to fourteenth centuries) was constructed from the oral tradition of the Manding. Son-Jara was the descendent of Bilal, companion of Muhammad, whose family migrated from Asia. *The Son-Jara* is a political epic, focused on the rivalry of two brothers for succession to their father's throne. The epic had a moral tone of good versus evil as well as an ideological function, which was to construct a Manding common identity under a founding hero. The tale, an accumulation of oral accounts, contains three distinct generic layers: the first layer provides a narrative framework of structural episodes and genealogies; the second layer recounts praise poems and songs; and the third layer, called "The Task of the Griot," brings the narrative to life and reenacts it dramatically.

Poetry and Thought in Early China

Historical Background

Chinese civilization first developed in the Yellow River Basin with the establishment of the Shang dynasty (1600–1046 BC). Chinese writing was based on characters developed during this dynasty. From 1045 to 256 BC, a great migration from the west occurred, establishing the Zhou dynasty. Zhou people argued that because the Shang Dynasty had been guilty of misrule and caused hardship, Heaven had transferred power to them. Thus there were high expectations for those in power to rule virtuously, and rulers recorded models and statutes on how to rule. Texts circulated most frequently among the aristocracy. The Lu province of the Zhou dynasty was the birthplace of Confucius, and his beliefs emphasizing the connection between idealized history and social history pervaded spiritual life. Midway through this period, however, the Zhou dynasty lost much power, and bordering new kingdoms grew stronger but culturally absorbed many Zhou ways. During this time, most regions were ruled by aristocratic families with officials chosen from lesser clans, but by the mid-400s BC, regions battled each other for power. This was called the warring states period, which saw the emergence of Taoism (meaning "path" or "way"), which focused on the individual rather than the polity.

Eventually all states evolved into a centralized state, but this time marked political and intellectual upheaval. By 256 BC, the Zhou dynasty ended with Qin Shi Hwang becoming the first emperor of a unified China. Qin Shi Hwang outlawed Confucianism, burned many books, buried many scholars, and encouraged legalism, the idea that subjects of the state should adhere completely to laws and policies. In 220 BC, the Han dynasty began. The Han dynasty is considered one of the greatest periods in history of China. During this time, China became an official Confucian state.

Literary Elements

Works generally reflected Confucian ideals, which emphasized government and morality, the correctness of social relationships, justice, and sincerity. Works also reflected the three jewels of the Tao: compassion, moderation, and humility. Taoist writing also addressed the concepts of nature, health, longevity, and *wu wei* (meaning "effortless action"). Writing often took the form of song, including hymns, temple songs, hunting songs, and love and marriage songs. Poetry was written in metaphors.

Major Writers and Works

The Book of Documents is a collection of statements and proclamations from early Zhou period.

Classic of Poetry is a collection of lyric poetry that began the Chinese literary tradition.

The Book of Change I Ching Yijing (ca. 800 BC) is a handbook for foretelling the future directions of the universe.

Analects, recorded by Confucius's disciples, represents a fusion of ethical thought idealizing Zhou traditions.

Chuang Tzu, written by Chuang Tzu (fourth century BC) is a book of philosophical meditations in many forms, including jokes, parables, and intricate philosophical arguments that were based on Taoism and that illustrate how Tao represents the natural course of things.

Laozi tzu, written by Lao-Tzu (ca. 300 BC), is a silk manuscript containing eighty-one short stanzas: part old adages, and part commentary on or interpretations of sayings that address political and personal issues and offer the key to great and illusive wisdom.

Historical Records, by Ssu-ma Ch'ien, is a comprehensive history of the lives of ruling families and dynasties in China up to time of Emperor Wu.

China's Middle Period

Historical Background

Between AD 220 and 280, China was divided into three regional states; this resulted in the crumbling rule of the Han dynasty and the decline and demise of social order, which was reflected in writing that questioned Confucian values. In 280, China briefly reunified under the Chin dynasty, but by 316, China fell into the hands of non-Chinese invaders, and the court moved to the south, marking a period of northern and southern dynasties. By 589, the Sui, the northern dynasty, reunified China. The Tang dynasty eventually supplanted the Sui in 618, expanding the political, economic, cultural, and military realms. The century spanning 1000 to 1100 marked the development of printing.

Literary Elements

The middle period of Chinese literature occupies a central place in the nation's cultural history. This was an era during which Chinese thought and letters achieved its highest form. Confucianism declined in importance because of the crumbling Han Dynasty during the second century, with Taoism and Buddhism acquiring more important status. The Tang dynasty, a time of cultural vibrance and expansion, saw the flourishing of poetry that focused more on understanding nature and the nature of the individual or recluse. A stronger presence of Buddhism and Taoism changed the nature of poetry and thought; departing from the Confucian emphasis on denying the importance of the self, many new literary works focused on understanding the psyche, spiritual enlightenment, and the natural world. Taoist imagery reflected contemplation and mystical union with nature, wisdom, learning, and purposive action abandoned in favor of simplicity and *wu-wei* (nonaction, or letting things take their natural course). *Jueju*, the five to seven character quatrain, emerged, and Chinese poems (*Yue fu*) were composed in folk-song style. Furthermore, the development of printing caused an increased awareness of literary traditions and classical literature.

Major Writers and Works

Li Po (701–762), a wandering poet who is recognized as the greatest Tang poet, produced an abundance of poems on subjects such as nature, wine, friendship, solitude, and the passage of time. With its air of playfulness, hyperbole, and fantasy, his poetry captures the nuances of the human experience of nature and friendship.

Literature of India from 3000 BC to AD 100

Historical Background and Literary Elements

The history and the literature of this period are so connected that this section will generally focus on the literary developments of this period. There was extreme diversity in the written and oral literary tradition of India: Sanskrit, the language of the Hindu culture, was introduced in 1500 BC; Pali and Praki became the preferred languages of Buddhists and Jains; Tamil was the language of south India; and Islam, not introduced until AD 1100, was represented in Islamic, Arabic, and Persian literature.

The core concepts of Hinduism permeated early Indian literature as Hinduism was able to synthesize tenets and ideas from other religions. Dharma, a significant core concept, addresses the guiding principle of human conduct that preserves the social, moral, and cosmic integrity of universe. Such conduct is righteous and requires sacred duties, which impact three spheres that govern ideal life: *artha* (wealth, profit, political power), *kama* (love, sensuality), and *moska* (release, liberation). Another core concept, karma, holds that all things are responsible for their own actions. Buddhism, an egalitarian and populist religion that focuses on ways that creatures can be freed from cycle of suffering, is also reflected in Hinduism. The enduring motif of Hinduism is that idea that moral and spiritual conquest is superior to conquest by sword.

Major Writers and Works

The *Vedas* (ca. 3000–1500 BC) is the first known writing originating from the Aryans. This text addresses the primary scriptures of Hinduism, which consist of four books of sacred hymns that were chanted by priests at ceremonies marking rites of passage. Sanskrit entered India about 1500 BC. This writing includes mantras or sacred utterances used to recite the *Vedas*.

The *Upanisads (Mystic Doctrines)* were mystical and philosophical mediations that de-emphasized role of the ritualistic present in the *Vedas*.

Ramayana and *Mahabharatar*, two epic poems, are based on actual historical events in north India and express core values of Hinduism. *Ramayana*, which contains 50,000 couplets composed by Valmiki (500–200 BC), documents the adventures in exile of Prince Rama of Kosala. *Mahabharatar*, by Vyasa, focuses on the civil war between battling Aryans. Both texts reflect mythic tone and historical narrative, have been retold in all major Indian languages, and have inspired works of art and literature in India and Southeast Asia. Both works emphasize dharma.

Jakata, a popular Buddhist tale collection, suggests that all people can embark on a path toward enlightenment by detaching themselves from desire and focusing on the well-being of others, thus becoming a *Bodhisattva*.

Islamic Literature

Historical Background and Literary Elements

Circa 570, Muhammad was born into the Quraysh tribe of Mecca. During 610 to 632, the Koran was produced, marking the period of Muhammad's prophesy from first revelation, through the growth of his following, his flight (*hijra*) to Medina, and his final pilgrimage to Mecca. The Koran was responsible for the new religion and community known as Islam. In 653, the third caliph, Uthman, authorized the collection and establishment of the official text of the Koran. Written in Arabic, the text is greater than prophetic revelation as it is God's final revelation to humanity though Muhammad. Written in Arabic, the revelations came in verses, *åya*, of varying length and number, which were then assembled into larger divisions called suras, which were organized by subject. The Koran, with its unique rhythm, was written to be heard and recited and accompanied by music. Thus, a written version does not best convey the text effectively as the text is more dialogic than narrative. Furthermore, the style varies greatly with early and short suras that sound like charms and incantations and later and longer ones filled with legal prescriptions. The Koran differs from the Bible in style. The essence of the Koran is admonition and guidance. Unlike pre-Islamic literature, which was written in verse, the Koran, unlike the Bible, is written in prose and has no single narrative running through it as it is not embedded in the history of a single people. The prose style of this text influenced subsequent literature and became popular for the distribution of religious learning.

Japanese Literature

Historical Background and Literary Elements

During the ninth century, the Japanese syllabary developed, reflecting the tremendous impact and authority Chinese script and language had on Japan. During the eleventh century, Japan adopted Chinese as the official language of the government. The imperial court was no more misogynistic than European society in the Middle Ages. Women writers played a role in exploring the potential of Japanese language. During this time, men had a great deal of sexual freedom (authority over multiple wives, concubines, etc.), while women's identities were entirely constructed by how men recognized them in all contexts. The Japanese view of sexuality was relatively liberated; woman of the upper class were considered sexually alive but not licentious. The Japanese did not integrate marriage, romance, and erotic love; the purpose of marriage was procreation, continuation of the family line, and advantageous alliances with other families. By the end of this period, literature was distinguished from fanciful romance and privileged realism, psychological insight, and authenticity over romanticism.

Major Writers and Works

Murasaki Shikibu (1013) wrote *The Tale of Genji*, the first great Japanese prose novel. It is a story about the life and love of a prince and his descendents. The themes address loss, substitution, transgression, and retribution. Genji's life and the lives of his successors are presented as a search for the ideal woman and also represent the quest for the perfect man.

Golden Age of Japan (1100–1600)

Historical Background

During this age, Japan engaged in the Gempei wars, during which the Taira and Minamoto clans fought for aristocratic monopoly of power. The following period (1185–1333) was the Kamakura period, when the political center of Japan moved to eastern Kamakur. It was at this time that the samurai, or warrior elite, emerged. In the late 1200s, Marco Polo journeyed to China, opening trade routes and cultural ties between Europe and East Asia. The subsequent Muromachi period saw a flourishing culture in the arts despite social chaos. The fifteenth century marked the rise of Zen Buddhism and the arrival of the Portuguese, who brought firearms and Christianity. Until this time, Japan was primarily a racially homogenous country; historically nomadic, Japanese ancestors settled in this part of Asia, bringing with them a tolerance of impermanence. By the late 1500s, Japan became unified through civil war and built the printing press modeled after the Korean version. By this time, Japanese civilization possessed a keen awareness of changes brought by seasons, a taste for the natural and refined, and a disposition toward practicality. Cultivating wet rice, one of the most labor-intensive crops, taught Japanese people about economy in the use of space and the advantages of cooperation, which gave rise to the long-standing Japanese ideal that privileges societal needs over the individual.

Japan also absorbed the Chinese theories of sovereignty and a centralized state, which also reemphasized kinship ties from tribal times embedded within family and lineage. The Japanese were unlike the egalitarian Chinese, however. Significantly influenced by Buddhism, Japanese society subscribed to the doctrine of universal impermanence, which spoke to a country where earthquakes and typhoons were and still are common. Buddhism offered the hope of escape, as Buddhahood was attainable within each individual.

Literary Elements

It was at this time that Japanese poets introduced the haiku form of poetry into literary world. Literature was highly influenced by the impact of kinship on bureaucracy; thus literature focused on family fortunes, politics, economy, and the military. Due to the influence of Buddhism, however, the literature also explored the depths of longing and ambition.

The fifteenth century also saw the emergence of linked poetry. There are three different kinds of linked poetry: *renga*, *renku*, and *renshi* (developed during the twentieth century). *Renga* was first developed as a game between court poets. Ranging from lengths of 50 to 1,000 stanzas, this poetry contained numerous allusions to Chinese and Japanese literature. *Renku* was common among the rising middle class in Japan. Also called *haikai no renga*, this poetry was linked intuitively, based on what seemed logically connected. The primary goal of linking poetry is quick and easy movement from one topic to another without repeating any phrases. This kind of poetry is like the best party conversation: witty, engaging, and intelligent.

Major Writers and Works

Matsuo Bashō (1644–1694) was the most famous poet of the Edo period in Japan. During his lifetime, Bashō was recognized for *renga*, and today, he is recognized as a master of haiku.

Tale of the Heike (thirteenth to fourteenth centuries, author unknown) is an account of the Gempei wars, which led to aristocracy's loss of wealth and political power.

Yoshida Kenkō wrote *Essays in Idleness* (1330), which recounts observations about aesthetic issues. He also wrote *Nō*, which are short, simple, plotless tragic plays often highlighting the teachings of Buddha; titles include *Atsumori* and *Haku Rakuten*.

Shinkei, a poet, wrote *Murmured Conversations* (1463), a treatise on the principles of linked poetry.

Sōgi, Shōhaku, and Sōchō, three poets, created *Three Poets at Minase* (1488), a 100-verse sequence that epitomizes the linked-poetry tradition.

WORLD LITERATURE FROM THE FIFTEENTH CENTURY TO THE PRESENT

The Renaissance: Europe (1500–1650)

Historical Background

This was clearly a period of rebirth and change. Christopher Columbus proved that the earth is not flat with his arrival in the West Indies (1492). Leonardo da Vinci painted the *Mona Lisa* (1503), and Michelangelo, the ceiling of the Sistine Chapel (1512). Nicolaus Copernicus theorized that the earth moves around the sun (1514). Martin Luther published Ninety-five Theses, denouncing the abuses of the Roman Catholic Church in 1517, while Henry VIII broke with Rome and became the head of the Church of England in 1534. England declared war on France in 1549 and defeated the Spanish Armada in 1588. Galileo Galilei proved Copernicus's theory of the earth's rotation around the sun (1610), Pilgrims settled in Jamestown, Virginia, in 1607 and in Plymouth, Massachusetts, in 1620. Louise XIV became king of France in 1643, and Charles I was beheaded in 1649, leaving Oliver Cromwell to rule England until his death in 1658.

The Renaissance saw a rebirth of ancient culture. Renaissance authors lived in a world of widespread revolutionary change, and scholars began to study and understand the cultural legacy of the ancient Greek and Roman world, which gave them a sense of their own place in history. This period saw the invention of the compass, printing press, and gun, forging a kind of global unity. These discoveries were positive in that they spread ideas and negative in that they profoundly impacted those who could not handle the uncertainty. People became preoccupied with this life rather than life beyond. Human actions were judged in terms of effectiveness, memorability, delight, and beauty. Tension between values of worldly goods and spiritual renunciation emerged. The political forces of the Catholic Church and the Protestant Reformation influenced a period more preoccupied with earthly princes than a heavenly king. The period was characterized by a strongly affirmed awareness of the intellectual and physical virtues of humankind and the individual's place in creation.

Literary Elements

Characters in Renaissance literature had more autonomy and more fully realized personalities. Deliberation and action were equally important. Literary characters and writers had almost no firm ground to stand on as they lived in an increasingly complex world. European intellectuals and writers were highly influenced by ancient literature, classical mythology, philosophy, and scriptures. Literature reflected a taste for the harmonious and memorable, spectacular effects, and "striking of a pose." Writing addressed themes of virtue, fame, and glory as well as melancholy, puzzling doubts, and mistrust. Poets celebrated high deeds and dispensed glory. Writing joined the philosophical and the imaginative.

The Enlightenment: Europe (1600–1800)

Historical Background

The Enlightenment was considered the age of rationality. Thinkers emphasized reason over passion and believed that reason could provide solutions to all problems. The dramatic conflict between reason and passion played out in society; therefore, the ruling class wished to control passion and institutionalize reason. There was a rigid class system during this time which confronted difficult challenges as the eighteenth century approached, bringing with it new commerce, which generated new wealth. Those who accumulated new wealth felt entitled to their share of social power, which threatened kings. The mortality of kings led to the instability of the social order over which kings presided. People became preoccupied with the human condition and no longer automatically assumed God's omnipotence or carried out Christian obligations. Religious differences led to divisions in social class and political conviction; divisions within nations were more important than divisions between nations (France and England).

Philosophers realized the possibility of the mind's isolation and the impossibility of knowing the reality of the external world. Society provided standards and instruments of control that might help counter the tumult of individual impulse. Public life mattered more than private life for the English and French upper classes. The good of the group dominated the good of the individual. Enlightenment thinkers also emphasized common aspects of humanity more than cultural differences. Convention served as the mode of control, reflecting the period's constant struggle toward stability. The classical past provided the emblem for stability. Ancients believed that Greece and Rome established standards applicable to all accomplishments and provided models of achievement never to be surpassed. The Moderns held the view that the new always surpassed the old and that figures of classical past were flawed and fresh possibilities were always likely.

During the late 1600s, Russian czar Peter the Great visited western Europe and England and resolved to westernize Russia. England and Scotland united to form the United Kingdom of Great Britain (1707) and transported 100,000 slaves per year across the Atlantic. Colonists in North America fight the American War of Independence, and the French Revolution followed soon after. In 1799, Napoleon Bonaparte became the first consul of France.

Literary Elements

Eighteenth-century writers in France and England dramatized intricate interchanges and conflicts between reason and passion. Jean-Baptiste Poquelin Molière regarded religion as a sham, Jonathan Swift institutionalized hypocrisy, Alexander Pope emphasized the ambiguities in sexual mores, and Voltaire recounted the world's inconsistencies of profession and practice. Across Europe eighteenth-century writers assumed the superior importance of the social group and of shared opinion. French writers used domestic situations to examine larger problems. England and France assumed marriage as the normal goal for men and women, making erotic love less important and the position of women increasingly insignificant. Writers located the sense of permanence particularly in the idea of nature, which offered comfort to those aware of flaws in actual social arrangements. Writers identified that human nature and the fundamental aspects of personality remained constant in spite of social divergence. If an author depicted a character who failed to conform to what eighteenth-century readers understood as human nature, the work might be viewed as inadequate. Literary themes emphasized the conventions of eighteenth-century society and agreed-on systems of behavior declared appropriate for specific situations, noting that commitment to decorum helped preserve society's important standards. Literature existed to delight and instruct readers. Realism attempted to convey the literal feel of experience, shape the occurrence of events, and inform the way people really talked in social circles. Formalities of literature attempted to make stable what experience demonstrated as unstable.

MTEL Tip

Realism attempted to convey the way people really talked in social circles.

Major Writers and Works

Miguel de Cervantes (1547–1616), Spanish dramatist, poet, and author, wrote the epic poem *Don Quixote de la Mancha* when he was fifty-eight years old. His work satirized tales of chivalry presented in classical literature. Poking fun at European and particularly

Spanish society, Cervantes believed that although humankind was inherently good, it was prone to mischief. Cervantes based most of his work on personal experiences and adventures. *The Exemplary Novels of Cervantes* (*Novelas ejemplares*, 1613) presents tales of pirates.

Sor Juana Inés de la Cruz (1658–1695), a nun and Mexican poet, defended a woman's right to be treated as a human being. In *"Hombres necios"* ("Stubborn Men"), she criticized the sexism of the society of her time, poking fun at and revealing the hypocrisy of men who publicly condemn prostitutes but have them themselves.

Johann Wolfgang von Goethe (1749–1832), considered a genius, was a German poet, dramatist, novelist, autobiographer, lawyer, diplomat, and scientific researcher. In his play (poetic drama) *Faust*, Dr. Faustus, a scholar who lived from 1480–1549, makes a contract with Mephistopheles (the Devil) in order to test the limits of possibility. In this text, Goethe explored the issue of imagination verus social obligation and questioned the functions and limitations of desire.

Jean-Baptiste Poquelin Molière (1622–1673), a comedic playwright, enjoyed pointing fun at ruling and rich aristocrats. His most famous works include *Tartuffe*, *The Misanthrope*, *The Blunderer*, *The School for Husbands*, and *The School for Wives*.

Michel de Montaigne (1533–1592), a French Renaissance thinker, used himself as the focus of a collection of personal essays. *Essays* sought to identify his and others' values, habits, beliefs, and natures to create a more realistic picture of humankind. While traveling, he meditated on his essays. Although his style was light and simple, his work incorporated skepticism and fideism, which argues against the rationalization of God and for belief based on faith. A theme that pervades *Essays* is that man is not superior but rather inferior to the beasts of the world.

Jean Racine (1639–1699), considered one of the three major dramatists of the period (in addition to Molière and Pierre Corneille), wrote primarily tragedy such as *Phaedra*. His work was often criticized for its lack of historical veracity.

François de la Rochefoucauld (1613–1680), a French classical writer, focused on morality in his work. Best known for his maxims and epigrams, he wrote *Reflections* and *Maximes*, which linked the essay form of the previous period to a more contemporary form of maxims.

Jean-Jacques Rousseau (1712–1778) believed in the destructive nature of institutions, the gradual corruption of humankind throughout history, and the importance of nature and feeling in individual development and society. Rousseau was often forced to leave France because of his controversial writing. *Confessions* recounts how men and boys strive to express natural impulses but are frustrated by society's demands and assumptions. In his texts, the character's own nature has much more significance than anything that happens to him, and the common people are morally superior to those in the upper classes. His work expresses the narcissistic side of romanticism.

The Americas (1500–1650)

Historical Background

In 1519, Hernán Cortés arrived in the Aztec capital of Tenochtitlán and met with Montezuma, the Aztec emperor. Two years later the Spanish conquered the Aztecs. Francisco Pizarro followed suit, conquering the Incas in Peru in 1533. The sequence of events preceding and following Cortés's meeting with Montezuma was recreated in Spanish chronicles and many other literary works. Mayan and Aztec cultures exchanged ideas with Spain, and the area developed into the Mexican–Central American region known as Mesoamerica.

Literary Elements

Aztec art was recorded in the alphabetical script of western Europe, translated into Spanish, and preserved in Europe. Mesoamerican contact with Europeans influenced recording of Mesoamerican historical narratives, prayers, and song texts, which resulted in growing native literature preserved in western European script available to the world in European languages. Maya, Zuni, and Navajo literature based on oral tradition were written down and published. Three genres of Mesoamerican literature emerged: song, narrative, and oratory. Songs were most perfectly memorized and included the interjection of vocables and song syllables, which created patterns leading to paired stanzas. Narrative, the most expansive genre, followed a prescribed plot line, but the performer improvised and added details at will. The hero was usually a trickster who was gullible, clownish, ribald, and conniving. Oratory was comprised of prayer, educational monologues, ceremonial colloquy, and prose poems. Mesoamerican (native) literary themes addressed supernatural power, problems of humanity versus nature, social obligation, and development of individual. Despite rich symbolism and imagery, literature was regarded as functional rather than aesthetic.

China (1400–1800)

Historical Background

The link between classical literature, an education in Confucian classics, and service in government was temporarily broken after the Mongols conquered the southern Sung dynasty in 1279. In 1421, the capital moved to Peking. The late Ming dynasty (1580–1644) was a period of radical individualism, subjectivism, and questioning of authority and tradition. In 1664, the Manchus conquered China and established the Ch'ing dynasty. Early Ch'ing intellectual culture posed a strong reaction against radical individualism of the last part of the Ming dynasty, during which personal freedom was celebrated at the expense of social responsibility. The Literary Inquisition between 1736 and 1794 censored many of the earlier works, and many writers were imprisoned for suspected critical references to Chi'ing dynasty. During the latter seventeenth and early eighteenth centuries, intellectuals turned away from Ming "subjectivism." The eighteenth century was the last period of glory and self-confidence for traditional Chinese civilization as European colonial powers began to make major inroads on Chinese autonomy in the early nineteenth century. British merchants dominated the opium trade, draining away Chinese silver and creating social problems. Christian missionaries spread throughout country. Ultimately the Ch'ing government was unable to adapt to a world thrust upon it and slowly disintegrated until the first decade of the twentieth century.

Literary Elements

Classical literature remained as an important part of life for intellectuals through the rest of the imperial period, but its general role diminished as an important part of social life but not at its core (like literature in the Western civilization). Instead, literature such as plays, verse romances, and prose fiction were published in Chinese vernacular during the thirteenth to fourteenth centuries. Yuan and Ming vernacular lacked the subtlety of classical literature, but much that had been repressed in classical literature emerged in the vernacular: sex, violence, satire, and humor. The rise of the bourgeoisie in great cities spread literacy to urban areas. There was no drama in ancient China as classical prose fiction was generally considered pure entertainment. In cities, theater, oral-verse romance, and storytelling flourished. Popular Chinese literature included murder mysteries, stories of bandits, and fantasy. High culture favored neo-Confucianism, an attempt to discover the philosophical grounds of Confucian classics, but the rigid strictures imposed on self-cultivation and ethical behavior failed to address complexities of human nature and pressures of living in an increasingly complex world. Vernacular literature celebrated liberty, violent energy, and passion.

Major Writers and Works

Cao Xueqin (1715–1763) authored *The Story of the Stone* (1740–1750), an embodiment of China's cultural identity in recent times. A story of an extended family, centered on women and relationships within the family, this text represents the best and worst of traditional China in its final phase.

Chin P'ing Mei wrote *Golden Lotus* in 1617, a satirical novel about the manners of a corrupt sensualist.

K'ung Shang-jen (1648–1718), author of *The Peach Blossom Fan* (1699), wrote long plays in the tradition of southern drama known as *ch'uan-chi'i* with intricate and sprawling affairs, numerous characters, and multiple story lines.

Li Yü (1611–1680) was a comic dramatist, storywriter, and champion of vernacular literature. Whether or not the focus of his plays celebrated Monkey's free spirit and turbulent ingenuity or serious allegory of *Monkey* and Tripitaka's journey toward Buddhist enlightenment is debated.

Romance of the Three Kingdoms (1522) is a long historical novel about the fall of the Han dynasty.

T'ang Hsien-tsu (1522), a major dramatist, developed the *ch'uan-ch'i* play into a literary form.

Wu Ch'eng-en (1592) wrote *Monkey*, a story based on the journey of a T'ang Buddhist monk named Hsüan Tsang or Tripitaka, who journeyed from China to India in search of Buddhist scriptures.

In 1788, *Ssu-k'u ch'üan-shu*, a massive collection of all important earlier literature, was completed.

The Ottoman (Turkish) Empire (1500–Present)

Historical Background

The Ottoman state was the last of the great Muslim empires. The Ottomans were originally leaders of an Oghuz (Turkomen) tribal confederation that came to Anatolia (Turkey) from central Asia as part of the Aljuqid army. They established themselves as an independent dynasty after the destruction of the Saljuqid state in the thirteenth century and expanded into Europe. Mehmed was the first Ottoman sultan to see himself as successor to the Muslim caliphs and Byzantine emperors and initiated a policy of imperial expansion that gave the Ottoman state dominance over a vast region. The Ottoman Empire extended from Crimea to Aden to Iran to Morocco and successfully waged war against European rivals during the sixteenth and seventeenth centuries. A more powerful European military and economy checked further Ottoman advances, weakening the empire and ultimately causing its decline.

Literary Elements

Ottoman literature was linguistically Turkish but drew heavily on Arabic and Persian vocabulary, themes, and literary forms. The poetry and prose of the Ottoman Turks achieved richness and complexity that made it the third great literature of Islamic tradition.

Major Writers and Works

Evliya Çelebi (1611–1684) was the most prolific and celebrated writer of this period. He was supposedly inspired by a dream about the prophet Muhammad, who encouraged him to wander and travel throughout the Ottoman Empire for the next forty-four years. *The Book of Travels* details a panoramic view of the Ottoman Empire in the mid-seventeenth century, when its geographic extent was the greatest and most powerful. There are no comparable records of any Islamic state.

India (1800–1900)

Historical Background

In 1816, a group of Bengali and English men founded Hindu College in Calcutta. At the same time, James Mill wrote *History of India*, justifying British rule in India. By the late 1820s, Bengali reformer Ram Mohun Roy had founded Brahmo Samaj, an organization dedicated to Hindu religious and social reform, and in 1835, Thomas Macaulay published *Minute on Education in India*, arguing for English education for Indians. In 1885, a group of Indian and English intellectuals founded the Indian National Congress, an organization devoted to Indian representation in the British colonial government of India. Writing of the Indo-Muslim culture was mainly in Persian, the court language, but eventually turned more to Urdu because of a desire to express Indian sensibilities and experiences through an Indian idiom.

Literary Elements

Ghazal, the quintessential lyric genre in Urdu, a language that evolved out of interaction of dialects of Hindi with Persian, reached perfection between the sixteenth and eighteenth centuries. Imported from Persian poetry, this lyric genre emerged as mature and productive form of Urdu. This poetry was of introspection and reflection but was also a public, performed genre, a critical and essential element of South Asian culture. Typical *ghazal* poems were reflections on love and idealized the beloved and God. Such poetry was a lyrical contemplation of love as a metaphor for the relations that exist among people, God, and the world. The poetry contained stringent and complex formal conventions: three to seven couplets, each focusing on a separate thought, image, and mood, connected by a common meter and rhyme scheme. The rhyming element, a *qafiyah*, was a syllable or sequence of sounds that appeared in both lines of the first couplet and the second line of following ones. The *takhallus* is the poet's pen name or signature.

Major Writers and Works

Bankim Chandra Chatterjee (1838–1894) wrote *Anandamath*, an allegorical novel of resistance to colonial rule, establishing prose as a literary vehicle for the Bengali language, and helped create in India a school of fiction on the European model.

Michael Madhusudan Datta (1824–1873), a Christian convert in India, published *Meghanadvadh*, a Bengali version of the *Ramayana* epic in blank verse.

Mrza Asadulla Khan Ghalib (1820–1865) wrote ghazal lyric poems expressing the aesthetic of Islamic culture in India.

Henry David Thoreau around 1840 read and, was influenced by, the *Bhagavad Gita*.

Japan (1600–1900)

Historical Background

From 1600 to 1868 was considered the Edo period, during which the Tokugawa family established a dynasty of shoguns that ruled from Edo. During this time, the imperial family commissioned artists Sotastu and Korin to create masterpieces of Japanese screen painting. During the early 1600s, the shoguns proclaimed a policy of national isolation, expelling the Portuguese, outlawing Christianity, and forbidding foreign travel. The Tokugawa clan managed to dominate its rivals, ending 150 years of violence and war among rival clans, and reunifying the nation under strict yet peaceful rule of the shoguns. The clan also attempted to stop time by freezing political, social, and economic conditions that favored foreign influence, and the bourgeois emerged as a mercantile class when peace and stability returned to Japan. Samurai staffed the shogun bureaucracy. Urban samurai developed new needs, which were met by enterprising merchants, artisans, and laborers, who grew in numbers in response to economic opportunity. These upstart merchants were absorbed in a culture completely of their own making, the urban culture. Japanese townspeople of the seventeenth and eighteenth centuries were impatient and competitive. This new urban culture developed organically, its members creating their own cosmopolitan customs, and few had ever heard of the Enlightenment brought on by the scientific revolution.

Literary Elements

Puns and parodies occupied popular literature. Woodblock prints, short stories, novels, poetry, and plays depicted city life, which was fast, varied, crowded, and competitive. People lived by and appreciated wit. Literature that came to the urban masses had to fit their tastes, and the impatience of Japanese townspeople showed in their fiction. The new tradesmen class demanded realism, and playwrights, poets, and novelists captured bourgeois life: blunt, expansive, iconoclastic, and playful.

Major Writers and Works

Ueda Akinari authored a collection of supernatural stories called *Tales of Moonlight and Rain* (1776).

Matsuo Basho, a haiku poet, wrote *The Narrow Road of the Interior* (1694), a travel memoir written in verse.

Takeda Izumo II, a playwright, wrote *The Treasury of Loyal Retainers* (1742), a play immortalizing the fealty of samurai who avenge their master's death.

Chikamatsu Monzaemon wrote *The Love Suicides at Amijima* (1721), a tragedy of fatal love written for puppet theater.

Ihara Saikaku, a comic realist, wrote popular fiction: *The Life of a Sensuous Man* (1682) and *The Barrelmaker Brimful of Love* (1686), a novella introducing realistic literature and portraying bourgeois experience.

The Modern World (1900–Present)

Historical Background

The two most important historical events influencing modernism were World War I and World War II. Modern consciousness in the twentieth century took a major turn because it began to be truly global for the first time. There were no more frontiers or large areas of the globe to discover. The century saw advances in technology, transformations of modern states, and the rapid spread of international corporations. Cultural exchanges occurred rapidly and inevitably, and communication and transportation networks linked all sections of the world. The essential reality became interconnectedness rather than isolation, and these connections changed the system, disrupted tradition, and gave people more choices. Western modernization led to industrial progress, refusal of positivist certainty about the nature of the world, and a desire to transcend narrowly nationalist politics. Western countries became models for regions beset by poverty, disease, and social unrest. Political leaders believed that westernization and progress were synonymous, and sought prosperity. Individualism and democracy, attention to literacy and education, private ownership and a thriving middle class, religious freedom, scientific method, public institutions, and emancipation of women were considered modernizing and Western ideas of the twentieth century. Colonial governments considered it their duty to disseminate values by promising advances in literacy and the standard of living as well as by suppressing indigenous traditions, including literature. Western modernity emerged as the Industrial Revolution, which transformed social, economic, and political life. Unprecedented developments in science encouraged westerners to believe that they would master the secrets of the universe and that the scientific method constituted a total worldview in which everything would be ultimately explained, including human society. Western social theorists envisioned creation of a perfect society by understanding social "laws." Karl Marx's proposal of a scientific theory of world history was driven by broad economic forces and believed in the power of rational systems to find solutions for society's ills. There was ongoing debate of knowledge and human values. Friedrich Nietzsche focused on the individual, not society, by rejecting paradigms of nationalism, Christianity, faith in science, loyalty to the state, and bourgeois civilized comfort. He focused on the individual's complete freedom without God and attacked the unimaginative mediocrity of mass society in the modern industrial world.

World War I radically changed everything inherited from the recent past, involved the whole continent of Europe and the United States for the first time, and was the first total war that spared no one, including civilians. An entire generation was lost in the trenches, and survivors resolved to reexamine bases of certainty, structures of knowledge, systems of belief, and repositories of authority. The modern philosophy of phenomenology, the study of phenomena as they literally appear, struggled to understand the relationship between appearance and reality.

Post-World War II saw the emergence of the idea of absurdity. Existentialism of the 1940s and 1950s attempted to recover a clear vision in a meaningless world. Philosophical absurdity corresponded to real confusion caused by radical historical changes. A view of cultural parochialism, belief in one correct view of the world, became much harder to maintain when people traveled widely and experienced different ways of life.

Literary Elements

Modernism was a literary and artistic movement with roots in Europe. Works were translated and republished in great numbers, and exported around the globe with the general expansion of Western culture. The new aura of modernist works rejected traditional authority and represented the change in attitudes and artistic strategy that occurred in Europe and America at beginning of the twentieth century. Indebted to the evolution of scientific thought and with an emphasis on randomness and shifting perception, each literary work could be categorized as a combined product of its race, milieu, and time. Reaction to World War I was reflected in literature with a new use of language, new ways of representing our knowledge of the world, and new hesitations about subscribing to any single mode of understanding the new world. The literature drew on new areas beyond intellect, interrogating modes of human consciousness and feeling, attempting to go beyond limitations of previous rationalism. Henri Bergson refuted scientific rationality as unreal and artificial as it froze everything in conceptual space; he wished to register the immediate impact of senses with great precision and proposed immediate data of consciousness. This gave rise to stream-of-consciousness writing, a way to convey stream of consciousness in the written flow of words. Sigmund Freud insisted on a fundamental and universally true image of human sexuality, interpreted as a defensive reaction against racial and social discord, including anti-Semitism. Freud and others believed that there was significant importance in clari-

MTEL Tip

Modernism rejected traditional authority.

fying patterns of human thought and emotion and that everyday, "rational" behavior is shaped by unconscious impulses and hidden motivations and by the way human beings create and modify their images of self through dialogue with others. This belief influenced every writer after Freud to consider psychological undercurrents of human behavior in their writing. Experimental language in fiction and poetry reflected the influence of psychoanalysis and symbolist poetics of free associations. Modernist literature shows how words reshape the world we know; descriptions are not accurate because they can never grasp absolute reality. All language can do is to create socially agreed-upon labels. Literature and linguistic systems were seen as "games": combinations of words and rules. Writers stressed the game like nature of language and combined words and fragments to portray the play of relationships instead of struggling to find the "right" word.

Post-World War II resulted in existentialism, the theater of the absurd, which consists of choosing our actions at each point, avoiding the bad faith of pretending that others are responsible for our choices, and choosing not just for oneself but for all. This is a time of literary movements leading to many "isms." So many groups tried to find appropriate artistic response to contemporary history, all embraced by modernism. Dadaism represented disgust with traditional middle-class values blamed for World War I and a subversion of authority to liberate creative imagination. Surrealism combined two unrelated elements and suggested buried connections and possible relationships overlooked by the logical mind. Surrealism incorporated intensity, playfulness, and openness to change and proved to be most influential of all movements. Futurism expressed enthusiasm for the dynamic new machine age. It involved experiments in typography, free association, rapid shifts and breaks of syntax, manipulation of sounds and word placement for special effects, harshness and stark vision, and eagerness to depict a new age. There were also those who took a narrow view of modernism, a group of Anglo-American writers who favored clear, precise images and common speech, thought of work primarily as an art object produced by consummate craft. These included James Joyce, Ezra Pound, T. S. Eliot, William Faulkner, and Virginia Woolf. These writers used language in an exploratory way, disassembling to reconstruct, playing with shifting and contradictory appearances to suggest the shifting and uncertain nature of reality. They broke up logically developing plot lines; used interior monologues, free association, and image clusters; drew attention to style; blended fantasy with reality; and explored ancient non-Western literature in search of universal themes. Modernist works displayed highly self-conscious use of language in order to change the way we understand language, but still assumed a rich and unified core to human experience.

Major Writers and Works

Australia, Europe, Eurasia, and South America

Guillaume Apollinaire (1880–1918) was a French poet who wrote during the early years of the twentieth century, an era named the *belle epoque* ("beautiful epoch") in France because the years were marked by great economic prosperity and progress. Guillaume Apollinaire's poems reflected this "beautiful epoch" through his distaste for the old styles (naturalism) and his passion for new stylistic experiments, such as eliminating punctuation. Apollinaire's first collection of poetry was *L'enchanteur pourrissant* (1909), but *Alcools* (1913) formed his reputation. Apollinaire, along with other poets of the early twentieth century, is credited with coining the word "surrealism" and writing one of the earliest surrealist works, the play *Les Mamelles de Tirésias* (1917).

Thea Astley (1925–2004) was an Australian novelist and short-story writer who, by the time of her death, had won more Miles Franklin Awards (a major Australian literary award) than any other author. Her more infamous works include *The Well Dressed Explorer* (1962), *The Slow Natives* (1965), *The Acolyte* (1972), and *Drylands* (1999). Astley was remarkably unsentimental and funny, and her work usually satirically examined individuals she viewed as morally or intellectually isolated in Australia.

Pío Baroja (1872–1956) was a writer from the Basque region of Spain who saw the world as a cruel place and for most of his life repudiated all tradition, religion, and government organization. Many of his works, including *La Raza* (*The Race*, 1908–1911), *La Lucha por la Vida* (*The Struggle for Life*, 1922–1924), and *Agonías de Nuestro Tiempo* (*Agonies of Our Time*, 1926) are focused on dirty living conditions, prostitutes, criminals, and the ignorance of mankind. His most-read work, *El Arbol de la Ciencia* (*The Tree of Knowledge*, 1974), exposes the shortcomings of the medical field and the poverty and filth in many poor villages in Spain. Baroja's picaresque, pessimistic style of writing follows in the Spanish literary tradition; his novels came to be considered a type of precursor to Spanish fascism.

Samuel Beckett (1906–1989) was an Irish writer, dramatist, and poet who wrote primarily in English and French. His work offered a bleak view of the world and of human existence and became increasingly minimalist throughout his lifetime. Beckett wrote during the delicate time during which modernism ended and postmodernism began. He was a student and friend of James Joyce, was an important contributor to the theater of the absurd, and was the recipient of the Nobel Prize in Literature in 1969. One of Beckett's most famous works is *Waiting for Godot*, an absurdist drama.

Jorge Luis Borges (1889–1986) is considered one of Argentina's greatest literary figures. Educated in English and Spanish, Borges wrote imaginative and enigmatic stories and poetry, within which difficult themes were embedded. His 1944 collection of short stories, *Ficciones*, is widely regarded as his best work. Prolific, Borges also wrote allegories, fantasies, and even detective stories. Highly influenced by Walt Whitman, Miguel de Cervantes, and Thomas Carlyle, Borges wrote pure fiction about the famous and not so famous in *The Universal History of Infamy* (1935). A master of fanciful tales, Borges wrote *Spain in My Heart* (1937), *Twenty Love Poems and a Song of Despair*, and *The Garden of Forking Paths*.

Albert Camus (1913–1960), a world famous French existentialist and Nobel Prize-winning novelist, director, actor, and playwright, wrote about the profound anxiety experienced by humankind living in a century of fear. Born in Algiers, Camus was intensely involved in Algerian political struggles and later worked in the underground during the German occupation of France. His most famous works, which addressed the absurdity of man's existence and how man must make the most of his life because it is what gives meaning to human existence, include *The Wrong Side and the Right Side* (1937), *Nuptials* (1937), *Caligula* (1942), *The Stranger* (1942), *The Myth of Sisyphus* (1942), *The Plague* (1947), and *The Rebel* (1951).

Anton Chekhov (1860–1904) eventually became one of the most cherished storytellers, but his tragedies made him one of the greatest dramatists of all time. Fond of farce, his one-act plays like *The Bear* (1888), in which a creditor hounds a young widow but is so impressed when she agrees to fight a duel with him that he proposes marriage, and *The Wedding* (1889), in which a bridegroom's plans to invite a general to his wedding ceremony backfire when the general turns out to be a retired, low-ranking naval captain, are considered exemplars of comic sketches. Chekhov's first success, *The Seagull*, was followed by *Uncle Vanya* (1899), *The Three Sisters* (1901), and *The Cherry Orchard* (1904), which became one of the masterpieces of the modern theater. Chekhov considered his work comic satire that identified the unhappy nature of existence in turn-of-the-century Russia.

Fyodor Dostoevsky (1821–1881), a Russian novelist, was a central figure in the formation of modern sensibility, strongly influencing modern literature in China and Japan. *Notes from the Underground* (1864), *Crime and Punishment* (1866), *The Idiot* (1868), and *Brothers Karamazov* (1880) used fiction to formulate some of the central predicaments our time: God versus atheism, good versus evil, freedom versus tyranny, and the recognition of limits versus the fall of humanity. His personal version of extreme mystical Christianity suggested that although humanity is fallen, man is still free to choose between evil and Christ. Choosing Christ means taking on oneself the burden of humanity in love and pity. Dostoevsky supported a conservative Russian nationalism with a messianic hope for Russian Christianity. Dostoevsky's psychology derived from theories proposed by German writers about the unconscious, the role of dreams, ambivalence of human feelings, epiphanies, split personalities twisted by isolation, lust, humiliation, and resentment. His novels utilized the narrative of confession to create novel as drama.

Miles Franklin (1879–1974) was born into an Irish family in the Alps of New South Wales. An Australian author and feminist, Franklin was committed to the pursuit of an authentic and original Australian literature. Her first work, *My Brilliant Career* (1901), which was an autobiographical piece written at the age of sixteen, is considered by many people the first authentic Australian novel. Her later work, titled *All That Swagger* (1936), is set in World War I and traces the life of Dennis Delacy and his family as they migrate to New South Wales. *All That Swagger* highlights the contributions of Irish immigrants (such as Franklin's family) to twentieth-century Australia.

Eugene Ionesco (1909–1994) was a Romanian playwright who developed his dramas first as short stories. Inspired by Camus, Ionesco is considered one of the most significant writers in the theater of the absurd. His work combines surrealism, naturalism, tragedy, and comedy to describe the way contemporary society has destroyed and brutalized man. In *The Rhinoceros* (1959), Ionesco watches as his friends each turn into a rhinoceros and submits to conformity. At the end of the novel he alone stands unchanged and nonconformist.

Franz Kafka (1883–1924), a novelist of German-Jewish descent, is considered one of the most influential writers of the twentieth century. His unique work, most of which was published posthumously, including novels such as *The Trial* (1925), *The Castle* (1926), and *Amerika* (1927), concerns profoundly troubled individuals living horrible and depressing lives in a cold industrial world. *The Metamorphosis*, a novella written in 1915, recounts the life of Gregor, a traveling salesman who wakens as a beetle, unable to right himself or communicate with the outside world. Although Gregor is the only breadwinner in a family struck by economic hard times, his family ignores and loathes his presence, eventually regarding him as merely a repulsive insect, leaving him to die. This novella and the short story "In the Penal Colony," a tale about an elaborate mechanical device of torture and execution, address the harsh reality and vulnerability of life.

Federico Garcia Lorca (1898–1936), Spanish poet, director, and playwright, wrote *El maleficio de la mariposa* in 1920, a verse play depicting the absurd love between a cockroach and a butterfly. Interested in Spanish art and Spain's avant-garde and inspired by Salvador Dali, Lorca wrote three collections of poems, including *Canciones* (*Songs*) and *Primer romancero gitano* (1928, translated as *Gypsy Ballads*, 1953), his best-known book of poetry. Dali created the stage settings for Lorca's second play, *Mariana Pineda* (1927), which earned much acclaim. Other plays include *The Shoemaker's Prodigious Wife* (1926), a farce about fantasy, based on the relationship between a flirtatious, petulant wife and a henpecked shoemaker.

Octavio Paz Lozano (1914–1998) was a Mexican writer, poet, and diplomat. His family lived in exile in the United States for a short time until Octavio returned to Mexico, encouraged by Pablo Neruda to follow his passion and write poetry. This led to the production of Lozano's first collection, *Luna Silvestre* (1933). Lozano spent time in the United States and Spain and was there influenced by the modernist and surrealist movements. He became established finally as a major literary figure with the publication of two works in particular: the collection *Piedra de Sol* (*Sun Stone*, 1957), and *El Laberinto de la Soledad* (*The Labyrinth of Solitude*, 1950). Eight years before his death, Lozano won the 1990 Nobel Prize for Literature. Lozano is still remembered for the complexity of his work: he delved as no author ever has into the connections between the fields of art, philosophy, politics, and religion.

Antonio Machado (1875–1939) was a Spanish poet who explored memory through the study of recurrent symbols, the lines between dream and reality, and the intersection of past and present. His first famous collection of introspective modernist poems, *Soledades* (*Solitudes*, 1903), emphasized a cultish view of beauty, which Machado soon abandoned in *Campos de Castilla* (*Fields of Castile*, 1912) for a more anguish-driven political message. This 1912 work, which griped about the conditions in Spain, actually echoed and anticipated many of the issues that would be fought over in the imminent Spanish civil war, which began in 1936.

Gabriel García Márquez (1927) started his career as a journalist in Colombia, where he is familiarly known as "Gabo." Considered one of the most significant authors of the twentieth century, Márquez uses a style of writing called magical realism, which blends magical elements into ordinary or realistic situations. He often confronts the topic of loneliness, especially as it is portrayed through the solitude of love. His best-known novels are *One Hundred Years of Solitude* (1967) and *Love in the Time of Cholera* (1985).

Ana María Matute (1926) is a Spanish author who uses a lyric and expressionistic style to represent the voices of the people living during the *posguerra*, or the time directly following the Spanish civil war. Because she was around ten years old when the war began, much of Matute's writing is concerned with the aftermath of war, specifically in themes of loss of innocence, alienation, violence, and misery. These themes are prevalent in her major works, which include *Los Hijos Muertos* (*The Lost Children*, 1958), the trilogy *Los Mercaderes* (*The Merchants*, 1959–1969), and *Olvidado Rey Gudú* (*Forgotten King Gudú*, 1996).

Vladimir Nabokov (1899–1977) was a famous Russian novelist noted for his fight against anti-Semitism and for his opposition to the Bolshevik Revolution. Having fled to Germany from Russia and to France from Germany, he eventually came to the United States. At this time, he wrote his first novel, *Bend Sinister* (1947), in English. Novels *Lolita* (1955), about a man's profound lust for a twelve-year-old girl, *Pnin* (1957), and *Pale Fire* (1962) followed. Nabokov spoke and wrote English, Russian, and French and was a celebrated lepidopterist (one who studies butterflies and moths).

Pablo Neruda (1904–1973) was the pen name of Chilean author Neftalí Ricardo Reyes Basoalto. The pseudonym was used to hide his identity from his practical father and was inspired by the Czech writer Jan Neruda. A political activist, Neruda served as a senator for the Chilean Communist Party until Chilean president Gabriel Gonzalez Videla outlawed communism; Neruda was forced to go into hiding for months in his friends' basement and later in Argentina. His works are still widely read today and appreciated for the growth they show throughout the author's lifetime. *Veinte Poemas de Amor y una Cancion* (*Twenty Love Poems and Songs of Despair*, 1924) is Neruda's most famous work; it has sold over one million copies to date. In exile, Neruda produced another of his more famous collections, titled *Canto General* (1950), which includes 340 poems. After Soviet premier Nikita Khrushchev's revelation of the crimes committed during the regime of Joseph Stalin, Neruda revealed his shaken spirit in his collection *Extravagario* (1958). Neruda died of leukemia in 1973 but left modern readers with more than forty volumes of poetry, translations, and verse drama.

Luigi Pirandello (1867–1936), a Sicilian author educated in Germany, translated German writing into Italian. Later in life, he wrote two plays that were widely acclaimed: *Right You Are If You Think You Are* and *Six Characters in Search of an Author*. Toward the end of his career, his writing focused on death, insanity, and old age.

Marcel Proust (1871–1922) was a well-known French novelist and critic who created the famed seven-part piece titled *À la recherche du temps perdu* (*Remembrance of Things Past*, 1913–1927). Proust received such acclaim for this work because it provided a vivid portrayal of France before and after World War I and explored the irrationality of human behavior and motivations, especially in relation to love. In Proust's *À la recherche du temps perdu*, time is seen as something in constant flux, a concept that is inspired by the work of Henri Bergson.

Rainer Maria Rilke (1875–1926) is considered one of Germany's greatest twentieth-century poets. His imagery focuses on the impossible relationships between man and the unknown in a time of disbelief, solitude, and anxiety. Writing in verse and lyrical prose, Rilke positioned himself in the transition between the traditional and modern poets. He wrote more than 400 poems in French, which he dedicated to Switzerland, his homeland of choice, but his most famous poetic works are *Sonnets to Orpheus* and the *Duino Elegies*. His two most famous prose works are *Letters to a Young Poet* and the semi-autobiographical *The Notebooks of Malte Laurids Brigge*.

Jean-Paul Sartre (1905–1980) was a leading figure in twentieth-century French existentialist philosophy during *L'Âge de Raison*, or the Age of Reason. Sartre was born in Paris, studied in Berlin, and taught at the Lycée Pasteur in Paris. In Sartre's philosophical view, the lack of God in one's life is the norm. He believed that man must face his undeniable freedom if he ever wishes to become a moral being and establish his own existence. Sartre said that man, once he commits to being totally free from all authority and accepts that he must make meaning himself, needs to find solidarity with others. One way in which to create that solidarity is through literature; Sartre saw art and literature as moral activities. Sartre's early psychological studies went largely unnoticed in the political sphere, but his first novel, *La Nausée* (*Nausea*, 1938), and collection of stories, *Le Mur* (*The Wall and Other Stories*, 1938), brought him fame. His central philosophical work, *L'Etre et le néant* (*Being and Nothingness*, 1943), is a text that attempts to compartmentalize Sartre's concept of being and his early ideas of existentialism. However, Sartre is best known as a playwright. He wrote *Les Mouches* (*The Flies*, 1943) and *Huis Clos* (*No Exit*, 1947), which are loaded with symbolism in order to make clear his philosophical message. One famous line from *Huis Clos* is, *"L'enfer, c'est les autres,"* translated most often as "Hell is other people."

Kenneth Slessor (1901–1971) was an Australian poet and journalist often touted as the most talented Australian poet to write during the twentieth century for his use of modernist influences. Some of his best-known poems include "Beach Burial" (1944), which is a tribute to Australian soldiers who served in World War II, and "Five Bells" (1939), a melancholy poem that confronts death with despair.

Aleksandr Solzhenitsyn (1918–2008) was a Russian novelist, dramatist, and historian. Through his writings, he made the world aware of the gulag, the Soviet Union's forced labor camp system, and for these efforts Solzhenitsyn was exiled from the Soviet Union in 1974. He was awarded the Nobel Prize in Literature in 1970. He returned to Russia in 1994. He was the father of Ignat Solzhenitsyn, a conductor and pianist. Aleksandr Solzhenitsyn continued the realistic tradition of Dostoevsky and Leo Tolstoy and complemented it with his views of the flaws of both the East and West. In the 1960s and 1970s, he produced a number of major novels based on his own experiences of Soviet prisons and hospital life. Later he saw that his primary mission was to write the history of the Russian revolutionary period in the multivolumed work *The Red Wheel* (1983–1991).

Leo Tolstoy (1828–1910), a count and public figure, gave up his wealth to live the simple life of a Russian peasant. Tolstoy was a leader of a religious cult that espoused a highly simplified primitive Christianity reduced to a few moral commandments that condemned modern civilization, the state, courts and law, war, patriotism, marriage, modern art, science, and medicine. *War and Peace* (1812), a historical novel about the Napoleonic invasion of Russia in 1812, interprets history as a struggle of anonymous collective forces moved by unknown irrational impulses and waves of communal feeling. Heroes are insignificant puppets, and the best general is one who does nothing to prevent the unknown course of Providence. *Anna Karenina* (1887) is a novel of contemporary manners, adultery, and suicide that ends with the promise of salvation. Rich in vivid imagery, Tolstoy's works emphasize physical traits, deep spirituality, rejection of basic materialism, and the value of community.

Derek Walcott (1930), born in Saint Lucia and a descendent of slaves, worked as a theater and art critic. At eighteen, he wrote *25 Poems* but gained critical acclaim in 1962 for *In a Green Night*, a collection of plays. His work addressed the tension between Caribbean and European cultures but reflected performance, drama, carnival, music, and the color of his culture. His first play, *Henri Christophe: A Chronicle* (1950), is the popular story of a nineteenth-century slave who becomes king of Haiti. *Dream on Monkey Mountain* (1971) depicts how a charcoal vendor attempts to preserve tribal culture in a rigid and sterile colonial world. Walcott's poetic work varies from narratives like *The Fortunate*

Traveler (1981) to epics like *Omeros* (1990). Walcott received the Nobel Prize in Literature in 1992.

Patrick White (1912–1990) was an Australian author who used stream of consciousness and shifting narrative perspectives in his writing. White was born in London to Australian parents, but his family moved back to Sydney by the time he was six months old. In his middle years, he studied in England, befriended painter Roy de Maistre, spent a short time living in the United States, and joined the Royal Air Force at the start of World War II, at which time he was posted to the Middle East. After all of his traveling, White wrote *The Twyborn Affair* (1979), which is a three-part novel designed to confront and challenge the concept of identity. *The Twyborn Affair* traces the transmigration of the soul through three distinct identities, two of which are distinctly female: "Eudoxia" on the French Riviera before World War I, "Eddie" on a sheep station in the mountains of Australia between wars, and "Eadith" in London just prior to the start of World War II. For his contributions, White was awarded the Nobel Prize in Literature in 1973.

Judith Wright (1915–2000) was one of the most widely read poets in Australia during the twentieth century. Her writing is often described as "clear" and "lucid," and she was the first white Australian poet to explore the experiences of Australia's indigenous people. Wright's work is noted for its focus on the Australian environment as well as on the tense relationship between settlers, indigenous Australians, and the land itself. Some of her best-known collections of poetry include *The Moving Image* (1946), *Woman to Man* (1949), *The Gateway* (1953), *The Two Fires* (1955), *Birds: Poems* (1962), and *The Other Half* (1966).

Mikhail Zoshchenko (1895–1958) was the foremost Russian satirist of the Soviet period. Zoshchenko's father was a mosaicist responsible for the exterior decoration of the Suvorov Museum in Saint Petersburg. The future writer attended the Faculty of Law at the Saint Petersburg University, joined the army during World War I, and shared the views of the Serapion brothers. He attained particular popularity in the 1920s but lived in poverty after his denunciation in the Zhdanov decree of 1946. He developed a simplified deadpan style of writing, which simultaneously made him accessible to "the people" and mocked official demands for accessibility: "I write very compactly. My sentences are short. Accessible to the poor" (quoted in Volkov, p. 40). Volkov compares this style to the nakedness of the Russian holy fool or *yurodivy*. This style was much admired by composer Dmitri Shostakovich, who adopted it as a part of his own persona.

Africa

The modern literature of Africa is more well-known to Western readers than to readers in any other country. Many works were originally written in English, French, and Portuguese. Pervading African literature is the importance of "negritude," or consciousness of black identity.

Chinua Achebe (1930), a Nigerian novelist, composed his first novel, *Things Fall Apart*, in 1959. In contrast to previous African literature that addresses folklore and stories of urban life, *Things Fall Apart* addresses the grave impact of colonialization on a warrior hero who refuses to relinquish his traditional cultural beliefs and values. Achebe's other novels, *No Longer At Ease* (1960) and *Arrow of God*, also address the profound difficulties Africans face when worlds collide, resulting in rapid cultural change.

Doris Lessing (1919), a Zimbabwean British writer, authored the novels *The Grass Is Singing* and *The Golden Notebook*. In 2007, she won the Nobel Prize in Literature. Her writing depicts the horror and savagery of apartheid and nuclear war.

Wole Soyinka (1934), a Nigerian, writes drama, poetry, and novels. In 1960, he founded The 1960 Masks, a theater group, and in 1964, the Orisun Theatre Company, where he performed his own plays. Basing his writing on the mythology of his own tribe—the Yoruba—with Ogun, the god of iron and war, he wrote *The Swamp Dwellers* and *The Lion and the Jewel* (1963). Among Soyinka's serious philosophic plays are *The Strong Breed* (1963), *The Road* (1965), and *Death and the King's Horseman* (1975). Soyinka's novel *The Interpreters* (1965), a complicated narrative in which six Nigerian intellectuals share interpretations of their African experiences, has been compared to the works of Joyce and Faulkner. *Ake: The Years of Childhood* (1981) and *The Man Died: Prison Notes* (1972) are accounts of his childhood and later political imprisonment for allegedly conspiring with Biafran rebels.

Ngũgĩ wa Thiong'o (1938) is a Kenyan author and is the founder and editor of the Gikuyu-language journal *Mutiiri*. Ngũgĩ is well-known for his novel *Weep Not, Child* (1964) due to the text's prominence as the first major novel in English by an East African. Another aspect of Ngũgĩ's life that makes his works so popular is the fact that he was imprisoned for the strong political message of his play *I Will Marry When I Want*. After his release, Ngũgĩ made two bold choices: one was to abandon English as the language of his works in favor of Gikuyu, his native Kenyan language, and the other choice was to go into self-imposed exile in London. In 1980 Ngũgĩ published the first modern novel written in Gikuyu, called *Caitaani muthara-Ini* (*Devil on the Cross*, 1980).

China

China privileged the nation, not the individual, and government-established conservatism in writing. Chinese travelers who went abroad adapted literary models and made changes in the use of the vernacular. Contemporary Chinese writers strived to develop literature in both modern language and Chinese.

Bing Xin (1900–1999), a literary woman, is known for her *morbidezza* style of writing, so called as she wrote as though painting a picture with the finest and most tender detail. Her works provide insights of mother love and innocence. Early works advocated "the philosophy of love" and expressed strong individualism. Among her prose works, *An Orange-peel* Lamp, *We Have No Winter*, and *Cherry Blossoms and Friendship* are pieces that maintain her usual fresh and beautiful artistic style but replace misty and melancholy sentiments with a bright and optimistic tone. She is best remembered for *Ji xiao duzhe* (*To Young Readers*, 1926).

Lao She (1899–1966) was skillful in utilizing the Peking dialect. *Camel Xiangzi* and the drama *Tea House* are his masterpieces, which reflect the helplessness of the lower classes in old China. A novelist and dramatist, he was one of the most significant figures of twentieth-century Chinese literature. Among Lao She's most famous stories is "Crescent Moon," which depicts the miserable life of a mother and daughter and their deterioration into prostitution. His other important works include *Si Shi Tong Tang* (abridged translation is *The Yellow Storm*, directly translated into *Four Generations under One Roof*, 1944–1950), a novel describing the life of the Chinese people during the Japanese occupation, and *Cat Country*, a satire that is sometimes seen as the first important Chinese science fiction novel.

Lin Yutang (1895–1976), an essayist and novelist, was nominated for the Nobel Prize in Literature for his novel *Moment in Peking*. His informal but polished style in Chinese and English made him one of the most influential writers of his generation. Dr. Lin popularized classical Chinese literature in the West, developed *Gwoyeu Romatzyh*, a new method of romanizing the Chinese language, and created an indexing system for Chinese characters. At the behest of Pearl Buck, he wrote *My Country and My People* (1935) and *The Importance of Living* (1937). Since Chinese is a character-based rather than an alphabet-based language, with many thousands of separate characters, it was difficult to employ modern printing technologies in producing Chinese-language books until Lin invented a workable typewriter that was marketed during World War II.

Lu Xun (1881–1936) is called the father of modern Chinese literature. Lu Xun or Lu Hsün was a pen name of Zhou Shuren. His first story, "A Madman's Diary," is considered the first story written in modern Chinese. His first set of stories was published as the book *Call to Arms* or *Na Han*. He retold old Chinese stories from his own perspective. He also published *Wild Grass*, a collection of prose poems, in 1924, a work of dreams, including nightmares: dogs speak, insects buzz, and the sky tries to hide itself from onlookers.

Xu Zhimo (1915–1931) was a Chinese lyric poet who promoted modern Chinese poetry. His poetry consistently romanticized love, freedom, and beauty, although the forms through which he expressed these ideas varied greatly. It was at King's College that Xu became inspired by the English romantic poetry of Keats and Shelley as well as the French romantic and symbolist poets.

India

India's writing reflects the tension between "Indianness" and "Westernness," portraying the tensions between Western imperialism and an emerging national identity.

Mohandas K. Gandhi (1869–1948) was a major political and spiritual leader of India. He is regarded as one of the major leaders of the Indian independence movement. Ghandi believed in *satyagraha*, or resistance, to unjust rule through mass civil disobedience. He also promoted *ahimsa*, or total nonviolence. Often called Mahatma, which means "great soul," or Bapu, which means "father," Ghandi is seen as the father of the nation of India. He was also a prolific writer, and his autobiography, *My Experiments with Truth*, written in the Gujarati language originally between 1927 and 1929, is a classic text.

Amitav Ghosh (1956) was born in Calcutta, India, and grew up in Bangladesh, Sri Lanka, Iran, and India. In 1980, Ghosh completed anthropological field work in the village of Lataifa, Egypt, which resulted in his publication of *In an Antique Land* (1993). Ghosh published his first novel, *The Circle of Reason* (1986), and his second, *The Shadow Lines* (1988), and has since worked on journalistic endeavors. He is currently a professor at Columbia University.

Qurrat-ul-Ain Haider (1926–2007) is one of the most-talked-about names in Urdu literature. A novelist and a short-story writer, Haider wrote a total of twelve novels and four collections of short stories, and translated many classic texts. Her magnum opus, titled *Aag Ka Darya* (*Ring of Fire*), tells a story that spans from the fourth century BC to the postindependence period of India and Pakistan. Haider was known as Ainee Apa to her friends and admirers.

R. K. Narayan (1906–2001), or Rasipuram Krishnaswami Ayyar Narayanaswami, is one of the best-known Indian novelists to English-speaking audiences. Narayan's style is often compared to Faulkner's in that it celebrates the energy of ordinary life. His first novel, *Swami and Friends* (1935), set the tone for his other well-known works, *The English Teacher* (1980), *The Vendor of Sweets* (1983), and *Under the Banyan Tree* (1985). Narayan's works are usually set in the fictitious town of Malgudi through which the author is able to vividly convey the details of rural village life in India.

Sir Ahmed Salman Rushdie (1947) is a British Indian novelist and essayist whose novels use magical realism mixed with historical fiction. Rushdie has made major contributions to Indian writing in English, and his second novel, *Midnight's Children* (1981), which follows the life of a special child born at midnight on the day India gained its independence, declared that Rushdie, early on in his career, was a force to be highly regarded. Other texts include *Shame* (1983), which discusses the political turmoil in Pakistan and displays Rushdie's personal connection to the Indian diaspora; *The Satanic Verses* (1988), which is highly controversial; and *Shalimar the Clown* (2005), which won many international awards. Rushdie continues to write works that focus on the interchange of thought between the Eastern and Western world.

Rabindranath Tagore (1861–1941) was a Bengali poet and Brahmo philosopher who also delved into the realms of visual art, mysticism, and music. He was also the first Asian novelist to receive the Nobel Prize for Literature in 1913. At sixteen years old, Tagore published his first compilation of poetry under the pen name Bhanushingho ("Sun Lion"). He is most well-known for his poetry, although his short stories are also very popular. Tagore often wrote about very simple-sounding subject matter—ordinary people—and used language that flows well and sounds harmonious. His literature is humanistic and depicts a strong compassion for the poor. Some of Tagore's most popular works include *Gitanjali* (1913), *Saddhana, The Realisation of Life* (1916), *The Crescent Moon* (1913), *Fruit-Gathering* (1916), *Stray Birds* (1916), *The Home and the World* (1915), and *Thought Relics* (1921). These works reshaped Bengali literature in the early twentieth century.

Nirmal Verma (1929–2005) was a Hindi novelist and activist who helped to bring about the *Nayi Kahani* ("new short story") literary movement of Hindi literature. His best-known short story, "Parinde" ("Birds,"1959), is supposed to be the exemplar of the Nayi Kahani movement. Verma also wrote other notable stories such as "Ve Din" (1964), "Lal Teen Ki Chhat" ("Red Tin Roof," 1974), and "Kavve Aur Kala Pani" (1983), which have been translated into English, Russian, Polish, and French, among other languages. Verma's writing is rich in symbolism with a style that is deceptively simple.

Japan

Modernism in non-Western cultures assumed similarities and differences to the modernism of the West. Japanese authors attempted to reinvent themselves as equal to Western countries by undertaking the tortuous process of cultural absorption and transformation. Curiosity about the world and traditional receptivity to foreign ways transfigured the fabric of Japanese life. Modernism had more in common with realism and served as a literary compass for situating the confusion of identity, self-interest, and "belonging" within cultural ambiguity.

Oe Kenzaburo (1935) became Japan's second Nobel Prize recipient for literature in 1994. He used his experience of growing up with a brain-damaged father to write two of his works, *Kojinteki na Taiken* (*A Personal Matter*, 1963) and *Manen Gannen no Futtoboru* (*The Silent Cry*, 1967). In his novels, Oe intertwines poetry and prose, and reality and myth. He also writes about the isolation from the outside world felt within the twentieth-century Japanese culture.

Makoto Ôoka invented *renshi* (a type of linked poetry) in 1981. He and the American poet Thomas Fitzsimmons collaborated on the first international *renshi*. *Renshi* differs from *renga* and *renku* in that it is written in contemporary free verse instead of linked stanzas.

Kawabata Yasunari (1899–1972), who was awarded the Nobel Prize for Literature in 1968, is the author of *Tade-kuu Mushi* (*Some Prefer Nettles*, 1928). In this work, Yasunari uses the cities of Tokyo and Osaka as symbols of the conflict between modern and traditional thought in his country.

Banana Yoshimoto (1964) is a contemporary Japanese author whose given name is Yoshimoko Mahoto. She is the daughter of Yoshimoto Takaaki, an influential Japanese philosopher, but her writings have little to do with her upbringing. Yoshimoto's works have received mixed reviews but are noteworthy nonetheless because of their harsh, or brutally honest, insights into modern Japanese society. Yoshimoto's first popular story was a novella titled *Kitchen* (1987), a coming-of-age tale that deals with the topics of loneliness, death, and a girl who loves kitchens.

Mishima Yukio (1925–1970) was a talented writer who was capable of writing kabuki plays (highly stylized Japanese dance-dramas) in the traditional style. Yukio was homosexual and proudly professed his love for the human body; he had a strong appreciation for physical decline as well. His first major work, *Kamen no Kokuhaku* (*Confessions of a Mask*, 1949), and his last novel, *Hojo no Umi* (*The Sea of Fertility*, 1965–1970), highlighted these ideas. Yukio was opposed and despised the westernization of Japan and thus did not do his military service during the war. After forming a small private army and failing to inspire a revolt in the government's ranks, Yukio took to bodybuilding and eventually committed ritual suicide with other members of his fanatical army. His 1956 work, *Kinkakuji* (*The Temple of the Golden Pavilion*), echoes Yukio's own thoughts; in the story, a monk burns down the Kyoto pavilion in order to avoid seeing the United States gain control of it.

The Middle Eastern

The Middle East saw the introduction of the novel. The modern short story also emerged in Middle Eastern writing. Some Middle Eastern writers accepted Western modernity, while others regarded this as a radical transformation of society and near annihilation of culture. This tension became the subject of a series of novels and short stories.

Yehuda Amichai (1924–2000) was a significant contemporary Hebrew poet whose work helped to create modern Israeli poetry. Born in Germany, Amichai immigrated to Palestine in 1936 and later settled in Jerusalem. After fighting in World War II and the Israeli war of independence, which led to the formation of the state of Israel, Amichai attended Hebrew University and produced his first collection of poetry, *Achshav Uve-Yamim HaAharim* (*Now and in Other Days*, 1955), which established his position that poetry must reflect contemporary issues. Therefore, in his poetry readers must confront his surprising subjects and images, which include tanks, airplanes, fuel, administrative contracts, and technological terms. Also new to the poetic scene was the way in which Amichai played with words from the Hebrew language and mixed classical Hebrew, postmodern colloquialisms, newly coined idioms, and slang expressions in his work. Amichai received the Israel Prize in 1982 for the changes he introduced to poetry's diction. Some of his other notable works include *Collected Poems* (1963), *Selected Works* (1981), *Shirei Yerushalayim* (*Poems of Jerusalem*, 1987), and *Two Hopes Away* (1958).

Naguib Mahfouz (1911–2006), an award-winning Egyptian novelist, was one of the first Egyptians to explore existentialism in his work. Mahfouz began writing at age seventeen and published eleven works before taking a short reprieve during the Egyptian revolution of 1952. In 1957, Mahfouz published his famous Cairo Trilogy, *Bayn al Qasrayn* (*Between-the-Palaces*), *Qasr al Shawq* (*Palace of Longing*), and *Sukkariya* (*Sugarhouse*), which made him famous for the way in which he depicted urban life in the Arab world. Mahfouz then took a different route with *The Children of Gebelawi* (1959) and wrote with much symbolism in order to conceal his political statements. At the time of his death, Mahfouz was the author of no fewer than 30 novels, more than 100 short stories, and more than 200 articles in newspapers and magazines.

Amos Oz (1939) is an author whose prose for both children and adults has been widely translated and highly praised. Oz uses the turbulent history of Jerusalem in his writing to present the tribulations and stories of the people of Israel. He calls his readers to end ambivalence, to channel present emotions into future work, and to be open to dialogue. His texts examine human nature in all of its variety and frailty. His most famous works include *A Tale of Love and Darkness* (2003), *A Perfect Peace* (1982), and *To Know a Woman* (1989).

Orhan Pamuk (1952) is an important contemporary Turkish novelist and is often the only one widely known to most Western readers. The settings of his novels are usually varied in *when* they take place but not *where*; Pamuk focuses mostly on the country of Turkey or the former Ottoman Empire. One of Pamuk's early novels that brought much fame was *Beyaz Kale* (*White Castle*, 1985), which is a mystery story set in the early Renaissance. Two of Pamuk's most recent novels include *Benim Adım Kırmızı* (*My Name Is Red*, 1998) and *Kar* (*Snow*, 2002).

Marjane Satrapi (1969) is an accomplished Iranian and French graphic novelist, illustrator, animated film director, and children's book author. Satrapi grew up in Tehran, studied at the Lycee Francais, and went on to further study illustration in Strasbourg. In addition to her award-winning graphic novels, *Persepolis I* and *Persepolis II* (2003 and 2004, respectively), Satrapi has written several other books for children and adults. Some of these include *Embroideries* (2005), *Chicken with Plums* (2006), and *Monsters Are Afraid of the Moon* (2006) in English, and *Sagesses et malices de la Perse* (2001), *Ulysse au pays des fous* (2001), and *Le Soupir* (2004) in French.

Abraham B. Yehoshua (1936) is an internationally known Israeli author. He was born in Jerusalem, studied at the Hebrew University, and later lived and taught in Paris. Yehoshua's works include novels, short stories, plays, and essays. One of his newest works, *Five Seasons*, was published in 2007. In it, the main character Molkho's wife dies and the story traces Molkho's fantasies season by season as he struggles with his new freedom. *Five Seasons* is regarded as one of the most important books written since the creation of the state of Israel.

CHARACTERISTICS OF VARIOUS GENRES AND TYPES OF LITERATURE

The following section defines the various genres and types of literature. In addition, this section provides a detailed list of literary devices a reader uses to analyze, interpret, explicate, or read a text closely.

Genres and Characteristics

Fiction

Fiction is any text that is invented or imagined, usually in the form of prose narrative. Fiction may be based on personal events or experiences, but the characters in the story are invented. Even if a story is set in an actual place and involves a recognizable character, the story is still fictitious.

Elements of Fiction

Character

Character refers to the person in a work of fiction. There are two general types of characters: the protagonist and the antagonist. The **protagonist** is the character, usually a hero, who is central to the story and for whom all major events in the story have some importance; Harry Potter, for example, is the protagonist in J. K. Rowling's highly successful book series. The **antagonist** is the character who opposes the main character, in either an openly cruel or subtle way, for example, Lord Voldemort from the *Harry Potter* series or Cruella Deville in *101 Dalmations*.

Characterization

Characterization is the process by which the author provides the reader information about the characters. The author develops characterization in the following ways:

- By describing the character's physical, emotional, and social characteristics

- By explaining what the character thinks, feels, or dreams. In this case, the author is being psychologically introspective. Holden Caulfied in *Catcher in the Rye* is a first-person psychologically introspective character. Jane Austen is the master of creating a psychologically introspective, objective (albeit loosely) third-person narrator.

- By divulging what the character does or does not do or the actions or decisions the character makes (ethics)

- By describing what other characters in the story say about the character (dialogue) and how they react to the character's behavior (external evidence)

Characters may be round or flat, dynamic or static. **Round characters** are fully developed, acting according to complex and believable patterns of emotion, motivation and behavior. Nora Helmer in Henrik Ibsen's *A Doll House* is a round character. **Flat characters** are one-dimensional, predictable, and uncomplicated. Lennie in John Steinbeck's *Of Mice and Men* is a flat character. **Dynamic characters** develop and grow in response to events or motives. **Static characters** remain the same throughout the course of the narrative, untouched by events or the people they encounter.

Plot

Plot is the sequence of events in a story or a play, a series of events planned by the author that has a beginning, middle, and end. There are five essential parts of a plot:

Introduction: the beginning of the story, in which the author introduces the characters and the setting

Rising action: the part of the story in which the conflict is revealed, in essence a "leading up" to the climax. These are all the events between the introduction and the climax.

Climax: usually the most interesting and revealing part of a story, a turning point, which begs the question of whether or not the conflict will be resolved

Falling action: the point at which the events and complications that occur in the rising action and climax resolve themselves. At this point, the reader now knows whether or not the conflict has been resolved.

Denouement: the final outcome or untangling of events in a story.

Setting

Setting is the time, context, and location in which a story takes place. A reader should consider several aspects of the setting when analyzing a work of fiction:

Place: geographical location, where the action of the story occurs

Social conditions: daily life, speech, dress, mannerisms, customs. The social conditions and customs of a novel like *Jane Eyre* will obviously be very different from that of a William Burroughs novel like *Naked Lunch* (a modern work in which the author talks openly of drug addiction).

Time: the chronological flow of the story's events, the historical time period, the time of year, and the time of day

Weather: the weather and other physical conditions affecting the story and its characters, including things like rain, the color of the sky, and natural phenomenon like mountains and brooks

Mood or **atmosphere**: the feeling of the setting; for example, the beginning of Leo Tolstoy's *Anna Karenina* establishes a less cheery, somewhat troubling but somewhat matter-of-fact mood: "Every family is dysfunctional."

Theme

The theme of a fictional text is its controlling idea or insight. It is the underlying meaning or central idea of the work and essentially what the author is trying to tell the reader. For example, one theme in F. Scott Fitzgerald's *The Great Gatsby* is that one cannot relive the past, as Daisy Buchanan became an "unattainable object" for Jay Gatsby.

Types of Fiction

A **novel** is a fictional narrative in prose, usually longer than a short story. The author is not restricted by historical facts but is free to create fictional personalities in a fictional world (e.g., *Lord of the Flies* by William Golding).

A **short story** is narrative prose fiction that is shorter than a novel. Short stories often vary in length, with some no longer than a few hundred words and some are over 50,000 words (e.g., "The Lottery" by Shirley Jackson). An extended short story is referred to as a **novelette** (e.g., *First Contact* by Murray Leinster), or when longer, a **novella** (e.g., *The Metamorphosis* by Franz Kafka). The literary elements of plot, setting, and character are compressed in a short story.

Types of Fictional Narratives

Allegory is a form of extended metaphor in which objects, persons, and actions in a narrative are equated with meanings that lie outside the narrative itself. The underlying meaning has moral, social, religious, or political significance, and characters are often personifications of abstract ideas like charity, greed, or envy. An allegory has both literal and symbolic meanings. Nathaniel Hawthorne's *Young Goodman Brown* is an allegory that describes what happens when one abandons one's faith and becomes associated with the devil.

Fable is a brief story or poem that is told to present a moral or practical lesson. The characters in fables are often animals that speak or act like humans. *Aesop's Fables*, told by Aesop, a slave in ancient Greece, used animals to tell stories about important virtues.

Folk legend is a traditional narrative or collection of narratives, supposedly historically factual but usually a mixture of both fact and fiction, which has its origins in oral storytelling. The story of Pecos Bill, who apparently was raised out west by wolves, is an infamous tall tale created during westward expansion in the United States. He was a legendary cowboy, and akin to other folk figures like Paul Bunyan.

Myth is a traditional or legendary story that usually concerns some being, hero, or event without a determinable basis of fact or a natural explanation. Myths are often created to explain what humankind cannot understand, such as the actions of deities or demigods, practices, rites, or phenomena of nature. For example, the Greek myth of the Labors of Hercules describes how he ventures to the land of the dead and proves himself by accomplishing inhuman feats, eventually becoming a "complete god."

Romance is fictional prose narrative about improbable events involving characters that are different from ordinary people. King Arthur on a quest for a magic sword (Excalibur) aided by characters like fairies or trolls is an example of romance. Oftentimes, Gothic and romantic literature is mixed. For example, *The Castle of Otranto* takes place in a Gothic castle, but its hero, Theodore, a peasant, has "knightly blood," and ends up taking the throne. *Don Quixote* by Miguel de Cervantes is also an example of romance.

Modern fantasy is a kind of fiction in which the author creates a magical world where anything is possible. Fantasy may include magical beings, talking animals, and gods and goddesses. The *Harry Potter* series by J. K. Rowling is a perfect example of a fantasy.

Science fiction is a type of futuristic or high fantasy that explores scientific fact and often poses ethical questions about current scientific trends and predictions. The author often focuses on exploring an unknown world that has been affected by "extrapolations" of current technological advancement. The science fiction novel *Neuromancer* by William Gibson chronicles the life of Henry Dorsett Case, who is living in the futuristic dystopia of Chiba City, Japan. Case is a computer geek who hacks into a global computer network using a brain-computer interface. In this text, Gibson took the primitive notion of the Internet and imagined a world in which our brains were cybernetically "logged in."

Modern realistic fiction presents a problem to be examined through prose narrative (e.g., *The Chocolate War* by Robert Cormier).

Historical fiction is a story that takes the reader back to a particular time period and describes the life of a person who lived during that period. Good historical fiction is as true as possible to the time period being represented. The main character may (and often does) interact with actual historical characters, but usually the main character is not based on a real person. A historical artifact or person that appears out of place in a historical fiction is called an **anachronism**. For example, *Waverly*, written by Sir Walter Scott, depicts a fictional character named Edward Waverly who takes part in the Jacobite rebellion of 1745. Although he is English, he takes the side of the Highland Scottish and even meets the deposed King Charles (Bonnie Prince Charlie), who was a real historical figure.

Mystery fiction is a novel in which a crime has been committed. The reader and protagonist have to figure out the perpetrator. Mystery fiction is noted for intense suspense and intrigue. Agatha Christie's mystery novels follow protagonists such as Miss Marple and Hercule Poirot as they work to figure out crimes. A more recent example is Dan Brown's *The Da Vinci Code*, which recounts symbologist Robert Langdon's efforts to uncover a Biblical "secret" that Jesus was married and fathered a child with Mary Magdalene.

Nonfiction

Autobiography and biography are the most common forms of nonfiction, but periodicals and scientific papers also fall under this heading. Nonfiction is any prose narrative that recounts events or stories as they actually happened or that possesses factual information.

Types of Nonfiction

Autobiography is a person's account of his or her own life (e.g., *The Story of My Life* by Helen Keller).

Biography is a book someone else has written about (usually) a famous historical figure. A good example is Doris Kearns Goodwin's *No Ordinary Time* about Franklin and Eleanor Roosevelt.

Essay is usually a short piece written from an author's personal point of view. Essays can be literary criticism, political manifestos, arguments, observations of daily life, recollections, and reflections of the author. Early essays like Alexander Pope's *An Essay on Criticism* is written in verse, while most modern essays are written in prose.

Informational books and **articles** are books and shorter texts about topics of particular interest, such as Jared Diamond's *Guns, Germs, and Steel*, which traces the anthropological reasons for why the Western world rose to its modern status.

Memoir is a form of autobiography that is objective and anecdotal.

Newspaper accounts are supposedly un-biased, objective writing that tells exactly how an event happened. Newspaper articles are written in an "inverted pyramid" format in which the most important details are provided at the beginning and less important details are explained in the rest of the article.

Drama

Drama is a story that is acted out, usually on a stage, where actors and actresses take the parts of specific characters. Dramas are usually either tragedies, in which the protagonist meets a disastrous end, or comedies, in which a humorous plan ends happily[3].

---

[3] http://library.thinkquest.org/23846/library/terms/index.html

Genres of Drama

Serious drama or **tragedy** explores the notion that life is finite, and deals with serious subjects and characters who are confronted with their own mortality. Many tragic plots revolve around a crisis over succession to a throne, as in *Antigone*, and subsequent breaking of familial and societal ties. Murder and death occur frequently in tragedy and usually result from a transgression of sacred principles or morals, as in *Oedipus Rex*. Tragic characters like Oedipus act alone and take responsibility for their actions. The audience usually empathizes with tragic characters, identifying with their suffering, experiences, and catharses. Arthur Miller's *Death of a Salesman* is a modern tragic play.

Commons terms used in analyzing tragedy include

anagnorisis: self recognition

catharsis: purge of emotion

hamartia: tragic flaw

hubris: excessive pride

peripeteia: reversal of fortune

Comic drama or **comedy** celebrates the continuation of life and the success of generations through love and rebirth. Comic plots usually involve an outrageous idea or fantastic scheme that disrupts the normal workings of the community and leads to chaos. Comedy often examines characters from a particular social class, and comic characters tend to reflect human weakness. Comedy usually occurs in the realm of the ludicrous and ends with a reconciliation or happy resolution, such as an engagement or marriage.

Farce is a form drama designed to create laughter, emphasizing clowning and slapstick humor. Farce

- contains exaggerated physical action by stereotypical characters

- exaggerates characters so intensely that they are highly unlikely to be found in the real world

- incorporates absurd situations, improbable events, and unexpected experiences

- includes complex plots with character and dialogue less important to plot and situation

Aristophanes (*The Clouds)* and Plautus (*Miles Gloriosus*) were Greek masters of the farce. The movies of the Monty Python troupe and the Marx Brothers are modern examples of farce.

Melodrama[4] has its origins in music as it incorporated music to increase emotions or to signify characters with signature music. Such works

- reflected interest in morality and virtue stemming from the ideas of philosophers like Kant and Rousseau

- were set in the medieval world, with castles, dungeons, and torture chambers

- simplified the moral universe with good and evil embodied in stock characters

- occurred in an episodic form: villain poses a threat, and the hero or heroine escapes with a happy ending

- used many special effects: fires, explosions, drowning, and earthquakes

Tragicomedy is drama that mixes the elements and styles of tragedy and comedy. In the Jacobean era of Great Britain, these plays had romantic and exciting plots in which disaster persisted throughout the play, eventually reaching a happy conclusion. An example of such a play is Shakespeare's *The Winter Tale*. Modern drama explores existential themes that describe human activities that have no fixed meaning and are always in flux, uncertain, and ambiguous. Loneliness and alienation are significant themes in modern tragicomedy. More modern tragicomedy writers are Samuel Beckett (*Endgame* and *Malloy/Malone Dies*, though these are novels, not plays) and Anton Chekhov (*Three Sisters*).[5]

Poetry

Genres of Poetry

Poetry is language arranged in lines, with a regular rhythm and definitive rhyme scheme. Nontraditional poetry or "free verse" does away with regular rhythm and rhyme,

---

[4] http://novaonline.nv.cc.va.us/eli/spd130et/melodrama.htm

[5] *www.**drama**.uwaterloo.ca/**Genre-2005**.ppt*

though it is still usually written in lines. The sounds of words and the strong feelings evoked by images distinguish poetry from other forms of literature.

Concrete poetry, also often referred to as visual poetry, relies on the typographical arrangement of words to convey the meaning of the poem, along with other conventional elements of a poem, such as rhythm, meter, and word choice.[6] A simple example is

I

Like

Triangles

Dramatic poetry is written in either a monologue or a dialogue and in the voice of a character assumed by the poet. Famous dramatic monologues include Alfred Lord Tennyson's "Ulysses" and Robert Browning's "My Last Duchess."

The **epic poem** is a long narrative poem, often extending to several books with sections of several hundred lines. The poem usually focuses on a significant and serious subject. Homer's *Odyssey* is an example of an early and historic epic poem. Another example of this type of poem is Edmund Spenser's *Faerie Queene*, which, if you remember from this chapter's section on the Elizabethan literature of Great Britain, is an allegorical poem about the English Reformed Church and its struggle with paganism. Other examples are John Milton's *Paradise Lost*, and Elizabeth Barrett Browning's *Aurora Leigh*. In the twentieth century, epic poetry took on a freer, less formal structure, as in William Carlos William's *Paterson* and Ezra Pound's *Cantos*.

Lyric poetry originally consisted of songs performed in ancient Greece accompanied by a small harp-like instrument called a lyre. The current definition of lyric poetry is a short poem presented in the voice of a single speaker. The speaker, however, may quote others. The speaker's **voice** is frequently different from that of the actual author's, so readers should remember that the author often invents a fictional character in the poem to speak. The majority of poems that we read nowadays in English classes are lyric poems.

There are several types of lyric poetry:

Ballad: a type of quatrain, or stanza of four lines. The ballad stanza's lines are in iambic tetrameter, alternating with a rhyming *abcb* (lines 1 and 3

---

[6] http://members.optushome.com.au/kazoom/poetry/concrete.html

are unrhymed), less commonly, *abab*. Samuel Taylor Coleridge's *Rime of the Ancient Mariner* is a ballad.

Blank verse: unrhymed (blank) iambic pentameter, found in Shakespeare's plays

Couplet: two lines of verse, usually coupled by rhyme. Geoffrey Chaucer was the first poet to use this form in the "General Prologue" to *The Canterbury Tales*. Alexander Pope used a couplet in "An Essay on Man":

> *Why has not Man a microscopic eye?*
> *For this plain reason, Man is not a Fly.*

Heroic couplet: two consecutive lines of rhyming poetry that are written in iambic pentameter and that contain a complete thought. In a heroic couplet, there is usually one pause at the end of the first line and another heavier pause at the end of the second line.[7] Here is an example from John Keats's *Endymion*:

> *A thing of beauty is a joy forever;*
> *Its loveliness increases, it will never*
> *Pass into nothingness; but still will keep*
> *A bower quiet for us, and a sleep*

Elegy: poem that laments the loss of someone who has died, as in A. E. Housman's "To An Athlete Dying Young"

Limerick: a five-line stanza that comes from an old custom at parties where each person was required to sing an extemporaneous nonsense verse, which was followed by a chorus with the words "Will you come up to Limerick?" The master of the limerick was Edward Lear (1812–1888), who wrote "There Was an Old Man with a Beard." The first and fifth lines of the limerick must end with the same word, which is usually a place name. Lear, however, deviates from this convention.

Ottava rima: an eight-line stanza that rhymes *abababcc*; was introduced to English literature by Sir Thomas Wyatt. Lord Byron used in it *Don Juan*.

Sonnet: traditionally a poem of fourteen iambic-pentameter lines linked together by a rhyme scheme. This is one of the oldest verse forms in

---

[7] http://library.thinkquest.org/23846/library/terms/index.html

English. The sonnet originated in Italy and was introduced into England by Sir Thomas Wyatt in "Whoso List to Hunt." The three basic types of sonnet are the Italian or Petrarchan sonnet, the English or Shakespearean sonnet, and the Spenserian sonnet. The Italian sonnet has an octave, consisting of eight lines, and a "turn" in the poem called a sestet, a series of six lines. The difference between the English and Spenserian sonnets are as follows:

- A **Spenserian stanza** has nine lines, in which the first eight are iambic pentameter and the last is an iambic hexameter (called an alexandrine, defined later in the section on meter); the lines rhyme ababbcbcc.

Tercet: a stanza of three lines usually linked together with a single rhyme

Villanelle: a French verse form that consists of five tercets rhyming *aba* followed by a quatrain rhyming *abaa*, with the first line of the initial tercet recurring as the last line of the second and fourth tercets, and the third line of the initial tercet recurring as the last line of the third and fifth tercets

Criteria for Evaluating Poetic Works

The following are a few guidelines to consider when a reader analyzes, interprets, explicates, or reads a poem closely:

Pattern of the sound and rhythm

- Free verse has neither regular rhyme nor regular meter.

The visible shape or structure

- Consider the line structure, especially in concrete poetry.

Rhyme

End rhymes are rhymes that appear at the end of a line.

Feminine rhymes consist of a stressed syllable followed by an unstressed syllable, as in *flying/crying*.

Internal rhymes are rhymes whose internal syllables sound the same, as in *when/men*.

Masculine rhymes consist of single stressed syllable, for example, *bly/fly*.

Perfect rhyme occurs when the correspondence of rhyme sounds is exact.

Imperfect rhyme

Off-rhyme, or half rhyme, near rhyme, or slant rhyme, differs from perfect rhyme in changing the vowel sound and or concluding consonants in a sound, as in *gone/alone*.

Vowel rhyme occurs when the rhyme words have only their vowel sounds in common, for example, *boughs/towns*.

Similar consonants can also be used to create imperfect rhyme, as in *trod/trade*.

Literary Devices

Alliteration: the repetition of initial sounds in neighboring words, for example, the repetition of the *p* sound in *Peter Piper picked a peck of pickled peppers*.

Allusion: a reference to a person, event, or place, real or fictitious, or to a work of art. May be drawn from history, geography, literature, or religion. For example, in Mary Shelley's *Frankenstein*, the creature reads *Paradise Lost* by John Milton.

Analogy: a rather fully developed comparison between two things or ideas that are basically unlike although they share something in common. Frequently, something unfamiliar or complex will be described in terms of something familiar or simple. For example, in Henry Wadsworth Longfellow's "The Arrow and the Song," he analogizes, *kindness*: *friend* :: *arrow* : *tree*.

Anaphora: the deliberate repetition of words or phrases at the beginning of verses, clauses, or paragraphs. Barack Obama's "The Audacity of Hope" speech given at the Democratic National Convention in July 2004 offers an example: "Hope—hope in the face of difficulty. Hope in the face of uncertainty. The audacity of hope!"

Anastrophe: inversion of the normal syntactic order of words: *A pie he ate.*

Apostrophe: a direct address to an absent or deceased person, abstract concept, or important or inanimate object, for example, "Oh water, giver of life!" Another example:

In Ovid's *Metamorphoses*, Pyramus and Thisbe address the wall that separates them in this way: "You envious barrier."

Archetype: a character, symbol, plot, or theme that recurs often enough in literary works to have universal significance. Archetypes appeal to readers on a fundamental level, as dreams and myths do. Don Quixote and Odysseus are archetypes of characters on a great quest.

Assonance: repetition of vowel sounds, for example, the repeating *ea* sound in *cheap leap*.

Bathos: an abrupt appearance or transition of a trite phrase or idea in the midst of elevated or lofty speech. Here is an example from John Dryden's *Annus Mirabilis* (1667):

> The Eternal heard, and from the heavenly quire
> Chose out the Cherub with the flaming sword
> And bad him swiftly drive the approaching fire
> From where our *naval magazines* were stored.

Blank Verse: unrhymed poetry in iambic pentameter, lines of five feet, with each foot having an unstressed syllable followed by a stressed one. Blank verse reflects the natural rhythms of the English language. For example, Milton uses blank verse to describe Satan's banishment from Heaven in *Paradise Lost*:

> Nine times the space that measure day and night
> To mortal men he, with his horrid crew,
> Lay vanquished, rolling in their fiery gulf,
> Confounded though immortal. But his doom
> Reserved him to more wrath; for now the thought
> Both of lost happiness and lasting pain
> Torments him: round he throws his baleful eyes,
> That witnessed huge affliction and dismay,
> Mixed with obdurate pride and steadfast hate.

Cacophony: harsh or disconcerting sounds, as in, *Screeching crows and howling hyenas ripped the night's silence with screams of terror.*

Catachresis: the violent yolking of two things that are completely dissimilar and should not be put together, as in the lyrics "Her fingernails shine like justice," from the song "Short Skirt, Long Jacket" by the rock group Cake.

Chiasmus: type of rhetoric in which the second part is syntactically balanced against the first, for example, "Flowers are lovely, love is flowerlike" (Samuel Taylor Coleridge).

Connotation: the emotional or cultural associations surrounding a word, as opposed to its strict, literal dictionary meaning. In *Romeo and Juliet*, for example, Romeo associates Juliet with the sun. Another example: The word *steed* conjures up associations of a noble and powerful horse, yet *hack* conjures up associations of a workhorse. Both are horses.

Consonance: the repetition of consonant sounds, as in the repeating *s* sound in *someone sees something*.

Denotation: The strict dictionary meaning of a word, presented objectively, without emotional associations. Here's the denotation for *horse*: A horse is a large hoofed mammal (*Equus caballus*) having a shorthaired coat, a long mane, and a long tail, domesticated since ancient times, used for riding and for drawing or carrying loads.

Epigram: A short, witty saying, often ending with a clever twist. Example: "The heart that is distant creates its own solitude" (from T'oa Ch'in's "I Built my Cottage. . .") or "Thy praise or dispraise is to me alike;/ One doth not stroke me, nor the other strike" (from Ben Jonson's *Epigrams*).

Euphemism: a commonly used term or phrase used to express an idea without bluntly declaring that idea. For example, one might say, "He kicked the bucket" instead of "He died."

Euphony: soothing or pleasant sounds, as in this line from John Keats's *The Eve of St. Agnes* (1820): "And lucent syrops, tinct with cinnamon."

Foreshadowing: the use of hints or clues to suggest what will happen later in literature. In John Steinbeck's *Of Mice and Men*, for example, Carlson's shooting Candy's dog is a foreshadowing of George's shooting Lennie.

Free verse: Verse that has no fixed pattern of rhyme, rhythm, or line length. Although "free" from the demands of regular rhythm and rhyme, free verse achieves its effects with sound devices and subtle patterns of rhythm, as in the following lines from Stephen Crane's "There Was Crimson Clash of War":

There was crimson clash of war.
Lands turned black and bare;
Women wept;
Babes ran, wondering.

Hyperbole: an exaggeration or overstatement: *I'm so hungry I could eat a horse.*

Imagery: language that evokes one or all of the five senses: seeing, hearing, tasting, smelling, or touching. These sensory details provide vividness by arousing complex of emotional associations. Consider the imagery in James Masao Mitsui's "When Father Came Home for Lunch":

Mother adds fried onions, a fried egg
and potatoes to his main bowl.
He adds catsup, shoyu
and mixes it with the white radish,
He works around to the mustard-caked bowl
before each mouth of rice,
sauce hanging from his moustache.
Hot coffee, heavy with sugar & cream,
steams from a china mug.
Half-an-hour of noisy manners
and he's gone, back to work
in oily bib overalls,
I can still smell sweat
soaking his long-sleeved workshirt.

Inference: a reasonable conclusion about characters or events based on the limited information provided by an author. The following excerpt from Charles Dickens's *David Copperfield* leads Davy to believe that his mother and this gentleman are romantically involved:

I never saw such a beautiful color on my mother's face before. She gently chid me for being rude; and, keeping me close to her shawl, turned to thank the gentleman for taking so much trouble as to bring her home. She put out her hand to him, as she spoke, and as he met it with his own, she glanced, I thought, at me.

Irony: a discrepancy between what is said and what is meant. There are three kinds of irony:

Verbal irony: when an author says one thing and means another. Example: A man says, "Lovely day for a stroll," when there is a blizzard outside.

Dramatic irony: when an audience perceives something that a character in the play/literature does not know. For example, in *Macbeth*, the audience knows that the movement of Birnham Wood is actually soldiers holding tree branches; Macbeth thinks that the woods *are* indeed moving.

Situational irony: a discrepancy between the expected result and the actual result. Example: You buy a special pair of earrings for yourself as a birthday gift, only to learn that your friend gives you the same pair as a birthday present.

Malapropism: the act of misusing a word, often in a humorous manner, usually because the words sound the same, as in the question, *What are you incinerating?* in which the word *incinerating* is used instead of *insinuating*.

Metonymy: the act of substituting one word for another that is closely associated with it. Using the phrase *the White House* in place of *the president* or *the cabinet* is an example of metonymy: *The White House made the decision to start a war in Iraq.*

Metaphor: the comparison of two dissimilar things without using *like* or *as*: *In the wrestling ring, he was a lion.*

Mood: the general atmosphere or prevailing emotion of a work, as created by the choice of words, setting, images, and details. Stephen Crane uses imagery to create a mood that turns from peaceful to foreboding, sleep to eagerness in *The Red Badge of Courage*:

The cold passed reluctantly from the earth, and the retiring fogs revealed an army stretched out on the hills, resting. As the landscape changed from brown to green, the army awakened, and began to tremble with eagerness at the noise of rumor. It cast its eyes upon the roads, which were growing from long troughs of liquid mud to proper thoroughfare. A river, amber-tinted in the shadow of its banks, purled at the army's feet; and at night, when the stream had become of a sorrowful blackness, one could see across it the red, eyelike gleam of hostile campfires set in the low brows of distant hills.

Onomatopoeia: a word that imitates the sound it represents. Examples include *buzz* for the sound that bees make, and *splash* for the sound of falling water.

Oxymoron: a phrase or expression the combines two contradictory words, as in *wise fool*.

Paradox: a statement, character, or situation that appears to be contradictory but that is nonetheless true. "Tis the love of right/Lures men to wrong" is a paradox found in Rumi's *"The Soul of Goodness in Things Evil."*

Parallelism: the use of phrases, clauses, or sentences that are similar or complementary in structure or in meaning. In the sentence *I enjoy cooking, eating, and reading*, the series *cooking, eating, and reading* exhibits parallelism: all its elements are gerunds ending in *-ing*.

Parody: a form of satire that is a humorous imitation of the style, characters, or subject matter of serious writing designed to ridicule a work or to point up or exaggerate its characteristics. The movie character Austin Powers, for instance, is a parody of James Bond.

Pathos: feelings of pity, sympathy, tenderness, or sorrow that are evoked from a literary work. For example, *In Lord of the Flies* by William Golding, the ending scene when Ralph sobs uncontrollably arouses feelings of sadness, sorrow, and loss not only in the reader but also in the rescuing captain.

Personification: the attribution of human qualities to animals or objects. Example: *The fire danced in the dark night*.

Point of view: the vantage point from which an author presents the actions and characters in a story. The story may be related by a character (first-person point of view) or by a narrator who does not participate in the action (third-person). Further, the third-person narrator may be **omniscient**—able to see into the minds of all characters; **limited**—confined to a single character's perceptions; or **objective**—describing only what can be seen. Most events, pictures, and stories can be presented from more than one perspective, or point of view. Because every story can be told from a number of perspectives, an author must decide on a particular point of view from which to present the narrative and select a narrator, who shapes how characters, actions, settings, and events are perceived by the reader.

Rhythm: the arrangement of stressed and unstressed syllables in speech or writing. Rhythm, or meter, may be regular, or it may vary within a line or work. The four most common meters are iamb, trochee, anapest, and dactyl. In daily conversation, certain words and syllables receive more emphasis than others. Like ordinary speech, poetry has patterns of accented and unaccented syllables that form a beat, or rhythm. Although poems may or may not use rhyme, all poetry—even free verse, to some extent—has rhythm that is regular or irregular.

Feet and Meter

An identifiable pattern of stressed and unstressed sounds in poetry called **meter**. To determine the meter or rhythm of a poetic passage, mark the stressed syllables and unstressed syllables. In addition, each line can be divided into smaller units, each with an accented syllable and one or more unaccented syllables. Such units of measure, called **feet**, are divided by a slash. Determining the metrical pattern in poetry is called **scansion**.

The number of feet within a line of poetry may range from one to eight. The terms listed in the following table are used to represent the number of feet that occupy a line of poetry. Pentameter, tetrameter, and trimester are probably the most common line lengths in English verse.

A single **foot** in poetry is often the combination of just two syllables, an iamb and a trochee. If the foot is anapestic or dactylic, then it will have three syllables.

Meter	Number of Feet	Examples*
Monometer	One foot	Herrick's "Upon His Departure Hence"
Dimeter	Two feet	Tennyson's "The Charge of the Light Brigade"
Trimeter	Three feet	Shelley's "To a Skylark"
Tetrameter	Four feet	Marvell's "To His Coy Mistress"
Pentameter	Five feet	Shakespeare's sonnets
Hexameter	Six feet	Hexameter is known as an alexandrine and is often used to provide a resonant termination to a stanza of shorter lines. An example is Hardy's "The Convergence of the Twain."
Heptameter	Seven feet	Kipling's "Tommy"
Octameter	Eight feet	Browning's "A Toccata of Galuppi's"

*Examples taken from *The Norton Anthology of Poetry*.

Metrical Foot	Stress	Examples*
Anapestic: two unstressed, one stressed	u u /	u u / u u / The Assyrian came down
Dactylic: one stressed, two unstressed	/ u u	/ u u Leningrad
Iambic: unstressed followed by stressed	u /	u / New York
Spondaic: two equally stressed syllables	/	/ / Stay back
Trochaic: stressed followed by unstressed	/ u	/ u / u / u / London bridge is falling *down*

*Examples taken from *The Norton Anthology of Poetry*.

Stress Patterns

Anapest: pattern of three syllables, two unstressed and one stressed: *u u /*.

An example from "The Boys" by Oliver Wendell Holmes:

> *u / u u / u u / u u /*
> And when we have done with our life-lasting toys,
> *u / u u / u u / u u /*
> Dear father, take care of thy children, THE BOYS!

Dactyl: a foot of three syllables, one stressed and two unstressed: */ u u*.

An example from Henry Wadsworth Longfellow's *Evangeline*:

> */ u u / u u / u u / u*
> This is the forest primeval; but where are
> *U / u u / u*
> the hearts that beneath it

Iamb: a foot of two syllables one unstressed followed by a stressed syllable: *u /*.

An example from Johann Wolfgang von Goethe's *Faust*:

u / u / u / u / u
Had you not left off laughing long ago.

Spondee*:* two equally unstressed syllables

Trochee*:* a foot of two syllables, one stressed and one unstressed syllable */ u.*

An example from Longfellow's "A Psalm of Life":

/ u / u / u / u
Tell me not in mournful numbers
/ u / u / u /
Life is but an empty dream!

Satire*:* a technique that exposes human weakness or social evils. Satire may use exaggeration, wit, irony, or humor to make its point. The satirist may adopt a tone ranging from good-natured humor to biting ridicule or scorn. Satire can entertain, instruct, or reform or bring about action. In "A Modest Proposal," Jonathan Swift satirizes Irish aristocrats for their handling of the Irish potato famine, by suggesting that the starving eat babies.

Simile: the comparison of two unlike things using *like* or *as*: *He eats like a pig.*

Style*:* an author's choice of structure; selection and arrangement of words; tone; and degree of reliance on sound effects, imagery, and figurative language. For instance, William Faulkner's use of foreshadowing, flashbacks, symbolism, narration, and characterization as well as his immensely long sentences in *The Sound and the Fury* creates an unusual writing style.

Symbolism: the use of an object or action that means something more than its literal meaning; representing things by means of symbols or attributing symbolic meanings or significance to objects, events, or relationships. For example: the hammer and sickle were once a symbol of Soviet communism.

Synecdoche: the use of a part to represent the whole, as in, *All hands on deck!*

Synethsesia: the conflation of the senses. In Vladimir Nabokov's novel, *The Gift*, the main character Fyodor is a gifted young poet who experiences synesthesia. Note the use of words, letters, and sounds that conflate the senses:

If I had some paints handy, I would mix burnt sienna and sepia for you as to match the color of a "ch" sound . . . and you would appreciate my radiant "s" if I could pour into your cupped hands some of those luminous sapphires that I touched as a child.

Theme: the underlying meaning of a literary work. A theme can be stated or implied. Theme differs from the subject of a literary work in that it usually makes an observation about the subject. Some literary works have no theme; others have more than one. For example, the theme of William Blake's "A Poison Tree" is about anger, not a tree.

Tone: the attitude a writer takes toward a subject, character, or audience, such as serious, humorous, sarcastic, ironic, pessimistic, formal, critical, objective, or playful. Although tone and mood are related, they should not be confused. Mood is the overall effect that a work has on the reader, while tone involves the voice and attitude of the writer.

Voice: the author's style or the quality that makes his or her writing unique, and which conveys the author's attitude, personality, and character.

LITERARY THEORY AND CRITICISM

Classical Criticism

Aristotle and Plato are credited with establishing the parameters of literary critical study in their search for truth. Plato banned poetry from the ideal republic because it was three times removed from truth, imitated imitation, and appealed to our lower nature. Aristotle, on the other hand, viewed poetry as productive art but with an embedded moral purpose. Horace extended this view, observing that poetry must be both pleasing and morally and intellectually useful.

Neoplatonic Criticism

Plotinus (225), an Egyptian philosopher, developed a system of philosophy, which was later called neoplatonism, that held literature as a direct expression of eternal essences and a vehicle for providing access to higher spiritual realms and to the divine.

Neoplatonists elaborated allegory that enabled the harmony between the Old and New Testaments. Augustine also attempted to trace appropriate connections between literal and figurative language in the reading of scripture.

Medieval Criticism

St. Thomas Aquinas and Alighieri Dante refined neoplatonic notions of allegory, observing that meanings of language encompassed not only literal levels but also allegorical, moral, anagogical, or mystical levels. Thus, medieval aesthetics emphasized beauty, order, and harmony of God's creation. Literature, therefore, was one part of an ordered hierarchy of knowledge leading to the divine, its climax being theology.

Renaissance Criticism

Renaissance criticism assumed a more humanistic and secular view, reviving classical learning, reexamining the notions of imitations, the didactic role of literature, classification of genres, and vernacular as the medium of poetic expression and reassessment of classical heritage.

Neoclassic Criticism

Literary criticism of the neoclassicist period during the eighteenth century was rooted in the work of Dr. Samuel Johnson, Alexander Pope, and John Dryden. This period saw a return to the classical virtues such as rationality, moderation, balance, decorum, harmony of form and content, and dramatic unities of time and place and action. Johnson, a poet, critic, biographer, and political essayist, became a national sensation after writing *The Dictionary of the English Language*. The first writer to include quotations from other noteworthy authors to illustrate definitions, he took nine years to write his famous dictionary, which became the foundation of all subsequent dictionaries. His work established a common foundation on which forms of literature could be critiqued. A popular satirist and accomplished essayist, Pope published his first major essay, "An Essay on Criticism," which also paved the way for serious critique of literature.

Romantic Criticism

Immanuel Kant, influential philosopher of the eighteenth century, valued imagination as a higher and more comprehensive faculty than reason. His *Critique of Judgment* articulated for the first time a systematic formulation of the autonomy of art and literature, free of the constraints of morality or utility. This notion of autonomy was further developed into theories by Edgar Allan Poe, Charles-Pierre Baudelaire, and French symbolists and aestheticians such as Walter Pater, Oscar Wilde, and Henry James.

Realistic Criticism or Realism

Realistic critique emerged during the mid-nineteenth century. This approach to writing and critique described life, particularly setting, with objectivity, detail, and rich example. Another word for realism is *verisimilitude*, which reflects the author's attempt to present the setting or subject with such convincing detail that the reader easily visualizes the content. Although realism is not limited to any one century or group of writers, it is most often associated with the literary movement in nineteenth-century France, specifically with the French novelists Gustave Flaubert and Honoré de Balzac. George Eliot introduced realism into English literature, especially in *Middlemarch*. Poe was noted for his realistic and convincing depiction of the House of Usher. Contemporary author Sandra Cisneros uses description, vernacular, and vignettes to create accurate description in *The House on Mango Street*.

Naturalism

Whereas realism is a kind of literary technique, naturalism is a philosophy that emerged during the later nineteenth century that primarily focused on developing characterization using a more scientific approach. More pessimistic and unromantic, naturalists presented humankind as products of heredity, instinct, and environment. Using the objective technique of the realists, writers such as Emile Zola, Herbert Spencer, and Joseph LeConte combined a medical/historian approach to depict humans not as individuals but rather as beasts at a more physiological level.

CLASSICAL LITERARY CRITICISM

Formalism

Formalism, still commonly called new criticism, reveals how Anglo-American criticism has evolved over the last century. Associated with this particular kind of critique are Samuel Taylor Coleridge, T. S. Eliot, Cleanth Brooks, I. A. Richards, and John Crowe Ransom. The adjective *new* is somewhat ironic given that this form of criticism has its roots in classical literary criticism. When Aristotle discussed how six tragic elements should work together to create the ideal tragedy, he was demonstrating the intricate and complex balance between form and function. In this form of criticism, the poem (which refers to the text under study rather than "the poem" in the more traditional sense) is central to the meaning. In essence, the poem is meaning; form *is* meaning. Formalism emphasizes the unity of all parts to create a whole. A formalist analysis considers how all the elements, literary and syntactical, fit together to provide understanding and how understanding the whole gives relevance to the comprising elements. In formalism, content is *not* separated from form but rather inextricably linked to create meaning. All the parts of a poem are related to each other and to the poem as an organic whole. A formalist reading is a close reading or explication of a text in which the reader performs a detailed and subtle analysis of the complexities and ambiguities of the components or elements within a work. Analysis attends to the meanings and interactions of words, figures of speech, symbols, complexity, and coherence, regardless of literary genre.

A more appropriate descriptor of this kind of criticism is objective criticism, because of the status of the poem as "object." This implies that the reader can derive meaning from the poem regardless of knowing its historical context and author. Formalists assert that focused reading and rereading of a text will yield one, more justifiable meaning or truth that can be substantiated through textual evidence. Formalists ask questions such as, What is the motif, what does it mean, and how does it fit into the overall meaning of the poem? What word patterns emerge, and how do these patterns function in the text? What are the symbols and imagery, and how do they function in the text to create an overall meaning? For example, a poet might use the word *blue* in a text. Consulting a traditional and a historical dictionary would certainly uncover numerous definitions of the word *blue*, but formalists would argue that the reader can only know the correct definition when he or she understands how the word fits into the larger whole or scheme of the poem. Within this critique, the relationship between the reader and the text is unique. The meaning derives from the text; the reader does not impose meaning on the text.

This theory is much contested for several reasons. First, it asserts that there is one best meaning of a text. Historicists and other critics would claim that meaning depends on context, the reader, and the degree to which the meaning is congruent with reality. Other critics would assert that meaning is relative, political, and social. One person's truth or reality is not necessarily another person's truth or reality. Second, *form* has a number of meanings. Formalists use *form* to mean everything about the poem: words, patterns, rhyme, meter, sentence variety, literary elements and devices, and so on. Yet, a text may have a unique form such as haiku, sonnet, or limerick. Formalists concern themselves with the first meaning of *form*, which presents a sort of paradox. A limerick is an excellent example. A formalist would focus on the words, phrases, symbols, patterns, and rhyme (the first definition of *form*) inherent in a limerick; yet, the unique form (second definition) of a limerick is what makes it a limerick.

Historicism

Historicism emerged toward the end of the eighteenth century with German writers such as Johann Gottfried von Herder and continued through the nineteenth century with historians such Leopold von Ranke and Friedrich Meinecke, and to the twentieth century with thinkers such as Wilhelm Dilthy and R. G. Collingwood. Historicism, also called genetic criticism, views literary texts as integrally informed by the historical milieu. Authors associated with historicism are E. D. Hirsch, Jr., George Watson, and Alastair Fowler. Texts cannot be somehow dissected from history and analyzed in isolation outside of the historical process. Form and content are informed by specific historical circumstances and specific situation in time and place. Historicists believe that each past age possesses unique events, assumptions, values, and beliefs, and only someone who is an expert in the particular period during which the text was written can truly understand these events, assumptions, values, and beliefs. Historicism deals with the facts, the historical facts. Literature must be read and interpreted within a broader context that is grounded in the life, times, beliefs, class, privilege, and values of the author. Essentially, literature is not an imitation of life but rather the creation of a unique mind. This criticism is also referred to as objective interpretation. A reader might best approach a novel by Charles Dickens or Thomas Hardy through a historicist lens as these texts

MTEL Tip

Historicism deals with the facts.

truly reflect the social, political, and economic contexts of the time. Richard Wright's *Black Boy* and *American Hunger* would also benefit from this form of critique because they are autobiographical memoirs.

New Historicism or Cultural Criticism

New historicism is not radically new but represents a return to certain foci of analysis as developed by previous traditions of historicism. Emerging in the 1980s, this movement opposes the formalist view of literary critique but retains some of the influences of Marxist critique, which will be discussed later. A major influence on this theory is Michel Foucault, a French sociologist and philosopher who asserted that new historicism regards text as discourse situated within complex cultural, religious, political, economic, and aesthetic discourses, which shape the literature and are shaped by the literature. New historicists assert that history itself is a text, an interpretation that has no single history or any kind of unity or homogeneity to history and/or culture. History and culture are viewed as harboring networks of contradictory, competing, and unreconciled forces and interests. Much like historicists, new historicists believe that readers must interrogate and identify the historical causes of the text, but also contend that readers must examine the historical effects or consequences as well. Critics most aligned with new historicism include Stephen Greenblatt, Jerome McGann, and Jane Tomkins. The reader could use cultural critique to contextualize and understand Toni Morrison's *Beloved* or Arthur Miller's *The Crucible*, as these works integrate historical elements but also represent the contradictory, competing, and dissonant forces of the time.

Reader Response Criticism

Reader response criticism asserts that just as texts have authors, they also have audiences. Texts not only function independently of their authors but also have value that is independent from the time in which they were written. Reading, therefore, is not interpretation but a transaction between a reader and the text. The reader (audience) interprets texts based on his or her personal experiences, values, beliefs, and emotions; the reader reads text to gain insight into his or her own life. In *Literature as Exploration* (1938), Louise Rosenblatt explained that readers transact with text for different purposes. She developed a continuum that represented reader responses ranging from the efferent to the aesthetic stances. Embedded within an efferent stance is the purpose of taking away information from the text. An aesthetic stance addresses the purpose of experiencing the text. When one reads literature, one interacts with literature as event, and this interaction explores responses that reflect particular emotions, attitudes, beliefs, interests, and so on. The reader plays a vital role in this interaction; the text has meaning because the reader makes meaning from the text by bringing personal experiences, morals, social codes, and views of the world to reading the text. The range of reader responses will vary because each reader is unique. This lens is employed in teaching text particularly in elementary and middle school grades because it makes the reader and the reader's history more relevant to the text, but engagement with the text depends on the degree of the reader's personal interaction or transaction with the text, thus potentially limiting the overall experience and interpretation of the text. The form of critique privileges personal knowledge over textual knowledge. This criticism is also called phenomenological, speech-act, rhetorical, transactive, and subjective criticism. Other critics aligned with reader response criticism include Norman Holland (at the extreme end), German critic Wolfgang Iser, Joseph Campbell, and Stanley Fish. One can almost view any text from this perspective. Young adult fiction such as Robert Cormier's *The Chocolate War* or S. E. Hinton's *The Outsiders* invites the reader to interact because each text's theme addresses adolescent feelings of alienation.

Mimetic Criticism

Reality serves as the context for mimetic criticism. That literature is a reflection of reality was basically unchallenged until the mid-eighteenth century. Mimetic critics believe that great literature reveals particular truths in that it mimics reality. Such criticism requires the reader to construct meaning within a larger framework or reality. As a result, Marxism, feminism, and psychological critique fall within the broader category of mimetic criticism because each asserts a specific understanding of reality to inform interpretation. These will be explained more fully later on in this section. Mimetic criticism has allowed for more current literary techniques such as theater of the absurd, stream-of-consciousness writing, the meandering dialogue that Anton Chekhov inserts into his drama, techniques that paint characters and events as more true to life or realistic. A problem with this kind of criticism is addressed by the question, Whose reality? Plato criticized poetry because it gave readers a false view of reality, contending that the reality humans apprehend is truly just a manifestation of what our senses construct for us. Plato argued further that painting and poetry are essentially copies or imitations of a copy. For example, the ceramist fashions a bowl based on what we perceive as a bowl, which is already an imitation of a "real" bowl. The painter paints the bowl, providing indeed a copy of a copy, which begs a further question: What is real and what is art? Mimesis is prominent in modern thought because of the movement to view the world empirically, through the senses. Robert Alter, Erich Auerbach, Arne Melberg, and A. D. Nuttall are most aligned with this form of criticism. Julia Alvarez's *How the Garcia Girls Lost Their Accents* serves as a useful text to interpret through mimesis, because this lens allows the reader to see the layers of reality that exist for a girl who must negotiate two linguistic, cultural, and political realities, realities that were clearly different for mainstream Americans.

Marxist Criticism

A form of mimetic criticism, Marxist criticism has its roots in the work of Karl Marx and Friedrich Engels. Economic organization and relationships of power served as the context (reality) for their work. Asserting that human consciousness is constituted by an ideology or a set of concepts, beliefs, values, and ways of thinking and feeling, Marxism interrogates literature by posing social questions that address social context and issues of power, questions such as, Who has power? Who has money? Who has social capital? are embedded within Marxist critique. Thus, text is a social construction and is thus informed by conscious political doctrines and ideologies. Telling stories is a purposeful and political act that has different consequences given the storyteller; interpreting a text means identifying how issues of power, class, and ideology interact. Marxist critique focuses on the relationships between individuals, their roles and vocations in society, class systems, governments, and choice. Terry Eagleton observes that literature has powerful political and social implications and therefore is ideology. Marxist critique works especially well with texts such as Ray Bradbury's *Fahrenheit 451*, John Steinbeck's *Of Mice and Men*, and George Orwell's *Animal Farm*, which establish clearly the relationships of power between characters, classes, and political bureaucracies.

Feminism

A form of mimetic criticism, feminist discourse began to be addressed in literary texts in the 1970s. A derivative of Marxism, this critique is based on the cultural and economic limitations in a patriarchal society that have prevented women from realizing their potential and acquiring power. Gender is socially and culturally constructed within and influenced by patriarchal biases, because our civilization is patriarchal. Feminism focuses on the relationships between genders and examines the patterns of thought, behavior, values,and power relations between sexes. Feminists assert that women's cultural identity is the negative "object" or "other" to man, who is the "subject" or "self." In *The Second Sex* (1953), Simone de Beauvoir identifies the dominant group as "self" and the subordinate group as "other." She and others contended that women in literature written by men are generally cast as "other" and serve or detract from male protagonists. A critical tenet in judging literature from a feminist perspective is the authenticity of the females portrayed in the text. Authenticity implies that a female in the text governs her own actions, is reflective, and possesses a critical consciousness. Feminist film critic notes that women are portrayed in film as objects for the pleasure of the male and vehicles for male self-realization. Josephine Donovan asserts that feminist criticism is a form of moral criticism because it interrogates the function of women in literature: women either act as redemptive characters or scapegoats for the evil males' experience. Feminist critics include Elaine Showalter, Robyn Warhol, Diane Herndl, Judith Butler, and Teresa Ebert.

Kate Chopin's *Awakening* is fertile text for using the feminist lens as feminists would argue that Edna's final act of suicide represents a self-actualized female who takes her destiny into her own hands.

Psychological Criticism

Also a type of mimetic criticism, psychological criticism argues that characters that are believable are those that are most realistic. Psychological critics are interested in the character as a psychological being, a person whose mental reality is developed sensitively, complexly, and realistically. Bernard Paris observes that the beauty in bringing psychology and literature together is that the combination enables us to understand the character and her experiences in an analytical way to which we are not privy through a formalist read.

Psychological criticism derives from the work of Sigmund Freud and particularly Carl Jung. According to Jung, man is on an individual quest toward self-realization. Freud saw the individual as deeply dependent on society and anxious to conform to it, while Jung saw society as little more than a number of individuals of similar nature. Jung asserted that myths contain messages that speak to individuals in the same way. These myths contain archetypes, which have a fixed meaning. Among these are heroes, the self, the shadow, the villain, the serpent, the lion, the trickster, the magician, the fool, the sage, the child, gold, coal, and so on. Each of these archetypes serves as a powerful symbol. Jung also noted that these archetypes pervade all philosophies, ideologies, mythologies, literatures, and belief systems and are therefore common to all individuals. Although archetype meaning is fixed, each individual hears the message in the myth differently. Jung believed that these archetypes originated from constantly repeated experiences of humanity. Conrad Aiken's "Silent Snow, Secret Snow," Anton Chekhov's *The Bet*, and D. H. Lawrence's "The Rockinghorse Winner" provide rich fodder for psychological critique.

Intertextual Criticism

Donald Keesey summarizes the tenets of intertextual criticism in this statement: "Poems do not imitate life; they imitate other poems" (279). In other words, understanding the literary conventions and linguistic constructions inherent in all literature enables us to interpret text; interpreting text is by analogy. Northrop Frye identifies four principles that govern intertextual criticism: convention, genre, archetype, and the combination of the three. Literary conventions are literary devices that serve as a common language, which is used to discuss literature: plot, characterization, flashback, foreshadowing, and so on. Genres are the distinct forms of literature: poetry, essay, short story, and so on. Archetypes include the Jungian definition but also other symbols that appear throughout different genres of literature. Intertextualism subsumes structuralism and semiotics but itself is an old term as it recognizes the various influences that inform interpretation. For example, an epic poem is an epic poem because it includes all the features and characteristics that make it an epic poem: long narrative poem, often extending to several books with sections of several hundred lines. The poem usually focuses on a significant and serious subject and often describes a hero or heroic quest. Understanding *Beowulf*, the *Iliad*, or the *Odyssey* can help us understand more contemporary epics. Theorists associated with intertextual criticism are Northrop Frye, Roland Barthes, Umberto Eco, Jonathan Culler, and Robert Scholes. The romantic poetry of Great Britain not only offers excellent texts for close reading but also provides useful texts for intertextual analysis.

Structuralism

Structuralism forms the basis of semiotics, which is the study of signs or symbols. Structuralism assumes that meaning occurs through difference. A technique of structural analysis is identifying binary oppositions. Examples of binary oppositions include hot/cold, old/new, regression/progression, and the like. These oppositions can be used to construct meaning. For example, identifying the binary opposition in "Out! Out!" by Robert Frost reveals the pattern of nature versus technology, which helps the reader identify one of the major themes of this text. Structuralism concentrates wholly and completely on the text; structural criticism focuses on the universal qualities of literature.

Poststructural Criticism

Poststructural criticism assumes that the most effective way to interpret a text is to deconstruct it. Posited by Jacques Derrida, postructuralism assumes that language is unstable and ambiguous and therefore contradictory, that the author is not in full control of what he or she writes, and that literature means nothing because language means nothing, and therefore, there is no way of knowing what the "meaning" of a story is. This method of critique requires the reader to reflect deeply beyond surface of text in that text reveals meaning of which even the author might be unaware, to examine the relationships between appearance and reality, and to realize that language is creative and lively. Like the formalists, poststructuralists and deconstructionists use literary devices, conventions, and other formalist tools but use them to break down or deconstruct the text rather than derive a coherent and unifying whole. This view of criticism perceives text as not having a center or universal meaning, but an array of meanings; literature is political, cultural, and social. Also associated with this method of critique are Roland Barthes, Paul de Man, Stanley Fish, and Geoffrey Hartman. Chinua Achebe's *Things Fall Apart* clearly delineates how meaning is cultural, political, social, and gender related.

MTEL Tip

Poststructural criticism requires one to reflect beyond the surface meaning of a story.

STRUCTURE AND DEVELOPMENT OF THE ENGLISH LANGUAGE

Structural Features of the English Language

Linguistics

Linguistics is the science or study concerned with developing models of linguistic knowledge. The major core of theoretical linguistics includes phonology, morphology, syntax, and semantics. Phonetics, psycholinguistics, and sociolinguistics are usually excluded from the core components.

Linguistic Terms

Base word: standalone linguistic unit that cannot be deconstructed or broken down into smaller words. Example: *dog*; *house*

Compound word: two or more base words connected to form a new word. Example: *doghouse*

Contraction: shortened form of two words in which one or more letters have been deleted and replaced by an apostrophe. Example: *it's = it is*

Etymology: word or history origin

Grapheme: letter or letters that constitute a phoneme

Heteronyms: words that are spelled the same but differ in pronunciation and meaning

Root word: word from which another word is developed. For example, *symbol* is a root word for *symbolism, symbolize, symbolic, symbolical, symbolist, symbolistical, symbolizer, symbology, symbologist, symbolically, symbolicalness,* and *symbolics.*

Syllabication: the breaking down of words into each uninterrupted unit of spoken language

Morphology is the identification, analysis, and description of structure of words. A **morpheme** is the smallest structural unit with meaning. A **lexeme** is the different forms a phoneme can take; *sit, sat,* and *sitting* are all forms of the same lexeme.

Types of Morphemes

Free morphemes are units that stand alone, like *ditch* and *dog*, or can appear with other lexemes, like *dog house*.

Bound morphemes appear with other morphemes to form a lexeme. These are usually suffixes and prefixes like *un-, -able,* and *non-*: *unhappy, presentable, nonspecific.*

Derivational morphemes add to a word to create another word. For example, adding *ment* to *state* creates *statement*. These morphemes carry semantic information.

Inflectional morphemes change a word's number, tense, or other characteristics to create a new word. For example, adding *s* to *cat* creates the plural *cats*, or *ed* to *hint* creates the past tense *hinted*. Inflectional morphemes carry grammatical information.

Allomorphs are variants of the same morpheme. For example, the sound denoting the past tense can be *t*, *d*, or *td*.

Phonology (from the Greek *phon*, meaning "voice, sound," and *lógos*, meaning "word, speech, subject of discussion") is the systematic use of sound to encode meaning in any spoken human language. A **phone** is a speech sound. A **phoneme** is the smallest linguistically distinctive unit of sound, for example, the *d* sound in *dig* and *drill*. Phonemes have no semantic content. An **allophone** is one of several similar speech sounds that belong to the same phoneme, for example, *night rate* with a space or *nitrate* without a space.

Phonetics is the science of speech sounds. It deals extensively with the minute differences in sounds and the symbols used to represent these sounds. Phonetics is concerned with the physical apparatus involved in actually making the sound: the control and flow of breath, the placement of the lips, tongue, and teeth, and so on.

Phonics is a term that describes that part of phonetics applied to the teaching of reading. Phonics is concerned with sounds of word elements only to the extent that knowing these sounds aids in word recognition and subsequently reading. Phonics is also a method of teaching beginners to read using the phonetics of letters, groups of word, and syllables.

Phonics Patterns: Vowels

Short vowels are the five single letter vowels *a*, *e*, *i*, *o*, and *u* when they produce the sounds /a/ as in *cat*, /e/ as in *bet*, /i/ as in *sit*, /o/ as in *hot*, and /u/ as in *cup*. The term *short vowel* does not really mean that these vowels are pronounced for a particularly short period of time, but they are not **diphthongs** like the long vowels.

Long vowels are synonymous with the names of the single letter vowels, such as /a/ in *baby*, /e/ in *meter*, /i/ in *tiny*, /o/ in *broken*, and /u/ in *humor*. The way that educators use the term *long vowels* differs from the way in which linguists use this term. In classrooms, long vowel sounds are taught as being "the same as the names of the letters."

Schwa, a type of **reduced vowel**, is the third sound that most of the single-vowel spellings can produce. The schwa is an indistinct sound of a vowel in an unstressed syllable, represented by the linguistic symbol ə. Schwa, or /ə/, is the sound made by the *o* in *lesson*. Schwa is a vowel pattern that is not always taught to elementary school students because it is difficult to understand. However, some educators make the argument that schwa should be included in primary reading programs because of its importance in reading English words.

Barred vowels is the sound that /i/ makes in the word *medicine*. It is represented by /ɨ/.

Closed syllables are syllables in which a single vowel letter is followed by a consonant. In the word *button*, both syllables are closed syllables because they contain single vowels followed by consonants. Therefore, the letter *u* represents the short sound /u/. (The *o* in the second syllable makes the /ə/ sound because it is an unstressed syllable.)

Open syllables are syllables in which a vowel appears at the end of the syllable. The vowel will say its long sound. In the word *basin*, *ba* is an open syllable and therefore says /ba/.

Diphthongs are linguistic elements that fuse two adjacent vowel sounds. English has four common diphthongs. Others include /au/, /oy/, /aw/, /ou/ and /ew/, which partly accounts for the reason they are considered "long."

R-controlled vowels occur when an *r* follows a vowel, modifying that vowel's sound; for example, *a* followed by *r* as in *arms* has neither the short sound of *a* as in *apple* or the long sound of *a* as in *ale*.

Vowel digraphs are those spelling patterns wherein two letters are used to represent the vowel sound. The *ai* in *sail* is a vowel digraph. Because the first letter in a vowel digraph sometimes says its long vowel sound, as in *sail*. Other digraphs include /ea/, /oa/, /ay/, and /ee/.

Consonant-E spellings are those wherein a single vowel letter, followed by a consonant and the letter *e*, makes the long vowel sound. Examples of this include *bake*, *theme*, *hike*, *cone*, and *cute*. (The *ee* spelling, as in *meet*, is sometimes considered part of this pattern.)

Phonics Patterns: Consonants

> **Consonant digraphs** are those spellings wherein two letters are used to represent a consonant phoneme. The most common consonant digraphs are *ch-*, *ph-*, *sh-*, *th-*, *wh-*, *-ch*, *-ck*, *-sh*, *-tch*, and *-th*. Letter combinations like *wr* for /r/ and *kn* for /n/ are also consonant digraphs, although these are sometimes considered patterns with "silent letters."

Syntax and Syntactical Features

Syntax is the study of the principles and rules for constructing sentences in natural language. Syntax also refers directly to the rules and principles that govern the sentence structure of any individual language. There are several theories that address the study of syntax.

Generative grammar assumes that language is a structure of the human mind and that there are rules that can be used to produce or create any sentence. Pioneered by Noam Chomsky, this kind of grammar focuses on the form of a sentence rather than how it functions as communication. Chomsky's view is that all language has certain structures in common. For example, Lewis Carroll's "The Jabberwocky" presents an array of inane and made-up words, but because of syntax and rules of generative grammar, the reader is able to identify the purpose of the words, even though the reader does not know the meaning of the words:

> "Twas brillig, and the slithy toves
> Did gyre and gimble in the wabe:
> All mimsy were the borogoves,
> And the mome raths outgrabe.

Although the reader does not know the meaning of *brillig*, *slithy*, *toves*, *gimble*, *wabe*, and so on, the reader does have a sense of the function of each word in the phrases and sentences and can answer questions based on this understanding. For example, "What did the 'slithy toves' do?" They "did gyre and gimble in the wabe."

Syntactic terms are generally called the parts of speech. The following list, although not exhaustive, provides the most common parts of speech, their definitions, and examples.

Adjectives are words that modify a person, place, thing, or idea. Adjectives are generally used in four different ways:

Attributive adjectives modify or are attributed to the noun they modify.

Angry mob

Predicative adjectives—also called subject complements—are linked by a linking mechanism to the noun or pronoun they modify.

*The children are **quiet**.*

Absolute adjectives typically modify either the subject or whatever noun or pronoun they are closest to.

Angry about losing the game, the boy trudged home.

Substantive adjectives act almost as nouns.

*The **meek** shall inherit the Earth.*

Adverbs are words that modify any part of speech (sentence, clause, phrase, verb, or adjective) except for a noun.

Adverbs of manner answer the question "How?" by modifying verbs or adjectives. These often either begin with the prefix *a-* (e.g., *afloat*) or end in the suffixes *-ly* (e.g., *suddenly*) and *-wise* (e.g., *clockwise*). Example: ***surprisingly** simple*

Comparative and **superlative adverbs** indicate the degree to which something occurs or is true.

*He studies **harder** than his peers.*

Conjunctive adverbs can be used to join two clauses together.

*She has bruised her foot; **consequently**, she won't be able to race today.*

An **appositive** is a noun or phrase that renames or clarifies the noun next to it. It must always be separated from the rest of the sentence by commas.

> *Chess, **the ancient game of strategy**, is one of the world's most popular games.*

An **article** is a word that precedes a noun to indicate the type of reference or meaning made by the noun. An article often offers specific information about range or volume. There are four types of articles:

A **definite article** is used before either a singular or plural noun to refer to specific members of the group represented by the noun.

> ***The** zamboni resurfaced **the** ice rink.*

An **indefinite article** (*a* or *an*) is used before a singular noun that refers to any member of the group referenced by the noun. Example: ***a haunted house***

A **zero article** is the absence of an article in contrast to the presence of one.

> *Do you like fondue?*

An **auxiliary verb** is a verb preceding a main verb for some kind of added emphasis. Auxilliary verbs impact language in five ways:

Passive voice occurs when the auxiliary verb *be* is used with a past participle to indicate that some event happened but not who or what caused the event. One example might be a politician's apology:

> *It is unfortunate that people **were** hurt.*

Progressive aspect is formed when the auxiliary verb *am* is used with a present participle to indicate that the speaker is engaging in a specified action at the exact moment of speaking.

> *I **am** packing my bags and leaving town!*

Perfect aspect occurs when the auxiliary verb *have* is used with a past participle to indicate that an event in the past is still happening or has some connection to the present.

> *Brianna **has** lapsed in her study habits.*

Modal verbs can never be used as main verbs and must always function as an auxiliary verb. They express the speaker's opinion. There are ten modal verbs: *can, could, may, might, ought, shall, should, will, would,* and *must.*

> *We **shall** overcome.*

Dummy auxiliary refers to the insertion of *do* into a sentence to make it a question or to add negation or emphasis.

> ***Do** you understand?*
> *You **do** not understand.*
> *You **do** understand.*

A **clause** is a group of words that includes a subject and a predicate. A subset of clauses, dependent clauses, cannot function alone and must be part of a larger sentence. There are three types of dependent clauses:

Noun clauses are those in which a noun is replaced with a dependent clause.

> ***What happened** isn't important.*

Adjective clauses are dependent clauses that modify a noun.

> *The squirrel **I observed** stashed nuts.*

Adverb clauses are dependent clauses that modify the entire main clause.

> ***When the crumpets arrive**, tea will be served.*

Comparative refers to an adjective or adverb that modifies by making a statement about quantity, quality, degree, or grade. The comparative is used with a subordinating conjunction like *than* or *as . . . as.* Example: ***As rough as** sandpaper*

Null comparative occurs when no subordinating conjunction is used, so it is unclear to what standard the subject is being compared. Example: *Sun Shine Sunscreen works **better**!*

A **complement** is a word, phrase, or clause that is needed in the predicate of a particular sentence to complete its meaning.

*The zoo is **carefully maintained**.*

A **compound adjective** is a noun modifier created by combing two separate adjectives into one. The adjectives are separated by a hyphen, and there is no hyphen between the compound adjective and the noun. Example: *A **well-maintained** bridge*

A **compound noun** is a noun formed by the combination of two nouns, as in *doghouse*. There are four types of compound nouns:

Endocentric, in which the first portion denotes a specific type of the word represented by the second portion. Example: *backboard*

Exocentric, in which the words together describe an unexpressed idea. Example: *bittersweet*

Copulative, in which the words together describe a new idea. Example: *rundown*

Oppositional, in which each element describes a different aspect of the same subject. Example: *meatlover*

Conjugation is the creation of derived forms of a verb, adjective, or noun based on person, number, tense, gender (in some languages), and other factors.

*I **scream**.*
You (singular) ***scream**.*
*She, he, or it **screams**.*
*We **scream**.*
You (plural) ***scream**.*
*They **scream**.*

A **conjunction** is a word that connects two words, phrases, or clauses. There are three types of conjunctions:

Coordinating conjunctions join two words or phrases of equal significance. They include *for, and, nor, but, or, yet,* and *so.*

*Christy **and** Colleen are roommates.*

Correlative conjunctions are two words that work to coordinate to words or phrases, such as *both . . . and, either . . . or,* and *neither . . . nor.*

__Both__ Christy __and__ Colleen hope to be doctors.

Subordinating conjunctions introduce and connect a dependent clause. They include *after, although, if, unless, so that, therefore, because,* among others.

You cannot have dessert __unless__ you eat all of your dinner.

Dangling modifier refers to a mistake made by an author who places a modifier in a sentence so that it seems to modify a different word than the one intended.

I saw the electronics store __walking through the mall__.

Declension is a change in a noun, pronouns, or adjectives reflecting number, gender, or case. It is far more prevalent in European languages than in English; English words only decline to indicate number as singular or plural.

I had to return my old library __books__ before I could check out a new __book__.

An **expletive** is a word that is considered to be filler or padding in a sentence. They are often necessary grammatically but contribute nothing to the meaning of a sentence.

__It__ is so sunny outside!

Function words are those words that mean very little by themselves but which structure a sentence or express relationships of words within a sentence. Appositions, articles, auxiliary verbs, conjunctions, expletives, interjections, and pronouns are examples of function words. Function words are the opposite of content words like nouns, verbs, adjectives, and adverbs.

__The__ apple pie __and__ brownies are delicious!

Gender is the system used in many languages besides English, particularly Indo-European languages, in which words are assigned male, female, and sometimes neuter genders. Adverbs or adjectives are inflected differently to accommodate the gender of a specific noun in a sentence.

A **gerund** is a form of a verb ending with the suffix *–ing*. The gerund often looks exactly like the present participle of the verb, but it functions as a noun in a sentence. Gerunds can be subjects, direct objects, and objects of prepositions.

> *The girls love **shopping** in the city.*

The **infinitive** is the most basic form of a verb. In English, this can be with or without the particle *to*. Example: *find* and *to find*

Measure words, also known as numeral classifiers, are words that are used with a number to express the count of an item. Some measure words are fully independent grammatical particles. These types of words are rare in English and more common in Asian languages. Example: *The cowboy rounded up eighty **head** of cattle.* Most English measure words are actually units of measurement, as in *three **loaves** of French bread.*

A **noun** is a part of speech that represents a person, place, thing, or idea. Nouns can exist in the subject and predicate of a sentence or in a prepositional phrase. There are many more specific distinctions between nouns:

> **Proper nouns** are nouns that represent words that are specific entities. They are often capitalized. They differ from common nouns that refer to an entire group of similar things. Examples: *Bermuda, John, United States of America*

> Uncountable nouns are nouns that cannot be quantified, unlike countable nouns. Example: *laundry*

> **Collective nouns** refer to groups, even when singular. Example: *The **board** of the company voted to sell shares of controlling stock.*

An **object** is a noun in the predicate of a sentence that relates to the action of the verb. There are three types of objects:

> **Direct objects** are the immediate recipients of the action of the verb.

> > *I washed the **towel**.*

> An **indirect object** is a secondary recipient of a verb's action.

> > *She showed **me** her new dress.*

A **prepositional object** is an object at the end of a prepositional phrase.

*We put the pan in the **oven**.*

A **part of speech** is a classification of words determined by their function within a sentence. Nouns, adjectives, adverbs, prepositions, objects, and most of the other terms defined in this list are parts of speech.

A **participle** is a form of a verb that functions independently as an adjective. Participles can end in -*ing* (present participles): ***Blowing** in her face, the wind felt **refreshing***. Participles can also assume the past tense of the verb: *We ate baked beans.*

A **particle** is catchall phrase for words that do not fit within traditional grammatical classifications. Examples include *not* and *to* (as in the infinitive of a verb, not as a preposition).

Person is a language's way of referencing participants in an event described in a sentence through personal pronouns. In English, there are three persons:

First person refers to the speaker: *I, we.*

Second person refers to the listener: *you.*

Third person refers to another party: *he, she, it, they.*

A **phrase** is a group of words that function as a unit in a sentence. There are several types of phrases:

An **adjective phrase** begins with an adjective. Example: *speedy rabbit*

An **adverbial phrase** begins with an adverb. Example: *truly unexpectedly*

A **noun phrase** begins with a noun. Example: *Queen of hearts*

A **prepositional phrase** is composed of a preposition and an object. Example: *to the circus*

A **verb phrase** begins with a verb. Example: *Expect the worst.*

A **phrasal verb** is the joining of a verb with a preposition, adverb, or both so that they form a complete unit within the sentence. Example: *Swim underwater. Clean up.*

Plural is a form of a noun referencing either zero or more than one of the items in the group known by that noun.

> *The recipe calls for two **cups** of sugar but no **eggs**.*

The **predicate**, also known as the verb phrase, is the major part of any sentence containing the verb. It modifies the other main part of the sentence, the subject. It must include a verb, but it can also include various other parts of speech such as adjectives, adverbs, and others.

> *She **napped in the blue chair**.*

A **predicative** is a part of the predicate of a sentence that gives additional information after the verb. There are two types of predicatives:

An **adjectival predicative** occurs when an adjective follows the verb.

> *Dana looks **glamorous**.*

A **nominal predicative** occurs when a noun or pronoun follows the verb.

> *Carly lost her **phone**.*

A **preposition** is the first element of a prepositional phrase. Prepositions include *to, of, from, under, above, around, through, with, in,* and many other words. These words indicate the relationship between the other parts of the sentence and the prepositional object. Prepositions can modify verbs and nouns and complement verbs, nouns, adjectives, and other prepositions.

> *Let's ban Max **from** our room.*

A **personal pronoun** is a generic substitute for animate proper or common nouns. The three most common types of personal pronouns are:

First-person pronouns refer to the speaker: *I, we.*

Second-person pronouns refer to the listener: *you.*

Third-person pronouns refer to another party: *he, she, it, they.*

A **pronoun** is a generic substitute for any noun. In addition to personal pronouns, the category of pronouns also includes substitutes for inanimate objects.

> ***You*** *have to explain **it** to **them** when **you** arrive.*

A **sentence** is one or more words organized according to set grammatical rules to express an intended meaning. Sentences can vary in purpose as well. They can question, state, command, negate, or exclaim. There are four types of sentences:

Simple sentences have one independent clause.

> *Natalie is reading.*

Compound sentences have multiple independent clauses.

> *Natalie is reading, and Max is bored.*

Complex sentences have at least one independent clause with a dependent clause.

> *Cassie is a student who wants to be a nurse.*

Compound-complex sentences have multiple independent clauses and at least one dependent clause.

> *Cassie is a student who wants to be a nurse, and she is getting her degree soon.*

Singular is a form of noun referencing exactly one item. Example: *A **duck** likes to swim.*

The **subject** is one of the two parts of every sentence. It is a noun phrase that defines the object or topic to be modified by the sentence's predicate.

> ***Nikki*** *went to El Salvador.*

Superlative is the form of an adverb or adjective used to express that the modified object possesses the quality to the greatest degree of all the objects in question.

*Chris has the **happiest** smile of all our friends.*

Tense indicates the time at which an action expressed by a verb occurs. English has multiples tenses:

Present simple often expresses habit or routine: *I **study***.

Present continuous expresses action occurring at the moment of speech: *I **am studying***.

Present perfect indicates an action that has occurred at some, often vague, point in the past: *I **have studied***.

Preterite indicates that an action took place and has ceased to take place: *I **studied***.

Imperfect indicates a habitual action has ended: *I **used to study***.

Past continuous indicates an action that was taking place in the past at the time of a more specific action: *I **was studying***.

Conditional indicates a requirement or condition: *I **would study***.

Future indicates an action is going to occur: *I **will go***.

Pluperfect, also known as past perfect, indicates that an action ended before another began: *I **had studied***.

A **verb** is a part of speech that indicates action, occurrence, or state. It can vary with number, gender (in languages besides English), persona, and tense. There are three kinds of verbs:

Intransitive verbs have only a subject: *He **laughs***.

Transitive verbs have a subject and a direct object: *She **pets** the puppy*.

Ditransitive verbs have a subject, direct object, and indirect object: *I **showed** her my dance*.

Semantics

Semantics is the study or science of meaning in language. Semantic information addresses meaning in a variety of ways.

Vocabulary

Understanding vocabulary on specific, functional, and conceptual levels reflects an ability to understand semantic information:

Specific understanding refers to the literal definition of the word. For example, in the sentence *I run twenty miles every day*, the word *run* is a verb that means to move swiftly so that both feet leave the ground.

Functional understanding refers to the ability to use a word in writing and in speech.

Conceptual understanding refers to the ability to understand the word in a variety of contexts and syntactical forms. Examples:

> *There was a run on the bank.*
> *He knows how to run a campaign.*
> *I have a run in my stockings.*
> *The river runs through the canyon.*
> *He runs the printing press.*
> *The run of fabric is damaged.*

There are almost 100 ways the word *run* can be used. **Polysemy** is when one word has many meanings. *Run* is such a word.

Semantic information includes understanding not only the meaning of a word but also other meanings that relate to the word:

An **antonym** is a word that means the opposite of a word. For example, possible antonyms for the word *hot* include *cold*, *frigid*, *icy*, and *freezing*.

A **synonym** is a word that means the same or almost the same as another word. For example, possible synonyms for the word *hot* including *burning*, *boiling*, *ardent*, *feverish*, *scorching*, and *torrid*.

Homonyms or **homophones** are words that sound alike but have different meanings, as in *there*, *their*, and *they're*. Sometimes, homonyms can also be spelled the same, as in *bark* of a dog and *bark* of a tree.

Semantic shifts are ways meanings change:

Amelioration is the improvement or enhancement of a word's original meaning. Example: The word *sophisticated* derives from the Old French word *sophistrie*, which originally meant "contaminated" or "unnatural," or the more current word *sophistry*, which still means "specious, of fallacious reasoning." The current definition of *sophisticated* is "cosmopolitan, classy, or discriminating," demonstrating that the meaning has improved or been enhanced.

Deterioration or **pejoration** is the diminishing or lessening of a word's original meaning. Example: The word *villain* originally referred simply to an inhabitant of a village but has evolved to mean a scoundrel or criminal.

Expansion of a word means that the range of the word's meaning increases over time. Example: The word *arrive* derives from Latin *arrivare*, which originally comes from *ad ripam*, which means "at the shore." Currently *arrive* means "to reach a destination, achieve success, or take place."

Restriction is the opposite of expansion; it refers to the diminishing of a word's range. Example: The word *meat* comes from the Middle English *mete*, which generally meant "food." Now *meat* means "edible flesh."

Word meanings can also change metaphorically. Example: *Light* can be a metaphor for *hope*, *heaven*, *truth*, *understanding*, and the like.

A **euphemism** is the substitution of a more agreeable word for one that is offensive. Examples: The phrase *a reduction in force (RIF)* is a euphemism for being fired, let go, or laid off; *termination* can be a euphemism for murder; and *ethnic cleansing* is a euphemism for genocide.

History of the English Language

Speech developed between 100,000 to 20,000 BC. By the time period of 5,000 to 3,000 BC, there was one common language, which we now call Proto-Indo-European (PIE). After many migrations, by 1,000 BC, a number of distinct Indo-European languages formed. After more migration and increased trading with Africa and Asia, there emerged one branch of the PIE tree by AD 0: the Germanic language. Several characteristics differentiated Germanic language from other branches that broke away from PIE. The Germanic language placed accent or stress on the first syllable of a word (called Grimm's Law), inflected verbs only in the past and present tenses, and used the dental suffix *-ed* to form the past tense.

After AD 0, the Jutes, Saxons, and Angles—mercenaries that came from Denmark and what is now northern continental Germany—brought with them their own dialects, which fell within the Germanic branch of the Indo-European language family. Although writing was not common among these groups, the language had a Runic alphabet, called Futhroc.

By AD 600, the Germanic language began to differ somewhat from the continental German language because dialects had been intermingling for centuries in Briton away from the continent, therefore forming a new type of language. In addition, Briton was Christianized around AD 600, and the missionaries brought the Latin alphabet with them. This new language is what scholars today consider to be Old English.

Wars led to changes in language. Viking invasions occurred around AD 800, and the Danes invaded in the early eleventh century. Old English was not very standardized and spellings were inconsistent (e.g., *shield* could be spelled as *scyld*, *scild*, or *scield*). Although different dialects of Old English had been gaining strength, location and prominence caused the West Saxon dialect to become the dominant dialect, evolving into what we today call Middle English.

There is much debate about when Middle English usage actually began, but generally scholars refer to Middle English as the language spoken after the Norman conquest until the development of English as a full literary language during the sixteenth century. In 1066, William the Conqueror brought troops from Normandy and succeeded in becoming the king of England (while also remaining the king of France). Thus, for years, Norman French rulers dominated all spheres of society, including education, government, law, and the church. Latin and French became the languages of power, and English was left for the poor majority. There were many loanwords taken from French and Latin at this time, as seen in Geoffrey Chaucer's *Canterbury Tales*, which was written in the late 1330s in Middle English.

At the end of the fifteenth century, William Caxton brought standardization to English with the introduction of the printing press. This began the period we call Early Modern

English (1500–1650). During this time, the English language changed tremendously. First there was a phonetic shift in the way that long vowels were pronounced in English. This was called the great vowel shift. The language also became more standardized in the use of a more regular word order of subject-verb-object. Furthermore, greater trade with Asia Minor and the Middle East sparked an infusion of new vocabulary, and the Renaissance in England returned to classical learning, resulting in the translation of many of the classic Latin texts into English. William Shakespeare wrote during the late 1500s and early 1600s in Early Modern English, and in 1611, the King James Bible was written and was widely read. The Bible was still most often the only literature that the common people read, but now that the printing press had been introduced, many more people had access to books and therefore language.

By the 1700s, the English language was standardized and had become widely used. In this time of British imperialism, English spread around the globe to places such as Australia, India, and South Africa through colonialism. There was a great deal of linguistic borrowing from languages around the world, and in the nineteenth and twentieth centuries, the Scientific and Industrial Revolutions brought about the creation of technical vocabulary.

During the eighteenth to twentieth centuries, dictionaries and grammars gained much popularity with the growing belief that the English language had somehow been corrupted. Reformers called for a purer form of the language and generally fell into one of two groups: descriptivist, who wanted to describe language as it existed, and prescriptivist, who wanted to prescribe how language ought to be. One early work that was extremely popular was Samuel Johnson's *The Dictionary of the English Language*. As mentioned previously in this chapter, Johnson was the first writer to include quotations from other noteworthy authors to illustrate definitions; he took nine years to write his famous dictionary, which became the foundation of all subsequent dictionaries.

Linguists have been interested in the development of American English for centuries. After the settlement of Jamestown, Virginia, in 1607, the English language changed drastically from its British origins, so much so that many scholars of the seventeenth century thought American and British English would diverge and eventually become two totally separate languages. Although the languages have not yet become totally separate, there is much variation between not only American and British English but also between types of English spoken within the United States. Scholars have also studied regional dialects and social and racial variations in language. Dictionaries such as the *Dictionary of American Regional English* (*DARE*) are becoming more common.

Today, as we study the history of language development and the current changes that the English language is facing, it is important to realize that the language is in a state of flux and always will be, no matter how much people try to impede its changes. Whether one views this state of flux as progress or as regression, language change is nonetheless a natural part of life and of history.

Literary Timeline

MTEL English

LITERARY TIMELINE

Dates	Literary Period	Literary Elements of the Period
United States		
1500–1607	Precolonial/ Early Native American	**Poetic** and **symbolic**, this literature, viewed primarily as **folklore**, describes the beauty, power, and awe of nature. **Myths**, passed down from generation to generation, explain natural phenomena and cultural and religious rituals.
1607–1763	Colonial	First **printing press** was set up at Harvard in 1639. Two **themes** dominated literature: **religion** and **politics**; writing focused primarily on the **defense or explanation of religious beliefs**. **Protestantism** emphasized exclusive authority of the **Bible**; followers believed the Bible was the **revealed word of God**. **Sermons** by Puritan preachers constituted the first substantial literary genre in the English-speaking New World. The **rhetoric** was plain, emphasizing **logic** and **clarity**. Preachers combined **biblical imagery** and facts about **living in America**. Puritans used **allegories**, emphasizing the symbolic nature of the world. **Diaries**, to be handed down to sons or daughters, emphasized the irrelevance of human effort in transactions of grace and demanded righteous behavior. Other Puritan writing included **moral stories**, **elegies**, or poems lamenting the loss of a loved one, and meditations upon the end of things, **apocalyptic expectations**.
1764–1789	Revolutionary	Benjamin Franklin personified the peculiar genius of America. Franklin wrote the "**Dogood Papers**" with **common sense**, **humor**, and **free-thinking irreverence**. He dismantled Puritan elegy, reducing it to formulas and similes. Franklin's *Autobiography* was similar to the Puritan diaries. The difference was that Franklin's journey is secular; **reason** is the primary guide, and heaven has become a vague metaphor for the unknown. Beginnings of the American myth/story: a poor boy finds his way to wealth, the chartered servant earns his freedom

Dates	Major Writers and Works
1500–1607	**Delaware Tribe**: *The Walum Olum* **Navajo Tribe**: *The Navajo Origin Legend* and "Night Chant"
1607–1763	**William Bradford**: *History of Plymouth Plantation*, describes the Separatist movement in England, exile in Holland, and the voyage of the *Mayflower*; also authored *The Mayflower Compact* **Anne Bradstreet**: *The Tenth Muse, Lately Sprung Up in America*, poems written on philosophical subjects **William Byrd**: *A History of the Dividing Line*, about his journey into the swamp separating Carolinian territories from Virginia and Maryland **Jonathan Edwards**: "Personal Narrative" describes spiritual development and the idea that God in his infinite power permeates every part of the universe; well-known for his sermon "Sinners in Hands of Angry God," an influential text that describes man's corruption and God's justice **Richard Mather**: *Bay Psalm Book*, rhymed versions of psalms **Samuel Sewall**: wrote pamphlets against slavery and mistreatment of Indians, also the *only* one of the Salem witchcraft judges to confess publicly that he had been wrong in condemning witches **John Smith**: rescued by Pocahontas, the story of which provided a romantic parable characterizing the inevitability of white triumph over Indian opposition. Smith's account of Virginia in 1608 was the first book written in English in America, his *Description of New England* followed. **John Winthrop**: believed God sent his people to the New World and that all Europe had their eyes on them to see if they would succeed or fail; most known for his sermon "A Model of Christian Charity"
1764–1789	**John** and **Abigail Adams**'s letters in correspondence between Boston and Philadelphia: primary sources that document the dangerous period in history during Revolution **Benjamin Franklin**: *Pennsylvania Gazette*, a widely read weekly periodical; also authored *Poor Richard's Almanack*, containing rash weather predictions and brief sayings that urged virtue and good business practices **Alexander Hamilton**: along with James Madison and John Jay, wrote the series of eighty-five essays collected as *The Federalist*, in order to secure the ratification of the Constitution **Patrick Henry**: "Give me liberty or give me death" from his speech to the Virginia House of Burgesses **Thomas Jefferson**: authored almost all of the Declaration of American Independence and the Statue of Virginia for Religious Freedom　→

LITERARY TIMELINE

Dates	Literary Period	Literary Elements of the Period
United States		
1764–1789	Revolutionary (con't)	*(con't from pg. 168)* Poetry was pressed into the service of nationalism: Philip Freneau, propagandist in democracy's cause, wrote a poem called "The Rising Glory of America."
1790–1865	Romantic/ American Renaissance	Emergence of Early American **folktales** and distinctly American writing, not just copying English forms William and Mary established intellectual leadership. Southern writers were driven to **propagandize in defense of slavery** or wrote **escapist fantasies**. South produced **romance fictions** and **chivalric melodramas**. An indigenous southern genre was **the plantation novel**. **New England** was **center of American literature**. Belief in **transcendentalism** emerged. **Romanticism**, reaction against the Age of Reason: subordination of rationality to emotion and intuition; interest in the individual and nature, which offered harmony, joy, and spiritual refreshment American writers imitated British authors. A theme of **literary independence** emerged. Edgar Allan Poe and Nathaniel Hawthorne developed the **short story**. Walt Whitman wrote entirely on American topics. **Fireside poets** were read by American families in the harsh and enduring New England winters.

Dates	Major Writers and Works
1764–1789	**Thomas Paine**: appealed for complete political independence in *Common Sense*; also published sixteen issues of his paper, *The American Crisis* **George Washington**: wrote letters, diaries, and other pieces, which have been collected in thirty-seven volumes. "Farewell to the Army of the Potomac," his best work, written with the help of Hamilton and Madison, explains his reasons for leaving the presidency. **Philis Wheatley**: African-born black woman captured at the age of eight and sold to John Wheatley, a Boston merchant; Wrote her *Poems on Various Subjects* in English neoclassical style, imitative of Alexander Pope and Thomas Gray **Hartford Wits**: group of men who shared a Yale connection, produced satires, mock epics, and hymns to the New World. Conservative and Federalist, they intended to announce America's arrival on the national literary stage, relying on imitations of English models. **Gustavus Vassa**: *The Interesting Narrative of the Life of Olaudah Equiano, or Gustavus Vassa the African*, an abolitionist autobiography
1790–1865	**William Cullen Bryant**: produced austere and intellectual poems, most of which dealt with nature, the woods, or death **James Fenimore Cooper**: *The Last of the Mohicans*, depicts a young scout during the French and Indian war; also wrote *The Pioneers*, which features a middle-aged frontiersman **Ralph Waldo Emerson**: wrote about hard work, intellectual spirit of Americans, and the importance of learning about nature firsthand rather than through books **Nathaniel Hawthorne**: *The Scarlet Letter*, a book about Puritan New England society whose members left England to establish religious freedom **Oliver Wendell Holmes**: "The Deacon's Masterpiece: or, The Wonderful One-Hoss Shay" a *reduction ad absurdum* of logic of Calvinism and a parable of its breakdown **Herman Melville**: *Moby Dick*, in which Captain Ahab tries to capture a great white whale that has taken his leg; *Billy Budd*, an allegory of forces of evil to triumph over innocence and beauty **Edgar Allan Poe**: poet, wrote "The Raven," "To Helen," "Annabelle Lee," "The Tell-Tale Heart," "The Cask of Amontillado," and "The Fall of the House of Usher." Known for his gothic, psychologically thrilling tales, he believed that beauty was akin to truth and considered writing a religious and moral obligation. **William Gilmore Simms**: *The Yemasee*, the son of a Yemasee chief gives aid to the English against his own tribe and his Indian mother kills her son to prevent his dishonorable banishment from the tribe **Henry David Thoreau**: *On Walden Pond*. The second greatest of the transcendentalists, Thoreau lived a hermetic life on Walden Pond to test his transcendental philosophy of individualism, self-reliance, and spiritual growth. **Walt Whitman**: *Leaves of Grass*; also known for writing the famous elegy for Abraham Lincoln, "O Captain! My Captain!"

LITERARY TIMELINE

Dates	Literary Period	Literary Elements of the Period
United States		
1861–1865	Civil War	Significant literary themes focused on **abolition** and **polemics between advocates of slavery and abolitionists**. Writing of precipitated, rather than reflected, tensions in the country.
		Writing looked at in the context of new (or old) **historicism rather than formalism**.
		The transcendentalist tradition merged with John Brown's ideology, carrying over to the **abolitionist movement**.
1865–1930	Sectional Independence and Local-Color Literature	**Gilded Age** eradicated institutions that were centuries old, changed the social life in the country, and influenced literature and life in general.
		Themes included **conformity**, **self-discipline**, and **dreams of material comfort**.
		Moral tales and tales of **rags to riches** were popular. The voice of common people was heard from across the country, first in folk stories, then in passages written by humorists.
		Readers became conscious of regional differences: **romance of the Far West**, **rusticity of the Middle West**, and **glamour of the Deep South**.
		Literary works included **poetry, elegy, puns, allegory,** and **satire**.

Dates	Major Writers and Works
1861–1865	**Frederick Douglass**: in *Narrative of the Life of Frederick Douglass*, wrote about slavery and masters' desires to keep their slaves ignorant; noted that democracy and Christianity, although deformed by slavery, were worthy of allegiance **Abraham Lincoln**: most famous for the Gettysburg Address, a classic of oratory. His less famous second inaugural address was a blueprint for the reconciliation of the nation ("With malice toward none, with charity for all . . ."). **Harriet Beecher Stowe**: *Uncle Tom's Cabin*, notable characters include honest, black Uncle Tom, the mischievous slave girl Topsy, little angelic Eva, and the cruel slave driver Simon Legree **David Walker**: wrote a landmark pamphlet titled *Appeal to the Colored Citizens of the World*, which united history, classical rhetoric, and the Bible on behalf of a sustained and bitter denunciation of the inhumanity of slavery **William Lloyd Garrison**: one of the founders of the American Anti-Slavery Society and the editor of the abolitionist newspaper *The Liberator* **Benjamin Lay**: a Quaker and abolitionist **Susan B. Anthony**: an agent for William Lloyd Garrison's American Anti-Slavery Society of New York State; promoted women's rights, and although originally friends with Frederick Douglass, disagreed with his contention that only males should have the right to vote
1865–1930	**George Washington Cable**: one of the first to write about the rich color of New Orleans. *Old Creole Days* is a collection of short stories about a variety of ethnic groups mingled in New Orleans. **Willa Cather**: *O Pioneers!* describes the life of a Swedish immigrant who keeps her family together after the death of their father, building a prosperous farm on the "unfriendly" Nebraska prairie and finding happiness and love. "Paul's Case" is of one of Cather's most moving short stories about a troubled, bright, young gay man who eventually kills himself by being hit by a train. *One of Ours* won the 1923 Pulitzer Prize. In this text, Claude Wheeler finds meaning for his life in the front lines against Germany during World War I. **Kate Chopin**: *Bayou Folk* and *A Night in Acadia*; the latter, her most successful work, is a series of sketches based on the Creole people and customs **Samuel Langhorne Clemens**: known by his pen name "Mark Twain," wrote about local color and the particularities of the region in which he lived, along the Mississippi. *The Adventures of Tom Sawyer* depicts the carefree, primitive life Clemens had lived before his father died and he was forced to work at age twelve. Notable characters are Aunt Polly and Huck Finn. Tom is boyishly imaginative but more civilized than Huck. *The Adventures of Huckleberry Finn*, a sequel to *Tom Sawyer*, tells how a "half-civilized" Huck drifts down the river on a raft with a runaway slave named Jim, who is eventually freed by Tom. →

LITERARY TIMELINE

Dates	Literary Period	Literary Elements of the Period
United States		
1865–1930	Sectional Independence and Local-Color Literature *(con't)*	**Gilded Age** eradicated institutions that were centuries old, changed the social life in the country, and influenced literature and life in general. Themes included **conformity**, **self-discipline**, and **dreams of material comfort**. Moral tales and tales of **rags to riches** were popular. The voice of common people was heard from across the country, first in folk stories, then in passages written by humorists. Readers became conscious of regional differences: **romance of the Far West**, **rusticity of the Middle West**, and **glamour of the Deep South**. Literary works included **poetry**, **elegy**, **puns**, **allegory**, and **satire**. *(Text repeated from pg. 172 for reader's convenience.)*
1890–1920	Realism	**Realist literature** reflected scientific interest instigated by Charles Darwin, T. H. Huxley, and Spencer. Emergence of a **strong social consciousness** stimulated by Karl Marx and Russian novelists influenced writing. Realism went out of its way to point out the **cruel and ugly side of real life**. **Humanism** transcended the scientific method, drew upon classical and early Christian philosophers, and advised **self-restraint** as highest ethical principle and highest freedom, eliminating need for external compulsion. **New humanism** surfaced as a reaction against romanticism, realism, and naturalism.
1900–1914	Naturalism	**Naturalism** focused on man's subjection to natural law, while **humanism** distinguished between man and nature, emphasizing ethical concepts and **freedom of the will** as peculiar to man. Literature borrowed from French and Russian novelists, resulting in an **extreme degree of realism**. Works emphasized **natural selection**. Man is represented as lacking in free will; controlled by his passions and environment, man is an animal struggling against nature in impersonal, amoral universe; literature omits moral considerations and stresses unpleasant phases of life.

Dates	Major Writers and Works
1865–1930	**Emily Dickinson**: left over 1,700 poems upon her death, which her sister Lavinia collected and published**:** "I heard a Fly buzz—when I died," "I felt a Funeral, in my Brain," "My Life had stood—a Loaded Gun," and "What Soft—Cherubic Creatures," among others. Her poetry displays an extremely effective use of slant rhyme, and the tones of her poetry range from mild whimsy to impassioned delight to paralyzed despair, terror. **Bret Harte**: made the West a favorite realm of fiction. "The Luck of Roaring Camp" appeared in the *Overland Monthly*, the first literary presentation of a colorful section of the country (the West).
1890–1920	**William Dean Howells**: considered the father of American realism **Henry James**: *Daisy Miller* tells how a charming American girl offends her European friends and an American gentleman of European training by her innocent familiarity with a young Italian. In *The Portrait of a Lady*, Isabel Archer, James's prototypical heroine (young, beautiful, intelligent) is courted by an English nobleman, a wealthy, English invalid, and an earnest Yankee. **William James**: *The Varieties of Religious Experience*, an interesting inquiry into the various forms of faith and topics such as conversion, the sick soul, blind faith, etc. **Edith Wharton**: *Ethan Frome* recounts the struggle of an individual against convention.
1900–1914	**Stephen Crane**: considered the first naturalist. *The Red Badge of Courage* is a realistic psychological novel of a Civil War soldier. **Charlotte Perkins Gilman**: her *Women and Economics* offers a wide-ranging inquiry into what she called the sexuo-economic revolution. **Jack London**: *Call of the Wild* describes a tame dog, Buck, who is forced to revert to his original primitive state.

LITERARY TIMELINE

Dates	Literary Period	Literary Elements of the Period
United States		
1914–1945	American Modernism	Literature reflected the dominant mood of this period: **alienation and disconnection**.
		Writing was highly **experimental**, with extensive use of fragments, stream of consciousness, and interior dialogue in efforts to create a unique style.
		Regionalism reemerged, emphasizing the belief that history is socially constructed, thus paving the way for multicultural literature.
		Certain writers wrote from a particular social, cultural, and ethnic perspective, about social, cultural, and ethnic interests for a particular social, cultural, and ethnic audience.

Dates	Major Writers and Works
1914–1945	**William Faulkner**: *As I Lay Dying*; *The Sound and the Fury* (his masterpiece), examines the Compson family, demonstrated in the thoughts of its members: the mentally retarded Benjy, the intelligent Quentin who commits suicide after the marriage of his sister Caddy, whom he loved **F. Scott Fitzgerald**: *The Great Gatsby*, an ironic and tragic treatment of the American success myth **Ernest Hemingway**: *The Sun Also Rises* tells of the moral collapse of a group of expatriated Americans and Englishmen, broken by the war, who turn toward escape through all possible violent diversions; *A Farewell to Arms*, a love story of an English nurse and an American ambulance lieutenant during the war; *For Whom the Bell Tolls*, based on an incident in the Spanish Civil War whose thesis is that the loss of liberty in one place means loss of liberty everywhere; and *The Old Man and the Sea*, a parable of man against nature, for which he won the Pulitzer Prize. He won the Nobel Prize for Literature in 1954. **John Steinbeck**: *Grapes of Wrath* describes the Joads, a good-hearted family of sharecroppers; their eviction from their Dust Bowl farm, and their journey to California in a ramshackle car. *Of Mice and Men*, which reads like a play, is the objective description of the six distinct episodes, with thoughts revealed only through dialogue. The gigantic but feeble-minded Lennie Small is cared for by his pal, George Milton. Lennie loves animals, like mice and puppies, but kills them with his strength. When he inadvertently breaks the neck of the wife of their boss's son, George shoots Lennie to prevent his lynching. **Upton Sinclair**: *The Jungle* depicts poverty, horrendous living conditions, and hopelessness *Major Twentieth-Century Poets* **T. S. Eliot**: *The Waste Land* critiqued the failure of Western civilization as illustrated by World War I. **Ezra Pound**: for nearly fifty years, focused on the encyclopedic epic poem he titled *The Cantos*. Accused in 1945 of treason for spreading Fascist propaganda on the radio, Pound was acquitted but spent a decade in a mental institution. **e. e. cummings** (Edward Estlin Cummings): played around with form, punctuation, spelling, font, grammar, imagery, rhythm, and syntax. His works include *The Enormous Room*, *Tulips and Chimneys*, and *XLI Poems*. **Robert Frost**: considered America's best-known and -loved poet. Among his works are "Death of the Hired Man," "Birches," "Stopping by Woods on a Snowy Evening," "The Road Not Taken," "Out! Out!," and "Mending Wall." **Carl Sandburg**: one of Chicago's poets, described everyday Americans in a positive tone, with simple, easy-to-understand words and free verse; most well-known for his *Chicago Poems* **William Carlos Williams**: *The Young Housewife*, *The Red Wheelbarrow*, and *This is Just to Say*

LITERARY TIMELINE

Dates	Literary Period	Literary Elements of the Period
United States		
1915–1929	Harlem Renaissance	This era was marked by an outpouring of **black prose and poetry**. Publication of *The New Negro* in 1925, a special issue of the *Survey Graphic* devoted to the district of Harlem in Manhattan, provides a springboard for black artists and intellectuals. **African American writers asked questions** like, Is there, in fact or theory, "Afro-American art"? Are black literary norms the same as white literary norms? What is different and what should be held in common?
Twentieth Century–Present		The literature of this period represents a **blurring of the lines of reality** with a mix of fantasy and nonfiction. Writing is concerned with the **individual in isolation**, and is detached, unemotional, and generally humorless. Writers of the period include **Beat writers,** whose work was highly intellectual, antitradition, and pre-hippie; **Confessional poets**, who used their own anguish to explore America's hidden despair; and **ethnic and women writers**.

Dates	Major Writers and Works
1915–1929	**Countee Cullen**: considered the "black Keats" for his youth, skill as a poet, and use of traditional forms **Langston Hughes**: the most successful black writer in America; wrote poetry, drama, novels, songs, and movie scripts; noted for poetry such as "Harlem" **Zora Neale Hurston**: rediscovered by the women's movement in the 1970s with texts such as *Their Eyes Were Watching God* **Claude McKay**: wrote poetry that evoked the heritage of his native Jamaica. "If We Must Die" won critical acclaim as McKay was the first black poet to write in the form of an Elizabethan sonnet. **Jean Toomer**: wrote to establish his identity as a light-skinned black man in a rigid and racist society. *Cane*, a book of prose poetry based on his personal journey back to his Southern roots, described the Georgian people and landscape.
Twentieth Century–Present	***Beat Poets*** **William S. Burroughs**: *Naked Lunch*, an autobiographical account of his life as a drug addict **Jack Kerouac**: *On the Road* depicts the journey of two young men across America in search of a Bohemian life **Allen Ginsberg**: countered the hidden despair of the 1950s with wildly exuberant language and behavior in *Howl*; also wrote *A Supermarket in California* ***Confessional Poets*** **Sylvia Plath**: most famous for "The Bell Jar" and other poetry describing suicide **Anne Sexton**: won a Pulitzer Prize for her work *Live or Die*, also about suicide **Robert Lowell**: *Land of Unlikeness* and *Lord Weary's Castle*, for which he received a Pulitzer Prize in 1947. Full of intense anguish, Lowell's work, written in a rigidly formal style, explored the dark side of America's Puritan legacy. ***Prose and Theater (1950–Present)*** **Conrad Aiken**: poet, essayist, novelist, and critic. "Silent Snow, Secret Snow" depicts a young man who falls deeper and deeper into an almost autistic world, as if cut off from society by silence and snow. **Ray Bradbury**: prolific science-fiction writer, best known for novels such as *Fahrenheit 451*, a novel set in a totalitarian government in which a man whose job is to burn books begins to pilfer books and, when discovered, must run for his life; and *The Martian Chronicles*, a futuristic story about colonizing Mars **Shirley Jackson**: "The Lottery" presents the disconcerting side of a small midwestern farming town.　→

LITERARY TIMELINE

Dates	Literary Period	Literary Elements of the Period
United States		
Twentieth Century–Present		The literature of this period represents a **blurring of the lines of reality** with a mix of fantasy and nonfiction. Writing is concerned with the **individual in isolation,** and is detached, unemotional, and generally humorless. Writers of the period include **Beat writers,** whose work was highly intellectual, antitradition, and pre-hippie; **Confessional poets**, who used their own anguish to explore America's hidden despair; and **ethnic and women writers**. *(Text repeated from pg. 176 for reader's convenience.)*

Dates	Major Writers and Works
Twentieth Century–Present	**Arthur Miller**: regarded as one of the most famous contemporary playwrights. *Death of a Salesman* relates the story of typical and ordinary American Willy Loman, whose choices and their consequences lead to the destruction of the American dream. *The Crucible*, based on the actual events of the Salem witch trials, was also written in response to the McCarthy Hearings in the early 1950s. **Flannery O'Connor**: a writer in the genre of Southern Gothic, critiqued the weaknesses of humankind; saw humankind as not worthy of being redeemed. *A Good Man is Hard to Find*, a short story, shows a world infested with evil, corrosion, decay, and superficiality. **Dorothy Parker**: poet and critic, best known for quotable one-liners like "Men seldom make passes at girls who wear glasses"; wrote for magazines in New York, starting with *Vanity Fair*, *The New Yorker*, and *Life*; also wrote scripts for films, including *A Star Is Born* **J. D. Salinger**: fought in World War II, which resulted in his developing a serious nervous condition; has not been interviewed since 1980 and has never allowed his famous novel *The Catcher in the Rye* to be made into a movie. *The Catcher in the Rye* became the symbol for a generation of disaffected youth. **Gertrude Stein**: believed the traditional narrative was the enemy of language and reality because it relied on habit and continuity rather than spontaneity and memory; wrote *Composition as Explanation* **James Thurber**: known for witty short stories and lumpy cartoons, which appeared in *The New Yorker*. *The Secret Life of Walter Mitty*, the tale of a henpecked husband who escapes into heroic daydreams, is one of his best. Thurber's absurdist cartoons featured men, women, dogs and other strange animals. **Kurt Vonnegut**: satirical novelist; his experience as a soldier and prisoner during World War II influenced the novel *Slaughterhouse Five*, which depicts a soldier in World War II who experiences time travel. Although his work is often considered science fiction, Vonnegut used this genre to write black comedy. **Eudora Welty**: set most of her prose on Mississippi life. *The Robber Bridegroom* occurs in eighteenth-century Mississippi and is based loosely on a Brothers Grimm fairy tale. In this text, she combined actual and extraordinary events such that the two become indistinguishable. ***Contemporary Multicultural Literature*** *African American Literature* **Maya Angelou**: novels are part autobiography, part picaresque fiction, part social history; central characters are strong black women. *I Know Why the Caged Bird Sings* tells of her grandmother's religious influences and her mother's blues tradition. →

LITERARY TIMELINE

Dates	Literary Period	Literary Elements of the Period
United States		
Twentieth Century–Present		The literature of this period represents a **blurring of the lines of reality** with a mix of fantasy and nonfiction. Writing is concerned with the **individual in isolation**, and is detached, unemotional, and generally humorless. Writers of the period include **Beat writers,** whose work was highly intellectual, antitradition, and pre-hippie; **Confessional poets**, who used their own anguish to explore America's hidden despair; and **ethnic and women writers**. *(Text repeated from pg. 178 for reader's convenience.)*

Dates	Major Writers and Works
Twentieth Century–Present	**James Baldwin**: autobiographical novels like *Go Tell It on the Mountain* detail his experiences growing up in Harlem; became a preacher like his father, but felt writing would better detail the struggles of growing up poor in a racist society

Gwendolyn Brooks: first African American female poet to win the Pulitzer Prize, awarded for her poem *We Real Cool*. Her work in the 1970s, *Riot* and *Family Pictures*, focused on racial harmony, but her later work *Beckonings* (1975) and *To Disembark* (1980) demonstrated her disappointment at the conflict between members of the civil rights and black militant groups.

Ralph Ellison: *Invisible Man*, whose theme demonstrates that society willfully ignores blacks; collection of poems about critical social and political essays, *Shadow and Act*

Toni Morrison: first African American woman to receive the Nobel Prize for Literature. Her novels, which include *Sula*, *Beloved*, *The Bluest Eye*, and *Song of Solomon* combine fantasy, ghosts, and what she calls "rememory" or the recurrence of past events to elaborate the horrors of slavery and the struggles of African Americans after being freed.

Alice Walker: *The Color Purple* won her the Pulitzer Prize. Her novels focus on poor, oppressed black women in the early 1900s. One of her most widely read short stories, "Everyday Use," which appears in a collection of shorts stories *In Love and Trouble: Stories of Black Women*, tells the story of two daughters' conflicting ideas about identity and heritage.

Richard Wright: *Black Boy*, an autobiography, recounts his childhood growing up poor in racist Mississippi, and his struggle for individualism. *American Hunger* (published in 1977, after his death) tells of his disillusionments with the Communist Party.

Asian-American Literature
Maxine Hong Kingston: *The Woman Warrior: Memoirs of a Girlhood among Ghosts* tells of a shy girl protagonist who finds resolution as she breaks her female silence; *China Men* details male influences on her and celebrates strengths and achievements of the first Chinese men in America and prejudice they faced.

Amy Tan: *The Kitchen God's Wife* chronicles the early life of her mother, who escaped the turmoil of the Chinese civil war and the 1949 Communist takeover to come to America. *The Joy Luck Club* depicts four Chinese immigrant families who start the "Joy Luck Club," playing the game of mahjong.

Jewish American Literature
Saul Bellow: Canadian-born novelist received the Nobel Prize for Literature for his works *Herzog* (1965) and *Seize the Day* (1956). Bellow primarily wrote about urban Jews struggling to find spirituality and comfort in a racist and alienating society.

Bernard Malamud: *The Natural* is based on ballplayer Eddie Waitkus, who tries to make a comeback after being shot by a serial killer. ➤

LITERARY TIMELINE

Dates	Literary Period	Literary Elements of the Period
United States		
Twentieth Century–Present		The literature of this period represents a **blurring of the lines of reality** with a mix of fantasy and nonfiction. Writing is concerned with the **individual in isolation**, and is detached, unemotional, and generally humorless. Writers of the period include **Beat writers,** whose work was highly intellectual, antitradition, and pre-hippie; **Confessional poets**, who used their own anguish to explore America's hidden despair; and **ethnic and women writers**. *(Text repeated from pg. 178 for reader's convenience.)*
Great Britain		
450–1066	Old English or Anglo-Saxon	**Heroic age** of English literature; represented **epic battles**, **heroic feats**, and **almost supernatural characters**. *Beowulf* is a major example of Old English literature; this epic poem told in narrative verse addresses themes of **order versus disorder** and **man versus nature**. Some literary devices found in *Beowulf* include: **alliterative meter**, making the poem suitable for oral performance **kenning**, a complex phrase that replaces a simpler word to add color to a poem or to evoke imagery **stock epithet,** descriptive word or phrase used repeatedly in place of a name **caesura**, a break in a line or poetry or a grammatical pause, indicative of how the poem was to be read

Dates	Major Writers and Works
Twentieth Century–Present	**Elie Wiesel**: a Holocaust survivor has authored almost forty works that address Judaism, the Holocaust, racism, hatred, and genocide. *Night*, a memoir, depicts Wiesel's struggle and guilt having been the only one in his family to survive the Holocaust. *Latino American Literature* **Julia Alvarez**: *How the Garcia Girls Lost Their Accents* describes the difficulties of learning American English and being called a "spic" at school. **Sandra Cisneros**: Mexican American writer born in Chicago. Her stories reveal the misogyny present in both these cultures. *The House on Mango Street* is a novel about a young girl, Esperanza, growing up in the Latino section of Chicago and coming into her own. *Native American Literature* **Louise Erdrich**: member of the Turtle Mountain Band of Chippewa, was very close with her extended family, who had a tradition of storytelling. Her collection of short stories, *Love Medicine*, features characters and speakers from four Anishinaabe families. **N. Scott Momaday**: a Kiowa Native American, grew up on the reservations and pueblos of the Southwest, far from centers of learning and letters. He won the 1969 Pulitzer Prize for Fiction for *House Made of Dawn*, a semiautobiographical account of his life at Jemez Pueblo.
450–1066	**Bede**: the first English historian, wrote *The Ecclesiastical History of the English People* in 731. His text recounts that St. Augustine's mission was to bring literary materials from Rome to England to support worship and service of the church. He also introduced the Roman alphabet to Britain. The *Junius* manuscript, the *Vercelli Book*, and the *Exeter Book*: three significant collections of English verse, all produced in monastic *scriptoria* or "writing rooms" *The Seafarer*: an anonymous lyric poem, describes the speaker's nostalgia for his past life on shore but a deep love of the sea, despite its loneliness. A metaphor for the Christian path of self-denial, the sea symbolizes a life on earth of struggle and difficulty, which is brief, however, compared to an everlasting life of happiness in heaven.

LITERARY TIMELINE

Dates	Literary Period	Literary Elements of the Period
Great Britain		
1066–1510	Medieval English or Middle English	Literary forms emerged from the oral tradition, providing venues through which the church could instruct and guide parishioners, and permitting illiterate peoples to hear and see literature. **Morality Plays** dramatized the abstract themes of **vice versus virtue** or mankind's struggle with his soul. characters personifed virtues, vices, or mental attributes. these plays imparted lessons to guide a moral life. **Allegories** had a moral, political, or spiritual meaning. **Mystery and Miracle Plays** dramatized biblical events. **Folk Ballads**, short, traditional narrative told in song and transmitted orally, adhered to the culture's own peculiar rhetoric and structure, unimpacted by literary conventions. **Frame Stories** told a story within a story. Geoffrey Chaucer used this device in *The Canterbury Tales*.
1510–1660	Renaissance	Intellectual and cultural movement that embraced the **reemergence of scholarship**, **ancient learning**, **religious and scientific inquiry**, and the liberation of the individual from intellectual tyranny, feudalism, and secular matters of the church. Influences included **humanism**, which revived the Greek and Roman emphasis on the "here and now"; and geographic exploration and discovery. **The Reformation**, which began in 1517, marked a time of challenge to the dogma and practices of the Church. King Henry VIII made himself head of the Church of England. Supported by Martin Luther's Ninety-five Theses published in 1517, which challenged the pope, the English Reformation represented **England's turn to Protestantism**.
1558–1603	Elizabethan	This was a period of unprecedented literary growth. "The Theater" gave rise to drama troops such as the Earl of Leicester's Men and other theater "companies."

Dates	Major Writers and Works
1066–1510	The *Domesday Book*: a survey of english land ownership commissioned by the King in 1086; recorded the church's wealth and catalogued the material and territorial possessions of the newly imported secular aristocracy **Geoffrey Chaucer**: The "Father Of English Literature," wrote *The Canterbury Tales* during the latter part of his life. *The Canterbury Tales*, most likely the greatest work produced in middle english, chronicles tales told by twenty-nine people representing various classes of society, During their four-day pilgrimage to the shrine of Thomas A Becket at Canterbury. The significance of *The Canterbury Tales* is that it offers a cross section of British life, including saints' biographies, a sermon, animal fables, romantic escapades, religious allegories, fabliaux (cynical, humorous, or crass stories), pious and moralistic tales, and lewd and vulgar tales told by different members of English society: a knight, a miller, a monk, a shipman, a parson, etc. *Sir Gawayne and the Grene Knight*: written by the Gawain Poet, a fourteenth-century contemporary of Chaucer. *Sir Gawayne and the Grene Knight* was the first great love story, a sophisticated tale of chivalry and emotion. **Sir Thomas Malory**: *Le Morte D'arthur* (meaning "The Death of Arthur"), which compiled French and English and Malory's own stories about King Arthur, Merlin, Guenevere, and the Knights of the Round Table.
1510–1660	*See major writers and works listed for Europe and other countries.*
1558–1603	**Thomas More**: *Utopia* advocates religious toleration and opposes organized war. All things are physically perfect, streets are twenty-feet wide, and every house has a garden. **Edmund Spenser**: *The Faerie Queene* fashioned the virtues and discipline of a gentleman or nobleman. Each of the twelve books features a knight that represents one of Aristotle's twelve virtues. **Sir Thomas Wyatt**: a contemporary of More, introduced the sonnet into English literature **John Lyly**: became immensely popular around 1580 after writing *Euphues, or the Anatomy of Wit* →

LITERARY TIMELINE

Dates	Literary Period	Literary Elements of the Period
Great Britain		
1558–1603	Elizabethan *(con't)*	**William Shakespeare** made his mark during this period, writing ten history, ten tragedy, and seventeen comedy plays, numerous sonnets, and several other poems. He developed a new form of the **sonnet**, which is characterized by an **octave** (set of eight lines) that presents some form of conflict, and a **sestet** (set of six lines), which typically resolves the conflict. Shakespeare wrote five types of plays: **Histories**, which dramatized power struggles **Tragedies**, in which the tragic hero possesses a **tragic flaw** that leads to his downfall **Comedies**, which always have a happy ending, usually involving marriage **Tragicomedies**, often referred to as **romances** or **pastorals**, in which the characters do suffer loss but overcome challenges through sacrifice, gaining forgiveness and ending happily **Problem plays**, in which the hero must negotiate a contemporary social problem or moral dilemma All plays needed to be registered before they could be published; this provided censorship of critique of the crown, public matters, and freedom of thought.
1603–1625	Jacobean	Literature marked by sophistication and literary rivalry. This was the age of **metaphysical poetry**; these works were **abstruse**, employing powerful **metaphors** as a means of structure rather than description; used striking phrases and witty **colloquialisms;** expressed anxiety about the crisis between church and court; and were intentionally **cerebral** and **difficult to understand**.

Dates	Major Writers and Works
1558–1603	**Christopher Marlowe**: wrote *The Tragical History of Doctor Faustus* and *The Jew of Malta*. Marlowe was the first playwright to use blank verse in drama. He is also known for his poetry, especially "The Passionate Shepherd," which begins "Come live with me and be my love . . ." to which Sir Walter Raleigh responded with "The Nymph's Reply to the Shepherd."
	Thomas Nashe: a satirist, poet, pamphleteer, playwright, and early progenitor of the novel; was one of many writers educated at Cambridge who wrote to earn money
	George Peele: dramatist and lyricist, known for his flowery diction and poetic beauty; wrote blank verse in a way that was musical and sweet, different from Marlowe or Shakespeare
	Sir Walter Raleigh: navigator, explorer, historian, poet, courtier, and member of Parliament and one of Queen Elizabeth's favorites; wrote *The History of the World* and a series of romantic poems, one which is a response to Christopher Marlowe's "The Passionate Shepherd"
	Sir Philip Sidney: Elizabethan courtier and poet who romanticized the pastoral and rustic way of life. Considered the flower of chivalry, he wrote numerous sonnets and *The Defense of Poetry*.
1603–1625	**Francis Bacon**: philosopher, lawyer, and essayist; challenged medieval beliefs about science and approached scientific inquiry inductively. Bacon championed the scientific method of inquiry, which focused on using data gathered via the senses to discover knowledge about the natural world.
	John Donne: metaphysical poet who wrote about worldly experiences in opposition to the Petrarchan love sonnets of his time. Among his works are *The Flea*, *An Anatomy of the World*, and *Holy Sonnets*.
	Ben Jonson: poet and playwright best known for his satiric comedies. His first major play, *Every Man in His Humour*, was performed in the Globe Theatre by an acting troupe called Lord Chamberlain's Men, in which William Shakespeare played the lead.
	Thomas Middleton: playwright, poet, and city chronologer; his work reflected a humorous cynicism about the human race. His works include *A Chaste Maid in Cheapside*, *Women Beware Women*, and *The Changeling*.

LITERARY TIMELINE

Dates	Literary Period	Literary Elements of the Period
Great Britain		
1629–1649	Carolinean	Literature marked by **Cavalier poetry**. All Cavalier poets aligned with Charles I and professed a **libertine lifestyle**; noted for their *carpe diem* or "seize the day" poems: erotic, libidinous, and candidly sexual poetry that reflected a philosophy of "life is too short so live it to the fullest." The Stuart monarchy encouraged the circulation of literature and **masques**, static, superficial, spectacular pageants, rich in costume, scenery, and song with a casual storyline.
1649–1660	Commonwealth Age	Theaters reopened following the death of Oliver Cromwell, giving rise to **Restoration comedies**, which were sexually explicit and addressed topics of the day through their busy plots. Celebrity actors and actresses emerge during this period. Popular dramas entertained **murder**, **incest**, and **madness** set in Italy or Spain, both Catholic countries. Macabre in nature, these plays included villains and other characters that went to their deaths.
1690–1780	Eighteenth-Century Literature / The Age of the Novel	Marked by **reasoned argument**, **good humor**, and **common sense** as opposed to the discord between superstition and enthusiasm, literature returned to **neoclassicism**. Writers tried to imitate characteristics of Virgil, Horace, Cicero, and Lucretius, and others of the Augustan Age in Rome. Marked the beginning of the **newspaper**, **the periodical**, and **journalism**. There was a **return to satire and comedic banter**.

Dates	Major Writers and Works
1629–1649	**Robert Herrick**: wrote *carpe diem* poetry. The often-quoted "Gather ye rosebuds while ye may" comes from his famous poem "To the Virgins, to Make Much of Time," which implores readers to live life to the fullest. **Richard Lovelace**: while imprisoned in Westminster Gatehouse, wrote "To Althea, from Prison," which includes the famous words, "Stone walls do not a prison make, nor iron bars a cage." He is also noted for "To Lucasta, Going to the Wars." **Andrew Marvell**: John Milton's assistant and prodigy, wrote *carpe diem* poetry and satire. "To His Coy Mistress" is a famous example *carpe diem* poem in which the speaker tries to convince his mistress to have sex. **John Milton**: a Puritan and countercultural poet, wrote sonnets and complex poetry that were solemn, religious, and puritanical. Famous for *Paradise Lost*, based on the Book of Genesis, Milton's religious work, written in blank verse, defied the clear, simple, and sensual *carpe diem* poetry of the period. Milton also wrote the elegy *Lycidas*, a moving poem that laments the demise of a dear school friend. **Sir John Suckling**: a Cavalier poet who wrote light, melodious lyrical poetry such as "Ballad Upon a Wedding"
1649–1660	**John Dryden**: considered one of the chief founders of modern English prose, the first great English critic, and the most representative writer of the Restoration, dominated during this literary period. His best-known plays are *All for Love*, *The Hind and the Panther*, and *The Rehearsal*. **John Bunyan**: a preacher and student of scripture most well known for his Christian allegory *The Pilgrim's Progress*, in which a character named Christian encounters various perils on his way to Heaven and where vices and virtues are personified. **Thomas Hobbes**: *Leviathan* encouraged humankind to surrender its power to the authority of an absolute sovereign; otherwise, consistent struggle over power would lead to an endless state of war. **Lucy Hutchinson**: *Memoirs of the Life of Colonel Hutchinson* describes the lust and intemperance James I wrought on the throne as opposed to the honor, glory, and wealth his predecessor Queen Elizabeth I established.
1690–1780	**Daniel Defoe**: *Robinson Crusoe* fixed the form of the historical novel, led to Sir Walter Scott's *Waverly* and *Ivanhoe*. **Henry Fielding**: considered the founder of the English prose epic; produced *Tom Thumb*, which is his most famous and popular drama. Fielding wrote twenty-five plays, but his novels gained critical acclaim, such as *The History of Tom Jones, a Foundling* and *The History of the Adventures of Joseph Andrews*, a parody of Samuel Richardson's *Pamela*. **Richard Sheridan**: reestablished the prominence of English comedies. His works *The Rivals*, *The School for Scandal*, and *The Critic* won acclaim for their ingenious plots, playfulness of language, and social satire. ⟶

LITERARY TIMELINE

Dates	Literary Period	Literary Elements of the Period
Great Britain		
1690–1780	Eighteenth-Century Literature / The Age of the Novel *(con't)*	Marked by **reasoned argument**, **good humor**, and **common sense** as opposed to the discord between superstition and enthusiasm, literature returned to **neoclassicism**. Writers tried to imitate characteristics of Virgil, Horace, Cicero, and Lucretius, and others of the Augustan Age in Rome. Marked the beginning of the **newspaper**, **the periodical**, and **journalism**. There was a **return to satire and comedic banter**. *(Text repeated from pg. 188 for reader's convenience.)*

Dates	Major Writers and Works
1690–1780	**Jonathan Swift**: believed that humankind destroyed and ruined everything it touched and that men were generally odious beasts. His loathing of mankind is particularly evident in *Gulliver's Travels*, a political and social satire, which relegates humans to filthy horses. **Samuel Richardson**: the first psychological novelist. His first novel, *Pamela; or, Virtue Rewarded*, presented a heroine who resists the advances of a lascivious master until he marries her. **William Congreve**: considered the greatest master of the English comedy of "repartee" (banter); known for his highbrow, sexual comedy of manners, a type of comedy that satirizes the peculiar affectations of high society. His works include *The Way of the World*, *The Mourning Bride*, and *Love for Love*. **Dr. Samuel Johnson**: poet, critic, biographer, and political essayist who became a national sensation after writing *The Dictionary of the English Language*. Johnson also wrote *The Lives of the Poets* and *The Rambler*. **Oliver Goldsmith**: gained fame for publishing a collection of essays, *The Citizen of the World*; a hugely successful play, *She Stoops to Conquer*; and a novel about English country life, *The Vicar of Wakefield*. **Thomas Gray**: considered one of the most important poets of the eighteenth century; most noted for "Elegy Written in a Country Churchyard." His poetry was elegant, melancholic, and somewhat artificial, but reflected the literary elements of the period. **Joseph Addison** and **Richard Steele**: most famous for publishing *The Tatler*, which eventually became *The Spectator*, a magazine whose purpose was to provide English readers with topics suitable for educated conversations and social interactions **James Boswell**: earned major recognition for immortalizing Dr. Samuel Johnson, in *The Life of Samuel Johnson* **Horace Walpole**: wrote the first Gothic novel, *Castle of Otranto*. In this tale of curses, romance, terror, and fantasy, Walpole blended ancient and modern romance. **James Hogg**: noted for *The Private Memoirs and Confessions of a Justified Sinner*, in which he wrote about persecution, torture, delusion, and despair **Alexander Pope**: a master of Augustan (neoclassicist) poetry, wrote a mock heroic epic poem, *The Rape of the Lock*. This five-canto work, echoing *The Iliad*, humorously details the story of a young woman who flirts, drinks coffee, wears makeup, plays cards, and suddenly has a lock of hair stolen by an ardent suitor. His first major essay, *An Essay on Criticism*, contains the famous line, "A little learning is a dangerous thing."

LITERARY TIMELINE

Dates	Literary Period	Literary Elements of the Period
Great Britain		
1780–1830	Romantic	Romanticism rebelled against neoclassicism. Emphasizing **passion**, **imagination**, and a **deep sense of wonder and mystery**, writing moved from the objective view of the Enlightenment to a stronger focus on **subjective feelings**. Romantic poets revived the **Spenserian stanza and ode**. Poetry depicted the **triumph of the human spirit**. The movement elevated art in contrast to filthy factories and championed humanitarianism and democracy. **Gothic romance**, replete with sliding panels, secret chambers, rattling chains, eerie groans, shrouded figures, and bizarre torture also became popular. Literature also reflected a **break in political conformity**.

Dates	Major Writers and Works
1780–1830	**Robert Burns**: considered one of the great songwriters of his time; authored hundreds of works, including songs "Auld Lang Syne" and "Comin' thro the Rye," and poems such as "To a Mouse," "To a Louse," and "Highland Mary"

Pre-Romantic Poetry
William Blake: *Songs of Innocence*, which includes "Little Boy Lost," "Little Boy Found," and "Little Lamb," describes the natural world of spontaneity, innocence, and beauty; *Songs of Experience* assumes an ironic and darker tone where the beauty and innocence of childhood is met with the ugliness, truth, and fear often associated with adulthood.

First-Generation Romantic Poets
William Wordsworth: is attributed, along with friend Samuel Taylor Coleridge, with launching the romantic poetry movement with his first major work, *Lyrical Ballads*. His magnum opus, *The Prelude*, is considered to be semiautobiographical. Wordsworth also wrote "A Slumber Did My Spirit Seal," one of the Lucy poems; "An Ode to Duty," and "I Wandered Lonely as a Cloud."

Samuel Taylor Coleridge: collaborated with Wordsworth on *Lyrical Ballads*. *The Rime of the Ancient Mariner*, a supernatural tale of sin, penance, and salvation, opened the collaborative work *Lyrical Ballads*.

Second-Generation Romantic Poets:
John Keats: revered a return to nature and beauty as observed in works *Ode on a Grecian Urn*, *Ode to a Nightingale*, *Endymion*, and *Hyperion*.

Percy Bysshe Shelley: expelled from Oxford University for writing and distributing *The Necessity of Atheism*. His sister, Mary Shelley, would eventually write *Frankenstein*, a true tale of horror and man's inhumanity to man.

Lord George Byron: wrote *The Giaour*, a romantic, Oriental tale, and the successful, satirical epic *Don Juan*

Prose Writers
Jane Austen: known for her unhampered, indirect discourse; works include *Pride and Prejudice*, *Emma*, and *Sense and Sensibility*

Sir Walter Scott: particularly noted for *Ivanhoe*, which recounts the last important Jacobite movement of 1745 to place a Stuart on the throne

Charles Lamb: most noted for his collection *Essays of Elia*, a mixture of fact and fiction about his grandmother

LITERARY TIMELINE

Dates	Literary Period	Literary Elements of the Period
Great Britain		
1837–1857	Early Victorian	The English embraced sense of their **nation's identity**.
		A middle class emerged.
		A sense of the **lonely and complex individual** gained prominence.
		The year **1847-1848** was regarded as the **most significant period in the entire history of English novel**.
		The novel provided an understanding of and the vocabulary for articulating what it meant to be an individual in nineteenth-century Britain, and portrayed a sense of the changing **social order** (increasingly middle-class white simultaneously/paradoxically developing a sense of psychological complexity).
		Realistic novels reflected a middle-class tone of voice, imposed moral framework, and depicted the contradictions, complexities, and frustrations of respectable middle-class life.
		The **Newgate novel** was a form of fiction that dealt with lives of criminals.
		Poetry engaged more marginal, extreme, and unnerving dimensions of Victorian life, delving into the **strange and dark depths of the mind**.

Dates	Major Writers and Works
1837–1857	**Elizabeth Barrett Browning**: wife of Robert Browning; *Sonnets from the Portuguese*, written during her courtship, offers the most accurate representation of sonnets since the time of Shakespeare. Sonnet 43 from *Sonnets* begins with one of the most often-quoted lines, "How do I love thee? Let me count the ways." Her epic poem/novel *Aurora Leigh* played a central role in the debate about women and confronted fundamental questions about gendered identity.

Robert Browning: famous for "My Last Duchess"; also explored more bizarre states of mind, such as murderous jealousy and deepening insanity

Thomas Carlyle: most renowned for his spiritual autobiography *Sartor Resartus*, and detailed expositions on history, philosophy, and social problems in *Heroes and Hero-Worship* and *Past and Present*

Charlotte Brontë: *Jane Eyre* examines the position of women in Victorian Britain.

Emily Brontë: *Wuthering Heights* depicts characters caught between an old way of life and new world of Victorians and whose passion is so intense it transcends individualism.

Charles Dickens: wrote novels that reflected stories of social reconciliation and reconstitution. His *Oliver Twist* challenged the inhumane aspects of new social legislation, represented the fear of criminality and the mob, questioned how to control an increasingly complex society, and endorsed emerging middle-class values. In *David Copperfield* and *Great Expectations*, protagonists are at odds with and at the same time crave middle-class respectability. *Bleak House* and *Dombey and Son*, darker novels, recount death, murder, madness, despair, and suicide, negative but accurate consequences of a complicated, mechanized world.

Elizabeth Gaskell: portrayed the positive spirit encountered in fiction of the 1850s. *North and South* depicts social reconciliation of hostility and division, and engages the new reality of industrial Britain. Her works, such as *Wives and Daughters*, *Sylvia's Lovers*, and *Mary Barton*, suggest a personal answer to a political problem, but also present the conflict between creating and endorsing middle-class values that are flawed.

Thomas Macaulay: exuded a quiet confidence and wrote against slavery in the colonies and for establishing a national education system in India. His most acclaimed work is the *History of England*, a work of detail, diligence, and competence, and although he died before its completion, the text was considered a best seller.

Dante Gabriel Rossetti: his final work, *Ballads and Sonnets*, reflects the sadness, despair, grief, love, and mysticism he experienced during his nine-year engagement and two-year marriage to Elizabeth Siddal.

William Makepeace Thackeray: castigated the middle-class hero as selfish and offered little sympathy for heroine Becky Sharp in *Vanity Fair*. *The History of Pendennis* critiques the hero's loss of a role and direction in his life. In *The History of Esmond*, Thackeray not only critiques materialism but also portrays the shortcomings of the Victorian emphasis on the self. |

LITERARY TIMELINE

Dates	Literary Period	Literary Elements of the Period
Great Britain		
1857–1876	Middle Victorian	Mainstream authors offered **critical and dissenting voices**.
		Tension arose between questioning middle-class values and committing and embracing commitment to such values.
		Novelists favored stories about middle-class life and ordinary domestic experiences, narrated them in a tone that identified with the social and moral principles of such a society.
		Fiction reflected written confirmation of existence of middle-class values.
		Victorian realism shared a way of looking at the world.
		Novels assumed the **narrative form**.
		Sensation novels focused on ordinary middle-class life but included extravagant, horrible, and sensational events that simultaneously exposed convictions as hypocritical, fragile, and damaging.

Dates	Major Writers and Works
1857–1876	**Matthew Arnold**: wrote "Dover Beach," which identified the loss of religious faith as a central source of worry in Victorian life. His later novel, *Culture and Anarchy*, saw culture as the vehicle for helping the Victorians out of their difficulties and observed no central authority to control the drift of civilization toward anarchy.
	Mary Elizabeth Braddon: *Lady Audley's Secret* looked skeptically and critically at roles imposed upon women in Victorian society, revealing the complicated truths behind the façade of marriage and respectability.
	Lewis Carroll: called on alternative logic in *Alice's Adventures in Wonderland*, offering a different voice and constructing a different narrative in the midst of realistic fiction writing
	Wilkie Collins: *The Woman in White* reflected an age when people relied upon processes of law and questioned and undermined institutions and things of value that mid-Victorians relied upon. *The Moonstone* questioned British imperialism, specifically the British presence in India.
	Charles Darwin: *The Origin of Species*, which proposed and documented natural selection and survival of the fittest, moved people toward an evolutionary change with little moral or spiritual purpose.
	George Eliot (pen name for Mary Anne Evans): wrote novels that reflected an era of tremendous prosperity, portraying a central theme of egoism and the duties and obligations of the individual, as seen in *Adam Bede* and *Daniel Deronda*
	Gerard Manley Hopkins: Jesuit poet who believed that the purpose of his work was to glorify God and to display the significant nature of every creature. He called this focus inscape, which is observed in "Pied Beauty," "Thou Art Indeed Just, Lord," and "God's Grandeur."
	John Stuart Mill: wrote on logic, epistemology, economics, social and political philosophy, ethics, metaphysics, religion, and current affairs. His most well-known and significant works include *A System of Logic*, *Principles of Political Economy*, *On Liberty*, *Utilitarianism*, *The Subjection of Women*, *Three Essays on Religion*, and his *Autobiography*.
	John Ruskin: published *Traffic*, in which he condemned laissez-faire economics, commended the dignity of labor and moral and aesthetic value of craftsmanship, and attempted to reintroduce the human dimension into factory-based economy
	Alfred Lord Tennyson: identified individual identity as more haunted and lonely. Incorporating a sensuous and musical quality in work, he created *In Memoriam*, an elegy dedicated to his friend who died at the young age of twenty-two. His other works, "Mariana" and "The Lady of Shallott," simultaneously describe energy and guilt. *Idylls of the King* elaborates the stories of King Arthur and the Roundtable.
	Anthony Trollope: documented the story of Phineas Finn's rise to parliamentary power through a series of romantic attachments in *Phineas Finn*, in which he analyzed parliamentary society, seemingly celebrating British the political system, but at the same time suggesting that the parliamentary system is a pretence that is irrelevant to the true state of nation and with few real connections to those it claims to represent. In *The Way We Live Now*, Trollope created a satiric picture of decadent society corrupted by greed and gambling and living on borrowed time.

LITERARY TIMELINE

Dates	Literary Period	Literary Elements of the Period
Great Britain		
1876–1901	Late Victorian	Novel continued to be the most significant genre.
		Period was marked by new forms of **social analysis**, **resurgent socialism**, **new feminist voices**, and a **fresh expression of liberal values**.
		Literature illustrated protagonists not as heroes or heroines but as real people, replete with human foibles; reflected a sense of disintegration within society; and depicted crumbling social institutions such as family and marriage, and increasing **skepticism toward conventional morality**. Characters collided with society; themes expressed widespread feeling that society could not hold together. More sustaining fictions were replaced with troubling and disconcerting texts.
		Interests in **evolution** and **social Darwinism** coexisted with fears about regression, atavism, and decline, reflecting a loss of faith in goals traditionally pursed by middle-class hero and heroines.
		There was a prevailing idea that something dangerous and irrational would destabilize society.
		The period saw the emergence of **aestheticism**, where art has no reference to life and therefore nothing to do with morality and represents a refusal or inability to engage with reality.
		Romance novels embraced the idea of escape.
		Drama of the absurd revived the belief that life is ridiculous, without substance or depth.
Twentieth Century	Twentieth Century	Writers used literature to discuss and portray the **anxiety** of their changing society.
		New forms of media such as **photography and film** emerged, granting new aesthetic ways of looking at the world.
		Different styles reflected the age:
		Modernism played with shifting perspectives and "potentialities" of the first half of the twentieth century and the unreliable narration this shifting perspective implied.

Dates	Major Writers and Works
1876–1901	**Thomas Hardy**: depicted romantic, impractical, and disorganized characters that could not manage their lives. *Far from the Madding Crowd* and *The Return of the Native* emphasized a failure of relationships, breakdown of marriages, divorce, and sexuality. *The Mayor of Casterbridge*, about a vandal who steals sheep and is eventually executed, portrays the nature of indiscipline and a society that has instituted a system of law and order to regulate people. *Tess of the D'Urbervilles* presents an indignant portrayal of the ways social regulations and conventions ruin people's lives, and reflects the aggressive nature of patriarchal society, harshness of law, and lack of tolerance and understanding. *Jude the Obscure* critiques how education, class barriers, religious and moral conventions, and divorce laws conspire against protagonist Jude. **George Gissing**: represented late Victorian social pessimism, the despair of London's working-class life, presenting people as little better than savages. His works include *Workers in the Dawn*, *The Unclassed*, *Demos*, *Thyrza*, and *The Nether World*. *The Odd Women* is the most substantial novel about single women, noting that the least fortunate character is the one who marries. **Walter Besant** wrote about class, education, and the unprivileged in *All Sorts and Conditions of Men*. **Robert Louis Stevenson**: *Treasure Island* focuses on the romance of leaving Britain to embark on new adventures. *Doctor Jekyll and Mr. Hyde*, dark and sinister, represents the continual conflict between the irrational factors in mind and rational identity. **Rudyard Kipling**: in *Many Inventions*, proposed that social differences disappear when men agree to abide by same set of rules, a set of values that is relevant to all ranks. **George Bernard Shaw**: exposed social hypocrisy and presented a new kind of social analysis that reflected a commitment to socialism. His works include *The Philanderer*, *Heartbreak House*, *Widowers' Houses*. **Oscar Wilde**: expressed a radical, disconcerting vision of society, where characters use style and lack substance, drawing attention to themselves with no meaningful purpose. His plays included *Lady Windermere's Fan*, *A Woman of No Importance*, and *The Importance of Being Earnest*. Novels include *The Picture of Dorian Gray*, an example of aestheticism, as the portrait of Dorian Gray fades while the hero himself retains youthful beauty.
Twentieth Century	**Kingsley Amis**: *Lucky Jim*, an influential novel capturing the "angry young man" perspective in literature **W. H. Auden**: "found" by T. S. Eliot, who published his first book, *Poems*, in 1930. Auden went on to write more collections, including *The Orators* and *Look Stranger!* **Samuel Beckett**: Irish novelist and playwright. While living in France, he wrote *Waiting for Godot*, a play that put him in the vanguard of the theater of the absurd. He is also known for his plays *Endgame*, *Krapp's Last Tape*, *Breath*, and *Not I*. His various novels include the trilogy *Molloy*, *Malone Dies*, and *The Unnamable*. →

LITERARY TIMELINE

Dates	Literary Period	Literary Elements of the Period
Great Britain		
Twentieth Century	Twentieth Century *(con't)*	**Existentialism** asked what an individual was to do in such a topsy-turvy, absurd world where meaning seemed no longer relevant or reliable; finally explained that meaning could only be found in the self.
		Existential nihilism argued that life was intrinsically meaningless.
		Postcolonial literature was beginning to take shape and form a new genre around the world.
		Postmodernism began to suggest a total lack of social unity; postmodernism marks the point where such **deconstruction becomes the norm**.

Dates	Major Writers and Works
Twentieth Century	**The Bloomsbury Group**: an intellectual group headed by Virginia Woolf and her sister Vanessa Bell, a painter; welcomed the likes of E. M. Forster, Roger Fry and Lytton Strachey; fostered the rise of the avant-garde and modern thinking about sexuality, pacifism, and feminism in English literature **Anthony Burgess**: *A Clockwork Orange*, depiction of violent authoritarianism **A. S. Byatt**: *The Virgin in the Garden*, the first book in a quartet about twentieth-century family life in Yorkshire, England. *Still Life*, *Babel Tower*, and *A Whistling Woman* followed. These stories follow the life of a young female intellectual growing up in a still largely male-dominated intellectual world. Her best-known novel, *Possession*, won the Booker Prize. **Arthur C. Clarke**: one of the most prolific and influential science fiction writers of the twentieth century. His short story "The Sentinel" formed the basis for Stanley Kubrick's film *2001: A Space Odyssey*. **E. M. Forster**: a liberal realist, his major works include *Howard's End*, *A Room with a View*, and *A Passage to India*. His last novel, *Maurice*, published posthumously, was based on a strong homosexual theme. **William Golding**: *Lord of the Flies*, a pessimistic and violence-ridden view of humanity that echoes the feelings of the Western world after World War II. **Graham Greene**: *The Power and the Glory*, *Our Man in Havana*, *The Quiet American*, and *The End of the Affair*. **Seamus Heaney**: Pulitzer Prize-winner author of several collections of poetry, plays, and essays. His poems such as "North," "Field Work," and "Casualty" exalt the raw political power of words. **Aldous Huxley**: *Brave New World*, a science fiction story that warned against the overwhelming powers of technology. Some of his other works include *Point Counter Point*, *Ape and Essence*, and *Brave New World Revisited*. **James Joyce**: modernized and revolutionized literature and writing with his novel *Ulysses*. The book's narrative, taking place on one day in Dublin, uses various narrative styles, techniques, and viewpoints, including a stream-of-consciousness style. The novel explicitly calls upon his other writings, including *A Portrait of the Artist as a Young Man*, as much as it alludes to a compendium of world literature and classics, requiring a sense of inter- and intratextual knowledge, as well as an ability on the reader's part to go with the flow of the often strikingly sensual and poetic prose in the stream-of-consciousness passages. **D. H. Lawrence**: battled obscenity charges for his sexually explicit work, including *The Rainbow* and *Lady Chatterley's Lover*. He wrote daringly about personal and social hypocrisies, and he believed human nature is at its best when its consciousness is in harmony with its natural spontaneity. ➡

LITERARY TIMELINE

Dates	Literary Period	Literary Elements of the Period
Great Britain		
Twentieth Century	Twentieth Century *(con't)*	**Existentialism** asked what an individual was to do in such a topsy-turvy, absurd world where meaning seemed no longer relevant or reliable; finally explained that meaning could only be found in the self.
		Existential nihilism argued that life was intrinsically meaningless.
		Postcolonial literature was beginning to take shape and form a new genre around the world.
		Postmodernism began to suggest a total lack of social unity; postmodernism marks the point where such **deconstruction becomes the norm**.
		(Text repeated from pg. 200 for reader's convenience.)
Greece		
2000 BC–AD 100	Ancient Greece	**Greek comedy and tragedy** developed from choral performances.
		Greeks adapted language to the Phoenician writing system, adding signs for vowels to transform consonants.
		Literature included **commercial documents**, **poetry**, and **drama**.
		Homer developed metrical formulas, outline of the story.
		Lyric poems performed with the accompaniment of a lyre (hence, the word *lyric*).
		Sapphic meter was developed by the lyrical poet Sappho.
		Greek drama, primarily tragedy, emerged from choral performances.
		Thespis initiated dialogue between himself and a masked actor.
		Aeschylus created a prototype of later drama marked by conflict.
		Poetry, comic, reflected obscenity, farce, wit, satire, and parody (Aristophanes).
		Literature incorporated dialectic to undermine Socrates and Plato.
Rome		
Ancient World–Fifteenth Century	Ancient Rome	The **Romans borrowed Greek** sources, imitating the Greek epics and themes of heroism.
		Themes associated with **sophisticated and high-edge life of the Roman elite** also pervaded the literature.
		Hebrew literature addressed the personal, inner, and relational God.

Dates	Major Writers and Works
Twentieth Century	**V. S. Naipaul**: Indian-Trinidadian British writer; first Indian to win the Booker Prize in 1971; later awarded the Nobel Prize for Literature for "having united perceptive narrative and incorruptible scrutiny in works that compel us to see the presence of suppressed histories." However, he has also been criticized for making unsympathetic portrayals of the underdeveloped nations he writes about. His novels include *In a Free State* and *A House for Mr. Biswas*. **George Orwell**: his time in Burma in the Indian Imperial Police inspired much of his social criticism, evident in his most popular novels, *1984* and *Animal Farm*. **Sir Ahmed Salman Rushdie**: sets most of his novels in India, where he was born. His *Midnight's Children*, a magical realist novel, won the Booker Prize in 1981. He is well known for *The Satanic Verses* controversy but has written various novels and short stories since, including *The Moor's Last Sigh* and *Shalimar the Clown*.
2000 BC– AD 100	**Aeschylus**: *The Persians, Seven against Thebes, The Suppliants, The Oresteia* (*Agamemnon, The Libation Bearers, The Eumenides*), and *Prometheus Bound* **Aristophanes**: *The Acharnians, The Knights, The Clouds, The Wasps Peace, The Birds, Lysistrata, Thesmophoriazusae* (*The Women Celebrating the Thesmophoria*), *The Frogs, Ecclesiazusae* (*The Assemblywomen*), *Plutus or* (*Wealth*) **Aristotle**: *Poetics*, which was the first systematic work of Western literary criticism **Euripides**: *Alcestis, Medea, Trojan Women, The Bacchae, Cyclops* **Homer**: *The Iliad* and *The Odyssey* **Plato**: *Menwn* (*Meno*), *Faidwn* (*Phaedo*), *Politeia* (*Republic*), *FaidroV* (*Phaedrus*), *Sumposion* (*Symposium*), *ParmenidhV* (*Parmenides*), *QeaithtoV* (*Theaetetus*), *TimaioV* (*Timaeus*), *LegeiV* (*Laws*) **Sappho**: a lyrist, was the first author to write in the first person **Socrates** **Sophocles**: *Oedipus the King*
Ancient World– Fifteenth Century	**Virgil**: most noted for *The Aeneid*. Inspired by Homer, Virgil sought to create a national epic for the emerging Roman Empire under rule of Augustus Caesar and to link the dynasty of ancient Troy in the person of its surviving prince, Aeneas. **Ovid**: *Metamorphoses*, considered his masterpiece; known for subtlety and psychological depth, unrelated characters, and dactylic hexameter. This anti-*Aeneid* epic poem of fifteen books influenced all other epic poems thereafter. →

LITERARY TIMELINE

Dates	Literary Period	Literary Elements of the Period
Rome		
Ancient World–Fifteenth Century	Ancient Rome *(con't)*	The **Romans borrowed Greek** sources, imitating the Greek epics and themes of heroism. Themes associated with **sophisticated and high-edge life of the Roman elite** also pervaded the literature. **Hebrew literature** addressed the personal, inner, and relational God. *(Text repeated from pg. 202 for reader's convenience.)*
Europe		
500–1500	Middle Ages	**National literatures in the vernacular** appeared. Literature focused on religious faith and the appropriate use of physical force, but was nonetheless very diverse: literate and oral in **Germanic languages and Latin**, and secular and religious, tolerant and repressive, vernacular and learned, rural and urban, skeptical and pious, and popular and aristocratic reflecting, Arabs, Jews, and Christians. Literature incorporated **archetypal individuals** who sought to seek to better understand themselves and their destinies. The works **borrowed from non-Western traditions**, thus offering universal appeal, with characters being exported back from non-Western parts of the world. Styles ranged from the humblest signified by **colloquial humor** to the highest poetic tones.
China		
1600 BC–AD 100	Early China	**Confucian** ideals emphasized government, morality, social relationships, justice, and sincerity. **Three jewels of the Tao**: compassion, moderation, and humility **Taoist writing** addressed nature, health, longevity, and *wu wei* ("effortless action"). **Forms** include hymns, temple, hunting, and love and marriage songs. Poetry was written in metaphors.

Dates	Major Writers and Works
Ancient World– Fifteenth Century	*The Four Gospels of the Life and Sayings of Jesus and the Acts of the Apostles* was written in Greek about sixty years after the death of Jesus. Each Gospel addresses a different audience: Matthew, the Jewish public; Mark, the Gentile audience; and Luke, the cultured Greek readers. John's writing differs from his peers in that his work consistently refers to Jesus as Christ and Lord, representing Jesus as the Omnipotent. Final canon of the New Testament of the Christian Bible is established in 367.
500–1500	**Dante Alighieri**: *The Divine Comedy*, a poem that represents the supreme expression of the medieval mind in European imaginative literature, considered the greatest poem of Middle Ages; contains three divisions of identical length: *Hell* (*Inferno*), *Purgatory* (*Purgatorio*), and *Paradise* (*Paradiso*). The poem recounts Dante's descent through nine circles of Hell and seven divisions of Purgatory proper, ante-Purgatory, and Earthly Paradise (Garden of Eden).
1600 BC– AD 100	*The Book of Documents* *Classic of Poetry*: collection of lyric poetry *The Book of Change* I Ching Yijing *Analects*: recorded by Confucius's disciples *Chuang Tzu*: philosophical meditations of jokes, parables *Laozi tzu*: a silk manuscript, stanzas of wise, adages, political and personal issues *Historical Records*: a history of the lives of ruling families and dynasties in China up to time of Emperor Wu →

LITERARY TIMELINE

Dates	Literary Period	Literary Elements of the Period
China		
220–28	Middle Period	**Confucianism** declined in importance; **Taoism** and **Buddhism** acquiring more important status. **Flourishing poetry focused on understanding nature** and nature of the individual or recluse. Many new literary works focused on understanding the **psyche**, **spiritual enlightenment**, and the **natural world**.
220–28		**Taoist imagery** reflected contemplation and mystical union with nature, wisdom, and learning. Purposive action was abandoned in favor of simplicity and *wu wei* (nonaction, or letting things take their natural course). *Jueju*, the five- to seven-character quatrain emerged, and Chinese poems (*Yue fu*) were composed in folk-song style.
India		
3000 BC–AD 100		**Hinduism** holds that moral and spiritual conquest is superior to conquest by sword. **Hindu core concepts** permeated early Indian literature: dharma, karma, and Buddhism. **Sanskrit** entered India in 1500 BC.
Africa		
AD 200–600	Africa	200–350: **Christianity** was introduced and spread in **North Africa**. 500–1495: The West African savanna empires arose: Ghana in the northwest; and Kanem around Lake Chad, Mali, and Songhay in the Middle Niger. 600–1000: **Islam** was introduced and spread in **East and West Africa**. **Oral tradition** was an integral part of African life and comprised various expressive forms such as **folktale**, **legend**, **myth**, and **poetry**.
AD 570–653	Islamic Literature	The **Koran** was produced, marking the period of **Muhammad's prophesy** from first revelation, through the growth of his following, his flight (*hijra*) to Medina, and his final pilgrimage to Mecca; the Koran was the basis for Islam. Written in **Arabic**, the Koran was intended to be heard and recited, accompanied by music. The text is more dialogic than narrative, offering **admonition and guidance**.

Dates	Major Writers and Works
220–28	**Li Po**: a wandering poet; recognized as the greatest Tang poet; produced an abundance of poems on different subjects such as nature, wine, friendship, solitude, and the passage of time. With its air of playfulness, hyperbole, and fantasy, his poetry captured the nuances of the human experience of nature and human friendship.
220–28	None
3000 BC–AD 100	*Vedas*: Hindu scriptures *Upanisads* (*Mystic Doctrines*): philosophical meditations **Valkimi**: *Ramayana*, documented adventures in exile **Vyasa**: *Mahabharata*, expressed core values in Hinduism *Jakata*, a popular Buddhist tale collection, becomes *Bodhisattva*.
AD 200–600	*Epic of Son-Jara*: constructed from the oral tradition of the Manding, a political epic, focused on the rivalry of two brothers for succession to their father's throne. The epic had a moral tone of good versus evil as well as an ideological function, which was to construct a Manding common identity under a founding hero. It contains three distinct generic layers: first, a narrative framework of structural episodes and genealogies; second, praise poems and songs; third, the so-called task of the griot, which brings the narrative to life and reenacts it dramatically.
AD 570–653	The Koran

LITERARY TIMELINE

Dates	Literary Period	Literary Elements of the Period
Japan		
800–1100		**Japanese syllabary** reflected the tremendous impact and authority Chinese script and language had on Japan.
		Women writers played a role in exploring the potential of Japanese language.
		Literature privileged realism, psychological insight, and authenticity over romanticism.
1100–1600	Golden Age	**Japanese** poets introduced the **haiku** form of poetry.
		Literature reflected the influence of **kinship** on bureaucracy, focusing on **family fortunes**, **politics**, **economy**, and **the military**; it also explored the **depths of longing and ambition**.
		Two forms of **linked poetry** were developed during this period:
		Renga: first developed as a game between court poets; ranged from 50 to 1,000 stanzas; contained numerous allusions to Chinese and Japanese literature
		Renku: also called *haikai no renga*, was common among the rising middle class in Japan; linked intuitively, based on what seemed logically connected
Europe		
1500–1650	Renaissance	Characters had more autonomy and more fully realized personalities.
		Deliberation and action were equally important.
		Writers were highly influenced by **ancient literature**, **classical mythology**, **philosophy**, and **scriptures**; reflected a taste for the harmonious and memorable, spectacular effects, and striking of a pose; and addressed themes of **virtue**, **fame**, and **glory** as well as **melancholy**, **puzzling doubts**, and **mistrust**. Poets celebrated high deeds and dispensed glory.
		Writing joined the philosophical and the imaginative.
1600–1800	Enlightenment	Writers dramatized intricate interchanges and **conflicts between reason and passion**, one of the insistent themes of French and English literature in century beginning around 1660.
		Writers assumed the **superior importance of social group** and of shared opinion.
		French writers examined larger problems: marriage and other social and personal institutions.

Dates	Major Writers and Works
800–1100	**Murasaki Shikibu**: *The Tale of Genji*, the first great Japanese prose novel; a story about the life and love of a prince and his descendents. The themes address loss, substitution, transgression, and retribution. Genji's life and the lives of his successors are presented as a search for the ideal woman and also represent the quest for the perfect man.
1100–1600	**Matsuo Bashō**: recognized for *renga*, and after centuries, recognized as a master of haiku *Tale of the Heike*: an account of the Gempei wars, which led to the aristocracy's loss of wealth and political power **Yoshida Kenkō**: *Essays in Idleness* recounts observations about aesthetic issues; also wrote *Nō*, which are short, simple, plotless tragic plays (e.g., *Atsumori* and *Haku Rakuten*) often highlighting the teachings of Buddha **Shinkei**: poet; wrote *Murmured Conversations*, a treatise on the principles of linked poetry **Sīgi**, **Shīhaku**, and **Sīchī**: three poets who created *Three Poets at Minase*, a 100-verse sequence that epitomizes the linked-poetry tradition
1500–1650	*See also major writers and works listed under the Elizabethan, Jacobean, Carolinean, and Commonwealth Age periods for Great Britain.*
1600–1800	**Miguel de Cervantes**: Spanish dramatist, poet, and author; wrote epic poem *Don Quixote de la Mancha*, which satirized tales of chivalry presented in classical literature; based most of his work on personal experience and adventures. *The Exemplary Novels of Cervantes* (*Novelas ejemplares*, 1613), presents tales of pirates. **Sor Juana Inés de la Cruz**: a nun and Mexican poet, defended a woman's right to be treated as a human being. In *"Hombres necios"* ("Stubborn Men"), she criticizes the sexism of the society of her time. **François de la Rochefoucauld**: French classical writer, focused on morality in his work; best known for his maxims and epigrams, he wrote *Reflections* and *Maxime*. ➡

LITERARY TIMELINE

Dates	Literary Period	Literary Elements of the Period
Europe		
1600–1800	Enlightenment *(con't)*	Writers of the eighteenth century wrote on the basis of **established conventions**, among them the idea that commitment to **decorum** helped preserve society's important standards. Literature existed to delight and instruct readers.
		Realism attempted to convey the literal feel of experience, the shape in which events occur in the world, the way people really talked.
		Formalities of literature attempted to make stable what experience showed as unstable.
The Americas/Mesoamerica		
1500–1650		**Aztec art** was recorded in alphabetical script of western Europe, translated into Spanish, and preserved in Europe. Recording of **Mesoamerican historical narratives**, **prayers**, and **song texts** resulted in a growing native literature, preserved in western European script and available to the world in European languages.
		Maya, Zuni, and **Navajo literature** was based on the oral tradition Three genres of Mesoamerican literature emerged:
		Songs: most perfectly memorized; included the interjection of vocables and song syllables, which created patterns leading to paired stanzas
		Narrative: most expansive genre, followed a prescribed plot line; performer improvised; hero was usually a trickster who was gullible, clownish, ribald, and conniving
		Oratory: comprised of prayer, educational monologues, ceremonial colloquy, and prose poems
		Mesoamerican (Native) literary themes addressed supernatural power, problem of humanity versus nature, social obligation, and development of the individual.
		Rich symbolism and imagery, but literature was regarded as **functional rather than aesthetic**.

Dates	Major Writers and Works
1600–1800	**Michel de Montaigne**: French Renaissance thinker, used himself as the focus of a collection of personal essays, called *Essays* **Jean-Baptiste Poquelin Moliére**: comedic playwright who enjoyed pointing fun at ruling and rich aristocrats. His most famous works include *Tartuffe*, *The Misanthrope*, *The Blunderer*, *The School for Husbands*, and *The School for Wives*. **Jean Racine**: considered one of the three major dramatists of the period (the others being Moliére and Pierre Corneille); wrote primarily tragedy such as *Phaedra* **Jean-Jacques Rousseau**: forced to leave France because of controversial writing. *Confessions* recounts how men and boys strive to express natural impulses but are frustrated by society's demands and assumptions. **Johann Wolfgang von Goethe**: a German poet, dramatist, novelist, autobiographer, lawyer, diplomat, and scientific researcher. In his play (poetic drama) *Faust*, Dr. Faustus, a scholar who lived from 1480-1549, makes a contract with Mephistopheles (the Devil) in order to test the limits of possibility.
1500–1650	No written literature.

LITERARY TIMELINE

Dates	Literary Period	Literary Elements of the Period
China		
1400–1800		**Plays**, **verse romances**, and **prose fiction** were published in Chinese vernacular during thirteen to fourteenth centuries.
		Yuan and Ming vernacular lacked subtlety, voicing sex, violence, satire, and humor.
		Classical prose fiction was generally considered pure entertainment.
		Theater, **oral** verse romance, and storytelling flourished.
		Popular Chinese literature included **murder mysteries**, **stories of bandits**, and **fantasy**.
		Neo-Confucianism attempted to discover the philosophical grounds of Confucian classics.
		Literature celebrated **liberty**, **violent energy**, and **passion**.
Ottoman Empire		
1500– present	Ottoman Empire	Literature of the Ottoman Empire was **linguistically Turkish** but drew heavily on Arabic and Persian vocabulary, themes, and literary forms.
		Poetry and prose achieved richness and complexity that made it the **third great literature of Islamic tradition**.
India		
1800–1900		*Ghazal* was the quintessential lyric genre in **Urdu**, a language that evolved out of interaction of dialects of Hindi with Persian.
		Ghazal poetry was introspective, reflecting on love and an idealizing the beloved and God. But it was also a performative genre.
		Aesthetic effects of *ghazal* included:
		thematic and formal conventions: three to seven couplets
		qafiyah: rhyming element in which a syllable or sequence of sounds appears in both lines of first couplet and the second line of the following ones
		takhallus: the poet's pen name or signature

Dates	Major Writers and Works
1400–1800	**Cao Xueqin**: *The Story of the Stone*, an embodiment of China's cultural identity in recent times; story centered on women and relationships within an extended family; represents best and worst of traditional China in its final phase **Chin P'ing Mei**: *Golden Lotus*, a satirical novel about the manners of a corrupt sensualist **K'ung Shang-jen**: known for *The Peach Blossom Fan*; wrote long plays in the tradition of southern drama known as *ch'uan-chi'i* with intricate and sprawling affairs, numerous characters, and multiple story lines **Li Yü**: a comic dramatist, storywriter, and champion of vernacular literature *Romance of the Three Kingdoms*: a long historical novel about the fall of the Han dynasty **T'ang Hsien-tsu**: major dramatist who developed *ch'uan-ch'i* play into a literary form **Wu Ch'eng-en**: *Monkey*, a story based on journey of T'ang Buddhist monk named Hsüan Tsang or Tripitaka, who journeyed from China to India in search of Buddhist scriptures *Ssu-k'u ch'üan-shu*: a massive collection of all important earlier literature, completed in 1788
1500–present	**Evliya Çelebi**: *The Book of Travels*, a detailed, panoramic view of Ottoman Empire in mid-seventeenth century, when geographic extent was greatest and powerful; no comparable records for any other Islamic state
1800–1900	**Mrza Asadulla Khan Ghalib**: wrote ghazal lyric poems expressing aesthetic of Islamic culture in India **Michael Madhusudan Datta**: Indian Christian convert who published *Meghanadvadh*, Bengali version of *Ramayana*, an epic in blank verse **Bankim Chandra Chatterjee**: *Ananda Math*, an allegorical novel of resistance to colonial rule

LITERARY TIMELINE

Dates	Literary Period	Literary Elements of the Period
Japan		
1600–1900		**Puns and parodies** occupied popular literature. **Woodblock prints**, **short stories**, **novels**, **poetry**, and **plays** depicted city life: fast, varied, crowded, and competitive. **Impatience** of Japanese townspeople showed in their fiction. Playwrights, poets, and novelists captured **bourgeois life**: blunt, expansive, iconoclastic, and playful.
Australia, Europe, Eurasia, and South America		
1900–2000	Modern World Literature	New aura of modernist works **rejected traditional authority** and **represented the change in attitudes and artistic strategy** that occurred in Europe and America. Each literary work could be categorized as combined product of its **race**, **milieu**, and **time**. Literature interrogated modes of human consciousness and feeling, beyond limitations of previous rationalism. Many writers wrote in a **stream-of-consciousness style**. Sigmund Freud's idea that everyday, "rational" behavior is shaped by unconscious impulses influenced every writer thereafter. **Experimental language** in fiction and poetry reflected the influence of **psychoanalysis and symbolist** poetics of free associations. **Literature and linguistic systems were seen as games**: combinations of words and rules. Writers stressed the **game like nature of language**. **Existentialism**, the theater of the absurd, emerged in the post-World War II period. **Dadaism** represented disgust in traditional middle-class values blamed for World War I and a subversion of authority to liberate creative imagination. **Surrealism** buried connections and possible relationships overlooked by the logical mind, incorporating intensity, playfulness, and openness.

Dates	Major Writers and Works
1600–1900	**Ueda Akinari**: authored a collection of supernatural stories called *Tales of Moonlight and Rain*
	Matsuo Basho: haiku poet; wrote *The Narrow Road of the Interior*, a travel memoir written in verse
	Takeda Izumo II: playwright; wrote *The Treasury of Loyal Retainers*, a play immortalizing fealty of samurai who avenge their master's death
	Chikamatsu Monzaemon: wrote *The Love Suicides at Amijima*, tragedy of fatal love written for puppet theater
	Ihara Saikaku: comic realist who wrote popular fiction, including *The Life of a Sensuous Man*, and *The Barrelmaker Brimful of Love*, a novella introducing realistic literature and portraying bourgeois experience
1900–2000	**Guillaume Apollinaire**: French poet; first collection of poetry was *L'enchanteur pourrissant*, but *Alcools* formed reputation; credited with coining the word *surrealism* and with writing one of the earliest surrealist plays, *Les Mamelles de Tirésias*
	Thea Astley: Australian novelist, short-story writer; more infamous works include *The Well Dressed Explorer*, *The Slow Natives*, *The Acolyte*, and *Drylands*
	Pío Baroja: from the Basque region of Spain; works, including *La Raza* (*The Race*), *La Lucha por la Vida* (*The Struggle for Life*), and *Agonías de Nuestro Tiempo* (*Agonies of Our Time*) focused on dirty living conditions, prostitutes, criminals, and ignorance of mankind; most-read work, *El Arbol de la Ciencia* (*The Tree of Knowledge*), exposes shortcomings of medical field and poverty and filth in many poor villages in Spain
	Samuel Beckett: Irish writer, dramatist, and poet; most famous work is *Waiting for Godot*, an absurdist drama
	Jorge Luis Borges: one of Argentina's greatest literary figures; collection of short stories, *Ficciones*, is widely regarded as his best work; wrote of famous and not-so-famous in *The Universal History of Infamy*; other works include *Spain in My Heart*, *Twenty Love Poems and a Song of Despair*, and *The Garden of Forking Paths*
	Albert Camus: French existentialist whose works addressed the absurdity of man's existence and how man must make the most of his life; wrote *The Wrong Side and the Right Side*, *Nuptials*, *Caligula*, *The Stranger*, *The Myth of Sisyphus*, *The Plague*, and *The Rebel*
	Anton Chekhov: his tragedies made him one of the greatest dramatists of all time. *The Bear* and *The Wedding* are considered exemplars of comic sketches. His first success, *The Seagull*, was followed by *Uncle Vanya*, *The Three Sisters*, and *The Cherry Orchard*. →

LITERARY TIMELINE

Dates	Literary Period	Literary Elements of the Period
Australia, Europe, Eurasia, and South America		
1900–2000	Modern World Literature *(con't)*	**Futurism** expressed enthusiasm for the dynamic new machine age. Writers experimented with typography, free association, rapid shifts and breaks of syntax, manipulation of sounds and word placement, and harshness and stark vision; these experiments showed an eagerness to depict a new age.
		Some took a narrow view of modernism: those who favored clear, precise images and common speech, and who thought of work primarily as an art object produced by consummate craft. This group included James Joyce, Ezra Pound, T. S. Eliot, William Faulkner, and Virginia Woolf. These writers **disassembled to reconstruct**, played with **shifting and contradictory appearances** to suggest shifting and uncertain nature of reality. They **broke up logically developing plot lines**, **used interior monologues, free association**, and **image clusters**; **drew attention to style; blended fantasy with reality**; and **explored ancient non-Western literature in search of universal themes**. Modernist works assumed a rich and unified core to human experience.

Dates	Major Writers and Works
1900–2000	**Fyodor Dostoevsky**: Russian novelist; works include *Notes from the Underground*, *Crime and Punishment*, *The Idiot*, and *Brothers Karamazov*; used fiction to formulate some of the central predicaments our time: God versus atheism, good versus evil, freedom versus tyranny, and the recognition of limits versus the fall of humanity

Miles Franklin: Australian author and feminist, committed to the pursuit of an authentic and original Australian literature; *My Brilliant Career*, an autobiographical piece written at age sixteen, considered by many to be the first Australian novel; later work, titled *All That Swagger*, is set in World War I

Eugene Ionesco: Romanian playwright, considered one of the most significant writers in the theater of the absurd. In *The Rhinoceros*, Ionesco watches as his friends turn into rhinoceroses and submit to conformity.

Franz Kafka: novelist of German-Jew descent. His unique work, including *The Trial*, *The Castle*, and *Amerika*, concern profoundly troubled individuals living horrible and depressing lives in a cold industrial world. *The Metamorphosis* recounts the life of Gregor, a traveling salesman who wakens as a beetle, unable to right himself or communicate with the outside world.

Federico Garcia Lorca: Spanish poet, director, and playwright; wrote *El maleficio de la mariposa* in 1920, a verse play depicting the absurd love between a cockroach and a butterfly

Octavio Paz Lozano: a Mexican writer, poet, and diplomat; first collection was *Luna Silvestre*, but publication of the collection *Piedra de Sol* (*Sun Stone*) and *El Laberinto de la Soledad* (*The Labyrinth of Solitude*) established him as a major literary figure

Antonio Machado: Spanish poet; first famous collection of introspective modernist poems, *Soledades* (*Solitudes*), emphasized a cultish view of beauty that was soon abandoned for the more anguish-driven political message of *Campos de Castilla* (*Fields of Castile*)

Gabriel García Márquez: started as a journalist in Colombia; uses a style called "magical realism;" best-known novels are *One Hundred Years of Solitude* and *Love in the Time of Cholera*

Ana María Matute: Spanish author concerned with the aftermath of the Spanish Civil War, specifically in themes of loss of innocence, alienation, violence, and misery; major works include *Los Hijos Muertos* (*The Lost Children*), the trilogy *Los Mercaderes* (*The Merchants*), and *Olvidado Rey Gudú* (*Forgotten King Gudú*)

Vladimir Nabokov: Russian novelist noted for his fight against anti-Semitism; wrote his first novel, *Bend Sinister*, in English; novels *Lolita,* about a man's profound lust for a twelve-year-old girl; *Pnin*, and *Pale Fire* followed

Pablo Neruda (pen name of Chilean author Neftalí Ricardo Reyes Basoalto): most famous work is *Veinte Poemas de Amor y una Cancion* (*Twenty Love Poems and Songs of Despair*); another of his more famous collections, *Canto General*, includes a total of 340 poems ➡

LITERARY TIMELINE

Dates	Literary Period	Literary Elements of the Period
Australia, Europe, Eurasia, and South America		
1900–2000	Modern World Literature *(con't)*	**Futurism** expressed enthusiasm for the dynamic new machine age. Writers experimented with typography, free association, rapid shifts and breaks of syntax, manipulation of sounds and word placement, and harshness and stark vision; these experiments showed an eagerness to depict a new age.
		Some took a narrow view of modernism: those who favored clear, precise images and common speech, and who thought of work primarily as an art object produced by consummate craft. This group included James Joyce, Ezra Pound, T. S. Eliot, William Faulkner, and Virginia Woolf. These writers **disassembled to reconstruct**, played with **shifting and contradictory appearances** to suggest shifting and uncertain nature of reality. They **broke up logically developing plot lines**, **used interior monologues**, **free association**, and **image clusters**; **drew attention to style; blended fantasy with reality;** and **explored ancient non-Western literature in search of universal themes**. Modernist works assumed a rich and unified core to human experience.
		(Text repeated from pg. 216 for reader's convenience.)

Dates	Major Writers and Works
1900–2000	**Luigi Pirandello**: Sicilian author two of widely acclaimed plays: *Right You Are If You Think You Are* and *Six Characters in Search of an Author*

Marcel Proust: French novelist and critic who created the famed seven-part piece titled *À la recherche du temps perdu* (*Remembrance of Things Past*), in which time is seen as something in constant flux, a concept inspired by the work of Henri Bergson

Rainer Maria Rilke: one of Germany's greatest twentieth-century poets; wrote more than 400 poems in French, which he dedicated to Switzerland, his homeland of choice, but his most famous poetic works are *Sonnets to Orpheus* and the *Duino Elegies*. His two most famous prose works are the *Letters to a Young Poet* and the semiautobiographical *The Notebooks of Malte Laurids Brigge*.

Jean-Paul Sartre: French existentialist philosopher; his first novel, *La Nausée* (*Nausea*), and collection of stories, *Le Mur* (*The Wall and Other Stories*), brought him fame. His central philosophical work, *L'Etre et le néant* (*Being and Nothingness*), is a text that attempts to compartmentalize Sartre's concept of being. Best known as a playwright, Sartre wrote *Les Mouches* (*The Flies*) and *Huis Clos* (*No Exit*), which are loaded with symbolism in order to make clear his philosophical message.

Kenneth Slessor: Australian poet and journalist; poems include "Beach Burial," which is a tribute to Australian soldiers who served in World War II, and "Five Bells," a melancholy poem that confronts death with despair

Aleksandr Solzhenitsyn: Russian novelist, dramatist, and historian; wrote the multivolumed work *The Red Wheel*, an epic history of the events that led to the Russian Revolution

Leo Tolstoy: gave up his wealth to live life of a Russian peasant. *War and Peace*, his historical novel about the Napoleonic invasion of Russia in 1812, interprets history as struggle of anonymous collective forces moved by unknown irrational impulses and waves of communal feeling. *Anna Karenina* is a novel of contemporary manners, adultery, and suicide that ends with the promise of salvation.

Derek Walcott: born in Saint Lucia and a descendent of slaves. A theater and art critic, he wrote *25 Poems* but gained critical acclaim in 1962 for *In a Green Night*, a collection of plays. Other works include *Henri Christophe: A Chronicle*, *Dream on Monkey Mountain*, *The Fortunate Traveler*, and *Omeros*.

Judith Wright: one of the most widely read poets in Australia during the twentieth century. Some of her best-known collections of poetry include *The Moving Image*, *Woman to Man*, *The Gateway*, *The Two Fires*, *Birds: Poems*, and *The Other Half*.

Mikhail Zoshchenko: the foremost Russian satirist of the Soviet period. He developed a simplified deadpan style of writing, which simultaneously made him accessible to "the people" and mocked official demands for accessibility. →

LITERARY TIMELINE

Dates	Literary Period	Literary Elements of the Period
Australia, Europe, Eurasia, and South America		
1900–2000	Modern World Literature *(con't)*	**Futurism** expressed enthusiasm for the dynamic new machine age. Writers experimented with typography, free association, rapid shifts and breaks of syntax, manipulation of sounds and word placement, and harshness and stark vision; these experiments showed an eagerness to depict a new age.
		Some took a narrow view of modernism: those who favored clear, precise images and common speech, and who thought of work primarily as an art object produced by consummate craft. This group included James Joyce, Ezra Pound, T. S. Eliot, William Faulkner, and Virginia Woolf. These writers **disassembled to reconstruct**, played with **shifting and contradictory appearances** to suggest shifting and uncertain nature of reality. They **broke up logically developing plot lines**, **used interior monologues, free association**, and **image clusters**; **drew attention to style; blended fantasy with reality; and explored ancient non-Western literature in search of universal themes**. Modernist works assumed a rich and unified core to human experience.
		(Text repeated from pg. 218 for reader's convenience.)

Dates	Major Writers and Works
1900–2000	*Africa*

Africa

The modern literature of Africa is more well-known to Western readers than to readers in any other country. Many works were originally written in English, French, and Portuguese. Pervading African literature is the importance of **negritude**, or consciousness of black identity.

Chinua Achebe: Nigerian novelist; *Things Fall Apart* addresses the grave impact of colonization on a warrior hero who refuses to relinquish his traditional cultural beliefs and values. His novels *No Longer At Ease* and *Arrow of God* also address the profound difficulties Africans face when worlds collide, resulting in rapid cultural change.

Doris Lessing: a Zimbabwean-British writer, authored novels *The Grass is Singing* and *The Golden Notebook*. She wrote of the horror and savagery of apartheid and nuclear war.

Wole Soyinka: Nigerian writer of drama, poetry, and novels; founded the 1960 Masks and in 1964, the Orisun Theatre Company, where he performed his own plays. He wrote *The Swamp Dwellers* and *The Lion and the Jewel*, *The Strong Breed*, *The Road*, and *Death and the King's Horseman*.

Ngũgĩ wa Thiong'o: Kenyan author and founder and editor of the Gikuyu-language journal, *Mutiiri*; well-known for his novel *Weep Not, Child* due to the text's prominence as the first major novel in English by an East African. Ngũgĩ was imprisoned for the strong political message of one play, "I Will Marry When I Want." In 1980, Ngũgĩ published the first modern novel written in Gikuyu, called *Caitaani muthara-Ini* (*Devil on the Cross*).

China

China privileged the nation, not the individual, and government established conservatism in writing. Chinese travelers who went abroad adapted literary models and made changes in the use of vernacular. Contemporary Chinese writers strived to develop literature both in modern language and Chinese.

Lao She: skillful in utilizing the Peking dialect. *Camel Xiangzi* and the drama *Tea House* are his masterpieces, which reflect the helplessness of the lower classes in old China. Among Lao She's most famous stories is "Crescent Moon," which depicts the miserable life of a mother and daughter and their deterioration into prostitution. Other important works include *Si Shi Tong Tang* (abridged translation titled *The Yellow Storm*, directly translated into *Four Generations under One Roof*) and *Cat Country*, a satire sometimes seen as the first important Chinese science fiction novel.

Bing Xin: known for her *morbidezza* style of writing, so called as she wrote as though painting a picture with the finest and most tender detail. Among her prose works, *An Orange-peel Lamp*, *We Have No Winter*, and *Cherry Blossoms and Friendship* are pieces that maintain her usual fresh and beautiful artistic style but replace misty and melancholy sentiments with a bright and optimistic tone. She is best remembered for her *Ji xiao duzhe* (*To Young Readers*). →

LITERARY TIMELINE

Dates	Literary Period	Literary Elements of the Period
Australia, Europe, Eurasia, and South America		
1900–2000	Modern World Literature *(con't)*	**Futurism** expressed enthusiasm for the dynamic new machine age. Writers experimented with typography, free association, rapid shifts and breaks of syntax, manipulation of sounds and word placement, and harshness and stark vision; these experiments showed an eagerness to depict a new age.
		Some took a narrow view of modernism: those who favored clear, precise images and common speech, and who thought of work primarily as an art object produced by consummate craft. This group included James Joyce, Ezra Pound, T. S. Eliot, William Faulkner, and Virginia Woolf. These writers **disassembled to reconstruct**, played with **shifting and contradictory appearances** to suggest shifting and uncertain nature of reality. They **broke up logically developing plot lines**, **used interior monologues**, **free association**, and **image clusters**; **drew attention to style**; **blended fantasy with reality**; and **explored ancient non-Western literature in search of universal themes**. Modernist works assumed a rich and unified core to human experience.
		(Text repeated from pg. 218 for reader's convenience.)

Dates	Major Writers and Works
1900–2000	**Lu Xun**: the father of modern Chinese literature; his first story, "A Madman's Diary," is considered the first story written in Modern Chinese. His first set of stories was published as the book *Call to Arms* or *Na Han*. He also published *Wild Grass*, a collection of prose poems depicting a work of dreams, including nightmares: dogs speak, insects buzz, and the sky tries to hide itself from onlookers. **Lin Yutang**: essayist and novelist; nominated for the Nobel Prize in Literature for his novel *Moment in Peking*. At the behest of Pearl Buck, he wrote *My Country and My People* and *The Importance of Living*. **Xu Zhimo**: Chinese lyric poet who promoted modern Chinese poetry. His poetry consistently romanticized love, freedom, and beauty, although the forms through which he expressed these ideas varied greatly. *India* India's writing reflected the tension between "Indianness" and "Westernness," portraying the tensions between Western imperialism and an emerging national identity. **Mohandas K. Gandhi**: major political and spiritual leader of India; regarded as one of the major leaders of the Indian independence movement. He was also a prolific writer and his autobiography, *My Experiments with Truth*, written in the Gujarati language, is a classic text. **Amitav Ghosh**: Indian-born novelist who grew up in Bangladesh, Sri Lanka, Iran, and India; wrote *In an Antique Land*; published his first novel, *The Circle of Reason*, and his second, *The Shadow Lines*, and has since worked on journalistic endeavors **Qurrat-ul-Ain Haider**: novelist and short-story writer; wrote a total of twelve novels, four collections of short stories, and translated many classic texts. Her magnum opus, titled *Aag Ka Darya* (*Ring of Fire*), tells a story that spans from the fourth century BC to the postindependence period of India and Pakistan. **R. K. Narayan**, or Rasipuram Krishnaswami Ayyar Narayanaswami: one of the best-known Indian novelists to English-speaking audiences. His first novel, *Swami and Friends*, set the tone for his other well-known works, *The English Teacher*, *The Vendor of Sweets*, and *Under the Banyan Tree*. **Sir Ahmed Salman Rushdie**: a British Indian novelist and essayist; see listing under twentieth-century writers and works of Great Britain. **Rabindranath Tagore**: a Bengali poet and Brahmo philosopher who also delved into the realms of visual art, mysticism, and music. He is most well-known for his poetry, although after his poetry his short stories are also very popular. Popular works include *Gitanjali*, *Saddhana*, *The Realisation of Life*, *The Crescent Moon*, *Fruit-Gathering*, *Stray Birds*, *The Home and the World*, and *Thought Relics*. →

LITERARY TIMELINE

Dates	Literary Period	Literary Elements of the Period
Australia, Europe, Eurasia, and South America		
1900–2000	Modern World Literature *(con't)*	**Futurism** expressed enthusiasm for the dynamic new machine age. Writers experimented with typography, free association, rapid shifts and breaks of syntax, manipulation of sounds and word placement, and harshness and stark vision; these experiments showed an eagerness to depict a new age. **Some took a narrow view of modernism**: those who favored clear, precise images and common speech, and who thought of work primarily as an art object produced by consummate craft. This group included James Joyce, Ezra Pound, T. S. Eliot, William Faulkner, and Virginia Woolf. These writers **disassembled to reconstruct**, played with **shifting and contradictory appearances** to suggest shifting and uncertain nature of reality. They **broke up logically developing plot lines**, **used interior monologues**, **free association**, and **image clusters**; **drew attention to style; blended fantasy with reality**; and **explored ancient non-Western literature in search of universal themes**. Modernist works assumed a rich and unified core to human experience. *(Text repeated from pg. 218 for reader's convenience.)*

Dates	Major Writers and Works
1900–2000	**Nirmal Verma**: Hindi novelist and activist who helped to bring about the *Nayi Kahani* ("new short story") literary movement of Hindi literature; his best-known short story, "Parinde" ("Birds"), is supposed to be the exemplar of the *Nayi Kahani* movement; Verma also wrote other notable stories such as *Ve Din*, *Lal Teen Ki Chhat* (*Red Tin Roof*), and *Kavve Aur Kala Pani*. *Japan* Modernism in non-Western cultures assumed similarities and differences to the modernism of the West. Japanese authors attempted to reinvent themselves as equal to Western countries by undertaking tortuous process of cultural absorption and transformation. Curiosity about the world and traditional receptivity to foreign ways transfigured the fabric of Japanese life. Modernism had more in common with realism and served as a literary compass for situating the confusion of identity, self-interest, and "belonging" within cultural ambiguity. **Oe Kenzaburo**: Japan's second Nobel Prize recipient for literature used his experience of growing up with a brain-damaged father to write two of his works, *Kojinteki na Taiken* (*A Personal Matter*) and *Manen Gannen no Futtoboru* (*The Silent Cry*). *Makoto Ôoka*: invented *renshi* (a type of linked poetry) in 1981; collaborate with the American poet Thomas Fitzsimmons on the first international *renshi*, which differs from *renga* and *renku* in that it is written is contemporary free verse instead of linked stanzas. **Kawabata Yasunari**: awarded the Nobel Prize for Literature in 1968; wrote *Tade-kuu Mushi* (*Some Prefer Nettles*), in which he uses the cities of Tokyo and Osaka as symbols of the conflict between modern and traditional thought in his country. **Banana Yoshimoto** (given name is Yoshimoko Mahoto): contemporary Japanese author; first popular story was a novella titled *Kitchen*, a coming-of-age tale which deals with the topics of loneliness, death, and a girl who loves kitchens. **Mishima Yukio**: homosexual writer who proudly professed his love for the human body; had a strong appreciation for physical decline as well. His first major work, *Kamen no Kokuhaku* (*Confessions of a Mask*), and his last novel, *Hojo no Umi* (*The Sea of Fertility*), highlighted these ideas. His *Kinkakuji* (*The Temple of the Golden Pavilion*) echoes his anti-westernization sentiments; in the story, a monk burns down the Kyoto pavilion in order to avoid seeing the United States gain control of it. *The Middle East* The Middle East saw the introduction of the novel. The modern short story also emerged in Middle Eastern writing. Some Middle Eastern writers accepted Western modernity, while others regarded this as a radical transformation of society and near annihilation of culture. This tension became the subject of a series of novels and short stories. $\longrightarrow$

LITERARY TIMELINE

Dates	Literary Period	Literary Elements of the Period
Australia, Europe, Eurasia, and South America		
1900–2000	Modern World Literature *(con't)*	**Futurism** expressed enthusiasm for the dynamic new machine age. Writers experimented with typography, free association, rapid shifts and breaks of syntax, manipulation of sounds and word placement, and harshness and stark vision; these experiments showed an eagerness to depict a new age.
		Some took a narrow view of modernism: those who favored clear, precise images and common speech, and who thought of work primarily as an art object produced by consummate craft. This group included James Joyce, Ezra Pound, T. S. Eliot, William Faulkner, and Virginia Woolf. These writers **disassembled to reconstruct**, played with **shifting and contradictory appearances** to suggest shifting and uncertain nature of reality. They **broke up logically developing plot lines**, **used interior monologues**, **free association**, and **image clusters**; **drew attention to style**; **blended fantasy with reality**; and **explored ancient non-Western literature in search of universal themes**. Modernist works assumed a rich and unified core to human experience.
		(Text repeated from pg. 218 for reader's convenience.)

Dates	Major Writers and Works
1900–2000	**Yehuda Amichai**: Israeli poet who wrote about everyday people, life, love, loss, aging, and mortality. His first book of poetry, *Now and in Other Days*, was criticized by Israeli writers because of its colloquial language but eventually became widely read and accepted. Some of his other notable works include *Collected Poems*, *Selected Works*, *Shirei Yerushalayim* (*Poems of Jerusalem*), and *Two Hopes Away*.
	Naguib Mahfouz: award-winning Egyptian novelist who was one of the first Egyptians to explore existentialism in his work. His Cairo Trilogy, *Bayn al Qasrayn* (*Between-the-Palaces*), *Qasr al Shawq* (*Palace of Longing*), and *Sukkariya* (*Sugarhouse*), made him famous for the way in which he depicts urban life in the Arab world. In contrast, his novel *The Children of Gebelawi* is filled with symbolism in order to conceal his political statements.
	Amos Oz: uses the turbulent history of Jerusalem in his writing to present the tribulations and stories of the people of Israel. His most famous works include *A Tale of Love and Darkness*, *A Perfect Peace*, and *To Know a Woman*.
	Orhan Pamuk: an important contemporary Turkish novelist, often the only one widely known to most Western readers. One of his well-known early novels is *Beyaz Kale* (*White Castle*), a mystery story set in the early Renaissance. His most recent novels include *Benim Adım Kırmızı* (*My Name Is Red*) and *Kar* (*Snow*).
	Marjane Satrapi: an accomplished Iranian and French graphic novelist, illustrator, animated film director, and children's book author. Her works include the award-winning graphic novels *Persepolis I* and *Persepolis II* as well as several other books for children and adults: *Embroideries*, *Chicken with Plums*, and *Monsters Are Afraid of the Moon* in English, and *Sagesses et malices de la Perse*, *Ulysse au pays des fous*, and *Le Soupir* in French.
	Abraham B. Yehoshua: an internationally known Israeli author; works include novels, short stories, plays, and essays. *Five Seasons*, published in 2007, is regarded as one of the most important books written since the creation of the state of Israel.

References

Adventures in American Literature. New York: Harcourt, Brace & World, 1970.

Adventures in English Literature. New York: Harcourt, Brace & World, 1970.

Adventures in Modern Literature, New York: Harcourt, Brace & World, 1970.

Adventures in World Literature. New York: Harcourt, Brace & World, 1970.

Appleman, Deborah. Critical Encounters in High School English. New York: Teachers College Press, 2000.

Cook, James Wyatt. *Encyclopedia of Ancient Literature*. New York: Facts On File, 2008.

Coyle, Martin, and John Peck. *A Brief History of English Literature*. New York: Palgrave, 2002.

Eagleton, Terry. *Literary Theory: An Introduction*. 2nd ed. Minneapolis, MN: University of Minnesota Press, 1996.

Habib, M. A. R. *Modern Literary Criticism and Theory, A History*. Malden, MA: Blackwell, 2008.

Karolides, Nicholas J., and Duane Roen. "Louise Rosenblatt: A Life in Literacy." *ALAN Review* (2005). 31 January 2009 <http://findarticles.com/p/articles/mi_qa4063/is_200507/ai_n14716674>.

Katamba, Francis. "English Morphology." *The Higher Education Academy* (2002). 6 February 2009 <http://www.llas.ac.uk/resources/gpg/209>.

Keesey, Donald. *Contexts for Criticism*, 3rd ed. London: Mayfield, 1998.

Lawall, Sarah, and Mack Maynard. *The Norton Anthology of World Literature: The Twentieth Century*. New York: W.W. Norton & Company, 2002.

Literature: Bronze. New York: Prentice Hall, 1994.

Literature: Copper. New York: Prentice Hall, 1994.

Literature: Gold. New York: Prentice Hall, 1994.

Literature: Platinum. New York: Prentice Hall, 1994.

Literature: Silver. New York: Prentice Hall, 1994.

Literature: The American Experience. New York: Prentice Hall, 1994.

Literature: The British Tradition. New York: Prentice Hall, 1994.

Literature: World Masterpieces. New York: Prentice Hall, 1994.

Maynard, Mack. *The Norton Anthology of World Masterpieces*. New York: W.W. Norton & Company, 1997.

Roberts, Edgar V., and Henry E. Jacobs. *Literature: An Introduction to Reading and Writing*, 5th ed. New York: Prentice-Hall.

Web Sites

About.com. 2009. Classic Literature. The New York Times Company. 6 February 2009 <http://classiclit.about.com/library/bl-etexts/wmbaskervill/bl-wmbaskervill-grammar-syntax-intro.htm>.

Buzzin. 2004. Knowsley LEA. 6 February 2009 <http://www.buzzin.net/english/syntax.htm>.

http://www.achievement.org/autodoc/page/mom0pro-1

Dr. Fidel Fajardo-Acosta. March 7, 2005. Creighton University. 6 February 2009 <http://mockingbird.creighton.edu/english/fajardo/teaching/eng520/phonology.htm>.

EnglishClub.com. 2009. English Club. 6 February 2009 <http://www.englishclub.com/english-language-history.htm>.

Humanistic Texts. 2007. Rex Pay. 6 February 2009 <http://www.humanistictexts.org/LiPo.htm>.

Isle of Lesbos. 1995–2007. Alix North. 1 February 2009 <http://www.sappho.com/poetry/sappho.html>.

Kazoom Poetry. 2007. 8 January 2009 http://members.optushome.com.au/kazoom/poetry/concrete.html.

Li Po. 6 February 2009 <http://homepage.uab.edu/yangzw/libai1.html>.

The Norton Anthology World Literature. 2003–2009. W.W. Norton & Company. 31 January 2009 <http://www.wwnorton.com/college/english/nawol/s1_overview.htm#1>.

Nova Online. 2008. 3 November 2008 <http://novaonline.nv.cc.va.us/eli/spd130et/melodrama.html>.

"The Origin and History of the English Language." *Krysstal.com*. 2002. 6 February 2009 <http://www.krysstal.com/english.html>.

Plato. 9 August 2006. Garth Kemerling. 1 February 2009 <http://www.philosophypages.com/ph/plat.htm>.

Traugott, Elizabeth Closs, and Richard B. Dasher. *Regularity in Semantic Change*. Cambridge, England: University Press. 2002. 3 February 2009 <http://www.ask.com/bar?q=semantics+amelioration&page=1&qsrc=2106&ab=2&u=http%3A%2F%2Fwww.uni-duisburg-essen.de%2FSHE%2FHE_Change_Semantic.html>.

University of Minnesota Biographies. 2 February 2009 <http://voices.cla.umn.edu/vg/Bios/entries/erdrich_louise.html>.

University of Waterloo. 2005. 11 December 2008 <http://www.drama.uwaterloo.ca/Genre-2005.ppt>.

Who2?. "Dorothy Parker Biography." 2009. 3 Februrary 2009. <http://who2.com/ask/dorothyparker.html>.

CHAPTER 3

Rhetoric and Composition

Chapter 3, "Rhetoric and Composition," first summarizes the development of rhetoric from a classical art of persuasive oratory to a modern discipline concerned with the analysis and interpretation of spoken, written, and media communications. Next, similarities and differences between language structures in spoken and written English are identified. Then, ways of interpreting and applying English grammar and language conventions in oral and written contexts are explored. Next, the role of cultural factors in oral and written communication is identified. The next section of the chapter identifies written language conventions. Finally, current approaches to the composition process are discussed as well as useful ways to evaluate written work.

THE HISTORY AND DEVELOPMENT OF RHETORIC

Simply stated, rhetoric is the art of using language or discourse. Discourse is written and spoken language, used to convey meaning. Richard Young, Alton L. Becker, and Kenneth L. Pike suggest that the word *rhetoric* derives from Greek *eiro*: "I say." The history of rhetoric in Western tradition begins with the ancient, highly inventive societies. Essentially citizens used rhetoric to plead their cases in court. Although the Sophists were the first teachers of rhetoric, Plato, Isocrates, Artistotle, Cicero, Quintillian, and St. Augustine of Hippo are credited with developing modern rhetoric.

Plato (ca. 428–ca. 348 BC)

Plato loathed false rhetoric and was a harsh critic of the Sophists. A protégé of Socrates, Plato developed philosophical rhetoric for interrogating the truth (*Phaedrus*).

The intent of Plato's oratory was to influence humankind's soul, which assumed that he knew the kinds of souls humankind possessed. Given the depths to which humankind's souls have plunged, Plato would indeed have much work to do to influence contemporary souls.

Isocrates (436–338 BC)

Isocrates founded the first school of rhetoric in Athens. Unlike his contemporary, Plato, Isocrates used rhetoric to probe practical problems. He was most interested in the kind of discourse that would defend causes that were good and honorable.

Aristotle (384–322 BC)

Plato's student Aristotle developed a complete theory of rhetoric called *The Rhetoric*. Aristotle developed principles of argumentation, which are still used today.

Cicero (106–43 BC)

Cicero was probably the most influential member of the Roman senate. He used rhetoric to persuade and convince. In his work *De Oratore*, he identified the qualities of the ideal orator. Cicero believed that a specific style of oratory corresponded to a particular purpose. Proving required plain and simple language. Pleasing required a language of charm. Persuading required vigorous and rigorous language.

Quintilian (ca .35–ca. 100)

Quintilian, also a famous Roman rhetorician, devoted his life to creating volumes of ancient rhetorical theory (*Insitutio Oratoria*). He believed that good orators had to be good men or they would not be able to speak eloquently. Like Plato, he would be disheartened to know that history has seen marvelous orators whose goodness and character are suspect.

St. Augustine of Hippo (354–430)

A lawyer and teacher, St. Augustine of Hippo used rhetoric to evangelize. He believed that eloquent rhetoric converted pagans to Christianity more effectively than simple rhetoric. In his fourth book of *On Christian Doctrine*, he justifies his use of rhetoric to spread Christianity.

Section 1.01   Classical Rhetoric

Classical rhetoric is divided into three branches: deliberative, judicial, and epideictic. The purpose of **deliberative rhetoric** is to convince, persuade, or dissuade, as demonstrated in Patrick Henry's speech before the Virginia House of Burgesses. The purpose of **judicial rhetoric** is to accuse, defend, or exonerate. As surmised, this kind of rhetoric is employed in courtrooms. Harper Lee incorporates this type of rhetoric in *To Kill a Mockingbird* when Atticus presents his closing remarks about the innocence of Tom Robinson in the rape of Mayella Ewell. Marc Antony's spoken soliloquy in *Julius Caesar* is an excellent example of **epideictic rhetoric**, whose purpose is to celebrate, commend, or commemorate his slain mentor, Julius Caesar.

Cicero defined five overlapping divisions or canons of the rhetorical process:

Inventio (Greek, *heuristics*), invention: discovery of valid arguments to support the thesis

Dispositio (Greek, *taxis*), arrangement: five parts of the oration, which include

exordium or introduction to position or thesis in which the speaker or writer establishes credibility and the argument's purpose

narratio or narrative in which the speaker or writer establishes the sequential account of events

confirmation or main part in which the speaker or writer presents the arguments in support of the position or thesis

refutation or counterargument in which the speaker or writer anticipates possible opposing arguments and presents counterarguments

peroration or closing in which the speaker or writer summarizes the arguments and appeals to the audience's pathos

Elocutio (Greek, *lexis*), style: the manner in which a speech or argument is spoken or written. Style includes all figures of speech.

Memoria (Greek, *mneme*), memory: "the practice of storing up common-places or other material arrived at through the topics of invention for use as called for in a given occasion" (*Silva Rhetoricae* http://rhetoric.byu.edu/canons/Memory.htm).

Actio (Greek, *hypocrisis*), delivery: the performance or delivery of the speech

Even before these orators, however, three functions of language were identified in the writing of Homer: *heuristic, eristic,* and *protreptic.* The *heuristic* function of discourse is to invent, learn, or discover. The *eristic* function of discourse is to use language as a device of power to charm, offend, anger, engage, captivate, and so on. The *protreptic* function of discourse is to use words to persuade others to act differently or to act as we wish them to act.

MODERN RHETORIC

Although modern rhetoric still employs all the rhetorical devices of classical rhetoric, modern rhetoric has shifted from the speaker to the author and to the audience. Everyday language and communication in its variety of uses comprises rhetoric. In thinking about rhetoric, it is useful to think about the context of rhetoric, or more specifically to assume a rhetorical stance. Context, which includes purpose, audience, subject, and medium, provides the framework for a rhetorical stance.

Audience includes the listener(s) or reader(s). A writer or speaker varies the type of discourse according to the audience. A student explicating a thesis of a literary text to a professor will (hopefully) use academic discourse, that is, rhetoric that follows formal language conventions, employs the appropriate use of literary devices and figurative language, incorporates effective organization, and addresses the principles of unity of thought, coherence, proportion, and emphasis. A student participating in a debate in front of peers may have three audiences: the opposing side, the judge, and the gallery. A skilled debater then must earn points by addressing all three audiences in ways that support a logical, clear, and coherent argument defended in an effective, persuasive, and even expressive manner. A student text messaging a friend will utilize a minimalist form of rhetoric replete with its own codes, abbreviations, and language. In considering audience, a good writer or speaker asks, Who is the reader or listener? What does the reader or listener know about the subject or topic? How receptive is the reader or listener to what I have to say? What is the reader or listener's bias? How can I help my reader or listener understand what I have to say?

Purpose: James Kinneavy identifies four purposes of discourse within the realm of communication: expression, persuasion, reference, and literary. These purposes are not mutually exclusive and are often combined in a piece of writing but in a careful and deliberate manner:

Expressive discourse serves the speaker/writer's goal of self-expression. Such discourse in speech includes conversations, protests, complaints, prayers, and so on. Such discourse in writing includes diaries, myths, journals, creeds, declarations, contracts, and so on.

Persuasive discourse serves the speaker/writer's goal of persuading or convincing the listener(s)/reader(s). Such discourse in speech includes oratory, debate, political speeches, advertising, homilies, propaganda, marriage proposals, attorney's arguments, and so on. In writing, persuasive discourse appears in editorials, written appeals, grant writing, and the like.

Referential discourse can be exploratory, scientific, or informative. The goal of this type of discourse is to depict the subject matter as clearly, authentically, and realistically as possible.

Exploratory discourse in speech includes interviews, dialogues, seminars, panel discussions, diagnoses, text messages, emails, and so forth. Written examples would include questionnaires and medical histories, among others.

Scientific discourse in speech or writing would include literary criticism, descriptive analysis, history, taxonomy, and the like.

Informative discourse in speech could include news broadcasts, infomercials, weather reports, stock market panels, and financial reports on television programs such as *Fast Money*, Jim Cramer's *Mad Money*, and *The Kudlow Report*. Written informative discourse includes summaries, articles, essays, textbooks, and Web sites.

Literary discourse serves the speaker/writer's goal of entertaining or providing pleasure in some way. Such discourse in speech would include comedy routines, television shows, films, plays, poetry reading, songs, jingles, jokes, puns, and so forth. In writing, examples include the various genres of literature. In considering purpose, a good writer or speaker asks, What is my objective, aim, or goal? What is the purpose of my discourse: to explain, persuade, describe, probe, entertain, illustrate, express, discover, learn? How do I want my audience to respond? Do I want them to laugh, take action, agree, disagree, learn?

Subject is the topic or focus of the spoken or written word. The topic also determines or influences the type of discourse. Writing about a controversial subject such as euthanasia requires a different type of rhetoric than writing about a day at the beach. Even within a very specific type of discourse, for example, persuasive discourse, language conventions will differ according to subject. Proposing a new law and proposing marriage should require different conventions, vocabulary, and grammar (although the language in a prenuptial agreement might indeed be similar to that in a piece of legislation). In considering subject a good writer or speaker asks, What content best serves my purpose? What thesis will I offer? What is my point, message, idea, belief?

Medium is the method or form of delivery, which can range from a campaign speech, academic paper, poem, commercial, or letter, to email or a Web site. In today's world, rhetoric is critical to effective communication but is often perceived negatively as in the term "empty rhetoric," or propaganda. Yet both are forms of rhetoric. By today's standards, the medium is the message, which requires writers, readers, speakers, and listeners to attend not only to the text but also to the visuals that accompany the text. The appeal of a Web page, textbook, billboard, commercial, trailer, poster, or press conference is as much about visual images as it is about text. Music and special effects may enhance the rhetoric but may also detract from the message. Modern rhetoric, replete with bells and whistles, demands a discerning audience and a skilled rhetor.

Section 1.02   Unity, Coherence, and Emphasis

Critical to effective modern rhetoric are three principles: the three unities, coherence, and proportion and emphasis. The three unities that must be incorporated to render rhetoric effective are unity of thought, unity of feeling, and unity of purpose.

> **Unity of thought:** all ideas, arguments, details, and rhetoric must support one main or central idea or thesis in speech and in writing.

> **Unity of feeling**: manipulating emotions in various ways must work to produce the desired mood or feeling.

> **Unity of purpose**: all spoken or written discourse must enable the purpose, to inform, convince, influence, enlighten, and so on.

Of additional importance is the **principle of coherence**. All ideas in speech or composition (writing) must connect and relate logically to each other and to the central idea to create a coherent and consistent whole. Finally, speakers and writers must adhere to the principles of proportion and emphasis. Speakers and writers must observe the **principle of proportion** to assure that the appropriate amount of text or space should be allotted to each part of the whole; an imbalance negatively impacts the symmetry of the work. The **principle of emphasis** asserts that significant and important ideas must appear in prominent positions, at the beginning or at the end, as these are parts of the speech and composition that the listener or reader is likely to remember.

Section 1.03   Ethos, Pathos, and Logos

Aristotle believed that argument or persuasive rhetoric must address ethos, pathos, and logos (Ramage and Bean 81-82). These appeals are still important in both modern spoken and written rhetoric. **Ethos** relates to the ethical appeal of the speaker or author. The speaker or author must appear as credible, worthy of respect and attention, expert, knowledgeable, and likeable. **Pathos** relates to the emotional appeal of the speech or writing. The speaker or author must elicit sympathies, suspend disbelief, stimulate the imagination, and move the listener or reader to assume a point of view or take action. **Logos** relates to the logical appeal of the speech or writing. The speaker or author must clearly establish the major argument, supporting it with substantial evidence in an organized and logical manner.

Section 1.04   Similarities and Differences between Language
Structures in Spoken and Written English

(a)   Spoken Language

Spoken language is like thinking aloud. The speaker must make sure that the listener knows what, where, and to whom an utterance refers (deictics). This requires an unambiguous use of pronouns such as *it*, *this*, and *that*. Spoken language can capitalize on affect to enhance appeal to pathos; a speaker can show a specific emotion of excitement through gestures at the same time using words that relate the same emotion. Affect is used to appeal to logos as well; a speaker may show one finger to correspond to text: "The first point of my argument is . . ." Spoken language makes use of pauses, repetitions, and fillers. Spoken language allows the speaker to establish a relationship with the audience through gestures, facial expressions, and emotion. Irony, ambiguity, statement, implication, emphasis, questioning, imperatives, and exclamation in spoken language are also aided by a speaker's affect. Thus, speaking relies on the immediate and present context, in which talk occurs. Speech in everyday contexts is socially constructed and contributes significantly to enhancing social

MTEL Tip

The relationship between a speaker and her audience is critical.

relationships of all types. Thus, the relationship between speaker and audience is critical. Individual speakers can make different lexical choices in speech depending on the context and purpose of talk. There is an underlying grammar in spoken language, but a speaker may make more use of disjointed forms, phrases, fragments, and clauses. Speaking also requires pragmatic competence, being able to differentiate between questions, statements, and commands by using inflection, intonation, pitch, and stress. This competence enables coding, or the speaker's ability to "convey a persona and an attitude towards an audience" (Kantor and Rubin 59). Motivational speakers will employ a different lexicon than a newscaster. **Prosody** (pitch, stress, rhythm, and intonation), a suprasegmental feature of speech that allows a sound to be extended over several sounds, is not easily demonstrated in written language but allows a speaker to switch codes given the context, purpose, and audience.

(b)   Written Language

Like spoken language, written language must make sure that the reader knows what, where, and to whom language refers (deictics). This is accomplished through establishing voice and point of view. Writing also requires an unambiguous use of pronouns such as *it*, *this*, and *that*. While speakers have the advantage of an immediate context, writers must develop the context using figurative language, literary devices, and vivid imagery to appeal to pathos. Written language follows a specific organization depending on the purpose, audience, subject, and medium. This organization may involve the use of transitions, topic and clincher sentences, and other language conventions to signal logic and flow. A writer, unable to use gestures and facial expressions, must make use of myriad rhetorical devices to appeal to pathos. Writers must develop irony and ambiguity through the use of explicit devices and figurative language. Writers use punctuation, italics, boldface type, font, ellipses, and other elements to indicate statement, emphasis, questioning, imperative, and exclamation. Like speakers, writers can make different lexical choices in speech depending on the context of the writing. A journalist will employ a different lexicon than a poet. There is a specific grammar in written language, which depends on the type of discourse, subject, purpose, medium, and audience.

THE ROLE OF CULTURAL FACTORS IN ORAL AND WRITTEN COMMUNICATION

Many theorists have developed hypotheses about second-language acquisition. S. Krashen posits two theories about how children develop oral and written communication: learning and acquisition. Learning language implies that the writer and speaker are conscious of learning a language, its rules, structures, and conventions. This kind of language development occurs in school. Acquisition implies that language learning is subconscious and natural and occurs in and out of school in a variety of contexts.

Subsumed under these views are hypotheses that suggest that there is a natural order to learning language, with certain aspects of language development appearing before others. Second-language development also follows a natural order. For example, learners of English as a second language understand the formation of plural forms designated by *s* before they learn the presence of *s* in the singular verb form in subject-verb agreement. Researchers suggest that the natural order of learning rarely parallels the order in which language is taught.

It is also suggested that speakers and writers use language rules, structures, and conventions to check if what they are saying or writing is correct. Monitoring spoken language is much more difficult than monitoring written language, because spoken language is more spontaneous, and monitoring often impacts fluency of ideas and language flow.

Another hypothesis suggests that there are affective variables that impact language learning. Variables such as an English language learner's accent, nervousness, fear of sounding incomprehensible or making a mistake, and anxiety are just a few of the variables that prevent second-language learners from using the language acquisition device (see chapter 4.).

Other research suggests that language learners not only need to hear and read language in a variety of contexts reflecting a variety of purposes, or more specifically receive language input, but also must speak and write language in a variety of contexts for a variety of purposes, more specifically language output.

J. Schumann explored specific cultural factors that may inhibit second-language acquisition. He posits that social distance or the capacity for second-language learners to integrate into the dominant culture may impede language learning. For example, if there is a large enough number of immigrants situated in one area, there is more opportunity for that culture to become self-sufficient and closed, requiring less need to integrate into mainstream culture, where opportunities to learn the second language are more plentiful. Thus, there is a larger social distance between the second-language learner and the second language. Other factors that impact social distance are culture shock, attitude, and motivation. Research also confirms that we all possess a language ego, as our language is critical to our identity. Learning a new language can be intimidating, impacting our language ego in a negative way, deterring us from learning a new language. Another variable that influences second language learning is fossilization. Fossilization is the persistence of particular errors in speech and writing of second language learners. For example, a native language may not use articles in its written and spoken forms. Although the second language learner may have developed significant written and spoken output in the second language to communicate intended ideas, the lack of article usage may still remain. In essence, these language errors become fossilized.

WHAT DO GOOD WRITERS AND SPEAKERS DO? WHAT IS GOOD WRITING AND SPEAKING?

Good writers and speakers take risks by posing innovative and original theses, sharing unusual or engaging ideas, or playing with words. Good writers and speakers put themselves on the line, presenting arguments; narrating stories; and describing events that take a stand, demonstrate point of view, and exhibit powerful voice. Good writers and speakers explore questions and probe ideas that engage, interest, and motivate themselves. Good writers and speaker have strong purpose and consider audience carefully. Good writers and speakers play with language, building powerful vocabularies, and manipulate words and language.

MTEL Tip

Good writing incorporates details to paint a picture.

Good writing focuses on specificity incorporating details that create pictures or develop the bigger issue. Good writing includes characters that are highly detailed "right down to the color of his socks, her earrings" (Fletcher A Writer's Notebook: Unlocking the Writer in You, 58). Good writing demonstrates a distinctive voice and personality, develops argument, mounts suspense, builds conflict, creates imagery using multiple literary and rhetorical devices and effective diction, and intersects characters, plot, and setting with balance, finesse, and competence. Good writing leaves a lasting impression on the reader/audience, accomplishing its established purpose.

THE COMPOSING OR WRITING PROCESS

The National Council of Teachers of English identifies writing as a recursive process, a process that emphasizes prewriting, drafting, revision, peer editing, self-editing, and publishing.

Prewriting: The composing process actually begins as soon as the writer or speaker assumes a rhetorical stance. This is a critical part of prewriting because the writer has identified the purpose, considered the audience, focused on the subject, and selected the medium. Any activity that the writer does before writing the first draft is prewriting. Prewriting includes thinking, brainstorming, jotting notes, talking with others, interviewing experts, researching in the library or online, gathering and assessing information, listing, mapping, charting, webbing, outlining, and organizing information. Rereading, marking up, and annotating a text that is the focus of analysis is prewriting. Reading and noting what experts write about a topic is prewriting. Reading poetry before writing poetry is prewriting. Reading memoirs prior to writing a memoir is prewriting. Ralph Fletcher suggests keeping a writer's notebook to store ideas, notes, phrases, annotations, events, descriptions, quotations, and other fodder for writing. "A writer's notebook gives you a place to live like a writer, not just in school during writing time, but wherever you are, at any time of the day" (A Writer's Notebook 3).

Drafting involves committing ideas on paper. This is the point when ideas become phrases, phrases become sentences, sentences become paragraphs, and paragraphs become essays. During the drafting process, writers concentrate on articulating a clear thesis statement and explaining and developing ideas fully, thoughtfully, and thoroughly. During this part of the process, the writer seeks unity, coherence, and emphasis. During this part of the process, the writer makes connections within and among the parts of the draft. During this part of the process, the writer attempts to integrate the most appropriate and useful rhetorical devices, incorporating figurative language to create imagery, and using details, facts, illustration, and examples to elaborate major points and elucidate the thesis. It is during this part of the process that the writer writes and reads like a writer. Grammar, punctuation, and spelling are not important during this step in the writing process. It is more important that the writer puts thoughts on paper as oftentimes, the very act of putting words on paper changes original ideas and inspires new ones.

Revision is probably the most difficult step in the composing process. During this part of the process, it is critical that the writer reads the first draft like a reader. This part of the process must be reader centered, that is, the writer must be cognizant of how the clarity, flow, balance, evidence, and organization of the writing impacts the reader. During this part of the process, the writer must revisit those questions about purpose, audience, subject, and medium and reread and rewrite to assure that the writing responds to those questions and addresses those tasks in the most effective, explicit, and engaging manner possible. Revision is the most critical step in the writing process.

The following are questions writers and peer editors should ask of the writing:

1. What is the purpose? What about the purpose is clear, focused, and worthy? Is the reader convinced, entertained, or informed?

2. Who is the audience? How and why is the writing appropriate to the audience?

3. What is the subject? What new insight, information, or interpretation does the writing offer? What has the reader learned that is new or different? What about the writing is engaging, interesting, or compelling?

4. How does the medium or form of the delivery utilize the most effective rhetorical devices appropriate to that medium? What specific rhetorical and literary devices did the writer incorporate to accomplish purpose, develop subject, and address audience? In what ways does the writing show instead of tell?

5. What is missing? What new ideas, details, examples, illustrations, and evidence could or should be added? What other rhetorical and literary devices would improve the writing?

6. How does the writer command and engage attention throughout the piece?

Honest responses to these questions provide fodder for and guide revision. These questions can be addressed in a variety of ways. One way is through student-teacher conferencing. Conferencing is critical to the revision process. Carl Anderson suggests that the writer set the agenda for conferencing by "describing her work" and "responding to the teacher's questions" (83) and then follow up by listening carefully to the teacher's responses, asking clarifying questions, and incorporating the teacher's feedback into the next draft.

In working with Somali students, A. A. Friedman ("Agents of Literacy Change: Working with Somali Students in an Urban Middle School") used small group work to aid revision, incorporating a peer-editing protocol that involved reading and talking aloud, questioning, and rewriting. In the first step of the process, each student read his or her paper aloud. Peers listened carefully so they might later ask questions to clarify understanding and meaning. Listeners did not have a draft copy because it was just as important for students to improve listening skills. Writers were also instructed to stop and correct any confusing phrases, ideas, and details discovered during their read aloud. This process reinforced self-evaluation and self-correction, and immediate corrections and changes aided in creating a second draft. Before each student read the self-corrected draft, the other students were invited to share at least two positive comments about the writing and to ask at least two questions to help improve writing and help the reader better understand what the writer was thinking and writing. Writers summarized feedback aloud and wrote notes on the second draft. During the next step, writers incorporated and highlighted answers to questions in a new draft, which was later read aloud, as the process was repeated until pieces were proofread and published.

Editing is the next step in the composing process. Editing involves checking or proofreading written work for accurate language conventions of grammar, mechanics, and spelling. Ralph Fletcher and JoAnn Portalupi suggest several areas that writers should evaluate during the editing process. They include paragraph indenting, comma usage, use of active voice, precise language and diction, strength of verbs, sentence variety, quotation and dialogue usage, and sentence flow.

Publishing is the final step in the process. During this step, writers share and celebrate their work in a public forum.

RHETORICAL DEVICES

Speakers and authors integrate specific rhetorical devices to appeal to ethos, pathos, and logos into their spoken and written word. Richard Nordquist offers terms and their definitions in the following "Tool Kit of Rhetorical Analysis." The following list is taken from Nordquist's work; most definitions have been modified and new examples have been provided.

Accismus: being coy; a form of irony in which a person fakes a lack of interest in something that he or she actually desires. Mark Antony's soliloquy from William Shakespeare *Julius Caesar* offers an example: "I come to bury Caesar, not to praise him" (act 3, scene 2). Praising Caesar is indeed Mark Antony's intent.

Accumulation: figure of speech in which a speaker or a writer gathers scattered points and lists them together. Example: "I'd much rather be a woman than a man. Women can cry, they can wear cute clothes, and they're the first to be rescued off sinking ships" (Gilda Radner: http://www.ask.com/bar?q=Gilda+Radner+quotes&page=1&qsrc=2417&ab=4&u=http%3A%2F%2Fwww.yuni.com%2Fquotes%2Fradner.html).

Allegory: literary device in which a metaphor is extended so that objects, persons, and actions in a text are equated with meanings that lie outside the text. Example: "The Allegory of the Cave" by Socrates.

Alliteration: repetition of initial consonant sound, as in the following from Graeme Base's *Animalia*:

Wicked
Warrior
Wasps
wildly
waving
Warlike
Weapons

Allusion: a brief, usually indirect reference to a person, place, or event—real or fictional. These lyrics to "Superman" by Brown Boy demonstrate allusion:

"I'll be your superman; I can love you like no one can; I can be your superman; Just take my hand let's fly away; I promise I'll be there everyday; Just close your eyes let's start to fly; I'm gonna love you until I die."

Ambiguity: the presence of two or more possible meanings in any passage. Example: "I am having a friend for dinner." Hannibal Lecter's comment to Clarice in the film *Silence of the Lambs*.

Amplification: all the ways an argument, explanation, or description can be elaborated, enhanced, enriched, and expanded. Amplification is accomplished using

- accumulation (see above definition)

- metaphor, hyperbole, and simile (see chapter 2)

- *copia*: extensive description. Example:

  Love is patient, love is kind.
  It does not envy, it does not boast, it is not proud.
  It is not rude, it is not self-seeking,
  it is not easily angered, it keeps no record of wrongs.

Love does not delight in evil but rejoices with the truth.

It always protects, always trusts, always hopes, always perseveres.

And now faith, hope, and love abide, but the greatest of these is love.

(1 Corinthians. 13:4-13)

- *epimone*: repetition of a question, as in, "Who is here so base that would be a bondman? If any, speak; for him I have offended. Who is here so rude that would not be a Roman? If any speak; for him have I offended" (*Julius Caesar*, act 3, scene 2).

- *synasthroesmus*: piling on the adjectives. Example: *You are a no-good, cheating, lying, deceitful, untrustworthy, malicious, and unscrupulous scoundrel.*

Anadiplosis: repetition of the last word of one line or clause to begin the next. Example: "I am Sam, Sam I am" (Dr. Seuss, *Green Eggs and Ham*).

Analogy: reasoning or arguing from parallel cases (see chapter 2).

Anaphora: repetition of the same word or phrase at the beginning of successive clauses or verses. Example: "I do not like them in a box, I do not like them with a fox" (Dr. Suess, *Green Eggs and Ham*).

Anticipation: argumentative strategies whereby a speaker or writer foresees and replies to objections. Example:

But Brutus says he was ambitious;

And Brutus is an honourable man . . .

He hath brought many captives home to Rome,

Whose ransoms did the general coffers fill:

Did this in Caesar seem ambitious?

When that the poor have cried, Caesar hath wept:

Ambition should be made of sterner stuff:

Yet Brutus says he was ambitious;

And Brutus is an honourable man.

You all did see that on the Lupercal

I thrice presented him a kingly crown,

Which he did thrice refuse: was this ambition?

(*Julius Caesar*, act 3, scene 2)

Anthymeme: an informally stated syllogism with an implied premise. Example: *Got milk?*

Anticlimax: abrupt shift from a noble tone to a less exalted one—often for comic effect. Example:

> Be respectful to your superiors, if you have any, also to strangers, and sometimes to others. If a person offends you, and you are in doubt as to whether it was intentional or not, do not resort to extreme measures; simply watch your chance and hit him with a brick. That will be sufficient. ("Advice for Youth," Mark Twain)

Antirrhesis: a type of refutation in which an argument is rejected because of its insignificance, error, or wickedness. Example:

> "A woman who gets beaten brings it upon herself by nagging or provoking her spouse." People are beaten for reasons as ridiculous as: the dinner is cold; the TV was turned to the wrong channel; the baby was crying. Abusive people refuse to control their violent impulses. Even where the person may have reason to be angry, they have no right to express their anger violently. (*Women's Rural Advocacy Program* "Domestic Violence Information" November 15, 2007 *http://www.letswrap.com/dvinfo/index.htm*) 29 April 2009.)

Antithesis: juxtaposition of contrasting ideas in balanced phrases. Example:

> It was the best of times, it was the worst of times, it was the age of wisdom, it was the age of foolishness, it was the epoch of belief, it was the epoch of incredulity, it was the season of Light, it was the season of Darkness, it was the spring of hope, it was the winter of despair, we had everything before us, we had nothing before us, we were all going direct to Heaven, we were all going direct the other way. (Charles Dickens, *A Tale of Two Cities*)

Antonomasia: substitution of a title, epithet, or descriptive phrase for a proper name (or of a personal name for a common name) to designate a member of a group or class.

For example, the characters in J. K. Rowling's *Harry Potter* series refer to the villain Lord Voldemort as "He who must not be named."

Aphorism: a tersely phrased statement of a truth or opinion; brief statement of a principle: *A penny saved is a penny earned.*

Aporia: expression of real or simulated doubt or perplexity. Example: "I come to bury Caesar not to praise him" (*Julius Caesar*, act 3, scene 2).

Aposiopesis: an unfinished thought or broken sentence. Example:

> I will have such revenges on you both
> That all the world shall—I will do things—
> What they are yet, I know not; but they shall be
> The terrors of the earth! (William Shakespeare, *King Lear*)

Apostrophe: breaking off discourse to address some absent person or thing. Example: "Laziness, have I ever offended thee?"

Apposition: placing side-by-side two coordinate elements, the second of which serves as an explanation or modification of the first. Example: *John, my husband*

Arrangement: parts of a speech or the structure of a text (See section: Unity, Coherence, and Emphasis)

Assonance: similarity in sound between internal vowels in neighboring words (see chapter 2).

Asyndeton: omission of conjunctions between words, phrases, or clauses; opposite of *polysyndeton*. Example: *He shouted, screamed, hollered, yelled.*

Auxesis: a gradual increase in intensity of meaning with words arranged in ascending order of force or importance. Example:

> Deep into that darkness peering, long I stood there wondering, fearing,
> Doubting, dreaming dreams no mortal ever dared to dream before.
>   (Edgar Allan Poe, "The Raven")

Bdelygmia: a litany of abuse; a series of critical epithets, descriptions, or attributes. Example:

> The Republicans are not stupid. They tagged the liberals as "latte-drinking, Volvo-driving, school-busing, fetus-killing, tree-hugging, gun-fearing, morally relativist and secularly humanist so-called liberal elitists," as commentator Jason Epstein described it, soft on communism, soft on crime, opposed to capital punishment, and soft on the new war on terrorism. (Mort Zuckerman, *U.S. News*, 6 June 2005)

Boosting: adverbial construction used to support a claim or express a viewpoint more assertively and convincingly. Example: *A hot fudge sundae is **certainly** the best cure for a bad day!*

Categoria: direct exposure of an adversary's faults. Example:

> **Jessep**: You can't handle the truth! Son, we live in a world that has walls. And those walls have to be guarded by men with guns. Who's gonna do it? You? You, Lieutenant Weinberg? I have a greater responsibility than you can possibly fathom. You weep for Santiago and you curse the Marines. You have that luxury. You have the luxury of not knowing what I know: that Santiago's death, while tragic, probably saved lives. And my existence, while grotesque and incomprehensible to you, saves lives . . . You don't want the truth. Because deep down, in places you don't talk about at parties, you want me on that wall. You need me on that wall.
>
> We use words like *honor*, *code*, *loyalty* . . . we use these words as the backbone to a life spent defending something. You use 'em as a punchline. I have neither the time nor the inclination to explain myself to a man who rises and sleeps under the blanket of the very freedom I provide, then questions the manner in which I provide it! I'd rather you just said thank you and went on your way. Otherwise, I suggest you pick up a weapon and stand a post. Either way, I don't give a damn what you think you're entitled to! (Aaron Sorkin, *A Few Good Men*)

Chiasmus: a verbal pattern in which the second half of an expression is balanced against the first but with the parts reversed. Example: "Fair is foul, and foul is fair" (Shakespeare, *Macbeth*, act 1, scene 2).

Chleuasmos: sarcastic reply that mocks an opponent, leaving him or her without an answer. Example: *Here is your knife, fork, spoon, glass, napkin, Wetnap, Pepsi, dinner, and dessert. If you like, I can eat it for you.*

Climax: mounting by degrees through words or sentences of increasing weight and in parallel construction with an emphasis on the high point or culmination of a series of events. Example:

> The hunters were looking uneasily at the sky, flinching from the stroke of the drops. A wave of restlessness set the boys swaying and moving aimlessly. The flickering light became brighter and the blows of the thunder were only just bearable. The littluns began to run about screaming. (William Golding, *Lord of the Flies*)

Commonplace: any statement or bit of knowledge that is commonly shared among a given audience or a community. For example, it is a commonplace statement that taxes and death are certain.

Commoratio: repetition of a point several times in different words. Example:

> "He's gone off his rocker!" shouted one of the fathers, aghast, and the other parents joined in the chorus of frightened shouting.
> "He's crazy!" they shouted.
> "He's balmy!"
> "He's nutty!"
> "He's screwy!"
> "He's batty!"
> "He's dippy!"
> "He's dotty!"
> "He's daffy!"
> "He's goofy!"
> "He's beany!"
> "He's buggy!"
> "He's wacky!"
> "He's loony!"
> "No, he is not!" said Grandpa Joe.
>
> (Roald Dahl, *Charlie and the Chocolate Factory*)

Confirmation: the main part of a speech or text in which logical arguments in support of a position are elaborated. Example:

Americans forced Native Americans to assimilate: to make them white. The U.S. government broke up their reservations into pieces of land and sold most of it to settlers or divided it among other Indians. The government also took away their religion, made them dress like white people, and forced them to go to boarding schools because it considered them uneducated. The government acquired money by killing the Indians' buffalo, their primary source of shelter, food, clothing, and fuel. Assimilation destroyed tribal life and broke the spirit of Native Americans.

Concession: argumentative strategy by which a speaker or writer concedes a disputed point or leaves a disputed point to the audience or reader to decide. For example, in Shakespeare's *Julius Caesar*, Mark Antony concedes that if Caesar was ambitious, then it was a grievous fault. He also concedes that Brutus is an honorable man:

The noble Brutus
Hath told you Caesar was ambitious:
If it were so, it was a grievous fault,
And grievously hath Caesar answer'd it.
Here, under leave of Brutus and the rest—
For Brutus is an honourable man;
So are they all, all honourable men—

Connotation: the emotional implications and associations that a word may carry. For example, the word *green* can imply jealousy, envy, rookielike status, plush, among other meanings.

Copia: expansive richness as a stylistic goal. The following passage from Samuel Taylor Coleridge's "Kubla Khan" illustrates copia:

In Xanadu did Kubla Khan
A stately pleasure-dome decree:
Where Alph, the sacred river, ran
Through caverns measureless to man
Down to a sunless sea.

So twice five miles of fertile ground
With walls and towers were girdled round:
And here were gardens bright with sinuous rills
Where blossomed many an incense-bearing tree;
And here were forests ancient as the hills,
Enfolding sunny spots of greenery.
But oh! that deep romantic chasm which slanted
Down the green hill athwart a cedarn cover!
A savage place! as holy and enchanted
As e'er beneath a waning moon was haunted
By woman wailing for her demon-lover!"

Crot: verbal bit or fragment used as an autonomous unit without transitional devices. Example:

Salvador with eyes the color of caterpillar, Salvador of the crooked hair and crooked teeth, Salvador whose name the teacher cannot remember, is a boy who is no one's friend, runs along somewhere in that vague direction where homes are the color of bad weather, lives behind a raw wood doorway, shakes the sleepy brothers awake, ties their shoes, combs their hair with water, feeds them milk and cornflakes from a tin cup in the dim dark of the morning. (Sandra Cisneros "Salvador Late or Early")

Deduction: a method of reasoning in which a conclusion follows necessarily from the stated premises. The following sentence demonstrates deductive reasoning: *If the black widow is a spider, and all spiders have eight legs, then the black widow has eight legs.*

Dehortatio: dissuasive advice given with authority. Example: " 'Fool,' said my Muse to me, 'look in thy heart, and write' " (Sir Philip Sidney, *Astrophel and Stella,* Sonnet 1).

Deliberative: speech or writing that attempts to persuade an audience to take (or not to take) some action. Consider the following deliberative passage from Dylan Thomas's "Do Not Go Gentle Into That Good Night":

And you, my father, there on the sad height,
Curse, bless me now with your fierce tears, I pray.
Do not go gentle into that good night.
Rage, rage against the dying of the light.

Delivery: one of the five traditional parts or canons of rhetoric, concerned with control of voice and gestures (see this chapter's section on classical rhetoric.)

Denotation: the direct or dictionary meaning of a word, in contrast to its figurative or associated meanings. For example, the denotation of *assimilate* is "to absorb (immigrants or a culturally distinct group) into the prevailing culture."

Diacope: repetition broken up by one or more intervening words. Example:

Is there anything more beautiful than a beautiful, beautiful flamingo, flying across in front of a beautiful sunset? And he's carrying a beautiful rose in his beak, and also he's carrying a very beautiful painting with his feet. And also, you're drunk." (Jack Handey, *Deep Thoughts*)

Diatyposis: recommending useful precepts or advice to someone else. Example:

Pick out a pleasant outlook,
Stick out that noble chin,
Wipe off that full-of-doubt look,
Slap on a happy grin!
Spread sunshine all over the place,
And just put on a happy face**!**
    ("Put on a Happy Face," from the musical *Bye, Bye, Birdie*)

Distinctio: explicit references to various meanings of a word to remove ambiguities. Example: For the purpose of this discussion, *assimilate* is defined as "to absorb (immigrants or a culturally distinct group) into the prevailing culture."

Dysphemism: substitution of a more offensive or disparaging word or phrase for one considered less offensive. For example, one might use the word *cripple* instead of *physically handicapped*.

Effectio: description a person's physical attributes or charms. Example: "My mistress' eyes are nothing like the sun/ Coral is far more red than her lips' red:" (Sonnet 130, William Shakespeare)

Ellipsis: omission of one or more words, which must be supplied by the listener or reader, as in the following sentence: *In case of fire, grade 1 will assemble in the front of the building, grade 2, the back lot, and grade 3, the driveway.*

Encomium: tribute or eulogy in prose or verse glorifying people, objects, ideas, or events. Mark Antony's funeral speech in Shakespeare's *Julius Caesar* is an encomium.

Epanalepsis: repetition at the end of a clause or sentence of the word or phrase with which it began. Example:

> Possessing what we still were unpossessed by,
> *Possessed* by what we now no more *possessed*.
>   (Robert Frost, "The Gift Outright"; italics added)

Epicrisis: circumstance in which a speaker quotes a passage and comments on it, as in the following: *You have heard the phrase "Absence makes the heart grow fonder." Well, from my experience, absence just gives the cat more time to play.*

Epideictic or **demonstrative rhetoric**: speech or writing that praises or blames (see this chapter's earlier section on classical rhetoric).

Epimone: repetition of a phrase or question; dwelling on a point. Example: *Are you nuts? Are you crazy? Are you mad? Have you lost all reason?*

Epiphora: repetition of a word or phrase at the end of several clauses. The repeated line "And Brutus is an honourable man . . ." in Shakespeare's *Julius Caesar* is an epiphora.

Epiplexis: the act asking questions to reproach rather than to elicit answers. Example: "Suppose you wake up some morning and find your sister dead? What would you think then?" she asked. "Suppose those rats cut our veins at night while we sleep? Naw! Nothing like that ever bothers you! All you care about is your own pleasure!" (Richard Wright, *Native Son*)

Epithet: an adjective or phrase used (often habitually) to characterize a person or thing. Example: "The *snotgreen* sea. The *scrotumtightening* sea" (James Joyce, *Ulysses*; italics added)

Epizeuxis: repetition of a word for emphasis (usually with no words in between). Example: *I am simply appalled,* appalled. *You hear me? Appalled by your behavior!*

Erotesis: a rhetorical question that implies strong affirmation or denial. Example: "If you prick us, do we not bleed?" (Shakespeare, *Merchant of Venice*).

Ethopoeia: putting oneself in place of another so as to both understand and express feelings more vividly. Example: *We are soul mates. Our lives our indistinguishable.*

Ethos: persuasive appeal based on the projected character of the speaker or narrator (see this chapter's earlier section on ethos, pathos, and logos).

Euphemism: substitution of an inoffensive term for one considered offensively explicit (see chapter 2).

Euphuism: elaborately patterned prose style, such as in Shakespearean sonnets.

Evidence: facts, documentation, or testimony used to strengthen a claim or reach a conclusion.

Exordium: the introductory part of an argument in which a speaker or writer establishes credibility (ethos) and announces the subject and purpose of the discourse (see earlier section on classical rhetoric).

Exuscitatio: emotional utterance that seeks to move hearers to a like feeling. Example: Martin Luther King, Jr.'s "I Have a Dream" speech

Fable: short narrative meant to teach a moral lesson (see chapter 2 and 4).

Figures of speech: the various uses of language that depart from customary construction, order, or significance. Examples include *turn on a dime*, *racking my brains*, *sweating bullets*, *raining cats and dogs*, and so forth.

Gradatio: sentence construction in which the last word of one clause becomes the first of the next, through three or more clauses. Example:

> There was an old lady who swallowed a bird;
> How absurd, to swallow a bird!
> She swallowed the bird to catch the spider
> That wiggled and wiggled and tickled inside her.
> She swallowed the spider to catch the fly.
> But I dunno why she swallowed that fly—
> Perhaps she'll die.

Hyperbole: the use of exaggerated terms for the purpose of emphasis or heightened effect (see chapter 2).

Hypophora: a figure of speech in which the speaker raises questions and answers them. Example: "What makes a king out of a slave? Courage! What makes the flag on the mast to wave? Courage!" (Frank Baum, *The Wizard of Oz*).

Hypotaxis: an arrangement of phrases or clauses in a dependent or subordinate relationship. Example:

I told her way up yonder past the caution light
There's a little country store with an old Coke sign
You gotta stop in and ask Miss Belle for some of her sweet tea
Then a left will take you to the interstate
But a right will bring you right back here to me.
                    (Billy Currington, "Good Directions")

Identification: any means by which an author may establish a shared sense of values, attitudes, and interests with his or her readers.

Induction: method of reasoning by which a speaker or writer collects a number of instances and forms a generalization that is meant to apply to all instances. Example:

We are the world, we are the children;
We are the ones who make a brighter day so let's start giving;
There's a choice we're making; We're saving our own lives;
It's true we'll make a better day; Just you and me.
                    (USA for Africa, "We Are the World")

Invective: denunciatory or abusive discourse that casts blame on somebody or something. Example: "A knave, a rascal, an eater of broken meats; a base, proud, shallow, beggarly, three-suited, hundred-pound, filthy worsted-stocking knave; a lily-livered, action-taking, whoreson, glass-gazing, super-serviceable, finical rogue; one-trunk-inheriting slave" (Shakespeare, *The Tragedy of King Lear*).

Invention: the discovery of the resources for persuasion inherent in any given rhetorical problem (see earlier section on classical rhetoric).

Irony: use of words to convey the opposite of their literal meaning; statement or situation where the meaning is directly contradicted by the appearance or presentation of the idea (see chapter 2).

Isocolon: succession of phrases of approximately equal length and corresponding structure, as in, *The nearer to church, the farther from heaven.*

Judicial: term used to describe speech or writing that considers the justice or injustice of a certain charge or accusation. The following is an example of judicial rhetoric: *Given eyewitness testimony that places the defendant at the scene of the crime, the murder weapon with the defendant's fingerprints on it, and the defendant's motive, you must find the defendant guilty of first-degree murder.*

Kairos: the opportune time and/or place, the right time to say or do the right thing. Example: proposing a toast at a fiftieth wedding anniversary

Litotes: a figure of speech consisting of an understatement in which an affirmative is expressed by negating its opposite. Example: "for life's not a paragraph / And death I think is no parenthesis" (e.e. cummings, "since feeling is first").

Logos: in classical rhetoric, the means of persuasion by demonstration of the truth, real or apparent; logic (see earlier section on ethos, pathos, and logos).

Meiosis: to belittle; to use a degrading epithet, often through a trope of one word; rhetorical understatement. Example: Referring to a psychiatrist as a *shrink*

Memory: one of the traditional five parts or canons of rhetoric, that which considers methods and devices to aid and improve the memory (see earlier section on classical rhetoric).

Metaphor: an implied comparison between two unlike things that actually have something important in common (see chapter 2).

Metonymy: figure of speech in which one word or phrase is substituted for another with which it is closely associated (see chapter 2).

Narratio: the part of an argument in which a speaker or writer provides a narrative account of what has happened and explains the nature of the case (see earlier section on classical rhetoric).

Onomatopoeia: the formation or use of words that imitate the sounds associated with the objects or actions they refer to (see Chapter 2).

Oxymoron: a figure of speech in which incongruous or contradictory terms appear side by side (see chapter 2).

Parable: a short and simple story that illustrates a lesson.

Paradox: a statement that appears to contradict itself (see chapter 2).

Paralepsis: emphasizing a point by seeming to pass over it. Example: *Let's not discuss the young man's poor academic record, his tardiness, and his disrespect. That is not our purpose.*

Parallelism: similarity of structure in a pair or series of related words, phrases, or clauses (see chapter 2).

Parataxis: phrases or clauses arranged independently; a coordinate, rather than a subordinate, construction. Example:

> Twenty-two years old, weak, hot, frightened, not daring to acknowledge the fact that he didn't know who or what he was . . . with no past, no language, no tribe, no source, no address book, no comb, no pencil, no clock, no pocket handkerchief, no rug, no bed, no can opener, no faded postcard, no soap, no key, no tobacco pouch, no soiled underwear and nothing nothing nothing to do . . . he was sure of one thing only: the unchecked monstrosity of his hands. (Toni Morrison, *Sula*)

Parenthesis: (1) either or both of the upright curved lines, ( ), used to mark off explanatory or qualifying remarks in writing. Example: *Her decision making improved to the reflective level (Stage 7).* (2) the insertion of a verbal unit that interrupts the normal flow of the sentence. Example: "In the still—du wap, du wah—of the night . . ." (The Five Satins, "In the Still of the Night")

Pathos: the means of persuasion in classical rhetoric that appeals to the audience's emotions (see earlier section on ethos, pathos, and logos).

Periodic sentence: long and frequently involved sentence, marked by suspended syntax, in which the sense is not completed until the final word—usually with an emphatic climax. Example:

> "They then go flashing down the wire that leads right into the back of the television set, and in there they get jiggled and joggled around until at last every single one of those millions of tiny pieces is fitted back into its right place (just like a jigsaw puzzle), and presto!—the photograph appears on the screen." (Roald Dahl, *Charlie and the Chocolate Factory*)

Peroration: the closing part of an argument (see earlier section on classical rhetoric).

Persona: voice or mask that an author or speaker or performer puts on for a particular purpose. Example:

> *In 2001: A Space Odyssey*, the author creates the persona, HAL (the talking computer) to apprise us of not only the flaws but also the immense power of technology.

Personification: figure of speech in which an inanimate object or abstraction is endowed with human qualities or abilities (see chapter 2).

Ploce: repetition of a word with a new or specified sense, or with pregnant reference to its special significance. Example: "What lies behind you and what lies in front of you, pales in comparison to what lies inside of you" (Ralph Waldo Emerson, original sources unknown).

Polyptoton: repetition of words derived from the same root but with different endings. Example: *Do not **speak** the **unspeakable**.*

Polysyndeton: a style that employs a great many conjunctions. Example: *He squirmed and wiggled and wormed and jiggled and spun and whirled around and around and around.*

Prolepsis: figurative device by which a future event is presumed to have already occurred. Example: "Consider the lilies of the field and how they grow; they neither toil nor spin" (Matthew 6:28).

Proverb: Short, pithy statement of a general truth, one that condenses common experience into memorable form. Example: "For many are called, but few are chosen" (Matthew 22:14).

Pun: play on words, sometimes on different senses of the same word and sometimes on the similar sense or sound of different words. Example:

> **Mercutio**: Nay, gentle Romeo, we must have you dance.
> **Romeo**: Not I, believe me. You have dancing shoes
> With nimble *soles*; I have a *soul* of lead . . .
> (Shakespeare, *Romeo and Juliet*, act I, scene 4, lines 13-15)

Refutation: the part of an argument wherein a speaker or writer anticipates and counters opposing points of view (see earlier section on classical rhetoric).

Rhetor: (1) a speaker or writer; (2) a teacher of rhetoric.

Rhetoric: the study and practice of effective communication.

Rhetorical canons: five overlapping offices or divisions of the rhetorical process (see earlier section on classical rhetoric).

Rhetorical question: question asked merely for effect with no answer expected. Example: *Did you think I would throw you to the sharks?*

Rhetorical situation: the context of a rhetorical act; minimally, made up of a rhetor, an issue, and an audience.

Running style: sentence style that appears to follow the mind as it worries a problem through. Example:

> My parents suffer from competing illnesses; it's a contest about who is
> sicker than the other, like dueling banjos but only illnesses. He has had a

lot of dizziness lately. Oh, I forgot to call the dentist; my mom has a tooth-ache. I really should be kinder, shouldn't I? They won't be here forever, I mean, how can they? No one is immortal except Shakespeare; that's what my English teacher said, but he's really dead, you know.

Scheme: a rhetorical device, which changes only the shape of a phrase with no impact on the meaning. "Shines the light brightly" instead of "The light shines brightly."

Series: a list of three or more items, usually arranged in parallel form. Example: *I love eating, drinking, dancing, and carousing.*

Simile: stated comparison (usually formed with "like" or "as") between two fundamentally dissimilar things (see chapter 2).

Sprezzatura: rehearsed spontaneity, studied carelessness, and well-practiced natural-ness that lies at the center of convincing discourse of any sort.

Style: narrowly interpreted as those figures that ornament speech or writing; broadly, as representing a manifestation of the person speaking or writing.

Syllogism: a form of deductive reasoning consisting of a major premise, a minor premise, and a conclusion. Example: *All cats are mammals. Fritz is a cat. Therefore, Fritz is a mammal.*

Synecdoche: a figure of speech is which a part is used to represent the whole, the whole for a part, the specific for the general, the general for the specific, or the material for the thing made from it (see chapter 2).

Tapinosis: undignified language that debases a person or thing. Example: *You are a dirty, rotten, conniving lowlife.*

Tenor: the underlying idea or the principal subject that is the meaning of a metaphor. In the following example, *prayer* is the tenor, or the subject, of the metaphors that follow:

> Prayer, the Church's banquet, Angels' age,
> *God's breath* in man returning to his birth.
>   (Herbert, "Prayer"; italics added)

Testimony: a person's account of an event or state of affairs.

Tetracolon climax: a series of four members. Example: *Determined, she rolled up her sleeves, turned toward the forest, picked up the axe, and chopped down the tree.*

Tricolon: series of three parallel words, phrases, or clauses. Example: *over the river, through the woods, and across the lake*

Trope: A figure of speech or rhetorical device that produces a shift in the meaning of words. An oxymoron, for example, is a trope: *cheerful pessimist*.

Understatement: figure of speech in which a writer deliberately makes a situation seem less important or serious than it is. Example: "I have to have this operation . . . It isn't very serious. I have this tiny little tumor on the brain." (J. D. Salinger, *The Catcher In The Rye*)

Vehicle: in a metaphor, the figure itself. A metaphor carries two ideas: the vehicle and the tenor, or underlying idea. Example:

> Prayer, the *Church's banquet, Angels' age,*
> *God's breath* in man returning to his birth.
> (Herbert, "Prayer"; italics added)

Voice: the quality of a verb that indicates whether its subject acts (active voice) or is acted upon (passive voice; see chapter 2).

Zeugma: use of a word to modify or govern two or more words although its use may be grammatically or logically correct with only one. Example: "He carried a strobe light and the responsibility for the lives of his men" (Tim O'Brien, *The Things They Carried*).

CRITERIA OF AND STRATEGIES FOR EVALUATING THE CONTENT AND EFFECTIVENESS OF WRITTEN AND SPOKEN LANGUAGE

The past sections of this chapter have identified and illustrated the more specific components of written and spoken language, the composing process, and rhetorical devices that enhance written and spoken language. The following section addresses traditional paragraph structures and types, essay structures, forms of writing, metrics for evaluating written and spoken language, and the most common language conventions that are essential to effective written and spoken language.

Section 1.05   Paragraphs and Essays

(a)   The Paragraph

A paragraph is a group of sentences assembled together around a main idea or topic. There are several kinds of paragraphs: enumerative, explanatory, "how to," descriptive, comparison, contrast, comparison/contrast, cause and effect, and problem solutions. The traditional paragraph contains a topic sentence, supporting sentences, and a concluding sentence, sometimes called a clincher sentence. The first word in a paragraph is always indented.

The **topic sentence** is the most general sentence that poses the main idea or focus of the paragraph. The topic sentence usually begins the paragraph but may be found in the middle and sometimes at the end of a paragraph, especially if the paragraph introduces an essay. The **supporting sentences** include reasons, details, examples, evidence, and illustrations that support the main idea or topic sentence of the paragraph. All supporting sentences should relate to the topic sentence. The **concluding sentence** ends the paragraph by reiterating (using different words) or summarizing the main idea of the paragraph. Sentences in a paragraph follow a logical order by including effective transitions.

(b)   The Five-Paragraph Essay

The five-paragraph essay is the most traditional form of the written essay. The five-paragraph essay includes an introductory paragraph, three supporting or "body" paragraphs, and a concluding paragraph.

The first paragraph, or **introductory paragraph**, hooks the reader into the essay, provides minimal background information, states the thesis statement, and establishes the framework or blueprint as to how the writer will prove the thesis statement. A **thesis statement** is a statement that takes a stand or position, expresses one main idea, justifies its value, and narrows the topic into a manageable, supportable argument. Generally the thesis statement includes three major points that support the main argument. Each of these points becomes the topic in each of the three body paragraphs.

Each of the **three body paragraphs** has a topic sentence that relates to one of the major points in the thesis statement, supporting sentences that include details, examples, reason, illustrations, and evidence that support the topic sentence and a concluding/transitional sentence that leads the reader into the next body paragraph.

The **concluding paragraph** summarizes the major points of the essay, rewords the thesis statement, and includes a clincher sentence that leaves the reader thinking.

Section 1.06   Rubrics: Evaluating Written and Spoken Language

Whether evaluating writing or speaking, evaluative criteria must establish high standards, value originality and diversity, encourage risk taking, encourage passion and voice, and support revision. There are numerous ways to evaluate writing, but rubrics provide a useful instrument that not only differentiates among quality criteria in writing and speaking but also, and more important, offers students clear foci for revision and improvement. Rubrics are usually generic or task specific. Truly generic rubrics can be used to evaluate any performance. Task-specific rubrics are tailored to the particular performance or purpose.

MTEL Tip

Rubrics offer students a clear focus to apply when they revise and improve their writing.

Holistic rubrics tend to be generic rubrics, which can be used to evaluate many performances. The advantages to such rubrics are that they "emphasize what learners do," are easy to use, save time, and can be applied by trained raters with good coefficients of reliability.

To learn more about rubrics and to download useful examples see: <*http://www.carla. umn.edu/assessment/VAC/Evaluation/rubrics/types/holisticRubrics.html*>). The primary disadvantage is that they provide little useful feedback to students that can improve performance. The Massachusetts Comprehensive Assessment System uses a holistic rubric to evaluate long compositions. See Tables 1 and 2.

Analytic rubrics address the more general categories of generic rubrics but are presented in distinct categories. In such rubrics, a student can receive points for each category, which are totaled at the end to create a final score. The following is a list of performance dimensions commonly found in analytic rubrics for speaking and writing:

1. Content
2. Vocabulary

3. Use of grammar, spelling, and punctuation

4. Originality

5. Diction

6. Voice

7. Organization

8. Coherence

9. Relationship between form and purpose

10. Style

11. Fluency

12. Intonation

13. Pronunciation

Section 1.07   English Grammar and Language Conventions in Oral and Written Contexts

English grammar has numerous definitions. *The American Heritage Dictionary* defines *grammar* as

- the study of how words and their component parts combine to form sentences

- the study of structural relationships in language or in a language, sometimes including pronunciation, meaning, and linguistic history

- the system of inflections, syntax, and word formation of a language

- the system of rules implicit in a language, viewed as a mechanism for generating all sentences possible in that language

- writing or speech judged with regard to such a set of rules

In this section, sentence types and structures, the most common English grammar and language conventions, and general punctuation rules are defined and illustrated. For a complete list of parts of speech and other language conventions, see chapter 2.

(a) Sentences

A sentence is commonly defined as "a complete unit of thought." Normally, a sentence expresses a relationship, conveys a command, poses a question, or describes someone or something. A sentence begins with a capital letter and ends with a period, question mark, or exclamation point. The basic parts of a sentence are the subject and the verb. The subject is usually a noun—a word that names a person, place, or thing—or pronoun. The predicate (or verb) usually follows the subject and identifies an action or a state of being. Consider the following simple sentence:

The wind blows.

The wind is the complete subject, and *wind* is the simple subject of the sentence. The predicate of the sentence is *blows*, which tells what the wind does or how the wind acts.

There are four kinds of sentences:

- A **declarative sentence** states, declares, describes or defines. A declarative sentence ends with a period (.).

  Hannah likes ice cream.

This sentence states a simple fact about Hannah.

- An **interrogative sentence** asks a question. An interrogative sentence ends with a question mark (**?**).

  What does Hannah like to eat?

This sentence asks for specific information about Hannah.

- An **exclamatory sentence** exclaims or shows excitement. An exclamatory sentence ends with an exclamation point (**!**).

  Hannah absolutely loves ice cream!

This sentence emphasizes the fact that Hannah loves ice cream and that she is excited about eating it.

- An **imperative sentence** poses a command. A verb often begins an imperative sentence. An imperative sentence can end with a period or an exclamation point.

> *Please step up to the plate.*
> Someone is being commanded to step up to the plate.
> *Hannah, eat your ice cream right now!*

Hannah is being commanded or ordered to eat ice cream at this very minute.

> *I want Hannah to eat her ice cream!*
> I am commanding Hannah to eat ice cream.

(b)   Sentence Variety

There are four varieties of sentence structures:

Simple sentence: a sentence that has one subject and one predicate. Another term for a simple sentence is an *independent clause, independent* because it can stand alone, and make sense.

> *Mary sells seashells by the seashore.*

Mary is the subject; sells seashells by the seashore is the predicate.

Compound sentence: two simple sentences or *independent clauses* that are joined by a conjunction. Conjunctions include *and, but, or, nor, for, yet,* and *so*.

> *Agatha peeled the vegetables **and** Joshua barbecued the hamburgers.*

The two individual sentences or independent clauses in this compound sentence are *Agatha peeled the vegetables and Joshua barbecued the hamburgers*. The conjunction *and* joins the two simple sentences together.

Complex sentence: a sentence in which an independent clause is joined by one or more *dependent clauses*. A clause is dependent because it cannot stand alone and depends on the independent clause to have complete meaning. A complex sentence always has a subordinating conjunction such as *because, since, after, although*, or *when* or a relative pronoun such as *that, who*, or *which*.

> *Sam is studying all night because he must pass the exam in order to graduate.*

Sam is studying all night is the independent clause and *because he must pass the exam in order to graduate* is the dependent clause.

Jenny is the girl who won the contest.

Jenny is the girl is the independent clause and *who won the contest* is the relative clause because it relates specific information (who won the contest) to the girl in the sentence.

Compound-complex sentence: a sentence that has both a compound sentence (two independent clauses joined by a coordinating conjunction) and a dependent clause joined to the compound sentence by a subordinating or a relative pronoun.

Ben brought his sister to soccer practice and his brother bought groceries, after their parents told them to assume more responsibilities around the house.

Ben brought his sister to soccer practice and *his brother bought groceries* are independent clauses joined by *and*. The dependent clause *after their parents told them to assume more responsibilities around the house* is connected to the compound sentence by *after*.

(c) Fragments and Run-ons

Fragments and run-ons are among the most common types of sentence errors students make in their writing. A sentence fragment takes one of the following forms:

1. a phrase that is missing either a subject or verb (predicate) and therefore does not form a complete thought:

The girl with the pink hair.	(What about her?)
Ran across the street.	Who ran across the street?)

2. a subordinate clause that has a subject and verb but does not form a complete thought:

After he finished writing the report.	(What did he do after writing the report?)
If I were you.	(What would you do?)
Because she was afraid to fail.	(What happened?)

MTEL Tip

Connecting two complete sentences with a comma is called a comma splice.

Run-on sentences consist of at least two complete sentences that are not joined correctly using a coordinating conjunction (*and, or, but, nor, for, so, yet*). If you do not use one of these words, you must either separate the run-on into two separate, complete sentences or connect them with a semicolon (;). Connecting two complete sentences with a comma is also incorrect; this is called a comma splice.

I missed my bus I had to walk. (run-on)
I missed my bus, I had to walk. (comma splice)

Correct forms:

I missed my bus, so I had to walk.
I had to walk because I missed my bus.
I missed my bus; I had to walk.

(d) Subject-Verb Agreement

Another very common error students make when writing is incorrect subject-verb agreement. In a sentence, the subject must agree with the verb, that is, the sentence must demonstrate subject-verb agreement. This means that a singular subject takes a singular verb, and a plural subject takes a plural verb. The following are only a few examples of how this rule is applied. Ex:

He doesn't understand the rules.   I don't understand the rules.
She eats vegetables.   I eat vegetables.
He goes to school.   I go to school.

General Rules for Subject-Verb Agreement

1. When the subject of a sentence is composed of two or more nouns or pronouns connected by *and*, use a plural verb.

    James and Carrie love to walk.

    James and Carrie forms a plural subject so they take a plural verb, *love*.

2. When two or more singular nouns or pronouns are connected by *or* or *nor*, use a singular verb.

   Running or jumping requires energy.

   The use of *or* makes the subject singular, which therefore takes a singular verb.

3. When a compound subject contains both a singular and a plural noun or pronoun joined by *or* or *nor*, the verb should agree with the part of the subject that is closest to the verb.

   Neither the girls nor he likes to work.

   In this sentence, the verb *likes* is singular because it is closest to the pronoun *he*, which is singular.

   Neither he nor the girls like to work.

   In this sentence, the verb *like* is plural because it is closest to the noun *girls*, which is plural.

4. The words *each, each one, either, neither, everyone, everybody, anybody, anyone, nobody, somebody, someone,* and *no one* are singular and require a singular verb.

   Everyone likes brownies.

5. Nouns such as *scissors, tweezers, trousers, shoes,* and *shears* require plural verbs because they come in pairs.

   Sharp scissors cut easily.

6. Nouns such as *civics, mathematics, dollars* (when talking about money as a whole), *measles,* and *news* require singular verbs.

   The nightly news shows bias toward the new governor.

7. When a phrase separates a subject and a verb, the verb agrees with the subject, not the noun or pronoun in the phrase.

   Jenny along with her sisters visits the beach every summer.

   The subject is *Jenny,* so it takes a singular verb.

   The sisters of Jenny visit the beach every summer.

   The subject is *sisters,* so it takes a plural verb.

8. Expressions such as *with, together with, including, accompanied by, in addition to,* or *as well* do not change the number of the subject. If the subject is singular, the verb is too.

Sam in addition to Joey likes carrots.

9. Collective nouns are words that imply more than one person but are considered singular and take a singular verb, such as: *group*, *team*, *committee*, *class*, and *family*.

   The family visits the beach every summer.

10. The contraction for *does not—doesn't—*is generally used with a singular subject. The only exception to this rule is when the pronouns *I* or *you* are the subjects of a sentence. Even though these pronouns may represent only one person, each takes the plural form of the contraction for *do not* which is *don't.*

    He doesn't understand the rules.

    I don't understand the rules.

(e) Punctuation

Punctuation is the use of standard marks and signs in writing and printing to separate words into sentences, clauses, and phrases in order to clarify meaning. There are fourteen punctuation marks used in written English.

The **apostrophe** (') is used to indicate the omission of a letter or letters from a word (as in contractions or abbreviations), to show possession, or to indicate the plurals of numbers, letters, and abbreviations.

*He **doesn't** wish to attend the dance.* (contraction)
*This matter is of **internat'l** importance.* (abbreviation)

***John's** dog has rabies.* (possession)

*Twenty-five phone numbers had **6's** in them.* (plural)

The **period** (.), **question mark** (?), and **exclamation point** (!) are used to end sentences (see earlier section on sentences).

A period is also used at the end of abbreviations:

***Dr.** Jekyll was kind, but **Mr.** Hyde was cruel.*

The **comma** (,), **semicolon** (;), and **colon** (:) are marks used to create a pause in a sentence.

Commas are used in several ways:

1. To separate items in a series:

    Adam loves broccoli, asparagus, and squash.

2. To conclude the salutation and closing of a letter:

    Dear John,

    Yours truly,

3. To separate two independent clauses; it appears before the conjunction:

    John likes broccoli, but Ted prefers carrots.

4. To separate an introductory phrase or clause from the rest of the sentence:

    After you complete your composition, please check it for punctuation errors.

5. To set off any group of words that can be taken out of the sentence without changing the meaning of the sentence, as in appositives, parts of dates, places, and interrupters:

    Dr. Smith, one of my physicians, was in Europe. (appositive)

    I was born June 11, 1950. (date)

    My hometown is Attleboro, Massachusetts. (place)

    Commas, for example, have many uses. (interrupter)

The semicolon is used to separate two independent clauses not joined by a conjunction or to separate elements in series that have internal punctuation:

The day grew long; he grew weary.

He yearned for a hot, nourishing meal to fill his stomach; a soft, cozy chair to rest his bones; and a warm, welcoming face to greet him.

The colon is used after a word that introduces a quotation, an explanation, an example, or a series, and after the salutation in a business letter:

Most researchers observe: "Punctuation is easy to correct."

This is the best way to boil lobster: fill a large pot with water up to the two-inch mark, heat to a boil, drop the lobster in, and cover the pot.

The following are examples of fruits: apples, peaches, and pears.

Dear Madam:

A colon is also used to separate the hour and minute in time: *3:45 a.m.*

(f) Dashes and Hyphens

There are several types of dashes.

Figure dash

The **figure dash** (-) is so named because it is the same width as a digit, is used within numbers, for example with telephone numbers: *617-867–5309*. This does not indicate a range (en dash is used for that), or function as the minus sign (which has its own glyph).

En dash

The **en dash**, or **n dash**, **n-rule**, etc., (–) is roughly the width of the letter *n*.

The en dash is commonly used to indicate a closed range (a range with clearly defined and non-infinite upper and lower boundaries) of values, such as those between dates, times, or numbers. Ex: He lived from 1639-1689.

The en dash can also be used to contrast values, or illustrate a relationship between two things. Ex: Boston College beat UNC 24-21.

The en dash is used instead of a hyphen in compound adjectives for which neither part of the adjective modifies the other. Ex: Anglo-Saxon Literature

Em dash

The **em dash** (—), or **m dash**, **m-rule**, etc., often demarcates a parenthetical thought—like this one—or some similar interpolation. It is wider than a hyphen, as wide as M, hence the term em dash or m dash.

It is also used to indicate that a sentence is unfinished because the speaker has been interrupted such as in Darth Vader's line "I sense something; a presence I have not felt since—" in *Star Wars Episode IV: A New Hope*.

The em dash is used in much the way a colon or set of parentheses is used: it can show an abrupt change in thought or be used where a full stop (or "period") is too strong and a comma too weak. Em dashes are sometimes used in lists or definitions, but that is a style guide issue; a colon is often recommended for use instead.

Hyphen

A hyphen (-) is used to form compound words and names and to separate words into syllables, when the complete word does not fit at the end of the line.

Sally Winston-Carver

back-to-back

Johnny kindly brought Mrs. Smith the muf-
fins his mother baked.

Parentheses ( ), **brackets ([ ])**, and **braces ({ })** are used to contain words or phrases that further explain or form a group.

Parentheses are used to contain further thoughts or qualifying remarks. Generally, commas can replace parentheses without changing the meaning:

Jessie and Danesha (who were also in the wedding) flew in from Florida.

Brackets are used to contain technical information:

[See www.ask.com for additional information.]

Braces are used to contain at least two lines of text or to group information in a unit. Braces are rarely used in writing but more often in computer language to indicate that all the information belongs in one line or command.

Quotation marks (" ") are used to set off a word, phrase, sentence, or sentences that are being directly quoted or that are being used as linguistic examples instead of italics. Examples:

Mom hollered, "Turn off that radio!"

"Wow!" she observed. "Can you believe that he left her at the altar?"

It is important to keep in mind that different style manuals (American Psychological Association, Chicago Manual, Modern Language Association, etc.) have different rules for citing information, especially with respect to quotations.

(g) Capitalization

Article II.   The following are the rules governing capitalization:

1. Capitalize the first word of a sentence:

    He lumbered toward the pool.

2. Capitalize the pronoun *I*:

    *The teacher and **I** will attend the debate.*

3. Capitalize people's names and titles used with people's names:

    Prime Minister Winston Churchill attended the ceremony.

4. Capitalize familial titles such as *mother*, *father*, *mom*, *dad*, *aunt*, *uncle*, *grandmother*, and *grandfather* only when they are used as a name:

    I went fishing with Grampa.

5. Capitalize titles of high importance, even without the person's name:

    The President of the United States; the Pope

6. Capitalize the proper names of geographical places, such as cities, states, countries, rivers parks, roads, mountains, and so on:

    Joshua toured the Vatican, Greece, and Crete.

7. Capitalize the names of languages, races, nationalities, religions, and related adjectives:

    Darnell studied Mandarin and lived with a Chinese family.

8. Capitalize days of the week, months, and holidays but *not* seasons:

    The first day of spring is Sunday, March 20.

9. Capitalize the names of organizations and institutions (such as schools, universities, churches, hospitals, clubs, businesses) and their abbreviations; historical events and documents; and ships, trains, airplanes, and automobiles.

    the United Nations, the U.N.

    Empire State Building

    Mt. Everest

    the Declaration of Independence

    Boston College

    Anaheim Chamber of Commerce

    the U.S.A.

    the Starship Enterprise (ship names are also italicized)

10. Capitalize and italicize the titles of literary works, textbooks, works of art, movies, and television shows; capitalize and put in quotes poem and song titles, chapter titles, and the titles of other works included within a larger work (such as short stories within an anthology). Also capitalize titles of specific courses:

    The Tragedy of King Lear

    Of Mice and Men

    Apocalypse Now

    Adventures in British Literature

    Life Magazine

    "To a Skylark"

    "Madman across the Water"

    Chemistry 101

11. Capitalize regions within a country but not compass directions:

    Massachusetts is located on the East Coast, far north of the Deep South.

References

Anderson, Carl. *How's It Going?: A Practical Guide to Conferencing with Student Writers*. Portsmouth: Heinemann, 2000.

Barilli, Renato. *Rhetoric*. Minneapolis: University of Minnesota Press, 1989.

Craig, Bob. "Rhetorical Theory." *Bob Craig's Web Home*. 2009. 2 April 2009 <http://www.ask.com/bar?q=Rhetorical+Theory&page=1&qsrc=6&ab=1&u=http%3A%2F%2Fwww.colorado.edu%2Fcommunication%2Fmeta-discourses%2FTheory%2Frhetorical_theory.htm>.

Espenshade, Harry A. *The Essentials of Composition and Rhetoric*. New York: D.C. Heath & Co., 1904.

Fletcher, Ralph. *Live Writing*. New York: Avon, 1999.

Fletcher, Ralph. *What a Writer Needs*. Portsmouth: Heinemann, 1993.

Fletcher Ralph. *A Writer's Notebook: Unlocking the Writer within You*. New York: Avon, 1999.

Fletcher, Ralph, and JoAnn Portalupi. *Writing Workshop: The Essential Guide*. Portsmouth: Heinemann, 2001.

Freeman, David S., and Yvonne S. Freeman. *Essential Linguistics*. Portsmouth: Heinemann, 2004.

Friedman, A. A. "Agents of Literacy Change: Working with Somali Students in an Urban Middle School." *The Power of Culture: Teaching across Language Difference*. Cambridge: Harvard Educational Publishing Group, 2002. 121145.

Friedman, A. A. "Writing and Evaluating Assessments in the Content Area." *English Journal 90*(1) (2000). 107–116.

Henning, Martha L. "Friendly Persuasion: Classical Rhetoric—Now! Draft Manuscript. August 1998. 25 March 2009 <http://www.millikin.edu/wcenter/workshop7b.html>.

Herrick, James A. *The History and Theory of Rhetoric: An Introduction*. Needham Heights: Allyn and Bacon, 2001.

Honeycutt, Lee. *Aristotle's Rhetoric*. 21 June 2004. 22 March 2009 <honeyl@iowastate. edu>.

Kantor, Kenneth K., and Donald L. Rubin. "Between Speaking and Writing: Processes of Differentiation." *Exploring Speaking-Writing Relationships: Connections and Contrasts*. Urbana: NCTE, 1981.

Kraschen, S. *Explorations in Language Acquisition and Use*. Portsmouth: Heinemann, 2003.

Moore, Andrew. "Structure of Speech." *Andrew Moore's Teaching Resource Site*. 7 April 2009 <http://www.teachit.co.uk/armoore/lang/speech.htm>.

National Council of Teachers of English. *Teaching the Writing Process in High School*. Urbana: NCTE, 1995.

Nordquist, Richard. "Tool Kit of Rhetorical Analysis." 2009. *About.com*. 16 March 2009 <http://grammar.about.com/od/rhetorictoolkit/Tool_Kit_for_Rhetorical_Analysis. htm>.

Ramage, John D., and John C. Bean. *Writing Arguments*, 4th ed. Needham Heights: Allyn & Bacon, 1998, 5 April 2009 <http://www.u.arizona.edu/ic/polis/courses021/ ENGL_102-78/EthosPathosLogos>.

Composition and Rhetoric. "Some Definitions of Rhetoric." 2009. 30 March 2009 <http:// www.stanford.edu/dept/english/courses/sites/lunsford/pages/defs.htm>.

Schumann, J. *The Pidginization Process: A Model for Second Language Acqusition*. Rowley: Newbury House, 1978.

17 Gough Square. 2007. 2 February 2009 <http://www.17goughsquare.com/ 17goughsquare/Pages/Writing%20and%20Editing/Kinds%20of%20Writing/ Methods%20and%20Purposes.html>.

Silva Rhetoricae. 2009. 5 April 2009, <http://www.ask.com/bar?q=five+canons+of+ rhetoric&page=1&qsrc=0&ab=0&u=http%3A%2F%2Frhetoric.byu.edu%2Fcanons %2FCanons.htm.>

Women's Rural Advocacy Program. Battering. The Facts. 2009. 3 March 2009 <http://www. ask.com/bar?q=What+Causes+Men+to+Abuse+Women&page=1&qsrc=6&ab=0&u= http%3A%2F%2Fwww.letswrap.com%2Fdvinfo%2Fwhatis.htm>.

Young, Richard, Becker, Alton, L., and Kenneth L. Pike. *Rhetoric: Discovery and Change*, 1970. New York: Harcourt Brace & World.

YourDictionary.com. 1996-2009. 1 April 2009 <http://www.yourdictionary.com/search? ydQ=definition+of+punctuation&area=entries&x=29&y=11>.

(George A. Kennedy, *A New History of Classical Rhetoric*, 1994)

Reading Theory, Research, and Instruction

Chapter 4, "Reading Theory, Research, and Instruction," focuses on two major areas: (1) the interrelationship among language acquisition, theories of reading, and reading processes; and (2) the effective research-based pedagogy for reading instruction and the role of children's and young adult literature in promoting reading proficiency. This chapter is further divided into several sections. The first section describes the most current theories of language acquisition. The next section describes the various theories of reading and theorists aligned with those theories. The third section describes the various processes of reading. The fourth section identifies the most effective research-based pedagogy in reading instruction. The final section explains the role and usefulness of using children's and young adult literature to enhance reading proficiency.

LANGUAGE ACQUISITION

First-Language Acquisition

The earliest theory of language acquisition emerged from the behaviorists, specifically B. F. Skinner, who wrote *Verbal Behavior*. He believed that language, like every behavior in the behaviorists' world, was simply a result of stimulus and response. Tiny Sarah produces a sound (stimulus), "Mom," that resembles *Mama*, Mom smiles and repeats the sound (response), and voilà, the baby repeats the sound back to Mom, and so the cycle continues. This theory of language development prevailed until the mid-1970s when Noam Chomsky posited that human language was too complex to be merely a result of stimuli and responses. Furthermore, other researchers such as J. Lindfors observed that if language development were simply a function of stimulus and response, other primates that had the capability to vocalize would be able to learn and produce language, giving more credence to Chomsky's theory of language acquisition.

Children learn language in social settings.

Since Skinner's work, experts in anthropology, developmental psychology, education, linguistics, and sociology have researched language acquisition. All agree that children learn language in social settings. Furthermore, research encourages teachers, caregivers, older siblings, and others to support language development in very specific ways. G. Wells, who studied language development in very young children, suggested four critical ways to encourage language development: (1) when a child speaks, assume she has something important to say and support the conversation; (2) work to understand what the child has said; (3) use the child's speech to inform what you next say to the child by confirming or extending what the child has said; and (4) phrase your language so that it is at "or just beyond the child's ability to comprehend" (50).

Chomsky's work in *Generative Grammar* is probably the most influential in the area of language acquisition. *Generative Grammar* assumes that language is a structure of the human mind and that there are rules that can be used to produce or create any sentence. This kind of grammar focuses on the form of a sentence rather than how it functions in communication. Chomsky's view is that *all* language has certain structures in common. All language has surface and deep structures. **Surface structures** are what is said or written, and **deep structures** are the underlying meaning of what is said or written. He also asserted that children may use a variety of surface structures in language, but develop much fewer deeper or underlying structures. Chomsky also observed that meaning ambiguity can be a result of surface stuctures or deep structures. He used these structures to develop his theory of syntax.

Example 1:   *Jack fell down and broke his crown.*

This sentence can have two meanings:

1. Jack fell and broke his head.
2. Jack fell and broke the crown on his tooth.

This sentence is ambiguous because the word *crown* has more than one meaning; the deep structures are different.

Example 2:   *Visiting cousins can be fun.*

This sentence can also have two meanings:

1.   Cousins who visit can be fun.

2.   Going to visit one's cousins can be fun.

This sentence, like that in Example 1, is ambiguous because the underlying deep structures are different.

Chomsky observed that children understand surface and deep structures without direct teaching. He called this instinctive ability a **language acquisition device** and asserted that all children are born with this ability. Chomsky called this innate knowledge of language **universal grammar**. Not all language is innate, however. Therefore, children need to be taught certain words and vocabulary because vocabulary is not as predictable as syntax.

THEORIES OF READING

Bottom-Up Theory

The bottom-up theory emphasizes a progression from the smallest unit of the English language to the whole of a text in constructing meaning. This progression usually goes from phoneme to syllable, syllable to word, word to phrase, and phrase to sentence. Bottom-up theory is the basis of phonics. In the phonics model, students identify letters, combine these into spelling patterns, then into words, sentences, and an understanding of the entire text. Bottom-up theory places less emphasis on the knowledge and preconceptions a reader brings to the text and asserts that meaning can be derived entirely from elements on the page. It has been criticized because it may overlook the role of prior knowledge in a reader's interpretation of a text.

Top-Down Theory

The top-down theory suggests that the basis for understanding a text is situated in reader's assumptions about the text. Unlike the bottom-up theory, it views reading as a progression from the whole of the reader's idea of what the text may mean to the smaller parts that they ultimately use to support their assumption that the text has significance.

This theory recognizes the reader's prior cultural and factual knowledge, reasoning skills, and assumptions. Proponents argue that readers using the top-down model can use context clues to identify unfamiliar elements of a text and focus on the meaning of the text as a whole. This model manifests itself in the popular whole-language approach to teaching reading. Criticism of this model focuses on the assumption that the basis of meaning in a text does not come from the foundations of the text itself.

Interactive Theory

Interactive theory combines the top-down and bottom-up theories by incorporating elements from both, observing that these processes occur simultaneously during reading.

PROCESSES OF READING

Bottom-Up Models

Reading as Word Recognition

The bottom-up model places less emphasis on the knowledge and preconceptions a reader brings to the text and asserts that meaning can be derived entirely from elements on the page. Generally, this view contends the reader uses rules of phonics, learns sight words that do not follow phonics rules, and breaks words into patterns using structural analysis to decode words, phrases, and sentences. This view assumes that if the reader can identify the word, the reader will eventually derive meaning. This view also assumes that the reader can differentiate between sound patterns and can learn all the rules. This theory overlooks the role of prior knowledge in a reader's interpretation of a text, penalizes children that are nonnative English speakers, and assumes that all children learn the same way.

Reading as a Visual Process

Reading as a visual process assumes that "seeing" words is acquired through practice and that vision is the modality through which the mind and the text interact. Readers must be able to move their eyes and see in a way conducive to deriving meaning from text. Generally, nonreaders have not developed those skills. When a reader decodes a line of text, his or her eyes do not move along the line in a perfectly smooth motion; rather, they go, then stop on a word or words, and then go to the next word or words in a movement known as a **fixation**. Newer readers experience many fixations per lines and even multiple fixations per word, but as readers grow more experienced this number decreases. This view focuses on differences in readers' vision as a factor that can actually influence what they perceive while they read.

Top-Down Models

Reading as a Psycholinguistic Process

Reading is often viewed from a psycholinguistic perspective. Proponents of this outlook believe that an interaction between thought and words and both psychological and neurobiological factors allows readers to understand written language. They argue that human cognitive processes allow for understanding text. This view assumes various components of language:

Phonology refers to the way meaning is encoded in sound in language.

Phonemes are the smallest units of distinctive sound. While they have no meaning in and of themselves, they are the building blocks of the next-largest building block of language, morphemes.

Morphemes, composed of phonemes, are the smallest units of language that hold semantic meaning. Morphemes are not necessarily words, but they can be. They are called "free" if they can also stand alone as a word and "bound" if they must be part of a larger word. An example is the word *unbearable*, which has the morphemes *un*, *bear*, and *able*.

Tone and pitch refer to the use of raising or lowering one's intonation in language to give inflection to words. Often, tone and pitch serve to clarify grammar or meaning.

Stress is the extra weight or emphasis customarily given to various syllables of a word. Also called *accent*, stress affects the pronunciation of a word.

Juncture is the seam at which two syllables or words meet and are joined.

Semantics is the study of meaning in language, especially in text, speech, and signs. Good readers can utilize semantics to aid in their reading of a text, a practice commonly known as using context clues.

Syntax refers to the grammatical rules that exist in a particular language for organizing ideas into sentences.

Reading as a Sociopsycholinguistic Process

This view asserts that readers use background knowledge and cues from three language systems to construct meaning. These three systems include

> **graphophonics**: the relationship between orthography (letters) and phonology (sounds of the language)

> **syntax**: rules of grammar

> **semantics**: study of meaning in language

The reader integrates prior knowledge with information integrated from these systems to make predictions, use context clues, and derive meaning.

Reading as a Metacognitive Process

The idea of reading as a metacognitive process is important because it focuses on the power students have to improve their own reading by thinking about how they think while they read. It can improve reading skills in the short term and allow students to develop self-regulated reading skills and processes in the long run. When readers approach reading as a metacognitive process, they consciously apply purposeful steps or strategies to help decode and derive meaning.

EFFECTIVE READING INSTRUCTION

Ellin Keene and Susan Zimmermann (1997) have identified a fairly comprehensive list of strategies that proficient readers apply (22–23). Thus, it is important that effective reading instruction provide students with the most effective strategies for deriving meaning from a variety of texts. The following discussion includes critical aspects and strategies of effective reading instruction. Overall, a balanced literacy approach is the most effective way to address all classroom learners. Balanced literacy asserts that instruction includes a variety of interconnected activities and strategies that link reading, writing, listening, speaking, and thinking along with multiple and frequent forms of assessment. Although many of the following activities are more likely implemented in an elementary classroom, these actitivites and strategies work effectively for middle and high school readers and benefit learners of English as a second language as well.

Guided reading: The teacher introduces a selection at the student's instructional level, modeling specific strategies through a mini-lesson, interacting with text, and increasing the student's fluency level.

Independent reading: Students read independently, using strategies modeled during reading aloud, guided reading, and shared reading, thus extending reading stamina, improving comprehension, widening the kinds of texts that they read, and increasing familiarity and confidence with a new text.

Reading aloud: The teacher reads text aloud, modeling fluent reading, developing story line, modeling vocabulary development, encouraging prediction, asking questions, promoting active listening, making text connections, and building community.

Shared reading: The teacher and students read text together, developing fluency, correct phrasing, inflection, and intonation, modeling strategies, and increasing comprehension.

Activating prior knowledge: Students recall prior knowledge (schema) that relates to the reading, make connections to the reading, and compare the reading to what they already know. Keene and Zimmermann identify five kinds of connections proficient readers make before and during reading:

> **Text-to-self**: identifying personal connections and experiences that relate to the text

> **Text-to-text**: identifying how the text is like other texts that the student has read

> **Text-to-world**: identifying how the text relates to ideas that occur in the larger society or world

> **Text-to-author**: identifying the style of a particular author and making predictions based on what the reader knows about the author and his or her writing

> **Text-to-structure**: identifying forms of writing that occur in texts, dialogue, poetry, stream of consciousness. These structures are further broken down into narrative text elements and expository text elements:

Narrative text elements include character, setting, plot, conflict, title, figurative language, table of contents, dedication, prologue, epilogue, and illustrations.

Expository text elements include classification, categorization, listing, description, chronology, how-to, comparision/contrast, cause/effect, problem/solution, table of contents, chapter headings, subheadings, index, glossary, appendices, and graphics.

Determining important ideas: Students use conclusions to determine what is important, essential, or significant. Keene and Zimmermann observe that proficient readers automatically make decisions about what is important at three levels: word level, sentence level, and text level (94):

Word level: identifying two types of words: contentives, words that carry the meaning of the word; and functors, words that connect contentives

Sentence level: identifying key words, phrases, or sentences that carry the meaning: topic and clincher sentences, thesis statement, chapter headings and subheadings, bold-faced or italicized words and phrases

Text level: identifying key concepts, themes, and ideas. Readers are proficient at identifying word- and sentence-level information to reach text-level understanding. A proficient reader considers a variety of schema when identifying key concepts and the like: purpose, prior knowledge, personal beliefs, values, opinions, repeated ideas and text formats, concepts mentioned by peers, and nonexamples and examples.

Questioning the text: The teacher poses questions before, during, and after reading. These questions can clarify, explain, probe the author's intent, style, and format, predict, or focus reading for information. Bloom's Taxonomy offers six levels of understanding that help readers understand the text more effectively:

Knowledge: these questions seek factual information and address recall. Answers to such questions are text explicit. These questions generally ask, Who? What? When? Where?

Comprehension: these questions seek to elicit description in the reader's own words, retelling, ways to organize text, and so on. These questions generally ask, In your own words, what did the character say? What is the meaning of _____ in line 3 of the poem?

Application: these questions seek to elicit the application of information, rules, facts, and principles. These questions generally ask, What is the solution using this formula? How is this an example of . . . ? What is the simile in line 2 of the paragraph?

Analysis: these questions seek to elicit the breaking down of parts of the text, information, and so on. These questions generally ask, What textual evidence supports the thesis statement? How does the author's portrayal of this character compare to his portrayal of the other character? In what ways does the author develop characterization? What kinds of figurative language does the author use to develop setting?

Synthesis: these questions seek to elicit the combining of ideas to create a new and/or original whole. These questions generally ask, Based on the character's actions and archetype, what solutions would you pose to solve her problem? What do you predict will be the outcome of her decision? How would you characterize the author's style?

Evaluation: these questions seek to elicit an evaluation of an idea, event, decision, and so forth. These questions generally ask, How would you judge George's moral decision making based on his final action in the novel? Do you agree with Golding's overall perception of the nature of humankind in *Lord of the Flies*, and if so, why?

Visualizing the text: This enables the reader to create mental pictures or images using all senses, integrate details from reading to enhance those pictures, modify pictures as new information is learned from the reading or from others, and draw conclusions based on images.

Drawing inferences: This requires the reader to combine relevant prior knowledge with what is read to create meaning that is implict in the text but that can be supported with textual evidence. Proficient readers make predictions, interpret, analyze, draw conclusions, and evalute text.

Retelling and synthesizing: The reader refines interpretation for clarity, including the most important information and the most justifiable meaning. Proficient readers consistently add to concepts they form while reading, read on an inferential level, consider how literary devices work together to develop conclusions and inferences about the text, and revise or modify their interpretations based on new evidence.

Using fix-up strategies: Proficient readers know when to try a variety of strategies to enhance understanding. These strategies draw from different information systems:

Phonological: recognizing and pronouncing words

Morphological: knowing word meaning using inflection and affixes

Pragmatic: knowing the real-world uses of words

Syntactic: knowing how a word functions in a sentence

Semantic: knowing antonyms, synoymns, how words change, and so on

Developing Vocabulary Understanding

Few would disagree that many students encounter problems understanding narrative and content-area text because they do not understand difficult vocabulary. Knowing a definition does not mean knowing a word; knowing the word arises from making associations and connections with the word. Knowing the definition of the word, however, is not enough, especially when a word has a variety of meanings or shades of meaning. There are several levels of knowing a word (Tonjes, Wolpow, and Zintz). The following list demonstrates these levels using the word *assimilation*:

Specific: knowing the word in a general way; at this level, *assimilation* might be thought of as meaning "becoming something."

Functional: using the word appropriately in speaking and writing; at this level, *assimilation* would be defined as "the act of bringing or coming to be like or resemble something else."

Conceptual: knowing how to use the work in all its forms in a variety of contexts: at this level, *assimilation* is understood to be a euphemism for forced conformity and lost independence.

The following strategies help students learn vocabulary on a variety of levels.

Prereading, categorizing, and predicting using vocabulary: The teacher selects about fifty words, terms, and phrases from the passage that includes new technical vocabulary, new and old concept words, old vocabulary that should be reinforced, words that facilitate reading comprehension, as well as some words that most students should know.

For bilingual students, teachers should include

- Tier 1 words are those most commonly used in everyday language: *under*, *close*, *places*, *text*, and so on.

- Tier 2 words are those that are commonly used but are more complex: *illustrate*, *compare*, *contrast*, and so forth.

- Tier 3 words are those that are part of the technical vocabulary of the content area: *simile*, *metaphor*, *characterization*, *synecdoche*, and others.

Students work in small groups and read through your list of words, generating a new list of possible categories into which the words could fit. Not all words must fit into a category. For example, some possible categories are names of places, words that describe what people do, action words, names of people, words I don't know the meaning of, and so forth.

Students share lists with the whole class and talk about their categories. The teacher notes common categories and unusual ones and may add categories as well, especially if the words address important concepts that are important to the text.

Students choose any three categories and place the appropriate words in the categories.

Landforms	Tools	Sea Creatures

Then they find one category that has many words and write at least one paragraph that predicts what they think the passage is going to be about based on the list of words. After reading the text, students compare what they predicted with actual information from the text.

Before, during, and after chart: The teacher gives students a list of words or students select words themselves. Students then write what they think the word means before reading the passage and what they think the word means during reading; then teacher and students "correct" the meaning so that everyone understands the appropriate meaning.

Word	Before Reading	After Reading	After Discussion
assimilation	Making something similar	Making people similar	Process by which the dominant social class forces others to have the same values and beliefs.

Gipes cluing: The teacher identifies critical target words. For each word, students write a four-sentence paragraph. Sentence 1 uses the word exactly as it appears in the text. Sentence 2 defines and describes important characteristics of the word. Sentence 3 defines the word using concepts that are familiar to the reader. Sentence 4 applies the word to the student's life.

Visualization: The teacher selects a target word. Students close their eyes while the teacher reads a lengthy description of the word using sentences and phrases that create a mental picture of the word. Students individually or in small groups then draw what they visualize. Drawings can also be cartoons.

Using affixes: **Affixes** are words that are "affixed" or attached to the beginning of a word or to the end of a word to create a new word. Students can use affixes to figure out what words mean.

Prefixes are affixed before a base word or word stem (main part of a word) to add information. For example, in the word *predetermine*," the prefix is *pre-*, meaning "before," the base word is *determine*, meaning "decide or settle." *Predetermine* means "to decide or settle ahead of time or before."

Suffixes are affixed at the end of a base word or word stem to add information. Suffixes can denote tense or various parts of speech:

- Suffixes *-al, -ous, -ic, -y* make root words adjectives.

- Suffixes *-ment, -ion, -ism, -er, -or, -ist*, and *-ness* make root words nouns.

- Suffixes *-ize* and *-ing* can make root words verbs.

- The suffix *-ly* makes root words adverbs.

For a rather complete list of prefixes and suffixes, visit the Michigan Proficiency Exams Web site: *http://www.michigan-proficiency-exams.com/index.html*.

Using context clues: Students consider the meaning of the words, phrases, and sentences that surround the word, phrase, or sentence to glean meaning. The following list offers strategies for unlocking word meaning:

- Definition and restatement: The writer defines the word, especially if the word is a technical term.

    *The doctor used a **sphygmomanometer**, which is an instrument that measures blood pressure.*

    Words or phrases signaling definition and restatement include *which is, or, also known as, that is, in other words*, and *also called*.

- Example: The writer includes examples of what the word means.

    *The zoologist studied several types of **lepidoptera**, including butterflies and moths.*

    Words and phrases signaling examples include *like, including, such as, for example, for instance, especially, other, this, these*, and *these include*.

- Comparison: The writer makes a comparison between the word and something that is similar.

    *Similar to other members of the hog family, the **peccary** uses its snout and tusks to forage for roots.*

    Words and phrases signaling comparisons include *like, as, in the same way, similar to, resembling, likewise, similarity, also, identical*, and *related*.

- Contrast: The writer uses a statement of contrast to define the word.

    *Rather than adopt the **frugal** spending habits of her parents, Judith was generous with her money.*

    Words and phrases signaling contrast include *but, although, on the contrary, rather than, on the other hand, unlike, in contrast to, dissimilar, different*, and *however*.

- **Cause and effect:** The writer uses an unfamiliar word to define the cause but states the effect in familiar terms or vice versa.

    *Keisha was **emaciated** as a result of losing weight during her illness.*

    Words signaling cause and effect include *because, since, consequently, therefore, when*, and *as a result*.

- Inference from general context: The reader uses other clues in the sentence or sentences around the word and draws conclusions about the meaning of the word from those clues.

  The Wolfman *is a classic movie about a **lycanthrope**, who grew excessively hairy when the moon was full.*

Modeled and shared writing: The teacher models writing strategies, writing styles, and comprehension, provides different concepts of print, demonstrates how to support different purposes of writing using textual evidence, creates texts that students can read independently, and reinforces academic discourse.

Interactive writing: The teacher and students compose together using a "shared pen" technique in which students do some of the writing, collaborating about ways to organize and construct text, modeling application of learning, and increasing student knowledge of grammar, punctuation, spelling, text structures, literary devices, and other language conventions.

Independent writing: Students write independently, developing an understanding of and ability to write in multiple genres (e.g., narrative and expository texts) and learning to vary content, organization, style, and voice according to purpose.

Reading Assessments

Formal assessments include norm-referenced tests, standardized tests, district-based assessments, informal reading inventories, content informal reading inventories, and directed reading assessments

THEORIES OF SECOND-LANGUAGE ACQUISITION

There are two basic views of how second language is learned: the learning view and the acquisition view. The **learning view** or the traditional view asserts that the second language must be taught directly, that language must be broken into component parts, that students must learn through drill and practice, and that teachers must correct all errors (Freeman and Freeman 33). The **acquisition view** asserts that the second language must be made understandable through different linguistic techniques so students can use language for a variety of purposes, that students practice using language in a variety of contexts and settings, and that teachers focus on meaning and expression rather than errors, because making errors is a natural part of learning (Freeman and Freeman 33).

Bilingualism and Biliteracy

At the turn of the twenty-first century, an average of one in every nine U.S. students was an English learner. "Knowing two languages confers numerous obvious advantages: cultural, intellectual, cognitive, vocational, and economic" (Goldenburg 10). *Bilingualism* is the ability to use two languages with similar or nearly similar proficiency. **Biliteracy** means the ability to be literate in a variety of discourses in two languages. Bilingualism and biliteracy must go hand in hand in order for a student to achieve academically in the United States. Critical to all students' learning is proficiency in academic English or discourse.

Academic English or **discourse** requires knowing different forms and inflections of words and their appropriate use and possessing and using content-specific vocabulary and modes of expression in different academic disciplines such as mathematics and social studies. Academic English is abstract, complex and sometimes subtle, but necessary for academic success. Academic English is used both orally and in writing. Mastering the use of academic discourse is essential for English language as it impacts reading, writing, and speaking. Without the ability to use academic English in a classroom setting, students will inevitably feel discouraged and fall behind their native English-speaking classmates.

This challenge of teaching and learning academic English is one to be faced in almost every American classroom. The number of English language learners (ELLs) in U.S. classrooms has been increasing at a rapid rate. Currently, even states that have not typically been associated with ELLs have had a 300 percent population increase of non-English speakers.

Bilingual education describes any instructional approach that teaches at least some academic content (e.g., English, reading, or science) in the native language in addition to teaching students academic content in English. The state of Massachusetts does not permit bilingual education in its public schools. As a result, it is important that mainstream educators know how to implement effective strategies that enhance bilingualism and biliteracy in ELLs.

Best Practices

If ELLs are instructed in their primary language, the application of effective instructional models to their curriculum is transparent; all that differs is the language of instruction. Even when ELLs are instructed in English, however, effective instruction must reflect the critical aspects of literacy instruction for native English speakers. The following are best practices for teaching ELLs in mainstream classrooms:

- Establish clear goals, learning objectives, and language objectives.

- Provide meaningful, challenging, and motivating contexts.

- Assure that the curriculum is rich in content.

- Implement carefully designed and appropriately paced instruction.

- Elicit active engagement and participation.

- Provide opportunities to practice, apply, and transfer new learning.

- Offer useful feedback on correct and incorrect responses.

- Establish periodic review and practice.

- Employ frequent assessments to gauge progress, with reteaching as needed.

- Create multiple opportunities for interaction in a variety of contexts.

- Differentiate and teach three tiers of vocabulary:

  - Tier 1 words are those most commonly used in everyday language: *under*, *close*, *places*, *text*, and so on.

  - Tier 2 words are those that are commonly used but are more complex: *illustrate*, *compare*, *contrast*, and so on.

  - Tier 3 words are those that are part of the technical vocabulary of the content area: *simile*, *metaphor*, *characterization*, *synecdoche*, and the like.

Important Terms Related to Reading

Assessment: formal and informal data-gathering processes used to make a judgment about student performance.

> **Authentic assessments**: measures of what students know and are able to do that relate to realistic/real-world contexts. Such assessments might include open-ended problems, simulations, portfolios, and experiments.

Formal assessments: measures that use uniform and consistent methods of administration and scoring. These include norm-referenced and criterion-referenced measures:

- *Norm-referenced* measures are tests that compare the results of the individual with that of a group, called the norm group. Examples of these tests include the Iowa Test of Basic Skills, the Metropolitan Reading Readiness Test, and the College Board's SAT.

- *Criterion-referenced* measures are tests that report a student's performance in a particular area or domain but do not compare the students to a group. These are sometimes called mastery tests because they indicate what a student knows and is able to do with respect to a particular skill or concept, for example, vocabulary, literal comprehension, and the like.

Informal assessments: measures that do not utilize uniform and consistent methods of scoring and administration. These are usually teacher constructed and focus on a particular content, process, or skill. Five examples of informal assessments used in reading instruction are CLOZE, content area reading inventory (CARI), informal reading inventory (IRI), miscue analysis, and running record:

- CLOZE: an informal assessment that identifies the reader's ability to use understanding and coherence to fill in words in a sentence to make meaning. In a typical CLOZE assessment, the teacher selects a 250- to 300-word passage, leaving the first and last sentences intact, and replacing every fifth word with a blank line. The student fills in the blanks using context clues, syntax, schemata, and semantics.

- CARI: an informal assessment that identifies a reader's ability to use text structures, components of a textbook, reference skills, and learning aids to understand vocabulary, and to demonstrate literal and interpretive comprehension. In a CARI, the teacher selects a three- to five-page passage related to the content/discipline under study, creates six to eight questions for each of four areas: textbook components, reference skills, vocabulary, and literal, interpretive, and applied comprehension.

- IRI: an informal assessment that identifies the reader's **instructional**, **independent**, and **frustration** levels using a selected text. These assessments first determine word recognition competence, then use this level to select a text, which the reader reads aloud and silently and on which the reader is asked questions that address vocabulary understanding and different levels of comprehension. There are numerous published IRIs on the market.

IRI Levels:

Instructional level: level of text at which a reader can read and understand with instruction or faciliation

Independent level: level of text at which a reader can read and understand indepedently

Frustration level: level of text at which reader experiences frustration and difficulty while reading

Miscue analysis: originally developed by Kenneth Goodman, this assessment is used to diagnose how readers use phonemic, semantic, and syntactic cues to decode and understand a reading selection. In this analysis, the student reads a selection aloud while the teacher notes omissions and specific kinds of substitutions, such as phonic, graphic, syntactic, and contextual. As in the IRI tests, this information translates into instructional, independent, and frustration levels. Students are also required to retell the selection after reading. There are also numerous published miscue analysis assessments:

- **Running record**: developed by Marie Clay, this assessment identifies how readers use phonemic, semantic, and syntactic clues to decode a reading selection. While the student reads the text aloud, the teacher records a variety of conventions: omissions, substitutions, insertions, self-corrected errors, repetitions, appeals (student asks for help), and tells (teacher tells the word). The teacher also observes the reader for behaviors such as directional movement, expression, fluency and phrasing, pace, use of picture cues, inserting punctuation, finger pointing, pauses, and scanning.

Automaticity: parts of the reading process that the reader performs automatically, for example, immediate recognition of letters, syllables, words, phrases, and sentences; structural analysis, and so on.

Comprehension: the ability of a reader to understand written text. There are three levels of reading comprehension:

Literal/text-explicit: understanding that requires the reader to find or recall facts or information that can be found explicitly in the text; usually addresses who, what, when, where, and so on.

Interpretive/inferential/text-implicit: understanding that requires the reader to use information in the text to draw and support inferences, generalizations, and conclusions.

Applied/beyond the text: understanding that requires the reader to synthesize information from mupltiple texts and apply understanding to new situations or contexts.

Decode: the process of using conventions of spelling-sound relationships and knowledge about pronunciation of irregular words to derive a pronunciation of written words.

Fluency: the ability to read a text quickly and accurately.

Metacognition: a reader's awareness of comprehension during reading. Several metacognitive strategies are presented later in this chapter.

Readability: the difficulty of a text based on sentence structure, sentence length, vocabulary, and syntax. Other factors that impact readability of text include coherence and unity, elaboration, text length, text structure, familiarity of content, and text engagement. There are several readability formulas that can help a teacher determine the difficulty of a text. The Fry Readability Graph and the Gunning FOG Index are the most common. Most trade books that might be used in the classroom come with readability measures.

Schemata: chunks of knowledge that readers develop via multiple modalities. For example, American students are quite conscious of the economic system in the United States; they use money to purchase goods and services. Thus, American students have developed and stored this information in the form of schemata. Immigrant children from a society that barters for goods and services possess a different schemata and might find the U.S. economic system alien. Therefore, it is critical to help second-language learners develop schemata that enable them to understand new text.

Stamina: the ability to ready fluently with comprehension for sustained periods of time.

USING CHILDREN'S AND YOUNG ADULT LITERATURE IN READING INSTRUCTION

Children's and young adult literature serve as extraordinary vehicles for teaching not only reading and comprehension but also literary devices, criticism, genres, and forms or types of literature. Donna Norton's *Through the Eyes of a Child: An Introduction to Children's Literature* is probably one of the best texts in print that addresses reading, selecting, evaluating, and teaching children's and young adult literature. High-interest, easy-reading (low-readability) children's and young adult literature can provide valuable texts to engage nonreaders in exploring literature and improving reading fluency, stamina, and comprehension. Picture books and wordless books especially can offer nonnative English speakers and struggling readers a common focal point for identifying sequence, developing vocabulary, explaining and illustrating concepts and ideas, and deriving meaning. Alphabet books like *Animalia* by Graeme Base present exquisite illustrations of animals, idea, and objects that represent the letter accompanied by alliterative phrases composed of challenging vocabulary. Other picture books, such as *The Middle Passage* by Tom Feelings, which depicts the profoundly emotional, forced journey of African slaves to the New World, serve as a gripping prereading activity that contextualizes difficult content in a way that is accessible to all students. The following section describes the most common types (sometimes called genres) of children's and young adult literature and provides specific examples of quality selections of each genre by title and author.

> **MTEL Tip**
>
> **Picture books offer struggling readers a focal point for explaining and illustrating concepts and ideas.**

Types of Literature

Picture Books

Nodelman defines picture books as books that "communicate information or tell stories through a series of many pictures combined with relatively slight texts or no texts at all" (Norton vii). Pictures books help students learn sequence, characterization, story line, and vocabulary. Picture books include

alphabet books: books that present the letters of the alphabet using rich details, innovativeness, and numerous objects

- *Animalia* by Graeme Base

- *Bestiary: An Illuminated Alphabet of Medieval Beasts* by Jonathan Hunt

- *Ashanti to Zulu* by Margaret Musgrove

- *A Walk in the Rainforest* by Kristin Joy Pratt

concept books: books that help readers learn colors, shapes, trains, planes, night, day, and so on

- *The Grouchy Ladybug* by Eric Carle

- *Circles, Triangles, and Squares*; *Of Colors and Things*; and *Shapes, Shapes, Shapes* by Tana Hoban

- *Changes, Changes* by Pat Hutchins

counting books: books that usually show one large number, the word for the number, and a representation of the number using objects

- *Anno's Counting Book* by Mitsumasa Anno

- *Moja Means One: Swahili Counting Book* by Muriel Feelings

- *Count Your Way through Italy* by Jim Haskins

- *Eating Fractions* by Bruce McMilan

- *The History of Counting* by Denise Schmandt-Besserat

easy-to-read books: books designed for beginning readers and young children. These books, which can appear as Big Books, often reinforce phonics and linguistic patterns. Dr. Suess books appeal to any age and often address sophisticated concepts.

- *Oscar Otter* by Nathaniel Benchley

- *My Brother* by Betsy Byars

- *Sammy the Seal* by Syd Hoff

- *Frog and Toad* series by Arnold Lobel

- *The Butter Battle*; *Oh, the Places You'll Go*; and *One Fish, Two Fish, Red Fish, Blue Fish* by Dr. Seuss

Mother Goose books: books of rhymes and rhythms that tell stories about imaginative characters

- *Miss Mary Mac and Other Children's Street Rhymes* by Joanna Cole and Stephanie Calmenson

- *The Neighborhood Mother Goose* by Nina Crews

- *The Glorious Mother Goose* by Cooper Edens

- *Gregory Griggs and Other Nursery Rhyme People* by Arnold Lobel

wordless books: books that present a story using only pictures. Collections of artwork also serve as foci for writing, learning new vocabulary, and understanding satire, parody, and imagery.

- *Anno's Journey* by Mitsumasa Anno

- *Banksy*, *Banksy Graffiti*, and *Wall and Piece* by Banksy

- *Do You Want to Be My Friend?* by Eric Carle

- *Pancakes for Breakfast* and *The Hunter and the Animals* by Tomi dePaola

- *The Middle Passage* by Tom Feelings

- *Changes, Changes* by Pat Hutchins

- *A Boy, a Dog, a Frog, and a Friend* and *Frog Goes to Dinner* by Mercer Mayer

- *Circus, Dreams, Noah's Ark, People,* and *Rain* by Peter Spier

- *The Mysteries of Harris Burdick* by Chris VanAllsburg

- *Flotsam, Free Fall, Sector 7, The Three Pigs, Tuesday*, and *Hurricane* by David Wiesner

Traditional Children's Literature

Traditional children's literature includes forms that have emerged from the oral tradition of storytelling. The oral tradition is indigenous to every culture, race, class, and ethnicity. Traditional children's literature serves as an excellent model for writing in a particular genre form, particularly for middle and high school students. These texts also offer simple but engaging texts to teach theme, characterization, plot, and problem-solution, and can help students access prior knowledge or serve as "hooks" into more difficult texts that share similar themes and purposes. Types of traditional children's literature include

fables: tales whose main characters are animals that talk and act human. Tales usually teach a lesson or end with a moral.

- *Aesop's Fables* by Aesop

- *Ackamarackus: Julius Lester's Sumptuously Silly Fantastically Funny Fables* by Julius Lester

- *Squids Will Be Squids: Fresh Morals, Beastly Fables* by Jon Scieszka and Lane Smith

folktales: fictional narratives that tell about important characters, events, and beliefs and reflect the rich culture, setting, history, and ethnicity of the storyteller. Often, the main characters in folktales are animals that possess intelligence and wit. Human characters are often superheroes and heroines who demonstrate unusual abilities. Folktales may also tell stories that explain how or why a particular event happened or why an animal or character came to exist. Different types of folktales include cumulative, realistic, humorous, beast, magic, and pourquoi tales (Norton 209–211).

- *Why Mosquitoes Buzz in People's Ears* by Verna Ardeman

- *The Magic Gourd* by Baba Wague Diakite

- *More Tales of Uncle Remus: Further Adventures of Brer Rabbit* retold by Julius Lester

- *Nelson Mandela's Favorite Folktales* by Nelson Mandela

- *The Spring of Butterflies and Other Folktales of China's Minority Peoples* edited by Neil Philip

legends: narratives and poems that border on myths, folktales, and history (Cavendish 9). Legends provide important information about the cultures, beliefs, and societies that created them. Legends not only provide students a different way of thinking about the world and others but also expose students to literary devices of theme, figurative language, characterization, and conflict.

- *Beowulf*, anonymous

- *The Iliad* and *The Odyssey* by Homer

- *Sir Gawain and the Green Knight* by Michael Morpurgo

- *The Legend of Sleepy Hollow* by Washington Irving

- *The Merry Adventures of Robin Hood* by Howard Pyle

- *The Once and Future King* by T. H. White

myths: fictional narratives that are considered to be true in the culture depicted in the myth. Myths may explain the origin of an important event, person, concept, or natural phenomenon. Humans, animals, and deities are usually the main characters in myths. Myths are an essential part of early high school curriculum as their characters and themes form the basis for later works and describe gods, events, and phenomena that are alluded to in all genres of study.

- *Cupid and Psyche* by Edith Barth

- *A Book of Myths* by Thomas Bullfinch

- *The Golden God Apollo* by Doris Gates

- *In the Beginning: Creation Stories from Around the World* by Virginia Hamilton

- *The Adventures of Odysseus* by Neil Philip

Fantasy

Fantasy is considered among the most valuable forms of children's literature because it allows the reader to enter an imaginative world, expands curiosity, and "opens the mind to new possibilities" (Norton 272). Excellent examples of fantasy suspend disbelief, create characters that are believable, develop a magical setting, and pose universal themes, thus establishing characters that the reader believes are real, worlds that the reader believes could exist, and events that the reader believes could happen. Reading fantasy exposes the reader to rich description, vivid imagery, higher level vocabulary, intricate plots, various points of view, and differing methods of characterization.

Traditional fantasy includes

literary folktales or fairy tales that capitalize on the "Once upon a time. . ." story frame

- *The Tinderbox Box* and *The Wild Swans* by Hans Christian Andersen

religious and ethical allegories that address religious themes and moral quests

- *The Lion, the Witch and the Wardrobe* and the other books in the *Chronicles of Narnia* series by C. S. Lewis

- *At the Back of the North Wind* by George MacDonald

mythical quests and conflicts that address battles between good and evil or the adventures of characters seeking precious objects or power

- *Eragon* by Christopher Paolini

- *The Seeing Stone by Kevin Crossley-Holland*

- *The Golden Compass* by Philip Pullman

- *The Hobbit*, *The Lord of the Rings*, and *The Fellowship of the Ring* by J. R. R. Tolkien

- *The Black Cauldron* by Lloyd Alexander

- The *Harry Potter* series by J. K. Rowling

Modern fantasy includes

articulate animals: stories in which animals solve problems or get into mischief

- *The Tale of Peter Rabbit* by Beatrix Potter

- *Charlotte's Web* by E. B. White

- *Rikki-Tikki-Tavi* by Rudyard Kipling

- *The Wind in the Willows* by Robert Lawson

toy stories: stories told from the point of view of the toy or doll

- *The Velveteen Rabbit* by Margery Williams

- *Winnie-the-Pooh* by A. A. Milne

- *Pinocchio* by Carlo Collodi

preposterous characters and situations: stories in which characters find themselves in absurd or humorous situations and where language plays with words, parody, and satire

- *James and the Giant Peach, Charlie and the Chocolate Factory*, and *BFG* by Roald Dahl

- *Rootabaga Stories* by Carl Sandburg

bizarre worlds: stories that include unusual settings, elusive characters, and strange events

- *Alice's Adventures in Wonderland* by Lewis Carroll

- *Peter Pan* by James Barrie

little people: stories in which people like the reader solve problems and go on adventures

- *The Borrowers* by Mary Norton

- *The Hobbit* by J. R. R. Tolkien

spirits and ghosts: stories in which characters take on frightening spirits or ally with friendly creatures

- *The Boggart* by Susan Cooper

- *The Bartimaeus Trilogy* by Jonathan Stroud

- *The Children of Green Knowe* by Lucy Boston

time warps: stories in which characters travel to the future or back in time

- *The Devil's Arithmetic* by Jane Yolen

- *The Time Machine* by H. G. Wells

science fiction: stories that incorporate futuristic technology, scientific advancements, and space travel. This type of literature might also address dystopias.

- *Frankenstein* by Mary Shelley

- *Dr. Jekyll and Mr. Hyde* by Robert Louis Stevenson

- *Twenty Thousand Leagues Under the Sea* by Jules Verne

- *A Wrinkle in Time by* Madeleine L'Engle

- *The Giver* by Lois Lowry

Contemporary Realistic Fiction

Contemporary realistic fiction incorporates characters, themes, plots, settings, and conflicts that replicate real-life people, events, problems, and situations in honest and authentic ways. This form of literature offers readers characters that share similar social and emotional problems, thus helping readers feel that they are not alone or unique in their struggles. Realistic fiction often provides characters that serve as models for solving "challenging moral cognitive dilemmas" (Friedman and Cataldo 7).

Critical elements of contemporary realistic fiction include

conflicts that children and young adults encounter with peers, adults, authority, and external forces

- *The One-Eyed Cat* by Paula Fox

- *Taking Sides* by Gary Soto

characters that look, act, speak, and think like children and young adults in contemporary society

- *Homecoming* and *Dicey's Song* by Cynthia Voigt

themes that address human needs

- *Hope Was There* by Joan Bauer

style that incorporates believable dialogue and accurate and vivid description

- *Missing May* by Cynthia Rylant

Contemporary realistic fiction often addresses controversial issues that elicit criticism for its too-authentic content. These issues, which Norton calls "**New Realism**" (370), include sexism, sexuality, violence, profanity, family problems, desertion, divorce, and remarriage, death, growing up, alienation, individuality, racism, peer pressure, physical and emotional survival, and ageism. Norton counsels educators to consider such texts with care. Attention to mores, values, and beliefs of students in the classroom, citizens within the larger community, and the social context, culture, ethnicity, and race is essential when evaluating such texts for use in the classroom. Selections of contemporary realistic fiction that contain New Realism themes include

sexism: *Jacob Have I Loved* by Katherine Paterson, and *Dicey's Song* by Cynthia Voigt

sexuality: *Night Kites* and *"Hello" I Lied* by M. E. Kerr

violence: *Scorpions* and *Shooter* by Walter Dean Myers

profanity: *The Chocolate War* by Robert Cormier

desertion: *Walk Two Moons* by Sharon Creech

single-parent: *Where the Lilies Bloom* by Bill and Vera Cleaver

racism: *The Bluest Eye* and *Beloved* by Toni Morrison

war: *The Things They Carried* by Tim O'Brien

prejudice: *Snow Falling on Cedars* by David Guterson

physical survival: *Into the Wild* by Jon Krakauer

emotional survival: *Caramelo* by Sandra Cisneros

Multicultural Literature

"Multicultural literature is a body of literature that represents any distinct cultural group through accurate portrayal and rich detail" (Yokota 157). Multicultural literature appears throughout all genres and reflects the unique and varied perspectives, cultures, beliefs, traditions, and contributions of each cultural group in an increasingly diverse global society. Examples of multicultural literature appear throughout the various forms explained during previous discussions as well as in chapter 2. Additional selections of multicultural realistic fiction include

African American

- *Scorpions*, *The Mouse Rap*, and *Shooter* by Walter Dean Myers

- *The House of Dies Drear* by Virginia Hamilton

Asian American

- *Kira-Kira* by Cynthia Kadohata

- *Homeless Bird* by Gloria Whalen

- *Honeysuckle House* by Andrea Cheng

Native American

- *Walk Two Moons* by Sharon Creech

- *The Ceremony of Innocence*, *I Wear the Morning Star*, and *Legend Days* by Jamake Highwater

- *The Brave* by Robert Lipsyte

Latino

- *The House on Mango Street* by Sandra Cisneros

- *How the Garcia Girls Lost Their Accents* and *In the Time of the Butterflies* by Julia Alvarez

- *Taking Sides* by Gary Soto

- *Elya's Home at Last* by Susan Middleton

New Immigrant

- *Blue Jasmine* by Kashmira Sheth

- *The Sunita Experiment* by Mitali Perkins

- *Tangled Threads: A Hmong Girl's Story* by Pegi Dietz Shea

Historical Fiction

Historical fiction is a body of literature whose characters, setting, conflicts, theme, action, style, and perspectives are consistent with, relevant to, and reflective of the specific historical time period. Authenticity in language, setting, characterization, and theme is essential to effective historical fiction. Selections of historical fiction include

- *A Gathering of Days: A New England Girl's Journal* by Joan Bios

- *Code Talker* by Joseph Bruchak

- *Dust to Eat: Drought and Depression in the 1930s* by Michael Cooper

- *The Slave Dancer* by Paula Fox

- *Out of the Dust* by Karen Hesse

- *Dragonwings* by Laurence Yep

Nonfiction

Biographies

Historically, biographies for children were texts meant to educate them about politics, religion, and society. Texts tended to depict heroes and "reflected the belief that literature should save children's souls" (Norton 462). Eventually the religious focus was replaced by biographies of heroes that attained the American Dream, heroes in politics, science, music, sports, and other areas. Biographies also documented the struggle of various persons throughout history. Good biographies are engaging, factually accurate, and based on credible and reliable primary sources. Photographs and illustrations can also enhance the appeal of biographies. When read alongside historical fiction, biographies add clarity and authenticity. A selection of biographies includes

- *Maritcha: A Nineteenth-Century American Girl* by Tonya Bolden

- *Genius: A Photobiography of Albert Einstein* by Marte Ferguson Delano

- *Lincoln: A Photobiography* by Russell Freedman

- *The Voice That Challenged a Nation: Marian Anderson and the Struggle for Equal Rights* by Russell Freedman

- *Walt Whitman: Words for America* by Barbara Kerley

- *Wise Guy: The Life and Philosophy of Socrates* by M. D. Usher

- *Saladin: Noble Prince of Islam* by Diane Stanley

- *Anthony Burns: The Defeat and Triumph of a Fugitive Slave* by Virginia Hamilton

Informational Books

Informational books are texts that students use as sources for writing reports, enriching understanding in the disciplines, or learning about concepts and ideas out of curiosity. Informational books must contain accurate facts, pictures, and illustrations; be free of stereotypes; challenge analytical thinking; be organized for understanding; and possess an engaging style (Norton 502). Informational books also present technical vocabulary, which when accompanied by pictures, charts, and illustrations, enhances vocabulary understanding for both English language learners and native English speakers. Pairing an informational book with fiction text of a specific period also contextualizes the fictive work for readers. A selection of useful informational books includes

- *The Way Things Work* by David Macaulay

- *Four to the Pole! The American Women's Expedition to Antarctica* by Nancy Loewen and Ann Bancroft

- *Arrowhawk* by Lola Schaefer

- *Outside and Inside Killer Bees* by Sandra Markle

- *What's the Deal? Jefferson, Napoleon, and the Louisiana Purchase* by Rhoda Blumberg

- *The Golden City: Jerusalem's 3,000 Years* by Neil Waldman

- *Good Women of a Well-Blessed Land: Women's Lives in Colonial America* by Brandon Marie Miller

- *Remember D-Day: The Plan, The Invasion, Survivor Stories* by Ronald J. Drez

- *Scholastic Encyclopedia of the Civil War* by Catherine Clinton

- *Remember: The Journey to School Integration* by Toni Morrison

- *Now Is Your Time! The African American Struggle for Freedom* by Walter Dean Myers

Book Awards

The **Caldecott Medal** is an annual award given to a children's book for innovative, detailed, vivid, and rich illustrations, drawings, or pictures. The 2009 Caldecott Medal winner is *The House in the Night*, illustrated by Beth Krommes and written by Susan Marie Swanson. For a list of Caldecott Medal winners since 1938, visit the American Library Association's (ALA) Web site at <http://www.ala.org/ala/mgrps/divs/alsc/**awards**grants/bookmedia/>.

The **Newbery Medal** is an annual award given to a work written in English by an American citizen. Distinguished work is judged by the author's presentation or interpretation of theme with respect to accuracy, organization, clarity, characterization, setting, style, and plot development. The 2009 winner of the Newbery Medal is Neil Gaiman's *The Graveyard Book*. For a complete list of Newbery Medal winners since 1922, see <http://www.ala.org/alsc/**newbery**.cfm>.

The **Coretta Scott King Book Award** is presented by the Coretta Scott King Committee of the ALA's Ethnic Multicultural Information Exchange Round Table (EMIERT) to an African American author and an African American illustrator for an outstandingly inspirational and educational contribution that promotes understanding and appreciation of the culture of all peoples and their contribution to the realization of the American dream. The 2009 winner is *We Are the Ship: The Story of Negro League Baseball*, written and illustrated by Kadir Nelson. For a complete list of award winners, see <http://www.ala.org/ala/mgrps/rts/emiert/>.

References

Benchmark Education. 2006. 26 January 2009. <http://www.benchmarkeducation.com/educational-leader/reading/metacognitive-strategies.html#read4.html>.

Cavendish, Richard, ed. *Legends of the World*. New York: Schocken Books, 1982.

Clay, Marie. *Running Records for Classroom Teachers*. Portsmouth: Heinemann, 2000.

Components of a Balanced Literacy Approach. 2009. 5 March 2009 <http://www.ask.com/bar?q=Components+of+a+Balanced+Literacy+Reading+Program&page=1&qsrc=6&ab=0&u=http%3A%2F%2Finstech.tusd.k12.az.us%2Fbalancedlit%2Fhandbook%2Fblcomp.htm>.

Cunningham, Anne E., and Keith E. Stanovich. "What Reading Does for the Mind." *American Educator* Vol. 22, No. 1. (1998). 2 February 2009 <http://www.ask.com>.

Freeman, David E., and Yvonne S. Freeman. *Essential Linguistics*. Portsmouth: Heinemann, 2004.

Friedman, A. A., and Christina Cataldo. "Characters at Crossroads: Reflective Decision Makers in Contemporary Newbery Books." *The Reading Teacher* . Vol. 56, No. 2 (2002): 102–125.

Goldenberg, Claude. "Teaching English Language Learners: What the Research Does—and Does Not—Say." *American Educator* Vol 32, No. 2. (2008): 1–44.

Goodman, K. "Analysis of Oral Reading Miscues: Applied Psycholinguistics." *Language and Literacy: The Selected Writings of Kenneth Goodman*. Vol. I. Boston: Routledge & Kegan Paul, 1969. 123-134.

Keene, Ellin Oliver and Zimmermann, Susan. *Mosaic of Thought*. Heinemann: Portsmouth,NH. 1997

Lindfors, J. *Children's Language and Learning*. Englewood Cliffs: Prentice Hall, 1987.

Norton, Donna E., and Saundra Norton. *Through the Eyes of a Child: An Introduction to Children's Literature*. 7th ed. New York: Pearson, 2007.

Reutzel, D. Ray, and Robert B. Cooter. *Teaching Children to Read*. 4th ed. New York: Pearson Education, 2004.

Ryder, Randall J., and Michael F. Graves. *Reading and Learning in Content Areas*. New York: Merrill, 1994.

Savage, John. *For the Love of Literature*. New York: McGraw-Hill, 1999.

Savage, John. *Sound It Out! Phonics in a Comprehensive Reading Sy*stem. New York: McGraw-Hill, 2006.

Skinner, B. F. *Verbal Behavior*. New York: Appleton, 1957.

Tonjes, Marian, Ray Wolpow, and Miles Zintz. *Integrated Content Literacy*. New York: McGraw-Hill, 1992.

Wells, G. *The Meaning Makers: Children Learning Language and Using Language to Learn*. Portsmouth: Heinemann, 1986.

Yokota, J. "Issues in Selecting Multicultural Children's Literature." *Language Arts* March (1993): 156–167.

Integration of Knowledge and Understanding

In this chapter, you are assigned three tasks:

1. to compare, contrast, and connect literary periods and elements across three bodies of literature

2. to interpret a selected text based on a specific theory or theories of literary criticism

3. to identify, interpret, and explicate a theme based on a text of your choosing

Following each task is a graphic organizer or outline that will help you organize your ideas before drafting; a sample response; and an explanation about the elements of the sample response that make it an exemplar.

COMPARING AND CONTRASTING LITERARY PERIODS AND ELEMENTS ACROSS THREE BODIES OF LITERATURE

The later eighteenth century marked the romantic period in American literature, the romantic period in the literature of Great Britain, and the period of Enlightenment in world literature. In a cogent analysis, compare, contrast, and connect the historical and literary elements of these three periods, elaborating on pervasive themes and unique differences among the three. In your analyses,

identify representative works that demonstrate these similarities and differences and identify and support the connections or influences each period shared.

Approach

1. Prewrite: Read and outline the major literary and historical elements of each of the literary periods. A three-section graphic organizer is probably the easiest way to organize this information.

2. After each period, identify two to three key authors and their major works, including a brief summary of each work.

3. Review the information and identify the major similarities and differences among the three periods.

4. Outline an introductory paragraph that poses a thesis that identifies the major similarity and the major differences.

5. Outline the major body paragraphs (at least one for each period or "lens").

6. Write/draft your introduction and body paragraphs.

7. Write/draft your conclusion, reiterating your thesis and major points.

8. Revise the draft for clarity of thesis, supporting ideas, appropriate use of examples with clarifying explanation, appropriate application of literary lens, consistency of argument, continual reference to thesis, diction, style, voice, and so on.

9. Edit or proofread the draft, reviewing for errors in spelling, grammar, and punctuation.

Graphic Organizer

Literary Period	Historical Events	Literary Elements	Major Authors	Work and Summary
American Romantic				
British Romantic				
Enlightenment World				

Sample Response

For the English-speaking and European worlds, the eighteenth century is broadly called the period of Enlightenment, marked by exchanges and conflicts between reason and passion that played out in science, philosophy, and especially literature. During this century, the preceding Age of Reason eventually yielded to the romantic period. The romantic period in England, the United States, and other European countries dominated the later eighteenth century and prevailed into the first half of the nineteenth century. Its onset was for many heralded by the German writer <u>Goethe</u>, who wrote <u>The Sorrows of Young Werther</u>, a story about a psychologically flawed young artist who rejects the scholarship and rationality popular during his age but who describes himself with wonderfully poetic verse. Johann Wolfgang von Goethe, considered a genius, was a German poet, dramatist, novelist, autobiographer, lawyer, diplomat, and scientific researcher. In his play (poetic drama) Faust, Dr. Faustus, a scholar who lived from 1480 to 1549, makes a contract with Mephistopheles (the Devil) in order to test the limits of possibility. In this text, Goethe explores the issue of imagination versus social obligation and questions the functions and limitations of desire. Inspired by the works of Goethe and the French writer Rousseau, writers who embraced themes of subjectivity, passion, and imagination, Jean-Jacque Rousseau believed in the destructive nature of institutions, the gradual corruption of humankind throughout history, and the importance of nature and feeling in individual development and society. Rousseau, forced to leave France because of his controversial writing, presented characters whose nature had more significance than the events that impacted their lives and elevated the common people as morally superior to those in the upper classes. His work expresses the narcissistic side of romanticism. <u>Confessions</u> recounts how men and boys strive to express natural impulses but are frustrated by society's demands and assumptions. Literature of this period was influenced by the triumph of the French Revolution, the power of democratic ideals, and advocacy for the rights of women and children. The aesthetic of the romantics came to be defined as art over industry, and the individual and common man (and the rising middle class) over nobility. Overall, literature of this period, whether in England, Europe, or the United States, celebrated the triumph of the human spirit.

In the first paragraph, the author identifies the major historical elements that integrate all three literary periods, beginning with world literature, which was the major influence on writing in Great Britain and the United States. The author then identifies critical literary influences of the periods, their works, and their impact, the essential literary aesthetic that pervades all three periods, and finally an overarching thesis or theme that connects the periods.

Focusing on the power of human imagination, a resurgent interest in the Gothic naturally arose. In the United States, Edgar Allan Poe, emulating the Gothic style of English contemporaries, made the short story an American genre. Poe's stories and poems explored the supernatural and the strangeness in beauty and the beauty of strangeness as well as the psychological deterioration of imagination. Other dark themes pervaded the writing of American authors Herman Melville and Nathaniel Hawthorne, but instead their works interrogated the darkness of the human soul. Melville's Moby Dick, although posing natural imagery and settings like the works of other romantics, condemned human nature and sin, with nature symbolically triumphing over evil. Meanwhile, New England's Hawthorne was concerned with the flaws in human morality. His novel, The Scarlet Letter, criticized the religious hypocrisy of the Puritans. British poets also returned to nature, depicting conflicts between humankind and the natural world. Samuel Taylor Coleridge, like Poe, composed poetry of a dark, supernatural nature that articulated the consequences of upsetting the natural balance. His famous "Rime of the Ancient Mariner" tells the story of a mariner haunted by his sin of killing the albatross. Although replete with chilling imagery, the poem has a moral tale compelling its readers to revere all of earth's creatures; evildoers will be doomed to a life of penance and suffering. A respect for and love of nature was a theme in all romantic literature in Britain, from William Wordsworth (Coleridge's coauthor of Lyrical Ballads) to John Keats.

In the expanding United States, this sense of naturalism emerged in the form of transcendentalism, which thrived alongside romanticism. Similar to the Mariner's warning, transcendentalism teaches that the divine is manifested in all of nature. Ralph Waldo Emerson's Nature and Henry David Thoreau's On Walden Pond revered the natural world. However, these authors were also concerned with the more American theme of the romantic movement: individualism. Although this theme was also present in Europe—the rise of the common man and the middle class over pretentious nobility—individualism became a trope of a newly developing American sensibility in writing. Another genre American authors developed, as a national tradition, was the art of oratory, inspired by the great orator Abraham Lincoln. Emerson was also famous for his inspiring oratories. With this also came a love and desire for true democracy and freedom, as in Thoreau's "Civil Disobedience." Perhaps the best example of individualism is observed in American writers like Walt Whitman, who broke from the English literary tradition, totally disregarding traditional poetic diction and structure. In his frank rejection of all conventionality, however, he still revered his country and the desire for true democracy as observed in his ode to Lincoln, "O Captain! My Captain!"

In the preceding paragraphs, the author identifies how writers in the United States emulated the style and themes of British contemporaries, emphasizing the influence of world literature via the reiteration of the theme of human imagination. The writer then segues into the differences, noting how major U.S. authors worked to develop their own style and focus, but continues to compare and contrast U.S. and British authors, identifying major writers, summarizing their works, and noting how these examples reflect a common theme or a breaking away from the more traditional European and British themes.

While governments throughout the world were invading, appropriating, and colonizing territories, English and American writers also became interested in knowledge of the "other." James Fenimore Cooper, an American, mythologized the Native Americans in The Last of the Mohicans, borrowing the form of the historical novel from the contemporary British author of Ivanhoe, Sir Walter Scott. Meanwhile, as European governments expanded their "territories" through trade and colonialism, writers also sought a break from tradition, discovering an exoticism in what was called the "Oriental." While Thoreau's personal philosophies were influenced by new translations of the Bhagavad Gita from India, other writers like Lord Byron in England explored purely imaginative "Orientalist" themes, admiring and fantasizing upon the English idea of the East. It is conjectured that perhaps these English writers were mostly influenced by Eastern opiates, and the visions it allowed. Regardless, writers in the English-speaking world, influenced by Europe's growing colonial and economic expansion, became interested in the idea of the East, and as the global expansion of the West began its gradual domination of the rest of the world, the rest of the world became influenced by it. Thomas Babington McCaulay's "Minutes on Indian Education" foreshadows the dominance of the West and the English language, which became the accepted form for all subsequent literature.

In the final paragraph, the author returns to the world stage, demonstrating how colonialism influenced all literature and was inspired by an interest in the exotic "other," and illustrating just how connected the literature was during these periods. The writer then returns to an element articulated at the beginning of the piece: the dominance of English as the language of literacy, which ties the entire essay together and emphasizes the significant role of language in establishing literary identity.

Overall, the writer responds to the prompt, employing appropriate referential discourse. The writer develops each topic clearly and fully, offering specific examples of writers and their works, exposing critical and essential themes. Each example also supports the thesis, which either identifies the interconnectedness among the three literary periods or the particular elements that made the writing unique. Through integrated comparative and contrasting examples, the writer emphasizes the critical similarities among the literary themes, reemphasizing the interrelatedness and connectedness of literary themes. Sentences are varied, complex, and engaging, and the writing follows an organization that is easy to follow.

USING LITERARY CRITICISM TO INTERPRET TEXT

The lens through which a reader interprets a text contextualizes and situates the interpretation and meaning the reader derives according to particular criteria. The following excerpt appears at the end of chapter nine, "A View to Death," from *Lord of the Flies* by William Golding. Interpret the following excerpt using four forms of literary criticism: formalism, historicism, intertextualism, and one form of mimesis. Provide textual support to substantiate each interpretation. Then summarize the similarities and differences among interpretations again using supporting textual evidence.

Toward midnight the rain ceased and the clouds drifted away, so that the sky was scattered once more with the incredible lamps of stars. Then the breeze died too and there was no noise save the drip and trickle of water that ran out of clefts and spilled down, leaf by leaf, to the brown earth of the island. The air was cool, moist, and clear; and presently even the sound of the water was still. The beast lay huddled on the pale beach and the stains spread, inch by inch.

The edge of the lagoon became a streak of phosphorescence which advanced minutely, as the great wave of the tide flowed. The clear water mirrored the clear sky and the angular constellations. The line of phosphorescence bulged about the sand grains and little pebbles; it held them each in a dimple of tension, then suddenly accepted them with an inaudible syllable and moved on.

Along the shoreward edge of the shallows the advancing clearness was full of strange, moon-beamed bodied creatures with fiery eyes. Here and there a larger pebble clung to its own air and was covered with a coat of pearls. The tide swelled in over the rain-pitted sand and smoothed everything with a layer of silver. Now it touched the first of the stains that seeped from the broken body and the creatures made a moving patch of light as they gathered at the edge. The water rose farther and dressed Simon's coarse hair with brightness. The line of his cheek silvered and the turn of his shoulder became sculptured marble. The strange attendant creatures, with their fiery eyes and trailing vapors, busied themselves around his head. The body lifted a fraction of an inch from the sand and a bubble of air escaped from the mouth with a wet plop. Then it turned gently in the water.

Somewhere over the darkened curve of the world the sun and moon were pulling, and the film of water on the earth planet was held, bulging slightly on one side while the solid core turned. The great wave of the tide moved farther along the island and the water lifted. Softly, surrounded by a fringe of inquisitive bright creatures, itself a silver shape beneath the steadfast constellations, Simon's dead body moved out toward the open sea.

Approach

1. Prewrite: Prior to reading, summarize the essential characteristics of each of the theories and their guiding questions to focus your reading and note taking.

2. Read the excerpt, taking notes in response to the guiding questions for each lens.

3. Reread the excerpt to make sure you have adequate details and textual examples to support each interpretation.

4. Read all notes to create an overarching thesis that is supported by all three lenses.

5. Outline the introduction and major body paragraphs (at least one for each lens).

6. Write/draft your introduction and body paragraphs. Write/draft your conclusion being sure to reiterate your thesis and major points.

7. Revise your draft for clarity of thesis, supporting ideas, appropriate use of examples with clarifying explanation, appropriate application of literary lens, consistency of argument, continual reference to thesis, diction, style, voice, and so on.

8. Edit or proofread your draft, reviewing for errors in spelling, grammar, and punctuation.

Graphic Organizer

Literary Theory	Characteristics of Literary Theory	Guiding Questions of the Literary Theory	Interpretation Notes with Textual Examples
Formalism			
Historicism			
Intertextualism			

Sample Response

In this excerpt from <u>Lord of the Flies</u>, William Golding's rich use of imagery, symbolism, allusion, syntax, and rhetorical devices of figurative language set amidst the backdrop of devastating war offer a text worthy of formalist, historicist, and intertextual critique. Although each lens affords a particular way of "reading" the text, each framework substantiates one overpowering theme: man's innate and destructive beast.

Paragraph 1 introduces the text, identifies and links all three forms of literary criticism by listing those elements essential to all three forms, and articulates one overarching theme that each form of critique substantiates.

Formalism, an *objective* criticism, argues that the text *is* meaning. Formalism emphasizes the unity of all parts to create a whole and considers how all the elements, literary and syntactical, fit together to provide understanding and how understanding the whole gives relevance to the comprising elements. In formalism, content is inextricably linked to form to create meaning. Golding's use of language in this passage creates a mood of seductive beauty as ceasing rain and dissipating clouds give way to "incredible" starlit skies, drawing the reader into what appears a peaceful, illuminated natural world. Consonance in " ceased," "clouds," "sky," "scattered," "lamps," and "stars" suggests a soft, peaceful, and inviting setting and mood, but is abruptly replaced by harder sounds "breeze died" and the onomatopoetic "drip and trickle" of water running out of "clefts" and "spill[ing]" down to the "brown earth of the island," developing the motif of a cycle of events, in this case the water cycle, essential to human and earth's life. Downward motion implies a declining mood and establishes the contrast between starlit sky and brown earth. Although it has ceased raining, the air is "cool, moist, and clear," suggesting that the rain has not eliminated the humidity and that whatever it hoped to clear still remains. In addition, the drip and trickle of dripping water is suddenly still, a harbinger of the subject of the last sentence of the paragraph: a "beast . . . huddled on the pale beach" whose blood is invading the still waters "inch by inch," much like natural erosion or a slow-moving but deliberate cancer. Golding contrasts the stain with the pale beach, emphasizing the stark contrast between nature's beauty and human's evil nature.

Golding continues the "light" symbolism and imagery in the next sentences as the "lagoon" becomes a "streak of phosphorescence" controlled by the push and pull of the tides and the "clear water mirror[s] the constellations," further emphasizing the cycle motif and the constancy of nature and its events. Golding further contrasts the harsh sound of "bulging" and "dimple" with the "inaudible syllable," enhancing the "tension" between humankind and nature, evil and good, dark and light, sound and stillness. Bioluminescent creatures with "fiery eyes" enter the scene, not only enhancing the light imagery but also extending the cycle motif, this time the life cycle, as they surround the beast and begin to fulfill their function of burial at sea and eventual devouring and decaying of the corpse to atoms, continuing the life cycle, business as usual. But the business of burying the beast becomes sacred, as nature's "pearls" surround the "broken body" creating an aura or halo, implying that Simon is no ordinary beast, in fact not a beast at all, but rather a mystical creature whose demise is special and that this death is somehow healing and that this event is nature's supernatural response to man's inhumanity. Water, perhaps symbolic of a final baptism, "dresse[s] Simon's coarse hair," making the crooked and thick straight and fine, initiates Simon into the life hereafter. Simon's "silvered cheek" becomes "sculptured marble," providing additional tribute to this sacrificial lamb. "The strange attendant creatures, with their fiery eyes and trailing vapors," extend the cycle metaphor but also add to image of resurrection, and they gently turn Simon's body and carry him out to sea and into the metaphorical light of salvation where he will never be harmed again. Golding's reiteration of "fiery eyes" poses additional significance as fiery or red eyes can symbolize power and strength as in a dragon's fiery eyes, life and victory as in the amulets worn by Egyptian gods, or anger and fire as in the fiery nature of the angry sun. Contradictory interpretations further develop the tension between good and evil, however. Despite their size, these creatures "with the fiery eyes" are strong, powerful, and victorious in their mission to carry Simon either to salvation or to the next step in the planet's life cycle. The converse is that the creatures are angry at humankind's ineptitude and inability to recognize the true beast. The excerpt suggests that Simon's death is not accidental, as he has been fatally injured. Injured by whom? the reader asks. Someone or something evil enough to destroy a life whose burial is metaphorically spiritual, suggesting that good has been destroyed at least temporarily by evil. Golding ends the passage as he begins it, reiterating the pushing and pulling of the tides, controlled by the sun and the moon and the tilting of the earth. The "inquisitive bright creatures" that move Simon out to sea create a constellation of Simon, mirroring the initial starlit skies. And the cycle continues, as Simon becomes the spoils of humankind's inhumanity, part of the food chain or the resurrected soul, and his body pulled out to sea, a secret sad memory of a profoundly failed human experiment.

These preceding paragraphs first identify the elements of formalism and articulate why the text supports the use of this interpretive lens. Then the writer explicates the text almost line by line, identifying specific literary, semantic, and syntactic elements with examples that support the thesis. Throughout the explication, the writer consistently refers back to the thesis, emphasizing how the various elements work together to create a holistic interpretation. Within this persuasive discourse, the author also employs numerous literary devices that not only model formalist writing but also add to the formalist interpretation. Sentences are varied, complex, alliterative, and engaging. The writing engages the reader via questions that reemphasize and invite the reader to consider the theme. By beginning with a formalist analysis, the writer establishes a solid interpretive foundation, which contextualizes subsequent historicist and intertextualist readings.

A historicist interpretation further defends this theme. This passage portends an almost post apocalyptic world in which the fate of humanity is clearly bleak. Golding's cynical tone has roots in his personal experience, and as for any author, it is useful to explore his life itself as a source of explanation for his writings. Historicism argues that a text cannot be somehow dissected from history, standing alone as an entity outside of the historical context. Golding's values have origins in his life experiences, and his experiences are delineated by the values and events of his time. In this light, Golding's experience in the English Royal Navy during World War II, including the Battle at Normandy, inform the desolate perspective on human nature found in his writing. He joined the Royal Navy in 1940 and spent six years at sea. He witnessed sinking battleships and was present off the French coast for the D-Day invasion and later at the island of Walcheren, off the coast of the Netherlands. He saw people perish at sea, an impersonal depository of human folly and both a literal reflection of the deeds of men and a contrast to them, with its calming, soothing, and rhythmic soul, as suggested in the initial lines of the text. The horror of the Holocaust and the war itself did not paint a redeeming portrait of mankind. Golding's beast, Simon, represents not only humanity's capacity for evil but also the consequences of that evil. The tone of the passage reflects the postwar attitudes of the Western world toward itself. The West, once the epitome of civilization and order, must face its own capacity for evil and destruction. The horror of this realization served as Golding's sad inspiration for the novel and the source of the apocalyptic tone of the passage. Golding, also a biologist, realizes that life goes on. Bodies decay into atoms and reform new life, and in the end, nature assumes the upper hand. The question is whether or not humanity is worth redemption. Simon's burial is seemingly mystical suggesting that Simon was somehow heroic, and perhaps sacrificed for his attempts to see who or what the beast is. But what about the true beast, can it be saved?

The writer launches into the second interpretive framework by stating that historicism further explicates this theme and adeptly weaves Golding's tone, a critical historicist element, into the statement. Moving into the elements of historicism, the writer identifies those elements that the reader must explore in order to understand the fruits of this interpretive lens. The modus operandi is similar to the formalist read: the writer identifies critical examples from the text that expose historicist elements and consistently relates those elements and examples back to the theme. Again, the writer uses varied sentence type and structure, literary devices, and vocabulary appropriate to the lens in the explication. The last sentence poses a question that leads nicely into the intertextual analysis, suggesting that this is a question that has and continues to plague human existence.

Golding's text and tone echo other works that address the evil side of human nature. Intertextualism asserts that all literary texts in some ways speak to each other and that understanding the literary conventions and linguistic constructions inherent in all literature enables us to interpret text; interpreting text is by analogy. Northrop Frye identifies four principles that govern intertextual criticism: convention, genre, archetype, and the combination of the three. Joseph Conrad's <u>Heart of Darkness</u> offers a useful comparative text for numerous reasons. Both Conrad and Golding engage in a discussion about man's relationship to the sea and the sea's fate of absorbing and retaining a silent memory of human deeds. This archetypal imagery of the sea serves as a literary trope, the sea symbolizing both man's imagination and its watery depths as final home for the victims of human nature. Conrad writes that the tidal current, crowded with man's memories, continues its service of running to and fro. In both texts, the sea is personified as with the sky. Both brood over the fate of men and civilization. Conrad writes that the sky over the sea broods over London, the capital city of both writers, and the contemporary example of the hub of civilization. Similarly,

Golding's sea reluctantly accepts its fate as depository for humanity's lost hopes. It is described as holding pebbles and then sighing and moving on. This inaudible syllable, like a sigh of resignation, must also be heard when the sea finally accepts Simon. Thus, both authors engage in a very British and Western contemplation of the fate of man using the trope of nature as observer and mirror to human folly. Although either text may be first interpreted as an exploration of man's battle with nature and the elements of survival, each is actually a discussion of man's conflict with his own nature. The archetypal "beast" is the heart of darkness, and the heart of darkness is the bestiality of man's soul, just as the lord of the flies is the beast or the devil is within human nature. This idea is timeless as is the obvious religious intertextuality. Simon is the first name of Simon Peter, Jesus Christ's first apostle. Jesus called Peter his rock, upon which his future church would be built. Peter is considered a model for Christians to follow, for better or worse. Although Peter failed Christ several times, these failings symbolize man's sinfulness and weakness. In Golding's text, Simon is both the symbol of good and evil. He is good because he recognizes the beast for what it is, the darkness of man's soul; yet Simon's murder symbolizes the result of this darkness. Simon's mystical burial suggests a type of resurrection, a reward for trying to remain good despite a world of savage destruction, corruption, greed, and power. In essence, these themes and events explore the human condition, a focus of study and explication that is timeless.

Capitalizing on the essence of intertextualism, that all texts are analogous, the writer identifies another text whose conventions, theme, setting, and tone are similar. Exposing archetypes of the sea and the beast and comparing critical elements of both texts, the writer reminds the reader that literature has explored and exposed the nature of the human condition throughout time. The writer further emphasizes intertextualism by integrating and using religious intertextuality to illustrate theme and reconnect the interpretation to its formalist roots, summarizing that explication of humankind's evil nature is timeless.

Formalism, historicism, and intertextualism create a rich, holistic interpretation of Golding's passage. As the piece is allegorical, it fits into a wider genre of allegorical fiction that is instructive. Symbolism, figurative language, and *imagery seduce the reader into a worldview that although bleak and ominous, is one that humankind must nevertheless confront. Furthermore, Golding compels the reader to understand his cynical tone. Through the historicist's lens, the reader understands that Golding's experiences as a naval officer in World War II and a biologist inform his literary view of the world, that of a Westerner criticizing his own culture. Through intertextualism, Golding's engages an important historical and philosophical discussion about the nature of humanity. Ultimately, these lenses present an apocalyptic view about the fate of humankind if it does not conquer or at least tame the beast.*

In the conclusion, the writer summarizes the major interpretation derived from each theoretical framework with consistent reference to the overarching theme. The last sentence, like the excerpt itself, warns the reader of what lies ahead.

IDENTIFY, INTERPRET, AND EXPLICATE A THEME BASED ON A TEXT OF YOUR CHOOSING

Approach

1. Prewrite: Identify a text that you know deeply with respect to theme, conflict, figurative language, characterization, and so on, and can recall specific examples and textual evidence.

2. Identify a thesis that you believe you can substantiate with detailed examples and explication.

3. Outline as many specific examples as possible to support the thesis.

4. Outline the introduction and major body paragraphs.

5. Write/draft your introduction and body paragraphs. Write/draft your conclusion being sure to reiterate your thesis and major points.

6. Revise your draft for clarity of thesis, supporting ideas, appropriate use of examples with clarifying explanation, appropriate application of literary lens, consistency of argument, continual reference to thesis, diction, style, voice, and so on.

7. Edit or proofread your draft, reviewing for errors in spelling, grammar, and punctuation.

Graphic Organizer

Text and Author		
Theme	**Specific Examples**	**Explanation**

Sample Response

When Victor Frankenstein climbs Montanvert to console himself about the deaths of his family, murdered by his failed creation, his monster appears, approaching him at supernatural speed. Still refusing, and perhaps unable, to see his own guilt, Victor calls the monster an insect and orders him to stay so that he may destroy him. Ironically, the monster does not return anger with anger, but replies that Frankenstein can't play with life in this way. He has to do right by the monster so that the monster can do right by him and others. In this reply is the critical theme of Mary Shelley's <u>Frankenstein</u>: the creator must care for what he creates regardless of outcome; otherwise, the creator is truly the monster.

Initially, Victor Frankenstein's intentions appear altruistic. Like scientists before him (and to come), he believes that his work will be a gift for all mankind. If he can create life, perhaps he can cure and even eliminate disease. He thinks that in time he might be able to recreate life in sick and weak bodies. This all-consuming quest separates him from family, friends, and his beloved Elizabeth. As he gathers bones, limbs, and body parts, Victor remarks that his soul is lost and realizes that he now hides away from others as if guilty of a crime, Is he not here implying the immorality, sinfulness, and evilness of his deed?

Despite this realization, Victor continues his mission to become Creator; yet he is repulsed by the "catastrophe" he has created. Victor's deliberate and careful selection of only the most beautiful parts has yielded a hideous monster, a further irony. Remorseless, he asks how God could let this happen. Victor leaves his workshop in disgust, refusing to accept responsibility for his immoral act or to care for what he has created.

It is this rejection that fuels the monster's retaliation. Learning that his brother William has been killed, Victor knows that the monster is the murderer. Like an abused child, the monster punishes his father by inflicting abuse on others. Yet, consumed with arrogance, Victor still refuses to see his own culpability in the act, labeling the monster "evil," not knowing that the monster is only mimicking the evil and wickedness of his creator. It is only when innocent Justine is hanged for William's murder that Victor exhibits an intimation of guilt. Shelley's diction exacerbates and illustrates Victor's lack of genuine guilt. Referring to Victor as "author" diminishes the gravity of his actions, suggesting that like Shelley, Victor has only written a horror story, but in reality, Victor has birthed horror. Furthermore, Victor's suffering is not penitential but a result of fear that the monster might bring more violence, most likely on Victor himself.

Although Victor acknowledges his hand in the creation of evil, he feels no burden or responsibility to care for his creation. The monster, stronger, smarter, and wiser than his creator, clearly understands his father's responsibility, saying that he should be treated as if he were "Adam." Just as God cared for Adam by giving him Eve, Victor should provide the monster a companion. Instead, when the creature begs compassion, Victor gives none. When the monster identifies Victor and society's cruelty as the catalyst that perverted his original compassion and kind nature, Victor listens dumbfounded. It is only out of selfishness that Victor concedes to create a companion for the monster, but plagued by fears that this new creation will be even worse than the first, he inevitably refuses to create the companion. Not only does Victor deny the monster's request for genuine care and kindness, but he also attempts to destroy the creature. Not only will the creator not care for his creation, he will destroy it.

Victor flees to Ireland, but no one there will help him. He is rebuffed; being told that the Irish hate villains. Victor is arraigned for murdering a local gentleman (whom his monster has killed) and, delirious, spends three months in prison until acquitted and rescued by his father. The mistake is intentional; Victor is the villain.

Victor's hell deepens, as the monster makes good on his promise, killing Elizabeth on their wedding night. Totally consumed with revenge, Victor stalks his monster but unlike the monster does not apprehend his prey. Realizing that he cannot kill the monster, Victor asks Walton for mercy killing. In his madness, he admits that he created a rational creatuwre whose well being was his responsibility and duty. But, he discards this admission asserting that he had a greater responsibility to those of his own kind. Victor is ever remorseless, arrogant, and insane.

The final irony of Victor's deathbed scene further intensifies Victor's genuine lack of remorse and culpability for his cruelty. Extending the God metaphor through dramatic irony, the monster, a repentant sinner, seeks forgiveness and eventual salvation from Victor, his creator. Yet Victor is dispassionate, merciless, and unforgiving; even God forgave Adam through the resurrection, but Victor is neither God nor God-like. He assumes the power of creation but displeased and disgusted with the result, rejects his creation. Desiring to be loved and cared for, the monster leaves to build a fiery hell of torturing flames as penance for his sins, suggesting that the monster is superior to the creator, more human than the human.

Centuries later, Victor's quest is no longer fantasy. Engineering humans that are healthier, smarter, stronger, and more powerful not only pervades scientific research but also current legislation. Despite the brutality of Hitler's genocide in service of a master race, eugenics is emerging as an altruistic if not an admirable objective. Yet what is the outcome of creation without responsibility, Jurassic Park run amuck? Shelley's answer is clear: humankind must care for what it creates regardless of outcome; otherwise, we are all monsters.

The writer poses a theme that is thoughtful, engaging, and insightful. The theme is timely as the implication is that what once was considered science fiction is the nonfiction of today. The theme is also edgy as it subtly questions whether or not humankind has truly made progress since the publication of this text.

Each of the subsequent paragraphs poses a thoughtful element that supports the thesis, and each element is supported by numerous textual examples, which are analyzed and elaborated in a manner that supports the element, which in turn supports the thesis. Furthermore, the writer employs formalism and intertextualism, identifying rhetorical devices of figurative language, allusions, and other elements of the genre to develop each supporting element and the overall argument.

Finally, the writer offers a conclusion that not only reiterates the thesis and unites the supporting arguments but also contextualizes the theme in the present. This brings the argument full circle as it refers to the scientific advancement addressed in the introductory paragraph.

The persuasive discourse employs a variety of literary devices to explicate the argument, sentence types that vary in style and complexity, and transitions that are clear and effective, adding to the fluidness of the argument. Diction is precise. Language follows all conventions of spelling, grammar, and punctuation.

Practice Test 1

MTEL English

This practice test is also on CD-ROM in our special interactive MTEL English TestWare®. It is highly recommended that you first take this exam on computer. You will then have the additional study features and benefits of enforced timed conditions and instant, accurate scoring. See page 5 for instructions on how to get the most out of our MTEL book and software.

ANSWER SHEET FOR PRACTICE TEST 1

1 _____	21 _____	41 _____	61 _____	81 _____
2 _____	22 _____	42 _____	62 _____	82 _____
3 _____	23 _____	43 _____	63 _____	83 _____
4 _____	24 _____	44 _____	64 _____	84 _____
5 _____	25 _____	45 _____	65 _____	85 _____
6 _____	26 _____	46 _____	66 _____	86 _____
7 _____	27 _____	47 _____	67 _____	87 _____
8 _____	28 _____	48 _____	68 _____	88 _____
9 _____	29 _____	49 _____	69 _____	89 _____
10 _____	30 _____	50 _____	70 _____	90 _____
11 _____	31 _____	51 _____	71 _____	91 _____
12 _____	32 _____	52 _____	72 _____	92 _____
13 _____	33 _____	53 _____	73 _____	93 _____
14 _____	34 _____	54 _____	74 _____	94 _____
15 _____	35 _____	55 _____	75 _____	95 _____
16 _____	36 _____	56 _____	76 _____	96 _____
17 _____	37 _____	57 _____	77 _____	97 _____
18 _____	38 _____	58 _____	78 _____	98 _____
19 _____	39 _____	59 _____	79 _____	99 _____
20 _____	40 _____	60 _____	80 _____	100 _____

PRACTICE TEST 1

TIME: 4 hours   100 multiple-choice questions; 2 open-response questions

Directions: Read each question or statement carefully, and choose the response that BEST answers the question or completes the statement.

1. The literature of precolonial Native Americans is viewed primarily as

    A. narrative.

    B. folklore.

    C. epic.

    D. saga.

2. Which of the following sets of themes appeared in much of American colonial literature?

    A. Determinism, redemption, and salvation

    B. Righteousness, determinism, and liberalism

    C. Determinism, conservatism, and righteousness

    D. Redemption, liberalism, and determinism

3. Which of the following literary forms is **NOT** included in Puritan literature?

    A. Allegory

    B. Parable

    C. Sermon

    D. Legend

4. Which of the following texts most replicates the form and design of Puritan diaries?

    A. Benjamin Franklin's *Autobiography*

    B. Benjamin Franklin's *Poor Richard's Almanack*

    C. Benjamin Franklin's "The Dogood Papers"

    D. Benjamin Franklin's "Death is a Fisherman"

5.   Which of the following literary forms is **NOT** among American Revolutionary literature?

   A.   Oratory and essay

   B.   Poetry and satire

   C.   Autobiography and pamphlets

   D.   Novels and hymns

6.   Which of the following authors are associated with transcendentalism?

   A.   Henry David Thoreau, Edgar Allan Poe, and Ralph Waldo Emerson

   B.   Nathaniel Hawthorne, Herman Melville, and Walt Whitman

   C.   Ralph Waldo Emerson, Walt Whitman, and Henry David Thoreau

   D.   Walt Whitman, Harriet Beecher Stowe, and William Gilmore Simms

7.   Which form of narrative **BEST** describes Herman Melville's *Moby Dick* and *Billy Budd*?

   A.   Epic

   B.   Allegory

   C.   Parable

   D.   Parody

8.   Which of the following is **NOT** true of Emily Dickinson's work?

   A.   Her poetry included satire, elegies, puns, and allegory.

   B.   Her poetry displayed an extremely effective use of slant rhyme.

   C.   Her campaign for self-definition lead to suicide.

   D.   Tones ranged from mild whimsy to despair and terror.

9.   Which of the following writers is considered the first naturalist?

   A.   Jack London

   B.   Stephen Crane

   C.   Charlotte Perkins Gilman

   D.   Emily Dickinson

10. Writing that is highly experimental, making extensive use of fragments, stream of consciousness, and interior dialogue in efforts to create a unique style is most apparent in the works of

    A. Ernest Hemingway.

    B. William Faulkner.

    C. John Steinbeck.

    D. F. Scott Fitzgerald.

11. Which of the following novels was **NOT** written by John Steinbeck?

    A. *Grapes of Wrath*

    B. *As I Lay Dying*

    C. *Of Mice and Men*

    D. *East of Eden*

12. Which of the following authors wrote "The Young Housewife"?

    A. T. S. Eliot

    B. e. e. cummings

    C. Ezra Pound

    D. William Carlos Williams

13. Which of the following twentieth-century poets did **NOT** write in free verse?

    A. Carl Sandburg

    B. e. e. cummings

    C. Robert Frost

    D. T. S. Eliot

14. Which of the following poems by Robert Frost BEST depicts the binary opposition of nature versus technology?

    A. "Out! Out!"

    B. "The Road Not Taken"

    C. "Mending Wall"

    D. "Stopping by the Woods on a Snowy Evening"

15. Which of the following statements **BEST** describes the Harlem Renaissance?

    A. The Harlem Renaissance was a black cultural movement in the 1920s, during which the prose and poetry described alienation and disconnection through use of fragments, stream of consciousness, and interior dialogue.

    B. The Harlem Renaissance was a black cultural movement in the 1930s, during which the prose and poetry described alienation and disconnection through use of fragments, stream of consciousness, and interior dialogue.

    C. The Harlem Renaissance was a black cultural movement in the 1940s, during which the prose and poetry described alienation and disconnection through use of fragments, stream of consciousness, and interior dialogue.

    D. The Harlem Renaissance was a black cultural movement in the 1950s, during which the prose and poetry described alienation and disconnection through use of fragments, stream of consciousness, and interior dialogue.

16. Which of the following poems won the author critical acclaim and established the author as a black militant?

    A. "Ask Your Mama"

    B. "If We Must Die"

    C. *Cane*

    D. "Harlem"

17. Which of the following texts is **NOT** written by one of the Beat poets?

    A. *On the Road*

    B. *Naked Lunch*

    C. *Howl*

    D. *Lord Weary's Castle*

18. Which of the following texts uses the Salem witch trials to satirize the McCarthy hearings?

    A. "Silent Snow, Secret Snow" by Conrad Aiken

    B. *The Crucible* by Arthur Miller

C. *Fahrenheit 451* by Ray Bradbury

D. *The Catcher in the Rye* by J. D. Salinger

19. Which of the following modern female novelists did **NOT** consider humankind worthy of redemption?

    A. Dorothy Parker

    B. Flannery O'Connor

    C. Eudora Welty

    D. Shirley Jackson

20. Which of the following modern African American writers is noted for his novel *The Invisible Man*?

    A. James Baldwin

    B. Ralph Ellison

    C. Langston Hughes

    D. Richard Wright

21. Who was the first African American woman to receive the Nobel Prize for Literature?

    A. Toni Morrison

    B. Maya Angelou

    C. Gwendolyn Brooks

    D. Alice Walker

22. Which of the following African American writers developed and incorporates the technique of "rememory" in narrative?

    A. Toni Morrison

    B. James Baldwin

    C. Alice Walker

    D. Richard Wright

23. Which of the following Asian American writers depicts the struggles and achievements of the first Chinese men and the prejudice they faced in the United States?

    A. Amy Tan

    B. Bette Bao Lord

    C. Maxine Kingston Hong

    D. Laurence Yep

24. Which of the following Jewish American writers wrote *The Natural*?

    A. Elie Wiesel

    B. Bernard Malamud

    C. Saul Bellow

    D. Shel Silverstein

25. Which of the following texts or awards is **NOT** associated with Elie Wiesel?

    A. *Night*

    B. The Nobel Peace Prize

    C. *Seize the Day*

    D. The Congressional Medal of Honor

26. Which of the following Latin American writers draws from experiences with the Trujillo dictatorship?

    A. Julia Alvarez

    B. Sandra Cisneros

    C. Gary Soto

    D. Pablo Paez

27. Which of the following elements are **NOT** associated with Old English literature?

    A. Heroic feats

    B. Fairy-tale endings

C. Epic battles

D. Supernatural characters

28. Which of the following writers is considered the first English historian?

A. Bede

B. Junius

C. Exeter

D. Norman

29. Which of the following statements **BEST** characterizes the theme of *The Seafarer*?

A. The sea symbolizes a brief life on earth of struggle and difficulty in the context of a sophisticated tale of emotion and loss.

B. The sea symbolizes a brief life on earth of struggle and difficulty compared to an everlasting life of happiness in heaven.

C. The sea symbolizes a brief life on earth of struggle and difficulty compared to the profound suffering of life in hell.

D. The sea symbolizes a brief life on earth of struggle and difficulty, reflecting the political feudalism and chivalric code of time.

30. Which of the following literary devices is most often incorporated in Geoffrey Chaucer's work?

A. Frame story

B. Free verse

C. Stock epithet

D. Alliterative meter

31. Which of the following statements **BEST** describes Elizabethan literature?

    A. This period saw unprecedented literary growth, the creation of new and elaborate poetic forms and styles, advocacy for religious tolerance, and the use of blank verse in drama.

    B. This period saw unprecedented literary growth, the creation of new and elaborate poetic forms and styles, a new translation of the Bible, and the use of blank verse in drama.

    C. This period saw unprecedented literary growth, the introduction of the sonnet, a new translation of the Bible, and the use of euphuism.

    D. This period saw unprecedented literary growth, the creation of new and elaborate poetic forms and styles, advocacy of self-reliance and struggle, and the use of blank verse in drama.

32. *Much Ado about Nothing*, *A Midsummer Night's Dream*, and *Twelfth Night* are Shakespearean

    A. tragicomedies.

    B. tragedies.

    C. comedies.

    D. problem plays.

33. Which of the following literary periods **BEST** characterizes the literature of Great Britain from 1603 to1625?

    A. The Elizabethan Age

    B. The Jacobean Age

    C. The Carolinean Age

    D. The Puritan Age

34. Which of the following writers responded to each other's poetry?

    A. Addison and Steele

    B. Rosencrantz and Guildenstern

    C. Marlowe and Raleigh

    D. Nashe and Lyly

35. Whose essays challenged medieval beliefs about science and approached scientific inquiry inductively?

   A. John Donne

   B. Ben Jonson

   C. Sir Francis Bacon

   D. Thomas Middleton

36. Which of the following is **NOT** a poem written by John Donne?

   A. "To a Mouse"

   B. "The Flea"

   C. "No Man Is an Island"

   D. "The Canonization"

37. Literature of the Carolinean Age was marked by all of the following **EXCEPT**

   A. masques.

   B. Cavalier poetry.

   C. carpe diem poetry.

   D. metaphysical poetry.

38. Which of the following statements **BEST** describes John Milton and his poetry?

   A. John Milton was a countercultural poet whose style defied the simplicity and sensuality of Cavalier poetry.

   B. John Milton was a Cavalier poet whose style was compared to that of Homer and Virgil.

   C. John Milton was a Puritan poet whose style incorporated blank verse and simple vernacular.

   D. John Milton was a countercultural poet whose poetry included elegies, epics, and satire. His drama criticized King James II's extreme Catholicism and conservatism.

39.	"An allegory in which a character named Christian encounters various perils on his way to heaven and where vices and virtues are personified" BEST describes

	A.	*Leviathan.*

	B.	*The Pilgrim's Progress.*

	C.	*The Hind and the Panther.*

	D.	*All for Love.*

40.	Which of the following work-author pairs is incorrect?

	A.	*Robinson Crusoe* by Daniel Defoe

	B.	*Gulliver's Travels* by Jonathan Swift

	C.	*Pamela; or, Virtue Rewarded* by Henry Fielding

	D.	*Castle of Otranto* by Horace Walpole

41.	Which of the following statements is **NOT** true?

	A.	James Boswell earned acclaim by immortalizing the life of Dr. Samuel Johnson.

	B.	Joseph Addison is considered the greatest pamphleteer in English history.

	C.	William Congreve is considered the greatest master of English repartee.

	D.	Henry Fielding is considered the founder of the English prose epic.

42.	Which of the following is a satirical essay that suggests that Irish landlords eat children to compensate for the ravages of the Irish potato famine?

	A.	*A Modest Proposal*

	B.	*A School for Scandal*

	C.	*The Critic*

	D.	*An Essay on Man*

43.	Which of the following lines is attributed to Alexander Pope?

	A.	"A little learning is a dangerous thing."

	B.	"Gather ye rosebuds while ye may."

C. "Stone walls do not a prison make, nor iron bars a cage."

D. "A wrinkle in time saves nine."

44. Which of the following historical events occurred during the romantic period?

A. The Industrial Revolution, discovery of iron ore, and emergence of a powerful banking system

B. The Industrial Revolution, discovery of the cotton gin, and emergence of a powerful banking system

C. The Industrial Revolution, discovery of steam engine, and reemergence of an upper class

D. The Industrial Revolution, working mothers, and emergence of a powerful banking system

45. In which of the following poets' work do themes of heaven and hell, innocence and experience, and good and evil pervade?

A. William Blake

B. Samuel Taylor Coleridge

C. Robert Burns

D. Lord George Byron

46. For the purpose of continuity, historians and scholars divide the periods of English literature into various segments. Which of the following puts the segments in the correct chronological order?

A. Old English, Middle English, Victorian, Renaissance, neoclassical, romantic, modern

B. Old English, Middle English, Renaissance, neoclassical, romantic, Victorian, modern

C. Neoclassical, romantic, Victorian, Middle English, Old English, modern, Renaissance

D. Modern, Victorian, romantic, neoclassical, Renaissance, Middle English, Old English

47. Which of the following works is considered William Wordsworth's magnum opus?

   A. *Lyrical Ballads*

   B. *The Prelude*

   C. *Don Juan*

   D. *Christabel*

48. Which of the following female writers wrote during the romantic period in the literature of Great Britain?

   A. Elizabeth Barrett Browning

   B. Charlotte Brontë

   C. Jane Austen

   D. Mary Elizabeth Braddon

49. Which of the following texts did Emily Brontë write?

   A. *Jane Eyre*

   B. *Wuthering Heights*

   C. *Shirley*

   D. *The Professor*

50. Which of the following novels by Charles Dickens are darker novels, recounting death, murder, madness, despair, and suicide, negative but accurate consequences of a complicated, mechanized world?

   A. *Bleak House* and *Oliver Twist*

   B. *Dombey and Son* and *Bleak House*

   C. *Bleak House* and *David Copperfield*

   D. *Great Expectations* and *Bleak House*

51. Who was the most significant novelist in the late Victorian period?

   A. Oscar Wilde

   B. Rudyard Kipling

   C. Robert Louis Stevenson

   D. Thomas Hardy

52.   Which of the following novelists wrote under a pen name?

    A.   George Eliot

    B.   George Bernard Shaw

    C.   John Rushkin

    D.   Wilkie Collins

53.   Which of the following phrases **BEST** summarizes beliefs exemplified in the mid-twentieth-century literature of Great Britain?

    A.   Existential nihilism argued that life was intrinsically meaningless.

    B.   Existentialism asked what an individual was to do in such a topsy-turvy, absurd world.

    C.   Populations grew more accustomed and resigned to political and ethical hegemonies.

    D.   A technological revolution began to take place, but culture refused to be swept along.

54.   Which of the following authors is **NOT** a twentieth-century poet?

    A.   William Butler Yeats

    B.   Seamus Heaney

    C.   W. H. Auden

    D.   Anthony Burgess

55.   Which of the following playwrights wrote extensively for the theater of the absurd?

    A.   Samuel Beckett

    B.   Virginia Woolf

    C.   Graham Green

    D.   E. M. Forster

56.   Which of the following work-writer pairs is incorrect?

    A.   *Waiting for Godot* by Samuel Beckett

    B.   "The Second Coming" by William Butler Yeats

    C.   *The Satanic Verses* by Salman Rushdie

    D.   *Lady Chatterley's Lover* by James Joyce

57. Which of the following statements BEST describes early Greek literature?

    A. Literature included comedy, tragedy, lyric poetry, and dialectic.

    B. Literature included comedy, tragedy, epic poetry, and folklore.

    C. Literature included comedy, tragedy, epic poetry, and legend.

    D. Literature included comedy, tragedy, lyric poetry, and treatise.

58. Which of the following Greek writers created the prototype of later drama marked by conflict?

    A. Sappho

    B. Sophocles

    C. Aristophanes

    D. Aeschylus

59. In which of the following texts is the main character a prototype of the perfect or ideal Roman?

    A. *The Odyssey*

    B. *The Iliad*

    C. *The Metamorphoses*

    D. *The Aeneid*

60. In *The Four Gospels of the Life and Sayings of Jesus and the Acts of the Apostles*, each Gospel addresses a different audience. Which of the following statements is incorrect?

    A. Matthew addresses the Jewish public.

    B. Mark addresses the Gentile audience.

    C. Luke addresses the cultured Greek readers.

    D. John addresses the common Roman readers.

61. Which of the following texts is considered the greatest poem of the Middle Ages?

    A. *The Inferno*

    B. *The Purgatorio*

    D. *The Paradiso*

    C. *The Divine Comedy*

62.   Which of the following texts is **NOT** included in early Chinese literature?

  A. *Classic of Poetry*

  B. *The Book of Change*

  C. *Lao-tzu*

  D. *Epic of Son-Jara*

63.   Who is recognized as the greatest Tang dynasty poet?

  A. Li Po

  B. Confucius

  C. Qin Shi Hwang

  D. Laozi Tzu

64.   Which of the following statements about Hinduism is **NOT** true?

  A. Conduct that preserves the cosmic integrity of the universe requires profound self-denial and suffering.

  B. There are three spheres that govern ideal life: *artha*, *kama*, and *moska*.

  C. Karma holds that all things are responsible for their own actions.

  D. Moral and spiritual conquest is superior to conquest by sword.

65.   Which of the following statements is **NOT** true about the Koran?

  A. A written version of the Koran does not convey the text effectively, as its unique, rhythmic, narrative was meant to be recited and accompanied by music.

  B. Written in Arabic, the Koran is greater than prophetic revelation as it is God's final revelation to humanity through Uthman, the third caliph.

  C. The Koran, unlike the Bible, is written in prose and has no single narrative running through it as it is not embedded in the history of a single people.

  D. The style of the Koran influenced subsequent literature and became popular for the distribution of religious learning.

66. Which of the following statements is true about Japanese literature?

   A. Japanese poets introduced the haiku form of poetry into literary world.

   B. Japanese literature was highly influenced by Chinese Confucianism.

   C. Japanese literature focused on the doctrine of universal permanence.

   D. Japanese prose addressed righteousness and romanticism.

67. Which of the following statements does **NOT** describe eighteenth-century European literature during the Enlightenment?

   A. Eighteenth-century writers in France and England dramatized intricate interchanges and conflicts between reason and passion that exposed religion as a sham.

   B. England and France assumed marriage as the normal goal for men and women, making erotic love less important and the position of women increasingly significant.

   C. Across Europe, eighteenth-century writers assumed the superior importance of the social group and of shared opinion.

   D. Realism attempted to convey the literal feel of experience, shape the occurrence of events, and inform the way people really talked in social circles.

68. Poking fun at European society, observing that humankind is inherently good but prone to mischief is a central theme in the writing of

   A. Miguel de Cervantes.

   B. François de la Rochefoucauld.

   C. Jean-Baptiste Poquelin Molière.

   D. Jean-Jacques Rousseau.

69. Which of the following genres was **NOT** among Mesoamerican literature during the 1500s to 1600s?

    A. Essay

    B. Song

    C. Narrative

    D. Oratory

70. Which of the following statements **BEST** characterizes Chinese literature between 1600 and 1800?

    A. Literature included drama, oral romantic verse, and storytelling that celebrated freedom, energy, and passion.

    B. Literature included oral romantic verse, storytelling, and prose that were neo-Confucian but addressed complex human nature.

    C. Literature included oral romantic verse, drama, and prose that emphasized purity, sensuality, and freedom.

    D. Literature included oral romantic verse, drama, and poetry that focused on women, rigidity, and murder mysteries.

71. Which of the following texts offers a panoramic view of the Ottoman Empire?

    A. *The History of India*

    B. *The Book of Travels*

    C. *Crimea to Aden*

    D. *Muhammad to Mehmed*

72. Which of the following statements does **NOT** characterize literature of the modern world?

A. Indebted to the evolution of scientific thought and emphasis on randomness and shifting perception, each literary work could be categorized as combined product of its race, milieu, and time.

B. Experimental language in fiction and poetry reflected the influence of psychoanalysis and symbolist poetics as modernist literature described clearly the world as humankind experienced it.

C. The post-World War II period resulted in existentialism, the theater of the absurd, which consists of choosing our actions at each point, avoiding the bad faith of pretending that others are responsible for our choices, and choosing not just for oneself but for all.

D. Some writers used language in an exploratory way, disassembling to reconstruct, playing with shifting and contradictory appearances to suggest the changing and uncertain nature of reality.

73. Which of the follow texts was **NOT** written by Fyodor Dostoevsky?

A. *Crime and Punishment*

B. *Brothers Karamazov*

C. *War and Peace*

D. *The Idiot*

74. Whose writing **BEST** reflects the belief that man must face his undeniable freedom if he ever wishes to become a moral being and establish his own existence?

A. Jean-Paul Sartre

B. Albert Camus

C. Ranier Maria Rilke

D. Marcel Proust

75. Which of the following work-writer pairs is incorrect?

    A. *Lolita* by Vladimir Nabokov

    B. *Love in the Time of Cholera* by Gabriel García Márquez

    C. *No Exit* by Jean-Paul Sartre

    D. *Anna Karenina* by Fyodor Dostoevsky

76. Which of the following modern African writers is best known for work that explores the profound impact that colonization has had on Africans?

    A. Chinua Achebe

    B. Doris Lessing

    C. Wole Soyinka

    D. Ngũgĩ wa Thiong'o

77. Which of the following modern Chinese writers is considered the father of modern Chinese literature?

    A. Xu Zhimo

    B. Lin Yutang

    C. Lu Xun

    D. Bing Xin

78. Which of the following Indian authors was a *Hindi* novelist and activist who helped to bring about the *Nayi Kahani* ("new short story") literary movement of Hindi literature?

    A. Nirmal Verma

    B. Rabindranath Tagore

    C. R. K. Narayan

    D. Amitav Ghosh

79. Which of the following statements **BEST** characterizes medieval literary criticism?

    A. Medieval criticism assumed a secular view, addressing literature as a vehicle of teaching and reviving classical learning.

    B. Medieval criticism refined the neoplatonist views, suggesting that literature encompassed allegory, beauty, order, and harmony.

    C. Medieval criticism sought to find truth and viewed literature as embedded with moral purpose and intellectual function.

    D. Medieval criticism viewed literature as a reflection of eternal essence, providing access to higher spiritual realms.

80. Which of the following forms of literary criticism perceives text as **NOT** having a center or universal meaning, but an array of meanings, including political, cultural, and social?

    A. Formalism

    B. Intertextualism

    C. New historicism

    D. Poststructuralism

81. Which of the following **BEST** describes the order in the development of the English language?

    A. Proto-Indo-European, Germanic language, Old English, Middle English, the Great Vowel Shift, technical vocabulary, divergence of British and American English

    B. Indo-European, Germanic language, Old English, Middle English, the Great Vowel Shift, technical vocabulary, divergence of British and American English

    C. Proto-Indo-European, Germanic language, Old English, Middle English, technical vocabulary, the Great Vowel Shift, divergence of British and American English

    D. Indo-European, Germanic language, Old English, Middle English, the Great Vowel Shift, divergence of British and American English, technical vocabulary

82. Which of the following definitions is **NOT** correct?

    A. Linguistics is the science or study concerned with developing models of linguistic knowledge.

    B. Morphology is the identification, analysis, and description of the structure of words.

    C. Phonetics is concerned with sounds of word elements only to the extent that knowing these sounds aids in word recognition and subsequently reading.

    D. Phonology is the systematic use of sound to encode meaning in any spoken human language.

83. Which of the following is **NOT** an example of a digraph?

    A. *ea*

    B. *ck*

    C. *oa*

    D. *oy*

84. The emergence of the word *villain* from its original, *village*, is an example of

    A. pejoration.

    B. amerlioration.

    C. expansion.

    D. restriction.

85. Which of the following viewpoints is reflected in John Skretta's observation about teaching grammar: "To suggest that many of our students are grammatically impaired or in need of explicit grammatical instruction is both dehumanizing to our students and ludicrous from a linguistic standpoint"?

    A. Prescriptivist

    B. Descriptivist

    C. Generative

    D. Determinist

86. Which of the following processes of reading contends that the reader uses rules of phonics, learns sight words that do not follow phonics rules, and breaks words into patterns using structural analysis to decode words, phrases, and sentences?

    A. Reading as word recognition

    B. Reading as a visual process

    C. Reading as a psycholinguistic process

    D. Reading as a metacognitive process

87. Which of the following is **NOT** a reading strategy that a proficient reader applies to derive meaning from a text?

    A. Activating prior knowledge and summarizing

    B. Questioning and synthesizing

    C. Visualizing and retelling

    D. Inferencing and decoding

88. For a bilingual learner, words such as *characterization*, *simile*, and *metaphor* would be considered

    A. Tier 1 words.

    B. Tier 2 words.

    C. Tier 3 words.

    D. Tier 4 words.

89. Which of the following themes are **NOT** characteristic of new realism?

    A. Sexism and sexuality

    B. Maturity and perseverance

    C. War and violence

    D. Profanity and alienation

90. Which of the following texts is an example of historical fiction?

    A. *The Slave Dancer*

    B. *The Middle Passage*

C. *Taking Sides*

D. *The Cay*

91. Which of the following names the major branches of classical rhetoric?

    A. Invention, narration, and elocution

    B. Deliberative, judicial, and epideictic

    C. Inventive, narrative, and judicial

    D. Narrative, persuasive, and inventive

92. Which of the following definitions is incorrect?

    A. *Inventio*: discovery of valid arguments

    B. *Elocutia*: style or figures of speech

    C. *Memoria*: storing up all information to support the argument

    D. *Dispositio*: delivery or performance of the speech

93. Which of the following **BEST** describes the critical difference between classical and modern rhetoric?

    A. Modern rhetoric no longer incorporates all of the rhetorical devices of classical rhetoric.

    B. Modern rhetoric has shifted the focus from writing and speech to media.

    C. Modern rhetoric must now account for rapid growth of technology and diversity.

    D. Modern rhetoric has shifted from the speaker or author to the audience.

94. Which of the following identifies the four types of discourse?

    A. Persuasive, expressive, referential, and literary

    B. Expressive, informatory, literary, and scientific

    C. Persuasive, expressive, referential, and scientific

    D. Expressive, referential, informatory, and literary

95. A rhetor will manipulate emotions in various ways to elicit a specific mood or reaction in order to develop

    A. unity of thought.

    B. unity of feeling.

    C. unity of emphasis.

    D. unity of purpose.

96. When a writer or speaker carefully works to ensure that significant and important ideas appear in prominent positions, at the beginning or at the end, as these are parts of the speech and composition that the listener or reader is likely to remember, she is observing

    A. the principle of emphasis.

    B. the principle of proportion.

    C. the principle of coherence.

    D. the principle of consistency.

97. Which of the following is **NOT** a difference between spoken and written discourse?

    A. Speaking relies on the immediate and present context.

    B. Speaking makes use of pauses, repetitions, and fillers.

    C. Speaking makes use of body language and physical cues.

    D. Speaking demands more pragmatic competence.

98. Which of the following sets of factors affects social distance and therefore second language acquisition?

    A. Culture shock, attitude, accent, and ego

    B. Attitude, motivation, economics, and anxiety

    C. Culture shock, attitude, motivation, and ego

    D. Motivation, attitude, economics, and ego

99. Which part of the writing process includes charting, mapping, researching, interviewing, and outlining?

   A. Prewriting

   B. Drafting

   C. Revising

   D. Editing

100. Which of the following sentences is incorrect because of grammar, punctuation, and/or spelling?

   A. My mother, along with her sisters, visit their mother every summer.

   B. Nobody truly cares what you think, so why should I?

   C. Every spring the faculty votes on reinstating the university senate.

   D. Studying or thinking requires a great deal of cognitive energy.

OPEN-RESPONSE QUESTIONS

1. Respond to the following poem. Your response must include the identification of a theme; an analysis noting literary techniques, including genre features, literary elements, and rhetorical devices used to express the theme; and a conclusion.

The Chimney Sweeper

When my mother died, I was very young,
And my father sold me while yet my tongue
Could scarcely cry 'weep! 'weep! 'weep! 'weep!'
So your chimneys I sweep, and in soot I sleep.

There's a little Tom Dacre, who cried when his head,
That curled like a lamb's back, was shaved: so I said,
"Hush, Tom! never mind it, for when your head's bare,
You know that the soot cannot spoil your white hair."

And so he was quiet; and that very night,
As Tom was a-sleeping, he had such a sight,
That thousands of sweepers, Dick, Joe, Ned, and Jack,
Were all of them locked up in coffins of black.

And by came an angel who had a bright key,
And he opened the coffins and set them all free;
Then down a green plain leaping, laughing, they run,
And wash in a river, and shine in the sun.

Then naked and white, all their bags left behind,
They rise upon clouds and sport in the wind;
And the angel told Tom, if he'd be a good boy,
He'd have God for his father, and never want joy.

And so Tom awoke; and we rose in the dark,
And got with our bags and our brushes to work,
Though the morning was cold, Tom was happy and warm;
So if all do their duty they need not fear harm.

William Blake, *Songs of Innocence*, 1789

2. **Study the following statement:**

> *A book about one character and one country can become a book*
> *about other characters and the world.*

Choose TWO works from the list below and then write a well-organized essay in which you SUPPORT the statement above. Develop your thesis using specific references to elements of the works you select (such as characters, plot, and setting).

Literary Works

Maya Angelou, *I Know Why the Caged Bird Sings*

James Baldwin, *Go Tell It on the Mountain*

Charles Dickens, *Great Expectations* **or** *Oliver Twist*

F. Scott Fitzgerald, *The Great Gatsby*

Nathaniel Hawthorne, *The Scarlet Letter*

Isabel Allende, *The House of the Spirits*

Harper Lee, *To Kill a Mockingbird*

Arthur Miller, *The Crucible*

George Orwell, *Animal Farm* **or** *1984*

PRACTICE TEST 1 ANSWER SHEET
FOR OPEN-RESPONSE QUESTIONS

PRACTICE TEST 1 ANSWER SHEET
FOR OPEN-RESPONSE QUESTIONS

PRACTICE TEST 1 ANSWER SHEET
FOR OPEN-RESPONSE QUESTIONS

_____

_____

_____

_____

_____

_____

_____

_____

_____

_____

_____

_____

_____

PRACTICE TEST 1 ANSWER SHEET
FOR OPEN-RESPONSE QUESTIONS

PRACTICE TEST 1 ANSWER SHEET
FOR OPEN-RESPONSE QUESTIONS

_____

_____

_____

_____

_____

_____

_____

_____

_____

_____

_____

_____

_____

_____

ANSWER KEY—PRACTICE TEST 1

Question	Answer	Objective
1	B	I. Literature and Language
2	C	I. Literature and Language
3	D	I. Literature and Language
4	A	I. Literature and Language
5	D	I. Literature and Language
6	C	I. Literature and Language
7	B	I. Literature and Language
8	C	I. Literature and Language
9	B	I. Literature and Language
10	B	I. Literature and Language
11	B	I. Literature and Language
12	D	I. Literature and Language
13	C	I. Literature and Language
14	A	I. Literature and Language
15	A	I. Literature and Language
16	B	I. Literature and Language
17	D	I. Literature and Language
18	B	I. Literature and Language
19	B	I. Literature and Language
20	B	I. Literature and Language
21	A	I. Literature and Language
22	A	I. Literature and Language
23	C	I. Literature and Language
24	B	I. Literature and Language

Question	Answer	Objective
25	C	I. Literature and Language
26	A	I. Literature and Language
27	B	I. Literature and Language
28	A	I. Literature and Language
29	B	I. Literature and Language
30	A	I. Literature and Language
31	A	I. Literature and Language
32	C	I. Literature and Language
33	B	I. Literature and Language
34	C	I. Literature and Language
35	C	I. Literature and Language
36	A	I. Literature and Language
37	D	I. Literature and Language
38	A	I. Literature and Language
39	B	I. Literature and Language
40	C	I. Literature and Language
41	B	I. Literature and Language
42	A	I. Literature and Language
43	A	I. Literature and Language
44	B	I. Literature and Language
45	A	I. Literature and Language
46	B	I. Literature and Language
47	B	I. Literature and Language
48	C	I. Literature and Language
49	B	I. Literature and Language
50	B	I. Literature and Language
51	D	I. Literature and Language

Question	Answer	Objective
52	A	I. Literature and Language
53	B	I. Literature and Language
54	D	I. Literature and Language
55	A	I. Literature and Language
56	D	I. Literature and Language
57	A	I. Literature and Language
58	D	I. Literature and Language
59	D	I. Literature and Language
60	D	I. Literature and Language
61	D	I. Literature and Language
62	D	I. Literature and Language
63	A	I. Literature and Language
64	A	I. Literature and Language
65	B	I. Literature and Language
66	A	I. Literature and Language
67	B	I. Literature and Language
68	A	I. Literature and Language
69	A	I. Literature and Language
70	A	I. Literature and Language
71	B	I. Literature and Language
72	D	I. Literature and Language
73	C	I. Literature and Language
74	A	I. Literature and Language
75	D	I. Literature and Language
76	A	I. Literature and Language
77	C	I. Literature and Language

Question	Answer	Objective
78	A	I. Literature and Language
79	B	I. Literature and Language
80	D	I. Literature and Language
81	A	I. Literature and Language
82	C	III. Reading Theory, Research, and Instruction
83	D	III. Reading Theory, Research, and Instruction
84	A	III. Reading Theory, Research, and Instruction
85	A	III. Reading Theory, Research, and Instruction
86	C	III. Reading Theory, Research, and Instruction
87	D	II. Rhetoric and Composition
88	C	II. Rhetoric and Composition
89	B	I. Literature and Language
90	A	I. Literature and Language
91	B	II. Rhetoric and Composition
92	D	II. Rhetoric and Composition
93	D	II. Rhetoric and Composition
94	A	II. Rhetoric and Composition
95	B	II. Rhetoric and Composition
96	A	II. Rhetoric and Composition
97	B	II. Rhetoric and Composition
98	C	III. Reading Theory, Research, and Instruction
99	A	II. Rhetoric and Composition
100	A	II. Rhetoric and Composition

PRACTICE TEST 1 PROGRESS CHART

I. Literature and Language ——/83

1	2	3	4	5	6	7	8	9	10	11	12	13	14	15

16	17	18	19	20	21	22	23	24	25	26	27	28	29	30

31	32	33	34	35	36	37	38	39	40	41	42	43	44	45

46	47	48	49	50	51	52	53	54	55	56	57	58	59	60

61	62	63	64	65	66	67	68	69	70	71	72	73	74	75

76	77	78	79	80	81	89	90

II. Rhetoric and Composition ——/10

88	91	92	93	94	95	96	97	99	100

III. Reading Theory, Research, and Instruction ——/7

82	83	84	85	86	87	98

DETAILED EXPLANATIONS FOR PRACTICE TEST 1

1. **B.**

    Poetic and symbolic, the literature of pre-colonial Native Americans, viewed primarily as **folklore**, describes the beauty, power, and awe of nature. Most prevalent in this literature are **myths**, stories passed down from generation to generation that explain natural phenomena and significant cultural and religious rituals.

2. **C.**

    Although Puritan literature reflected the theme of determinism, the literature also preached the necessity of being righteous and conservative to a point of rigidity.

3. **D.**

    Allegory, sermon, and parable serve to teach lessons either through symbolic storytelling or explicit didactics, whereas legends are narratives that emerged from oral storytelling and combine fiction and factual history.

4. **A.**

    Benjamin Franklin's *Autobiography*, similar to the Puritan diaries in its design and structure, offers Franklin's life as a representative model of trial, pilgrimage, and success intended to teach and instruct others. *Poor Richard's Alamanack* (B) contains weather predictions and poetry, "The Dogood Papers" (C) offers humorous and irreverent tales, and "Death is a Fisherman" (D) is a poem that appeared in *Poor Richard's Almanack*.

5. **D.**

    As most of the written and spoken literature was political in nature during the Revolutionary period, the novel was not a form well suited to political rhetoric.

6. **C.**

    Henry David Thoreau and Ralph Waldo Emerson, whose works are clearly aligned with transcendentalism, significantly influenced the work of Walt Whitman.

7. **B.**

    Both *Moby Dick* and *Billy Budd* depict how forces of evil triumph over innocence and beauty, and therefore, are allegories.

8.   **C.**

Emily Dickinson did not commit suicide, but died in her hometown, Amherst, Massachusetts.

9.   **B.**

Although Jack London (A) and Charlotte Perkins Gilman (C) are naturalist writers, Stephen Crane is considered the first naturalist writer.

10.   **B.**

Although Ernest Hemingway (A), William Faulkner (B), John Steinbeck (C), and F. Scott Fitzgerald (D) were contemporaries, Faulkner is noted for his use of extensively long sentences, stream of consciousness, and fragments.

11.   **B.**

As I Lay Dying was written by William Faulkner.

12.   **D.**

William Carlos Williams, noted for representing females responsively, wrote "The Young Housewife."

13.   **C.**

Robert Frost wrote in traditional verse and the plain language of New Englanders.

14.   **A.**

"Out! Out!" describes a young boy who bleeds to death after the chainsaw he is using to cut wood "jumps" out of his hands and cuts off part of his arm.

15.   **A.**

The Harlem Renaissance emerged during the 1920s.

16.   **B.**

"If We Must Die," written in the form of an Elizabethan sonnet, won Claude McKay acclaim and the reputation as a black militant.

17.   **D.**

The Beat poets included Jack Kerouac (*On the Road*, A), William Burroughs (*Naked Lunch*, B), and Alan Ginsberg (*Howl*, C). Robert Lowell, the king of anguish, a confessional poet, wrote *Lord Weary's Castle*.

18.   **B.**

Arthur Miller's *The Crucible* compared Senator Joe McCarthy's House of Representatives' Committee hearings on Un-American Activities to the Salem witch trials.

19.   **B.**

Flannery O'Connor's *A Good Man Is Hard to Find* shows a world infested with evil and superficiality, suggesting that humankind is not worth redemption.

20.   **B.**

Ralph Ellison wrote *The Invisible Man*, whose theme demonstrates that society willfully ignores blacks, in 1953.

21.   **A.**

Toni Morrison was the first African American woman to receive the Nobel Prize for Literature (1993). Morrison's novels include *Sula*, *Beloved*, *The Bluest Eye*, and *Song of Solomon*.

22.   **A.**

Toni Morrison combines fantasy, ghosts, and what she calls "rememory" or the recurrence of past events to elaborate the horrors of slavery and the struggles of African Americans after being freed.

23.   **C.**

Maxine Hong Kingston grew up surrounded by other immigrants from her father's village hearing stories that influenced her later writing. *China Men* details male influences in her life and celebrates the strengths and achievements of the first Chinese men in America and the exploitation and prejudice they faced.

24.   **B.**

Bernard Malamud was a master of parables and myths. His best work, *The Natural*, is based on ballplayer Eddie Waitkus, who tries to make a comeback after being shot by a serial killer.

25.   **C.**

Saul Bellow wrote *Seize the Day*.

26.   **A.**

Julia Alvarez was born in New York City but spent her childhood in her parents' native Dominican Republic during the Trujillo dictatorship in the early 1950s. She returned to the United States in 1960. *How the Garcia Girls Lost Their Accents* describes the difficulties of learning American (conversational) English and being called a "spic" at school. The text is told in reverse chronological order and narrated from shifting perspectives, beginning with her four sisters' adult lives and moving to their childhood.

27.   **B.**

Old English or Anglo-Saxon literature (such as *Beowulf*) is noted for epic battles, heroic feats, and supernatural characters.

28.   **A.**

In 731, Bede, the first English historian, wrote *The Ecclesiastical History of the English People.* His text recounts that St. Augustine's mission was to bring literary materials from Rome to England to support worship and service of the church.

29.   **B.**

The Seafarer describes the speaker's nostalgia for his past life on shore but a deep love of the sea, despite its loneliness. A metaphor for the Christian path of self-denial, the sea symbolizes a life on earth of struggle and difficulty, which is brief, however, compared to an everlasting life of happiness in heaven.

30.   **A.**

Frame story, or a story within a story, is a technique that uses fictive narrative or a series of smaller stories. Chaucer used this device in many of his stories, in particular *The Canterbury Tales*.

31.   **A.**

Elizabeth I's reign marked forty-five years of literary growth. William Shakespeare and Edmund Spenser introduced new forms of the sonnet. John Lyly developed euphuism, an elaborate style of prose that has complex sentence structure using much parallelism and includes proverbs, similes from pseudoscience, and incidents from history. Thomas More offered a different literary focus when he described an imaginary commonwealth that incorporated the ideals of political, social order, education, and religion. More's *Utopia* advocates religious toleration and opposes organized war. Marlowe was the first playwright to use blank verse in drama.

32. **C.**

Much Ado about Nothing, *A Midsummer Night's Dream*, and *Twelfth Night* are Shakespearean comedies.

33. **B.**

The years 1603 to 1625 are considered the Jacobean Age in British literature.

34. **C.**

Christopher Marlowe is known for his poetry, especially "The Passionate Shepherd," which begins "Come live with me and be my love …" to which Sir Walter Raleigh responded with "The Nymph's Reply to the Shepherd."

35. **C.**

Sir Francis Bacon is the only essayist among the Jacobean writers. Ben Jonson (B) and Thomas Middleton (D) wrote plays and poetry, and John Donne (A), metaphysical poetry.

36. **A.**

"To a Mouse" was written by Robert Burns.

37. **D.**

Of the choices, only metaphysical poetry was not an element of Carolinean Age literature.

38. **A.**

John Milton was a countercultural poet whose style defied the simplicity and sensuality of Cavalier poetry. He incorporated blank verse and complex syntax into his epics and elegies.

39. **B.**

John Bunyan, a preacher and student of scripture, is most well-known for his Christian allegory, *The Pilgrim's Progress*. He used simple and plain language to preach and write about theology.

40. **C.**

Pamela; or, Virtue Rewarded was written by Samuel Richardson.

41. **B.**

Joseph Addison did indeed write pamphlets but never earned this distinction.

42. **A.**

Jonathan Swift considered being born in Ireland one of his misfortunes, yet he wrote extensively about Irish affairs during the Irish potato famine, best reflected in *A Modest Proposal*, in which he suggested that the Irish landlords eat the children. Swift spent significant time in a mental institution.

43. **A.**

Alexander Pope's first major essay, *An Essay on Criticism*, contains the famous line, "A little learning is a dangerous thing."

44. **B.**

The cotton gin was invented in the United States. A middle class emerged, and women stayed at home to attend to domestic needs.

45. **A.**

William Blake's pervasive themes of heaven and hell, innocence and experience, and good and evil heavily influenced the romantic poets.

46. **B.**

Only (B) sequences the periods chronologically. The list should read Old English, Middle English, Renaissance, neoclassical, romantic, Victorian, modern.

47. **B.**

The Prelude is considered William Wordsworth's magnum opus. He co-authored his first work, *Lyrical Ballads* (A), with Samuel Taylor Coleridge; it essentially launched both their careers. Lord George Byron wrote *Don Juan* (C), and Coleridge wrote *Christabel* (D).

48.   **C.**

Jane Austen, considered a great novelist and one of the few with manners, offered intensely perceptive psychology in her novels even though her plots are fairly placid romantic comedies (everyone marries at the end). Elizabeth Barrett Browning (A), Charlotte Brontë (B), and Mary Elizabeth Braddon (D) wrote during the Victorian period.

49.   **B.**

Emily Brontë wrote only one novel, *Wuthering Heights*.

50.   **B.**

Bleak House and *Dombey and Son* are Dickens's darker novels, recounting death, murder, madness, despair, and suicide, all negative but accurate consequences of a complicated, mechanized world. *Oliver Twist* (A) challenged the inhumane aspects of new social legislation, represented the fear of criminality and the mob (threatening herd of working-class people), questioned how to control an increasingly complex society, and endorsed emerging middle-class values. But the text is ultimately hopeful, documenting Oliver's progress as a hero who comes to terms with the world and embraces middle-class values while simultaneously remaining aware of the vulnerability and desires buried beneath the superficiality of polite manners. In *David Copperfield* (C) and *Great Expectations* (D), protagonists are at odds with and at the same time crave middle-class respectability.

51.   **D.**

Thomas Hardy was the most significant novelist in last quarter of the nineteenth century, writing from a perspective situated outside in the margins and questioning established values and distancing himself from the traditional or conventional social order.

52.   **A.**

George Eliot, the penname for Mary Anne Evans, wrote novels that reflected an era of tremendous prosperity, portraying a central theme of egoism and the duties and obligations of the individual, as seen in *Adam Bede* and *Daniel Deronda*.

53.　**B.**

　　This period saw new forms of social analysis, resurgent socialism, new feminist voices, and a fresh expression of liberal values. heroines, and the denunciation of Victorian values.

54.　**D.**

　　Anthony Burgess wrote the disturbing and nightmarish novel *A Clockwork Orange*, a depiction of violent authoritarianism. He is also the author of a wide array of other lesser known works, including criticism on language, music, and politics, and a biography of William Shakespeare.

55.　**A.**

　　Samuel Beckett, an Irish novelist and playwright, wrote *Waiting for Godot*, an existential play, and most of his other work, while living in France. This play put him in the vanguard of the theater of the absurd. He is also known for his plays *Endgame*, *Krapp's Last Tape*, *Breath*, and *Not I*.

56.　**D.**

　　D. H. Lawrence wrote *Lady Chatterley's Lover.*

57.　**A.**

　　Early Greek literature included comedy, tragedy, lyric and epic poetry, and dialectic.

58.　**D.**

　　Aeschylus created the prototype of later drama marked by conflict.

59.　**D.**

　　The Romans openly and proudly borrowed Greek sources, imitating the Greek epics and themes of heroism. In *The Aeneid*, Aeneas is the perfect prototype for the ideal Roman. Inspired by Homer, Virgil sought to create a national epic for the emerging Roman Empire under rule of Augustus Caesar and to link it to the dynasty of ancient Troy in the person of its surviving prince, Aeneas.

60. **D.**

The Four Gospels of the Life and Sayings of Jesus and the Acts of the Apostles was written in Greek about sixty years after the death of Jesus. Each Gospel addresses a different audience: Matthew, the Jewish public; Mark, the Gentile audience; and Luke, the cultured Greek readers. John's writing differs from his peers in that his work consistently refers to Jesus as Christ and Lord, representing Jesus as the Omnipotent.

61. **D.**

Dante Alighieri wrote the *Divine Comedy*, a poem that represents the supreme expression of the medieval mind in European imaginative literature. A comedy because it begins in misery and ends in happiness, *The Divine Comedy* is considered the greatest poem of the Middle Ages. Highly visual and symmetric, the work contains three divisions of identical length: *Hell* (*Inferno*), *Purgatory* (*Purgatorio*), and *Paradise* (*Paradiso*). The poem recounts Dante's descent through nine circles of hell and seven divisions of Purgatory proper, ante-Purgatory, and Earthly Paradise (Garden of Eden). Unlike the works of Homer, Virgil, or John Milton, this work is quiet, factual, and economical, rendering it an air of simplicity.

62. **D.**

The *Epic of Son-Jara* is an early African work.

63. **A.**

Li Po, a wandering poet recognized as the greatest Tang poet, produced an abundance of poems on subjects such as nature, wine, friendship, solitude, and the passage of time. With its air of playfulness, hyperbole, and fantasy, his poetry captured the nuances of the human experience of nature and human friendship. Confucius (B) was a Chinese philosopher; Qin Shi Hwang (C) was the first emperor of a unified China; and Laozi Tzu (D) is a silk manuscript containing eighty-one short stanzas.

64. **A.**

Dharma, a significant core concept of Hinduism, addresses the guiding principle of human conduct that preserves the social, moral, cosmic integrity of universe. Such conduct is righteous and requires sacred duties, which impact three spheres that govern ideal life: *artha* (wealth, profit, political power), *kama* (love, sensuality), and *moska* (release, liberation). Dharma does not require profound self-denial, as choice A suggests. Karma (C), another core concept, holds that all things are responsible for their own actions.

65.　**B.**

Written in Arabic, the Koran is greater than prophetic revelation as it is God's final revelation to humanity though Muhammad.

66.　**A.**

Japanese literature introduced the haiku circa 1100. Japanese literature was distinguished from fanciful romance and privileged realism, psychological insight, and authenticity over romanticism. The themes address loss, substitution, transgression, and retribution. Literature was highly influenced by the impact of kinship on bureaucracy; thus literature focused on family fortunes, politics, economy, and the military. Due to the influence of Buddhism, however, Japanese literature also explored the depths of longing and ambition.

67.　**B.**

As society once again focused on marriage as the norm, the position of women in society became increasingly insignificant.

68.　**A.**

Miguel de Cervantes (1547–1616), Spanish dramatist, poet, and author, wrote the epic poem *Don Quixote de la Mancha* when he was fifty-eight years old. His work satirized tales of chivalry presented in classical literature. Poking fun at European and particularly Spanish society, Cervantes believed that although humankind was inherently good, it was prone to mischief. Cervantes based most of his work on personal experiences and adventures.

69.　**A.**

Mesoamerican contact with Europeans influenced recording of Mesoamerican historical narratives, prayers, and song texts, which resulted in growing native literature preserved in western European script available to the world in European languages. Maya, Zuni, and Navajo literature based on oral tradition were written down and published. Three genres of Mesoamerican literature emerged: song, narrative, and oratory.

70.　**A.**

In cities, theater, oral-verse romance, and storytelling flourished. Popular Chinese literature included murder mysteries, stories of bandits, and fantasy. High culture favored neo-Confucianism, an attempt to discover the philosophical grounds of Confucian classics, but the rigid strictures imposed on self-cultivation and ethical behavior failed to address complexities of human nature and pressures of living in an increasingly complex world. Vernacular literature celebrated liberty, violent energy, and passion.

71.   **B.**

The Book of Travels details a panoramic view of Ottoman Empire in mid-seventeenth century, when its geographic extent was the greatest and most powerful. There are no comparable records of any Islamic state. The author, Evliya Çelebi, was the most prolific and celebrated writer of the Ottoman Empire. He was supposedly inspired by a dream about the prophet Muhammad, who encouraged him to wander and travel throughout the empire for the next forty-four years.

72.   **D.**

The post-World War II period resulted in existentialism, the theater of the absurd, which consists of choosing our actions at each point, avoiding the bad faith of pretending that others are responsible for our choices, and choosing not just for oneself but for all. This was a time of literary movements leading to many "isms." So many groups tried to find appropriate artistic response to contemporary history, all embraced by modernism. Dadaism represented disgust in traditional middle-class values blamed for World War I and a subversion of authority to liberate creative imagination. Surrealism combined two unrelated elements and suggested buried connections and possible relationships overlooked by the logical mind. Surrealism incorporated intensity, playfulness, and openness to change and proved to be the most influential of all the movements. Futurism expressed enthusiasm for the dynamic new machine age.

73.   **C.**

Leo Tolstoy wrote *War and Peace*.

74.   **A.**

In Jean-Paul Sartre's philosophical view, the lack of God in one's life is the norm. He believed that man must face his undeniable freedom if he ever wishes to become a moral being and establish his own existence. Sartre said that man, once he commits to being totally free from all authority and accepts that he must make meaning himself, needs to find solidarity with others. One way in which to create that solidarity is through literature; Sartre saw art and literature as moral activities.

75.   **D.**

Leo Tolstoy wrote *Anna Karenina.*

76.   **A.**

Chinua Achebe, a Nigerian novelist, composed his first novel, *Things Fall Apart,* in 1959. In contrast to previous African literature that addresses folklore and stories of urban life, *Things Fall Apart* addresses the grave impact of colonization on a warrior hero who refuses to relinquish his traditional cultural beliefs and values. Achebe's novels *No Longer At Ease* and *Arrow of God* also address the profound difficulties Africans face when worlds collide, resulting in rapid cultural change.

77.   **C.**

Lu Xun is called the father of modern Chinese literature. Lu Xun, or Lu Hsün, was a pen name of Zhou Shuren. His first story, "A Madman's Diary," is considered the first story written in modern Chinese. His first set of stories was published as the book *Call to Arms* or *Na Han.* He retold old Chinese stories from his own perspective. He also published *Wild Grass,* a collection of prose poems focused on dreams, including nightmares: dogs speak, insects buzz, and the sky tries to hide itself from onlookers.

78.   **A.**

Nirmal Verma was a Hindi novelist and activist who helped to bring about the *Nayi Kahani* ("new short story") literary movement of Hindi literature. His best-known short story, "Parinde" ("Birds"), is supposed to be the exemplar of the *Nayi Kahani* movement. Verma also wrote other notable stories such as "Ve Din," "Lal Teen Ki Chhat," and "Kavve Aur Kala Pani," which have been translated into several languages, including English, Russian, Polish, and French. Verma's writing is rich in symbolism with a style that is deceptively simple.

79.   **B.**

The medieval criticism of St. Thomas Aquinas and Alighieri Dante refined neo-platonic notions of allegory, observing that meanings of language encompassed not only literal levels but also allegorical, moral, anagogical, or mystical levels. Thus, medieval aesthetics emphasized beauty, order, and harmony of God's creation. Literature, therefore, was one part of an ordered hierarchy of knowledge leading to the divine, its climax being theology.

80.   **D.**

Poststructural criticism assumes that the most effective way to interpret a text is to deconstruct it. Posited by Jacques Derrida, postructuralism assumes that language is unstable and ambiguous and therefore contradictory, that the author is not in full control of what he or she writes, and that literature means nothing because language means nothing, and therefore, there is no way of knowing what the "meaning" of a story is. This method of critique requires the reader to reflect deeply beyond the surface of text in that text reveals meaning of which even the author might be unaware, to examine the relationships between appearance and reality, and to realize that language is creative and lively. Like the formalists, poststructuralists and deconstructionists use literary devices, conventions, and other formalist tools but use them to break down or deconstruct the text rather than derive a coherent and unifying whole. This view of criticism perceives text as not having a center or universal meaning, but an array of meanings; literature is political, cultural, and social.

81.   **A.**

The development of the English language occurred in the following stages: Proto-Indo-European, Germanic language, Old English, Middle English, the Great Vowel Shift, technical vocabulary, divergence of British and American English.

82.   **C.**

Phonics, *not* phonetics, is concerned with sounds of word elements only to the extent that knowing these sounds aids in word recognition and subsequently reading. Phonetics is the science of speech sounds. It deals extensively with the minute differences in sounds and the symbols used to represent these sounds. Phonetics is concerned with the physical apparatus involved in actually making the sound: the control and flow of breath, placement of the lips, tongue, teeth, and so on.

83.   **D.**

Choices A and C are vowel digraphs, those spelling patterns wherein two letters are used to represent the vowel sound. Choice C is a consonant digraph. Choice D, *oy*, is a diphthong, a linguistic element that fuses two adjacent vowel sounds.

84.   **A.**

Deterioration or pejoration is when a word's original meaning is diminished or lessened. The meaning of the word *villain* changed from "an inhabitant of a village" to "scoundrel."

85.　**A.**

During the eighteenth to twentieth centuries, dictionaries and grammars gained much popularity with the growing belief that the English language had somehow been corrupted. Reformers called for a purer form of the language and generally fell into one of two groups: descriptivist, who wanted to describe language as it existed, and prescriptivist, who wanted to prescribe how language ought to be. John Skretta fell into the latter group.

86.　**C.**

Reading as a psycholinguistic process is often viewed from a psycholinguistic perspective. Proponents of this outlook believe that an interaction between thought and words and both psychological and neurobiological factors allow readers to understand written language. They argue that human cognitive processes allow for understanding text. This view assumes various components of language: phonology, phonemes, morphemes, tone/pitch, stress, juncture, semantics, and syntax.

87.　**D.**

Decoding is a word recogntion skill, not a strategy.

88.　**C.**

Tier 3 words are those that are part of the technical vocabulary of the content area: *simile, metaphor, characterization, synecdoche,* and so on.

89.　**B.**

Maturity and perseverance are not among the themes characteristic of new realism. New realism often addresses controversial issues that elicit criticism for its too authentic content. These issues include sexism and sexuality (A), war and violence (C), profanity and alienation (D), among others.

90.　**A.**

The Slave Dancer by Paula Fox is an example of historical fiction. The *Middle Passage* by Tom Feelings (B) is a wordless book that documents the Middle Passage via pen-and-ink illustrations. *Taking Sides* by Gary Soto (C) is an example of new realism and multicultural literature, and *The Cay* by Theodore Taylor (D) is an example of multicultural literature.

91. **B.**

Classical rhetoric is divided into three branches: deliberative, judicial, and epideictic. The purpose of deliberative rhetoric is to convince, persuade, or dissuade, as demonstrated in Patrick Henry's speech before the Virginia House of Burgesses. The purpose of judicial rhetoric is to accuse, defend, or exonerate. As surmised, this kind of rhetoric is employed in courtrooms. Harper Lee incorporates this type of rhetoric in *To Kill a Mockingbird* when Atticus presents his closing remarks about the innocence of Tom Robinson in the rape of Mayella Ewell. Marc Antony's soliloquy in *Julius Caesar* is an excellent example of epideictic rhetoric, the purpose of which is to celebrate, commend, or commemorate; in his soliloquy, Marc Antony praises his slain mentor, Julius Caesar.

92. **D.**

Dispositio is the arrangement of an argument, which includes the introduction, narration, refutation, confirmation, and closing.

93. **D.**

Although modern rhetoric still employs all the rhetorical devices of classical rhetoric, modern rhetoric has shifted from the speaker or author and to the audience. Everyday language and communication in its variety of uses comprises rhetoric. In thinking about rhetoric, it is useful to think about the context of rhetoric, or more specifically to assume a rhetorical stance. Context, which includes purpose, audience, subject, and medium, provides the framework for a rhetorical stance.

94. **A.**

The four purposes of discourse are persuasion, expression, reference, and literary. These purposes are not mutually exclusive and are often combined in a piece of writing but in a careful and deliberate manner.

95. **B.**

Critical to effective modern rhetoric are three principles: the three unities, coherence, and proportion, and emphasis. The three unities that must be incorporated to render rhetoric effective are unity of thought, unity of feeling, and unity of purpose. Unity of thought requires that all ideas, arguments, details, and rhetoric support one main or central idea or thesis in speech and in writing. Unity of feeling requires that the author or writer manipulate emotions in various ways to produce the desired mood or feeling. And unity of purpose requires that all spoken or written discourse enable the purpose: to inform, convince, influence, enlighten, and so on.

96.   **A.**

The principle of emphasis asserts that significant and important ideas must appear in prominent positions, at the beginning or at the end, as these are parts of the speech and composition that the listener or reader is likely to remember. The principle of coherence states that all ideas in speech or composition (writing) must connect and relate logically to each other and to the central idea so that there is a coherent and consistent whole. The principle of proportion states that the appropriate amount of text or space needs to be given to each part of the whole so that it is balanced.

97.   **B.**

Both spoken and written discourse make use of pauses, repetitions, and fillers.

98.   **C.**

Social distance or the capacity for second language learners to integrate into the dominant culture may impede language learning. Culture shock, attitude, motivation, and ego, among other factors, can foster social distance, impacting negatively on language learning.

99.   **A.**

Any activity that the writer does before writing the first draft is prewriting. Prewriting includes thinking, brainstorming, jotting notes, talking with others, interviewing experts, researching in the library or online, gathering and assessing information, listing, mapping, charting, webbing, outlining, and organizing information.

100.   **A.**

The sentence should read: *My mother along with her sisters visits their mother every summer.* Expressions such as *with, together with, including, accompanied by, in addition to, along with,* or *as well* do not change the number of the subject. If the subject is singular, the verb is too.

HOW THE OPEN-RESPONSE ITEMS WILL BE SCORED

Two or more qualified educators will read your open-response responses, using scoring scales and standardized procedures that have been approved by the Massachusetts Department of Education. They will use scoring scales that describe varying levels of performance when they judge the overall effectiveness of each of your responses.

They will be looking to see that you demonstrate an understanding of the content of the Field and will score your work on the extent to which you achieve the purpose of the assignment, and your answers are appropriate and accurate in the application of subject matter knowledge, provide high-quality and relevant supporting evidence, and demonstrate a soundness of argument and understanding of the subject area.

Performance Characteristics Used by Scorers

Scorers use the following performance characteristics to guide them in considering your responses to the open-response items.

Characteristics Definitions

Purpose The extent to which your response achieves the purpose of the assignment.

Subject Matter Knowledge Accuracy and appropriateness in your application of subject matter knowledge.

Support The quality and relevance of your supporting details

Rationale The soundness of your argument and the degree of your understanding of the subject matter

Open-response questions will earn from a high of 4 to a low of 1. The following describes what you need to do to earn the highest score.

4	**The "4" response reflects a thorough knowledge and understanding of the subject matter.** • You fully achieve the purpose of the assignment. • You show substantial, accurate, and appropriate application of subject matter knowledge. • Your supporting evidence is sound; with high-quality, relevant examples. • Your response reflects an ably reasoned, comprehensive understanding of the topic.
3	**The "3" response reflects an adequate knowledge and understanding of the subject matter.** • You largely achieve the purpose of the assignment. • You have a generally accurate and appropriate application of subject matter knowledge. • Your supporting evidence is adequate; with some acceptable, relevant examples. • Your response reflects an adequately reasoned understanding of the topic.
2	**The "2" response reflects a limited knowledge and understanding of the subject matter.** • You have partially achieved the purpose of the assignment. • You have a limited, possibly inaccurate or inappropriate application of subject matter knowledge. • Your supporting evidence is limited; and have few relevant examples. • Your response reflects a limited, poorly reasoned understanding of the topic.
1	**The "1" response reflects a weak knowledge and understanding of the subject matter.** • You have not achieved the purpose of the assignment. • You show little or no appropriate or accurate application of subject matter knowledge. • Your supporting evidence, if present, is weak; you have few or no relevant examples. • Your response reflects little or no reasoning about or understanding of the topic.

Your response to an open-response item would be designated "unscorable" if it is unrelated to the assigned topic, is illegible and can't be read, not in the appropriate language, is too short insufficient to score, or merely repeats the assignment.

If you have not answered an open-response item, it will be designated "blank."

OPEN-RESPONSE QUESTION #1

Sample Response that would receive a top score of 4 points:

In William Blake's "The Chimney Sweeper," the images of a lonely child's misery, isolation, and suffering represent the Victorian philosophy that children were property to be used and then discarded when they outgrew their usefulness.

In the poem, the young orphaned narrator expresses his misery with sounds of "weeping." At first, his crying is the result of the loss or abandonment of his parents, "my mother died . . . and my father sold me . . ." and "father and mother . . . both gone to the church to pray," and secondly by the harsh and dangerous labor, the "chimneys I sweep," he is required to perform. In addition, the fact that the narrator is very aware that his father "sold" him speaks to the issue of Victorian children as a viable commodity.

At the same time that Blake paints the images of desolation, he presents his reader with the embodiment of death as in "coffins of black." The use of these references creates a somber atmosphere that reinforces the fact that the narrator who sleeps "in soot" lives in a blackened world filled with suffering and mortal danger, not allowing any chance for real rest.

The author suggests a heavenly redemption where God and angels will watch the "thousand of sweepers" who have been set free as they are "leaping, laughing" and running "down a green plain." However, Blake returns to the reality of the cold morning and implies that this faith in impending redemption may be unwarranted.

Overall, the poem's theme of the Victorian child's vulnerability and treatment as property are reinforced by the references to the child being "sold" into a dark and dangerous world, where he will know only sadness until his eventual death.

Evaluation of Response

This response demonstrates clear and consistent understanding of the images in the poem being discussed. The writer has fully identified the theme as the Victorian view of children as commodities. In identifying the theme, the writer has pointed to the poet's use of imagery and descriptive vocabulary. In stating his position, the writer has made specific reference to the actual words used by the poet. The writer used the final paragraph to conclude his essay with a brief summary. Overall, the writer has written a well-organized essay that is clearly focused and shows a smooth progression of ideas. In doing so, he has used varied, appropriate, and accurate vocabulary.

OPEN-RESPONSE QUESTION #2

Sample Response that would receive a top score of 4 points

The two books <u>The House of the Spirits</u> by Isabel Allende and <u>I Know Why the Caged Bird Sings</u> by Maya Angelou illustrate very well the statement: "A book about one character and one country can become a book about other characters and the world."

Allende's book—<u>The House of the Spirits</u>—takes place in an unnamed country in South America about the turn of the twentieth century. The fact that the setting is so unspecific perhaps makes the events in the book even more applicable to the reader in a different country and at another time; this lack of specificity makes the book even more a book for the entire world.

<u>I Know Why the Caged Bird Sings</u> is more specific in its setting than is <u>The House of the Spirits</u>. The events in Angelou's book occur during the Great Depression; the setting includes events in both the Northern and the Southern regions of the United States. This more specific setting in the United States, however, does not limit the applicability of the book to other parts of the world.

The main characters in both books are female. The female in <u>The House of the Spirits</u> lives in an earlier time and in a different country than does Angelou in the autobiographical <u>I Know Why the Caged Bird Sings</u>. The interesting feature is that the young females have many things and feelings in common. Again, "A book about one character"—or, in this case, one female—"and one country can become a book about other characters and the world."

Interestingly, the events of both books include muteness, a coping device that any person could use. In both writings the female protagonist displays the affliction of muteness. The condition in both cases is not one that had been present from birth; instead the condition of noncommunication is brought about by other factors. It is possible for events to change the lives of others in the world—regardless of the time or the place.

The two books <u>I Know Why the Caged Bird Sings</u> and <u>The House of the Spirits</u> both feature females. The stories in the books, the females in the books, the settings in the books are typical of others across the world—regardless of time, place, and gender.

Evaluation of Response

The test taker's response analyzes the literary issue introduced in the statement both systematically and completely. He develops a thesis and uses appropriate examples from two books to illustrate and support it. The writing is coherent and demonstrates control of the language using appropriate diction and syntax. The writing is well organized and observes the conventions of standard written English.

Practice Test 2

MTEL English

This practice test is also on CD-ROM in our special interactive MTEL English TestWare®. It is highly recommended that you first take this exam on computer. You will then have the additional study features and benefits of enforced timed conditions and instant, accurate scoring. See page 5 for instructions on how to get the most out of our MTEL book and software.

ANSWER SHEET FOR PRACTICE TEST 2

1 _____	21 _____	41 _____	61 _____	81 _____
2 _____	22 _____	42 _____	62 _____	82 _____
3 _____	23 _____	43 _____	63 _____	83 _____
4 _____	24 _____	44 _____	64 _____	84 _____
5 _____	25 _____	45 _____	65 _____	85 _____
6 _____	26 _____	46 _____	66 _____	86 _____
7 _____	27 _____	47 _____	67 _____	87 _____
8 _____	28 _____	48 _____	68 _____	88 _____
9 _____	29 _____	49 _____	69 _____	89 _____
10 _____	30 _____	50 _____	70 _____	90 _____
11 _____	31 _____	51 _____	71 _____	91 _____
12 _____	32 _____	52 _____	72 _____	92 _____
13 _____	33 _____	53 _____	73 _____	93 _____
14 _____	34 _____	54 _____	74 _____	94 _____
15 _____	35 _____	55 _____	75 _____	95 _____
16 _____	36 _____	56 _____	76 _____	96 _____
17 _____	37 _____	57 _____	77 _____	97 _____
18 _____	38 _____	58 _____	78 _____	98 _____
19 _____	39 _____	59 _____	79 _____	99 _____
20 _____	40 _____	60 _____	80 _____	100 _____

PRACTICE TEST 2

TIME: 4 hours   100 multiple-choice questions; 2 open-response questions

Directions: Read each question or statement carefully, and choose the response that BEST answers the question or completes the statement.

1. Which of the following statements is **NOT** true about Puritan literature?

    A. The Bible was the literal truth.

    B. Diaries were didactic and personal.

    C. Imagery was apocalyptic and meditative.

    D. Rhetoric was complex and enigmatic.

2. Which of the following works **BEST** describes man's corruption and God's justice?

    A. "Sinners in the Hands of an Angry God" by Jonathan Edwards

    B. *A History of the Dividing Line* by William Byrd

    C. *Relating to Witchcraft and Possessions* by Cotton Mather

    D. "A Model of Christian Charity" by John Winthrop

3. Which of the following themes characterize the literature of the American Renaissance?

    A. Transcendentalism and romanticism

    B. Romanticism and traditionalism

    C. Reason and transcendentalism

    D. Independence and revolution

4. Which of the following American writers was **NOT** allied with the abolitionist movement?

    A. Harriet Beecher Stowe

    B. David Walker

    C. Henry David Thoreau

    D. Ezra Pound

5.   All of the following are true about the Gilded Age **EXCEPT**

    A.   New England lost its monopoly on America's literary output.

    B.   the voice of the common people was heard from across the country.

    C.   tales of rags to riches became the fiction of the past.

    D.   literature reflected regional differences and local color.

6.   Which of the following is **NOT** an example of naturalist writing?

    A.   "To Build a Fire"

    B.   *The Red Badge of Courage*

    C.   *The Yellow Wallpaper*

    D.   *The Awakening*

7.   Which of the following styles of writing **BEST** characterize Ernest Hemingway?

    A.   Ironic and tragic

    B.   Natural and symbolic

    C.   Stoic and concise

    D.   Descriptive and rambling

8.   Which of the following texts depicts the corruption of the meatpacking industry in the early twentieth century?

    A.   *The Jungle*

    B.   *Cannery Row*

    C.   *The Fire Next Time*

    D.   *The Sun Also Rises*

9.   Which of the following twentieth-century poets incorporated imagism in his work?

    A.   T. S. Eliot

    B.   e. e. cummings

    C.   Ezra Pound

    D.   William Carlos Williams

10. Which of the following poems **BEST** characterizes humankind's struggle to find its place in the universe?

    A.   *The Waste Land*

    B.   "The Road Not Taken"

    C.   "The Love Song of J. Alfred Prufrock"

    D.   *The Cantos*

11. Which of the following twentieth-century poets wrote *Chicago Poems*?

    A.   Carl Sandburg

    B.   e. e. cummings

    C.   Robert Frost

    D.   T. S. Eliot

12. Which of the following authors did **NOT** write poetry during the Harlem Renaissance?

    A.   Langston Hughes

    B.   Claude McKay

    C.   Jean Toomer

    D.   Zora Neale Hurston

13. To which group of poets do Sylvia Plath, Robert Lowell, and Anne Sexton belong?

    A.   Fireside poets

    B.   Beat poets

    C.   Confessional poets

    D.   Muckraker poets

14. Who was the first African American woman writer to win the Pulitzer Prize for her poetry?

    A.   Maya Angelou

    B.   Toni Morrison

    C.   Gwendolyn Brooks

    D.   Alice Walker

15. Strong, black female characters who demonstrate extraordinary wisdom and mentoring are central to the work of which of the following writers?

    A. Toni Morrison

    B. Maya Angelou

    C. Gwendolyn Brooks

    D. Alice Walker

16. In which of the following novels do the action, characterization, and theme evolve around mahjong?

    A. *The Woman Warrior: Memoirs of a Girlhood among Ghosts*

    B. *The Joy Luck Club*

    C. *The Kitchen God's Wife*

    D. *China Men*

17. Which of the following writers is **NOT** a contemporary Native American writer?

    A. Sharon Creech

    B. Louise Erdrich

    C. N. Scott Momaday

    D. Marjorie Morningstar

18. Which of the following texts is **NOT** an example of Anglo-Saxon literature?

    A. *The Ecclesiastical History of the English People*

    B. *The Seafarer*

    C. *Eric the Red*

    D. *Beowulf*

19. Which of the following is **NOT** a form or technique that appears in medieval or Middle English literature?

    A. Frame stories

    B. Morality plays

    C. Folk ballads

    D. Kenning

20. Which of the following texts is **NOT** an example of medieval literature?

    A.　*The Canterbury Tales*

    B.　*Sir Gawayne and the Grene Knight*

    C.　*The Tragical History of Dr. Faustus*

    D.　*Le Morte d'Arthur*

21. All of the following were contemporaries of William Shakespeare **EXCEPT**

    A.　Sir Walter Raleigh.

    B.　Christopher Marlowe.

    C.　Thomas Nash.

    D.　Joseph Addison.

22. Which of the following statements is **NOT** true of the poetry of the Jacobean Age?

    A.　Poetry was sophisticated and cerebral.

    B.　Poetry was highly metaphorical and abstruse.

    C.　Poetry was metaphysical and difficult.

    D.　Poetry was political and satirical.

23. Which of the following writers is considered one of the greatest essayists of his time?

    A.　John Donne

    B.　Ben Jonson

    C.　Sir Francis Bacon

    D.　Thomas Middleton

24. Which of the following poems is **NOT** an example of carpe diem poetry?

    A.　"To His Coy Mistress"

    B.　"Ballad Upon a Wedding"

    C.　"Elegy Written in a Country Churchyard"

    D.　"To the Virgins, to Make Much of Time"

25. Which of the following is **NOT** a Cavalier poet?

    A. Sir John Suckling

    B. Andrew Marvell

    C. Richard Lovelace

    D. Sir Philip Sydney

26. Which of the following does **NOT** describe the literature of the Restoration period?

    A. Comedies were sexually explicit, addressing topics of the day and incorporating busy plots.

    B. The most popular dramas entertained murder, incest, and madness.

    C. Plays were macabre in nature and included villains and characters who went to their deaths.

    D. Drama criticized King James II's extreme Catholicism and conservatism.

27. Which of the following Restoration authors is considered the founder of modern English prose, noted for his contribution to literary criticism, and thought to have brought drama to the world?

    A. John Dryden

    B. John Bunyan

    C. John Donne

    D. Thomas Hobbes

28. Which of the following authors wrote *The Dictionary of the English Language*?

    A. Alexander Pope

    B. Dr. Samuel Johnson

    C. Oliver Goldsmith

    D. Richard Sheridan

29. Which of the following poems is a mock heroic epic poem?

    A. *The Rape of the Lock*

    B. *The Rambler*

    C. *The Private Memoirs and Confessions of a Justified Sinner*

    D. *Lives of the Poets*

30. Which of the following romantic poets gave dignity to the common man?

    A. William Blake

    B. Samuel Taylor Coleridge

    C. Robert Burns

    D. Lord George Byron

31. Which of the following is **NOT** true of William Blake and/or his poetry?

    A. William Blake was a pre-romantic poet, painter, and engraver.

    B. *Songs of Innocence* describes the natural world of spontaneity, innocence, and beauty.

    C. *Songs of Experience* describes the ugliness, truth, and fear often associated with adulthood.

    D. William Blake's style differed from Samuel Taylor Coleridge's simple diction and style.

32. Which of the following authors from the romantic period gave new popularity to the genre of historical fiction?

    A. Charles Lamb

    B. Charlotte Brontë

    C. Sir Walter Scott

    D. Mary Shelley

33. Which of the following texts was **NOT** written by Jane Austen?

    A. *Emma*

    B. *Pride and Prejudice*

    C. *Northanger Abbey*

    D. *Shirley*

34. Which of the following statements **BEST** describes early Victorian literature?

    A. This period is regarded as the most significant in the history of the English novel.

    B. This period is regarded as the most significant in poetry that addressed national identity.

    C. This period is regarded as the most significant in novels that addressed society versus the individual.

    D. This period is regarded as the most significant in poetry that addressed the deterioration of the psyche.

35. Reconciliation, restitution, humanity, and industriousness best characterize the Victorian novels of

    A. Charles Dickens.

    B. Charlotte Brontë.

    C. Emily Brontë.

    D. Elizabeth Gaskell.

36. Which of the following statements **BEST** characterizes the work of William Makepeace Thackeray?

    A. Thackeray's work elevated the middle-class hero's role in Victorian life to a higher level.

    B. Thackeray's work chastised the middle-class hero's selfishness and lack of direction.

    C. Thackeray's work critiqued materialism and the Victorian focus on social order.

    D. Thackeray's work critiqued materialism but lauded the Victorian focus on the individual.

37. Which early Victorian poet most accurately represented the sonnet since William Shakespeare?

    A.   Elizabeth Barrett Browning

    B.   Dante Gabriel Rossetti

    C.   Robert Browning

    D.   Emily Brontë

38. Which of the following novels was **NOT** written by Thomas Hardy?

    A.   *Far from the Madding Crowd*

    B.   *Jude the Obscure*

    C.   *Widowers' Houses*

    D.   *The Return of the Native*

39. Which of the following poets wrote during the middle Victorian period?

    A.   Lewis Carroll

    B.   Charles Darwin

    C.   Gerard Manley Hopkins

    D.   Anthony Trollope

40. Which of the following text-author pairs is incorrect?

    A.   *Idylls of the King* by Alfred Lord Tennyson

    B.   *Middlemarch* by George Eliot

    C.   "Dover Beach" by Matthew Arnold

    D.   *Phineas Finn* by John Rushkin

41. Which of the following late Victorian novelists painted a radical and disconcerting view of society?

    A.   Oscar Wilde

    B.   Rudyard Kipling

    C.   Robert Louis Stevenson

    D.   Thomas Hardy

42. Which of the following is **NOT** an author of science fiction novels?

    A.   Arthur Clarke

    B.   V. S. Naipaul

    C.   Aldous Huxley

    D.   George Orwell

43. Who was the first lyric poet?

    A.   Sappho

    B.   Homer

    C.   Aristophanes

    D.   Aeschylus

44. Which of the following is **NOT** a Greek tragedy?

    A.   *The Clouds*

    B.   *Oedipus the King*

    C.   *Antigone*

    D.   *Prometheus Bound*

45. Which cf the following poet's works focuses on the impossible relationships between man and the unknown in a time of disbelief, solitude, and anxiety?

    A.   Pablo Neruda

    B.   Ranier Maria Rilke

    C.   Kenneth Slessor

    D.   Derek Walcott

46. Which of the following statements is **NOT** true of early African literature?

    A.   The oral tradition comprised expressive forms such as folktale, legend, myth, and poetry, distinguishing it from ordinary speech.

    B.   The epic had a moral tone of good versus evil and an ideological function to construct a common identity under a founding hero.

C.   *The Son-Jara*, a political epic, focused on the rivalry of two brothers for succession to their father's throne.

D.   The early legends, myths, and folktales are readily available in print.

47.   Early Chinese writing includes all of the following types of songs **EXCEPT**

A.   temple songs.

B.   war songs.

C.   hunting songs.

D.   marriage songs.

48.   Which of the following elements do **NOT** appear in the literature of the Tang dynasty?

A.   A stronger presence of Buddhism and Taoism

B.   A stronger emphasis on spiritual enlightenment

C.   A stronger emphasis on self-denial and wisdom

D.   A stronger emphasis on the natural world and the psyche

49.   Literature from India from 3000 BC to AD 100 primarily includes all of the following EXCEPT

A.   epic poetry about civil war and exile.

B.   myths about preserving cosmic integrity.

C.   tales about enlightenment and well-being.

D.   mystical and philosophical meditations.

50.   *Renga*, *renku*, and *renshi* are examples of

A.   Japanese epic poetry.

B.   Japanese linked poetry.

C.   Japanese plotless drama.

D.   Japanese lyric poetry.

51. Which of the following work-writer pairs is incorrect?

    A. *Faust* by Johann Wolfgang von Goethe

    B. *Confessions* by Jean-Jacques Rousseau

    C. *Tartuffe* by Jean-Baptiste Poquelin Molière

    D. *Phaedra* by Sor Juana Inés de la Cruz

52. Which of the following themes did **NOT** pervade Mesoamerican literature during the 1500s to 1600s?

    A. Supernatural power

    B. Social responsibility

    C. Nature and humanity

    D. Power and wealth

53. Which of the following statements does **NOT** describe early Chinese literature?

    A. Works generally reflected Confucian ideals, which emphasized government and morality.

    B. Works reflected the correctness of social relationships, justice, and sincerity.

    C. Works reflected the three jewels of the Tao: compassion, moderation, and honesty.

    D. Works addressed the concepts of nature, health, longevity, and effortless action.

54. Which of the following Chinese texts is one of the best representations of Chinese vernacular literature?

    A. *Monkey* by Li Yü

    B. *Golden Lotus* by Chin P'ing Mei

    C. *The Story of the Stone* by Cao Xueqin

    D. *The Peach Blossom Fan* by K'ung Shang-jen

55. What is *ghazal*?

    A. *Ghazal* is a lyrical contemplation of love as a metaphor for the relations that exist among people, God, and the world.

    B. *Ghazal* is the poet's penname or signature in Indian poetry.

    C. *Ghazal* is a stringent and complex poetry form that includes three to seven couplets.

    D. *Ghazal* is the quintessential lyric genre in Urdu, a language that evolved out of interaction of dialects of Hindi with Persian.

56. Which of the following Hindu texts influenced the writing of Henry David Thoreau?

    A. *Anandamath*

    B. *Meghanadvadh*

    C. *Bhagavad Gita*

    D. *Ramayana*

57. In which category of modern fantasy does *Twenty Thousand Leagues under the Sea* by Jules Verne best fit?

    A. Time warps

    B. Spirits and ghosts

    C. Science fiction

    D. Bizarre worlds

58. Which of the following writers is among the countercultural authors of the modernist period?

    A. Virginia Woolf

    B. Eugene Ionesco

    C. Franz Kafka

    D. Federico Garcia Lorca

59. Which of the following statements about the writer and his or her work is incorrect?

    A. D. H. Lawrence, a great force in the modernist movement, is noted for his sexually explicit work and imagist poetry.

    B. James Joyce modernized and revolutionized literature by using a strikingly sensual stream-of-consciousness style.

    C. George Orwell drew inspiration for much of his social criticism from his experience as a Burmese policeman.

    D. E. M. Forster questioned the individual's compliance with social conventions, the unquestioned life, and society's liberal realism.

60. Which of the following statements does **NOT** characterize the difference between early and late Victorian literature?

    A. Late Victorian literature emphasized a failure of relationships, the breakdown of marriages, divorce, and sexuality.

    B. Late Victorian literature emphasized social class, education, poverty, and individuality.

    C. Late Victorian literature emphasized a researchlike investigation of humankind, the environment, and genetics.

    D. Late Victorian literature emphasized the widespread feeling that society could not hold together.

61. Which of the following modern authors did **NOT** win the Nobel Prize for Literature?

    A. Octavio Paz Lozano

    B. Aleksandr Solzhenitsyn

    C. Derek Walcott

    D. Vladimir Nabokov

62. What is a *morbidezza* style of writing?

    A. Writing that incorporates stream of consciousness and dreams into the plot

    B. Writing that paints a picture with the finest and most tender detail

    C. Writing that combines melancholic and optimistic tones

    D. Writing that integrates nightmares and insects

63. Which of the following elements **BEST** characterize the literature of the Japanese Edo period?

    A.   Playwrights, poets, and novelists captured bourgeois life: blunt, expansive, iconoclastic, and playful.

    B.   Playwrights, poets, and novelists captured bourgeois life: rich, witty, traditional, and classic.

    C.   Playwrights, poets, and novelists captured bourgeois life: rich, witty, cosmopolitan, and classic.

    D.   Playwrights, poets, and novelists captured bourgeois life: rich, witty, iconoclastic, and classic.

64. Which of the following statements **BEST** characterizes elements of setting?

    A.   Place, time, weather, social context, and tone

    B.   Place, time, weather, social conditions, and mood

    C.   Place, time, social context, mood, and tone

    D.   Place, time, social conditions, weather, and tone

65. Which of the following is **NOT** an example of an allegory?

    A.   "Young Goodman Brown"

    B.   *The Pilgrim's Progress*

    C.   *Animal Farm*

    D.   "The Raven"

66. Which of the following is **NOT** a type of nonfiction?

    A.   Legend

    B.   Biography

    C.   Autobiography

    D.   Memoir

67. Which of the following is the **BEST** example of a tragicomedy?

    A. *The Tempest*

    B. *King Lear*

    C. *Oedipus Rex*

    D. *As You Like It*

68. Which of the following is **NOT** an example of lyric poetry?

    A. *The Faerie Queene*

    B. "The Red Wheelbarrow"

    C. *Songs of Experience*

    D. *Leaves of Grass*

69. Which of the following does **NOT** provide a correct example of the given rhyme type?

    A. Feminine rhyme: *dying*, *sighing*

    B. Masculine rhyme: *joke*, *bloke*

    C. Internal rhyme: *grains*, *veins*

    D. Perfect rhyme: *bungee*, *agree*

70. The phrases *sea wood* (meaning "ship") and *mail armor* (meaning "helmet") are examples of

    A. caesura.

    B. kenning.

    C. stock epithet.

    D. elegy.

71. Which of the following is the **BEST** example of dramatic irony?

    A. Oedipus searches for the murderer of the King of Thebes only to find that *he* is the murderer.

    B. In the "Gift of the Magi," Della cuts her hair to buy Jim a special present and Jim sells his watch to buy her hair combs.

    C. While devouring all the potato chips, Sarah counsels her sister: "Junk food is absolutely not good for you!"

D.   In the *Rime of the Ancient Mariner* by Samuel Taylor
      Coleridge, the Mariner observes: "Water, water, every where, /
      And all the boards did shrink; / Water, water, every where, /
      Nor any drop to drink."

72.   Which of the following statements **BEST** characterizes realistic criticism?

A.   Realistic criticism is most often associated with Immanuel
      Kant, an influential philosopher of the eighteenth century
      who valued imagination as a higher and more comprehensive
      faculty than reason.

B.   Realistic criticism is most often associated with the later
      nineteenth century, primarily focusing on developing
      characterization using a more scientific approach.

C.   Realistic criticism is most often associated with Aristotle,
      who discussed how six tragic elements should work
      together to create an intricate and complex balance
      between form and function.

D.   Realistic criticism is most often associated with the literary
      movement in nineteenth-century France, specifically with the
      French novelists Gustave Flaubert and Honoré de Balzac.

73.   Which of the following types of literary criticism is **NOT** a form of mimetic
      criticism?

A.   Marxism

B.   Feminism

C.   Essentialism

D.   Psychological

74.   Which of the following texts would be **BEST** interpreted through the lens of
      historicism?

A.   *The House on Mango Street*

B.   *Crime and Punishment*

C.   *Things Fall Apart*

D.   *Great Expectations*

75. What is the study of signs and symbols called?

    A. Semiotics

    B. Structuralism

    C. Symbiosis

    D. Synergistics

76. What is the **BEST** definition of *dialect*?

    A. Regional vernacular

    B. Conversational speech

    C. A variety of language

    D. Intermingled language

77. Which of the following events in English language development was **NOT** a result of the Norman Conquest?

    A. Middle English developed as a language.

    B. Latin and French became languages of power.

    C. English became the language of the poor majority.

    D. William Caxton brought the printing press to Europe.

78. Which of the following is an example of a derivational morpheme?

    A. *ment*

    B. *un*

    C. *s*

    D. *dog*

79. Which of the following processes of reading asserts that readers use knowledge of graphophonics, syntax, and semantics to make predictions, decipher context clues, and derive meaning?

    A. Reading as word recognition

    B. Reading as a sociopsycholinguistic process

    C. Reading as a psycholinguistic process

    D. Reading as a metacognitive process

80. Which of the following assessments would be the most useful in determining how readers use phonemic, semantic, and syntactic clues to decode a reading selection?

    A. Informal reading inventory

    B. Content area reading inventory

    C. Miscue analysis

    D. Running record

81. Which of the following sentences contains a gerund and a participle?

    A. Listening to classical music and shopping for shoes are among my passions.

    B. Arrested for speeding, John was not permitted to drive Daneesha to the prom.

    C. It is not only insulting that you do not appreciate my offering you this opportunity but also infuriating that you have little motivation.

    D. My dog's favorite pastimes are fetching balls and catching Frisbees.

82. Which of the following processes of reading would be concerned with stress, pitch, morphemes, juncture, syntax, and semantics?

    A. Reading as word recognition

    B. Reading as a visual process

    C. Reading as a psycholinguistic process

    D. Reading as a metacognitive process

83. Which of the following types of children's literature would be useful in teaching sequence, story line, characterization, and vocabulary to early readers?

    A. Picture books

    B. Wordless books

    C. Concept books

    D. Chapter books

84. When readers develop chunks of knowledge gathered through multiple modalities, they

   A. decode text.

   B. improve fluency.

   C. enhance automaticity.

   D. develop schemata.

85. Which of the following types of children's literature would be useful in teaching satire and imagery and developing vocabulary for bilingual nonreaders?

   A. Picture books

   B. Wordless books

   C. Concept books

   D. Chapter books

86. Which of the following texts is **NOT** an example of modern fantasy?

   A. *James and the Giant Peach*

   B. *The Legend of Sleepy Hollow*

   C. *The Devil's Arithmetic*

   D. *The Giver*

87. Which of the following is **NOT** an essential element of contemporary realistic fiction?

   A. Conflicts that children and young adults encounter with peers and authority

   B. Themes that address moral cognitive dilemmas and human needs

   C. Style that includes dialogue, vivid description, and gripping imagery

   D. Characters that often say and do things that are not typical but reflect maturity

88. Which of the following sets of work, author, and culture is incorrect?

    A. *Scorpions* by Walter Dean Myers: African American

    B. *Walk Two Moons* by Sharon Creech: Native American

    C. *In the Time of the Butterflies* by Sandra Cisneros: Latino

    D. *Homeless Bird* by Gloria Whelan: Asian American

89. Which of the following awards is given to the author of the most distinguished example of children's literature?

    A. The Newbery Medal

    B. The Coretta Scott King Book Award

    C. The Caldecott Medal

    D. The Artistry Medal

90. Which of the following correctly lists the five canons of the rhetorical process?

    A. Inventio, dispositio, elocutia, memoria, and actio

    B. Exordium, narratio, confirmation, refutation, and peroration

    C. Inventio, dispositio, elocutia, memoria, and narratio

    D. Inventio, dispositio, elocutia, memoria, and narratio

91. According to Homer, which of the following is **NOT** a function of language?

    A. Invent or discover

    B. Charm or anger

    C. Persuade or convince

    D. Abuse or visualize

92. Which of the following would be included as examples of referential discourse?

    A. Scientific articles, diagnoses, textbooks, infomercials, weather reports, literary criticism

    B. Diaries, journals, prayers, complaints, creeds, declarations, myths

    C. Oratory, debate, political speeches, homilies, propaganda

    D. Poetry, novels, drama, songs, film, puns, satire, jokes

93. Which of the following is the **BEST** definition of *context* as it pertains to modern rhetoric?

    A.   Context addresses purpose, audience, voice, and medium in order to create the framework for a rhetorical stance.

    B.   Context addresses audience, voice, subject, and medium in order to create the framework for a rhetorical stance.

    C.   Context addresses purpose, audience, subject, and medium in order to create the framework for a rhetorical stance.

    D.   Context addresses purpose, audience, argument, and medium in order to create a framework for a rhetorical stance

94. A rhetor will manipulate emotions in various ways to elicit a specific mood or reaction in order to develop

    A.   unity of thought.

    B.   unity of feeling.

    C.   unity of emphasis.

    D.   unity of purpose.

95. Which of the following rhetorical devices would be used to appeal to ethos?

    A.   Aphorism

    B.   Apostrophe

    C.   Auxesis

    D.   Chleuasmos

96. A writer would use rhetorical devices of accumulation, amplification, hyperbole, effectio, and hypophora to appeal to

    A.   bathos.

    B.   ethos.

    C.   logos.

    D.   pathos.

97. Which of the following is **NOT** a characteristic of prosody?

    A.   Prosody includes pitch, stress, rhythm, and intonation.

    B.   Prosody is a suprasegmental feature of speech.

    C.   Prosody allows a sound to be extended over several sounds.

    D.   Prosody complicates a speaker's ability to switch codes.

98. Which of the following statements is true about spoken and written discourse?

    A.   Unlike writers, speakers can easily appeal to pathos.

    B.   Unlike writers, speakers make different lexical choices based on context.

    C.   Unlike speaking, writing requires an unambiguous use of pronouns.

    D.   Unlike writing, speaking must follow a rigid organization.

99. The revision process of writing asks all of the following questions **EXCEPT**

    A.   What new insight, information or interpretation does the writing offer and what is engaging, interesting, or compelling about the writing?

    B.   What specific rhetorical and literary devices does the writer incorporate to accomplish purpose, develop subject, and address audience?

    C.   What new ideas, details, examples, illustrations, and evidence could or should be added?

    D.   What are accurate conventions of spelling, grammar, and punctuation?

100. Which of the following sentences is incorrect?

    A.   Agnes pealed the vegetables while her mother prepared the tossed salad.

    B.   Jennifer decided that she would not be able to attend the concert because she has too much homework.

    C.   Neither Jess nor the boys care about visiting the park today.

    D.   Civics is a course that explores the purpose and function of the executive, judicial, and legislative branches of government.

OPEN-RESPONSE QUESTIONS

1. **Read the poem below and then answer the questions that follow.**

Ithaca

When you set out on your journey to Ithaca,
pray that the road is long,
full of adventure, full of knowledge.

The Lestrygonians and the Cyclops,
the angry Poseidon—do not fear them:
You will never find such as these on your path,
if your thoughts remain lofty, if a fine
emotion touches your spirit and your body.

The Lestrygonians and the Cyclops,
the fierce Poseidon you will never encounter,
if you do not carry them within your soul,
if your soul does not set them up before you.

Pray that the road is long.
That the summer mornings are many, when,
with such pleasure, with such joy
you will enter ports seen for the first time;
stop at Phoenician markets,
and purchase fine merchandise,
mother-of-pearl and coral, amber and ebony,
and sensual perfumes of all kinds,
as many sensual perfumes as you can;
visit many Egyptian cities,
to learn and learn from scholars.

Always keep Ithaca in your mind.
To arrive there is your ultimate goal.
But do not hurry the voyage at all.
It is better to let it last for many years;
and to anchor at the island when you are old,
rich with all you have gained on the way,
not expecting that Ithaca will offer you riches.

Ithaca has given you the beautiful voyage.
Without her you would have never set out on the road.
She has nothing more to give you.
And if you find her poor, Ithaca has not deceived you.
Wise as you have become, with so much experience,
you must already have understood what Ithacas mean.

—Constantine P. Cavafy (1911)

How does Cavafy use analogy and allusion in the work? Was the use of the devices effective? Explain why or why not.

2. You have noted that some of your students are not able to adequately read your subject text. You know that a content area textbook is often quite different from a typical reading textbook. You realize that even though you are a content area instructor, this does not excuse you from helping the students read a course text.

- Identify your grade and subject area.

- Describe some of the ways that the textbook for your course subject differs from a typical reading textbook.

- Describe some ways that you can help a student improve his/her reading of your subject matter book.

PRACTICE TEST 2 ANSWER SHEET
FOR OPEN-RESPONSE QUESTIONS

PRACTICE TEST 2 ANSWER SHEET
FOR OPEN-RESPONSE QUESTIONS

PRACTICE TEST 2 ANSWER SHEET
FOR OPEN-RESPONSE QUESTIONS

PRACTICE TEST 2 ANSWER SHEET
FOR OPEN-RESPONSE QUESTIONS

PRACTICE TEST 2 ANSWER SHEET
FOR OPEN-RESPONSE QUESTIONS

ANSWER KEY—PRACTICE TEST 2

Question	Answer	Objective
1	C	I. Literature and Language
2	A	I. Literature and Language
3	A	I. Literature and Language
4	D	I. Literature and Language
5	C	I. Literature and Language
6	D	I. Literature and Language
7	C	I. Literature and Language
8	A	I. Literature and Language
9	C	I. Literature and Language
10	C	I. Literature and Language
11	A	I. Literature and Language
12	D	I. Literature and Language
13	C	I. Literature and Language
14	C	I. Literature and Language
15	B	I. Literature and Language
16	B	I. Literature and Language
17	D	I. Literature and Language
18	C	I. Literature and Language
19	D	I. Literature and Language
20	C	I. Literature and Language
21	D	I. Literature and Language
22	D	I. Literature and Language
23	C	I. Literature and Language
24	C	I. Literature and Language

Question	Answer	Objective
25	D	I. Literature and Language
26	D	I. Literature and Language
27	A	I. Literature and Language
28	B	I. Literature and Language
29	A	I. Literature and Language
30	C	I. Literature and Language
31	D	I. Literature and Language
32	C	I. Literature and Language
33	D	I. Literature and Language
34	A	I. Literature and Language
35	A	I. Literature and Language
36	B	I. Literature and Language
37	A	I. Literature and Language
38	C	I. Literature and Language
39	C	I. Literature and Language
40	D	I. Literature and Language
41	A	I. Literature and Language
42	B	I. Literature and Language
43	A	I. Literature and Language
44	A	I. Literature and Language
45	B	I. Literature and Language
46	D	I. Literature and Language
47	B	I. Literature and Language
48	C	I. Literature and Language
49	B	I. Literature and Language
50	B	I. Literature and Language
51	D	I. Literature and Language

Question	Answer	Objective
52	D	I. Literature and Language
53	C	I. Literature and Language
54	A	I. Literature and Language
55	D	I. Literature and Language
56	C	I. Literature and Language
57	C	I. Literature and Language
58	A	I. Literature and Language
59	D	I. Literature and Language
60	B	I. Literature and Language
61	D	I. Literature and Language
62	B	II. Rhetoric and Composition
63	A	I. Literature and Language
64	B	II. Rhetoric and Composition
65	D	I. Literature and Language
66	A	I. Literature and Language
67	A	I. Literature and Language
68	B	I. Literature and Language
69	D	I. Literature and Language
70	B	I. Literature and Language
71	A	I. Literature and Language
72	D	I. Literature and Language
73	C	I. Literature and Language
74	D	I. Literature and Language
75	A	III. Reading Theory, Research, and Instruction
76	C	III. Reading Theory, Research, and Instruction
77	D	I. Literature and Language

Question	Answer	Objective
78	A	III. Reading Theory, Research, and Instruction
79	B	III. Reading Theory, Research, and Instruction
80	D	III. Reading Theory, Research, and Instruction
81	B	III. Reading Theory, Research, and Instruction
82	C	III. Reading Theory, Research, and Instruction
83	A	III. Reading Theory, Research, and Instruction
84	D	III. Reading Theory, Research, and Instruction
85	B	I. Literature and Language
86	B	I. Literature and Language
87	D	I. Literature and Language
88	C	I. Literature and Language
89	A	III. Reading Theory, Research, and Instruction
90	A	I. Literature and Language
91	D	II. Rhetoric and Composition
92	A	II. Rhetoric and Composition
93	A	II. Rhetoric and Composition
94	B	II. Rhetoric and Composition
95	A	II. Rhetoric and Composition
96	D	II. Rhetoric and Composition
97	D	II. Rhetoric and Composition
98	A	II. Rhetoric and Composition
99	D	II. Rhetoric and Composition
100	A	II. Rhetoric and Composition

PRACTICE TEST 2 PROGRESS CHART

I. Literature and Language   ——/78

1	2	3	4	5	6	7	8	9	10	11	12	13	14	15

16	17	18	19	20	21	22	23	24	25	26	27	28	29	30

31	32	33	34	35	36	37	38	39	40	41	42	43	44	45

46	47	48	49	50	51	52	53	54	55	56	57	58	59	60

61	63	65	66	67	68	69	70	71	72	73	74	77	85	86

87	88	90

II. Rhetoric and Composition   ——/12

62	64	91	92	93	94	95	96	97	98	99	100

III. Reading Theory, Research, and Instruction   ——/10

75	76	78	79	80	81	82	83	84	89

DETAILED EXPLANATIONS FOR PRACTICE TEST 2

1. **C.**

    Although Puritan literature reflected the theme of determinism, the literature preached the necessity of being righteous and conservative to a point of rigidity, therefore it was not apocalyptic or meditative.

2. **A.**

    Jonathan Edwards, a Calvinist minister, was best known for his "fire and brimstone" sermon "Sinners in the Hands of an Angry God," which preached the horrific consequences of liberalism and sin.

3. **A.**

    The American Renaissance marked a break from traditional thinking and reason, a change that was reflected in the romanticism and transcendentalism of the period.

4. **D.**

    Ezra Pound was a fascist and did not write until the modern period. All the other answer choices allied with the abolitionist movement: Harriet Beecher Stowe's *Uncle Tom's Cabin* (A) and David Walker's *Appeal to the Colored Citizens of the World* (B) sought to arouse antislavery sentiment and critique slavery as inhumane; Henry David Thoreau (C) and Ralph Waldo Emerson's transcendentalist philosophies merged with antislavery ideologies.

5. **C.**

    Rags-to-riches tales were a mainstay of Gilded Age literature. Men such as John D. Rockefeller and William Carnegie made fortunes in manufacturing and railroads, and writers such as Willa Cather narrated success stories of immigrants. The Gilded Age also marked the emergence of writers like Mark Twain from the South and others from the far west and Midwest who highlighted the countries regional differences (C) and thus moved the "literary" center out of New England (A). The voice of the common people was heard from across the country (B), initially in folk stories like "Johnny Appleseed," the "Hatfields and McCoys," "Paul Bunyan," and "Pecos Bill," then in the works of humorists like Twain.

6. **D.**

   The Awakening by Kate Chopin is considered an example of sectional literature, which appeared during the Gilded Age. "To Build a Fire" (A) by Jack London, *The Red Badge of Courage* (B) by Stephen Crane, and *The Yellow Wallpaper* (C) by Charlotte Perkins Gilman were written during the naturalist period.

7. **C.**

   Ernest Hemingway was noted for his sparse, precise, concise, and stoic prose.

8. **A.**

   The Jungle by Upton Sinclair describes the despicable corruption and conditions of meatpacking industry in the early twentieth century.

9. **C.**

   Ezra Pound used ordinary language, free verse, and concentrated word pictures, a technique used by Japanese and Chinese poets to create extraordinary imagery. This movement, called imagism, emphasized clarity, precision, and concise word choice.

10. **C.**

    "The Love Song of J. Alfred Prufrock" by T. S. Eliot addresses humankind's struggle to find its place in the universe and its ability or lack of ability to love and communicate.

11. **A.**

    Carl Sandburg is noted for his collection of poetry about Chicago.

12. **D.**

    Although Langston Hughes (A), Claude McKay (B), Jean Toomer (C), and Zora Neal Hurston (D) wrote during the Harlem Renaissance, Hurston was not a poet.

13. **C.**

    Sylvia Plath, Robert Lowell, and Anne Sexton are among the confessional poets who wrote about depression, suicide, and anguish.

14. **C.**

Gwendolyn Brooks was the first African American woman poet to win the Pulitzer Prize, for her poem *We Real Cool* (1959).

15. **B.**

The central characters in Maya Angelou's texts are strong black woman. In her autobiographical *I Know Why the Caged Bird Sings*, Angelou tells of her grandmother's religious influences and her mother's blues tradition, and describes the other exemplary women in her life, including one who teaches her to speak again after a rape has struck her dumb.

16. **B.**

Amy Tan's most famous book, *The Joy Luck Club*, depicts the lives of four Chinese American immigrant families who start the Joy Luck Club, playing the Chinese game of mahjong for money.

17. **D.**

Marjorie Morningstar is the title of a novel by Herman Wouk. Sharon Creech (A), Louise Erdrich (B), and N. Scott Momaday (C) are contemporary Native American writers.

18. **C.**

Eric the Red is a character in Norse mythology, not a piece of literature.

19. **D.**

Kenning is a literary device in which a complex phrase replaces a simpler word to add color to a poem or to evoke imagery, for example, *sea wood* in place of *ship*. The technique appears in Anglo-Saxon literature but not in medieval literature.

20. **C.**

All the answer choices except *The Tragical History of Dr. Faustus* are examples of medieval literature. Christopher Marlowe wrote *Faustus* during the Renaissance.

21. **D.**

Joseph Addison wrote during the eighteenth century.

22. **D.**

The poetry of the Jacobean Age was very involved, sophisticated, and difficult, but it was not political.

23. **C.**

Sir Francis Bacon is the only essayist among the Jacobean writers. Ben Jonson and Thomas Middleton wrote plays and poetry, and Donne, metaphysical poetry.

24. **C.**

The poem "Elegy Written in a Country Churchyard" is considered to be the definitive masterpiece of the graveyard school of poetry.

25. **D.**

Although Sir Philip Sydney wrote poetry about nature and women, he was an Elizabethan poet.

26. **D.**

The Restoration is called the Restoration because it marked the restoration of Charles II as king of Ireland, England, and Scotland. King James II succeeded Charles II.

27. **A.**

John Dryden, considered one of the chief founders of modern English prose, the first great English critic, and the most representative writer of the Restoration, dominated during this literary period.

28. **B.**

Dr. Samuel Johnson wrote *The Dictionary of the English Language*.

29. **A.**

Rape of the Lock is a mock heroic epic poem. This five-canto work, echoing *The Iliad*, humorously details a story of a young woman who flirts, drinks coffee, wears makeup, plays cards, and suddenly has a lock of hair stolen by an ardent suitor.

30. **C.**

Robert Burns, a Scottish poet noted for his almost musical poetry, sense of humor, and ability to give dignity to the common man through his use of only Scottish dialect, was considered one of the great songwriters of his time. Hailed the national poet of Scotland, Burns authored hundreds of works, including songs "Auld Lang Syne" and "Comin' thro the Rye" and poems such as "To a Mouse," "To a Louse," and "Highland Mary."

31. **D.**

William Blake anticipated Samuel Taylor Coleridge's simple diction and style, romanticism, and communion with nature.

32. **C.**

The novelist Sir Walter Scott brought popularity to the genre of historical fiction; he is particularly noted for *Ivanhoe*, which recounts the last important Jacobite movement of 1745 to place a Stuart on the throne.

33. **D.**

Charlotte Brontë wrote *Shirley*.

34. **A.**

The early Victorian period is regarded as the most significant in the entire history of the English novel. During the nineteenth century, the novel was the most dominant form of literature, occupying the middle ground as it helped people of the time make sense of their lives and guided people on how they could construct themselves in a changing world. Readers looked to the novel as a genre that could provide understanding and the vocabulary for articulating what it meant to be an individual in nineteenth-century Britain. The novel also portrayed a new sense of social order (increasingly middle-class white population simultaneously and paradoxically developing a sense of psychological complexity) by presenting characters who faced the difficult dilemmas that were inherent in such a society or who withdrew into themselves, unable to deal with the distress of the times.

35. **A.**

Charles Dickens wrote novels that reflected stories of social reconciliation and reconstitution. Replete with working-class characters, his novels depicted the lower class against a carnival-like backdrop and a middle class of morally advanced heroes and heroines. Success was represented by bourgeois virtues of industriousness, honesty, and charity. He used the novel to develop and strengthen individual identity by presenting role models of the idea of self and to provide reassurance for readers that they held the answers and solutions for social-class issues that emerged from a complicated and mechanized world.

36. **B.**

Characterized by his refusal to become enthusiastic about or accept the new values of the Victorian era, William Makepeace Thackeray rejected the new Victorian narratives, instead castigating the middle-class hero as selfish and offering little sympathy for heroine Becky Sharp in *Vanity Fair*. Adhering to this rhythm of disrupting the new rhythm of Victorian life, *The History of Pendennis* critiques the hero's loss of a role and direction in his life. In *The History of Henry Esmond*, Thackeray not only critiques materialism but also portrays the shortcomings of the Victorian emphasis on the self.

37. **A.**

Elizabeth Barrett Browning's *Sonnets from the Portuguese*, written during her courtship with Robert Browning, constitute the most accurate representation of sonnets since the time of Shakespeare. Sonnet 43 from *Sonnets* begins with one of the most often quoted lines, "How do I love thee? Let me count the ways."

38. **C.**

George Bernard Shaw wrote the play *Widowers' Houses*.

39. **C.**

Gerard Manley Hopkins is the only poet in this list. Lewis Carroll (A) and Anthony Trollope (D) were novelists; Charles Darwin (B) was a naturalist famous for his writings on natural selection.

40. **D.**

Anthony Trollope wrote *Phineas Finn*.

41. **A.**

Oscar Wilde, both playwright and novelist, expressed a radical, disconcerting vision of society, where characters use style and lack substance, drawing attention to themselves with no meaningful purpose.

42. **B.**

V. S. Naipaul is an Indian-Trinidadian British writer who has received both the Booker Prize and the Nobel Prize for Literature, but his novels, which include *In a Free State* and *A House for Mr. Biswas*, are not science fiction. He has been criticized for his unsympathetic portrayals of the underdeveloped nations he writes about.

43. **A.**

Sappho was the first lyric poet. These poems, designed to evoke the joys and sorrows of lovers, were performed with the accompaniment of a lyre (hence, *lyric*) and employed Sapphic meter.

44. **A.**

Aristophanes wrote *The Clouds*, a comedy that satirizes the Sophists and the intellectualism of the fifth-century BC Greeks.

45. **B.**

Rainer Maria Rilke is considered one of Germany's greatest twentieth-century poets. His imagery focuses on the impossible relationships between man and the unknown in a time of disbelief, solitude, and anxiety. Writing in verse and lyrical prose, Rilke positioned himself in the transition between the traditional and modern poets. He wrote more than 400 poems in French, which he dedicated to Switzerland, his homeland of choice.

46. **D.**

As with all early cultures, early stories are more difficult to find in print.

47. **B.**

Early Chinese writing often took the form of song, including hymns, temple songs, hunting songs, and love and marriage songs, but not war songs.

48. **C.**

The Tang dynasty, a time of cultural vibrancy and expansion, saw the flourishing of poetry that focused more on understanding nature and nature of the individual or recluse. A stronger presence of Buddhism and Taoism (A) changed the nature of poetry and thought; departing with Confucian emphasis on denying importance of the self, many new literary works focused on understanding the psyche, spiritual enlightenment, and natural world (B, D). Taoist imagery reflected contemplation and mystical union with nature, wisdom, learning, and purposive action abandoned in favor of simplicity and *wu-wei* (non-action, or letting things take their natural course).

49. **B.**

> Most Hindu literature included meditations (D), tales (C), and epic poems (A) grounded in historical fact.

50. **B.**

> *Renga, renku,* and *renshi* are examples of Japanese linked poetry.

51. **D.**

> Jean Racine wrote *Phaedra.*

52. **D.**

> Mesoamerican (native) literary themes addressed supernatural power (A), the problem of humanity versus Nature (C), social obligation (B), and the development of the individual. Despite rich symbolism and imagery, literature was regarded as functional rather than aesthetic.

53. **C.**

> Early Chinese literature did reflect the three jewels of the Tao, but these are compassion, moderation, and *humility*, not honesty.

54. **A.**

> Li Yü was a comic dramatist, storywriter, and champion of vernacular literature. Whether or not the focus of his plays celebrated Monkey's free spirit and turbulent ingenuity or serious allegory of *Monkey* and Tripitaka's journey toward Buddhist enlightenment is debated.

55. **D.**

> *Ghazal*, the quintessential lyric genre in Urdu, a language that evolved out of interaction of dialects of Hindi with Persian, reached perfection between the sixteenth and eighteenth centuries. Imported from Persian poetry, this lyric genre emerged as mature and productive form of Urdu.

56. **C.**

> In 1840, Henry David Thoreau read and was influenced by the *Bhagavad Gita.*

57. **C.**

  Twenty Thousand Leagues under the Sea by Jules Verne is science fiction, because it incorporates futuristic technology and scientific advancements.

58. **A.**

  Virginia Woolf was among those writers who took a narrow view of modernism, favoring instead clear, precise images and common speech; these writers, including Woolf, James Joyce, Ezra Pound, T. S. Eliot, and William Faulkner, thought of work primarily as an art object produced by consummate craft. They used language in an exploratory way, disassembling to reconstruct, playing with shifting and contradictory appearances to suggest the changing and uncertain nature of reality.

59. **D.**

  E. M. Forster questioned individuals' compliance with social conventions and the consequences of leading an unquestioned life as such, but he did not question liberal realism within society. He was himself a liberal realist. His major works include *Howard's End*, *A Room with a View*, and *A Passage to India*.

60. **B.**

  This period also saw new forms of social analysis, resurgent socialism, new feminist voices, and a fresh expression of liberal values. Sexuality was not as repressed and seen as dangerous as in previous years, and the late nineteenth century reflected the first presence of a homosexual subculture. Literature reflected protagonists not as heroes or heroines but as real people, replete with human foibles, who are entrapped and impacted by social conventions that only exacerbate their conditions. Literature reflected a sense of disintegration, with the center steadily falling apart, crumbling social institutions such as family and marriage, and increasing skepticism toward conventional morality. Characters collided with society, and themes expressed the widespread feeling that society could not hold together. Irrational forces just below the surface became evident, with texts exploring dark places of the mind. More sustaining fictions were replaced with troubling and disconcerting texts. Naturalist Emile Zola, whose style reflected an intense, research-like investigation of humankind, a strong presence of contemporary ideas of the environment and genetics, and the inevitable decline and downward spiral of the human condition due to disease, alcoholism, and madness, proved a significant influence in literature. Interests in evolution and social Darwinism coexisted with fears about regression, atavism, and decline, reflecting a loss of faith in goals traditionally pursed by middle-class hero and heroines, the denunciation of Victorian values with a move from solid moral convictions to mere emptiness, and the prevailing idea that something dangerous and irrational would destabilize society.

61. **D.**

Vladimir Nabokov, the author of *Lolita*.

62. **B.**

A *morbidezza* style of writing paints a picture with the finest and most tender detail. This style is most associated with Bing Xin, a twentieth-century Chinese author whose works provide insight of mother love and innocence. She is best remembered for her *Ji xiao duzhe* (*To Young Readers*).

63. **A.**

During the Japanese Edo period, playwrights, poets, and novelists captured bourgeois life: blunt, expansive, iconoclastic, and playful. Puns and parodies occupied popular literature. Woodblock prints, short stories, novels, poetry, and plays depicted city life, which was fast, varied, crowded, and competitive. People lived by and appreciated wit. Literature that came to the urban masses had to fit their tastes, and the impatience of Japanese townspeople showed in their fiction. The new tradesmen class demanded realism.

64. **B.**

The elements of setting include place, time, social conditions (social context), weather, and mood.

65. **D.**

"The Raven" is a narrative poem by Edgar Allan Poe, and though it is filled with literary devices—alliteration, allusion, and so on—it is not allegorical. An allegory is a form of extended metaphor in which objects, persons, and actions in a narrative are equated with meanings that lie outside the narrative itself. The underlying meaning has moral, social, religious, or political significance, and characters are often personifications of abstract ideas like charity, greed, or envy. An allegory has both literal and symbolic meanings. Nathaniel Hawthorne's "Young Goodman Brown" (A) is an allegory that describes what happens when one abandons one's faith and becomes associated with the devil. John Bunyan's *The Pilgrim's Progress* (B) is an allegory in which a character named Christian encounters various perils on his way to heaven and where vices and virtues are personified. *Animal Farm* (C) is an allegory through which George Orwell demonstrates the psychological foundation of revolution, its processes, and the irony of displacement of an oppressive regime by the new revolutionary order.

66. **A.**

A legend is a fictional narrative. Examples of nonfiction include biography (B), autobiography (C), essay, memoir (D), scientific articles, informational texts, and newspaper accounts.

67. **A.**

Tragicomedy is drama that mixes the elements and styles of tragedy and comedy. In the Jacobean era of Great Britain, these plays had romantic and exciting plots in which disaster persisted throughout the play, eventually reaching a happy conclusion. An example of such a play is William Shakespeare's *The Winter's Tale* or *The Tempest*. *King Lear* (B) and *Oedipus Rex* (C) are true tragedies, and *As You Like It* (D) is a true comedy.

68. **B.**

"The Red Wheelbarrow" by William Carlos Williams is an example of free verse.

69. **D.**

Bungee and *agree* are examples of end rhyme, not perfect rhyme. End rhymes appear at the end of a line; perfect rhyme occurs if correspondence of rhyme sounds is exact, as in *bend* and *send*. Feminine rhymes (A) consist of a stressed syllable followed by an unstressed syllable (*dying*, *sighing*). Masculine rhymes (B) consist of a single stressed syllable (*joke*, *bloke*). Internal rhymes (C) are those whose internal syllables sound the same (*grains*, *veins*).

70. **B.**

Kenning, common to Old English and Old Norse poetry, is a literary device in which a complex phrase replaces a simpler word to add color to a poem or to evoke imagery. For example, *sea wood* is used in place of *ship* or *mail armor* in place of *helmet*.

71. **A.**

   Dramatic irony occurs when an audience perceives something that a character in the literature does not know. The audience is aware that Oedipus murdered the King of Thebes, but Oedipus himself has no clue as he searches for the murderer. Choices B and D are examples of situational irony in that there is a discrepancy between the expected result and the actual result. Choice C is an example of verbal irony, when the speaker says one thing but means or does another.

72. **D.**

   Realistic criticism emerged during the mid-nineteenth century. This approach to writing and critique described life, particularly setting, with objectivity, detail, and rich example. Another word for realism is *verisimilitude*, which reflects the author's attempt to present the setting or subject with such convincing detail that the reader easily visualizes the content. Although realism is not limited to any one century or group of writers, it is most often associated with the literary movement in nineteenth-century France, specifically with the French novelists Gustave Flaubert and Honoré de Balzac.

73. **C.**

   Mimetic critics believe that great literature reveals particular truths in that it mimics reality. Such criticism requires the reader to construct meaning within a larger framework or reality. As a result, Marxism, feminism, and psychological critique fall within the broader category of mimetic criticism because each asserts a specific understanding of reality to inform interpretation.

74. **D.**

   The House on Mango Street (A), a coming-of-age novel about being a Latina, is best viewed through a lens of feminism. *Crime and Punishment* (B) depicts the profoundly emotional struggle from murder to love, suggesting psychological critique. *Things Fall Apart* (C) clearly delineates how meaning is cultural, political, social, and gender-related, rendering poststructuralism as the most appropriate interpretive lens. Charles Dickens wrote novels that reflected stories of social reconciliation and reconstitution. Replete with working-class characters, his novels depicted the lower class against a carnival-like backdrop and a middle class of morally advanced heroes and heroines. Success was represented by the bourgeois virtues of industriousness, honesty, and charity. He used the novel to develop and strengthen individual identity by presenting role models of the idea of self and to provide reassurance for readers that they held the answers and solutions for social class issues that emerged from a complicated and mechanized world. His work elaborated the complexity of the age and prompted new narratives of the self, as he portrayed crucial middle-class nature of nineteenth-century Britain.

75. **A.**

Structuralism forms the basis of semiotics, which is the study of signs or symbols.

76. **C.**

Dialect is a social or regional variety of language.

77. **D.**

The Norman Conquest occurred in 1066. At the end of the fifteenth century, William Caxton brought standardization to English with the introduction of the printing press. This began the period we call early Modern English (1500-1650).

78. **A.**

Derivational morphemes add to a word to create another word. For example, adding *ment* to *state* creates *statement*. These morphemes carry semantic information.

79. **B.**

Reading as a sociopsycholinguistic process asserts that readers use background knowledge and cues from the following three language systems to construct meaning:

graphophonics: the relationship between orthography (letters) and phonology (sounds of the language)

syntax: the rules of grammar

semantics: the study of meaning in language

The reader integrates prior knowledge with information integrated from these systems to make predictions, use context clues, and derive meaning.

80. **D.**

A running record, developed by Marie Clay, identifies how readers use phonemic, semantic, and syntactic clues to decode a reading selection. While the student reads the text aloud, the teacher records a variety of conventions: omissions, substitutions, insertions, self-corrected errors, repetitions, appeals (student asks for help), and tells (teacher tells the word). The teacher also observes the reader for behaviors such as directional movement, expression, fluency and phrasing, pace, use of picture cues, inserting punctuation, finger pointing, pauses, and scanning.

81. **B.**

In the sentence *Arrested for speeding, John was not permitted to drive Daneesha to the prom*, *Arrested* is a past participle that describes John and *speeding* is a gerund that is the object of the preposition *for*. In choice A, *listening* and *shopping* are gerunds because they serve as the subject of the sentence. In choice C, *insulting* and *infuriating* are part of verb phrases *is insulting* and *is* (implied) *infuriating*, and *offering* is a gerund that is the direct object of the verb *appreciate*. In choice D, *fetching* and *catching* are gerunds that act as subject complements.

82. **C.**

Proponents of reading as a psycholinguistic process believe that an interaction between thought and words and both psychological and neurobiological factors allow readers to understand written language. They argue that human cognitive processes allow for understanding text. This view assumes various components of language: phonology, phonemes, morphemes, tone and pitch, stress, juncture, semantics, and syntax.

83. **A.**

Picture books give information or tell stories through their pictures even with limited printed text or no text at all. Pictures books are excellent tools that help students learn sequence, characterization, story line, and vocabulary.

84. **D.**

Schemata are chunks of knowledge that readers develop via multiple modalities. For example, American students are quite conscious of the economic system in the United States; they use money to purchase goods and services. Thus, American students have developed and stored this information in the form of schemata. Immigrant children from a society that barters for goods and services possess a different schemata and might find the U.S. economic system alien. Therefore, it is critical to help second-language learners develop schemata that enable them to understand new text.

85. **B.**

Wordless books present a story using only pictures. Collections of artwork also serve as foci for writing, learning new vocabulary, understanding satire, parody, and imagery. These are useful in that bilingual learners and nonreaders in general can use pictures to develop vocabulary, talk about pictures without worrying about decoding, see the same visual image that everyone sees, create stories without fear of being incorrect, and so on.

86. **B.**

The Legend of Sleepy Hollow by Washington Irving derives from the oral tradition of storytelling and therefore is considered traditional fantasy.

87. **D.**

Critical elements of contemporary realistic fiction include conflicts that children and young adults encounter with peers, adults, authority, and external forces (A); characters that look, act, speak, and think like children and young adults in contemporary society; themes that address human needs (B); and style that incorporates believable dialogue and accurate and vivid description (C).

88. **C.**

In the Time of the Butterflies is written by Julia Alvarez, not Sandra Cisneros.

89. **A.**

The Newbery Medal is an award given to the author of the most distinguished example of children's literature.

90. **A.**

Cicero defined five overlapping divisions or canons of the rhetorical process:

inventio (Greek, *heuristics*) or invention: discovery of valid arguments to support the thesis

dispositio (Greek, *taxis*), arrangement

elocutio (Greek, *lexis*), style: the manner in which a speech or argument is spoken or written; style includes all figures of speech

memoria (Greek, *mneme*), memory: storing up information to support the argument

actio (Greek, *hypocrisis*), delivery: the performance or delivery of the speech

91. **D.**

Three functions of language were identified in the writing of Homer: heuristic, eristic, and protreptic. The heuristic function of discourse is to invent, learn, or discover (A). The eristic function of discourse is to use language as a device of power to charm, offend, anger, engage, captivate, and so on (B). The protreptic function of discourse is to use words to persuade others to act differently or to act as we wish them to act (C).

92. **A.**

Referential discourse can be exploratory, scientific, or informative. The goal of this type of discourse is to depict the subject matter as clearly, authentically, and realistically as possible. Referential discourse includes

- exploratory discourse: interviews, dialogues, seminars, panel discussions, diagnoses, text messages, emails, questionnaires, medical histories
- scientific discourse: literary criticism, descriptive analysis, history, taxonomy
- informative discourse: news broadcasts, infomercials, weather reports, stock market panels and reports, written summaries, articles, essays, textbooks, Web sites

93. **A.**

Everyday language and communication in its variety of uses comprises rhetoric. In thinking about rhetoric, it is useful to think about the context of rhetoric, or more specifically to assume a rhetorical stance. Context, which includes purpose, audience, subject, and medium, provides the framework for a rhetorical stance. Audience includes the listener or reader. Purpose may be expressive, persuasive, referential, or literary. Subject is the focus or topic of the written or spoken word. Medium is method of form of delivery.

94. **B.**

Critical to effective modern rhetoric are three principles: the three unities, coherence, and proportion and emphasis. The three unities that must be incorporated to render rhetoric effective are unity of thought, unity of feeling, and unity of purpose. Unity of thought requires that all ideas, arguments, details, and rhetoric support one main or central idea or thesis in speech and in writing. Unity of feeling requires that the author or writer manipulate emotions in various ways to produce the desired mood or feeling. And unity of purpose requires that all spoken or written discourse enable the purpose, to inform, convince, influence, enlighten, and so on.

95. **A.**

A speaker or writer might use an aphorism, which is a tersely phrased statement of a truth or opinion or a brief statement of a principle, to establish ethos, which relates to the ethical appeal of the speaker or writer. The speaker or author must appear as credible, worthy of respect and attention, expert, knowledgeable, and likeable. Breaking off discourse to speak to something or someone who is absent (apostrophe, B) might portray the speaker as mad, not contributing to a sense of credibility or expertise. Auxesis (C) is the manipulation of words in order of increasing intensity to appeal to emotion or to create a sense of impending doom or excitement. A chleuasmos (D) is a sarcastic reply that mocks an opponent, leaving him or her without an answer.

96. **D.**

All of these devices are used to elicit emotion and emphasize feeling in the audience; therefore, they are used to appeal to pathos.

97. **D.**

Prosody includes pitch, stress, rhythm, and intonation (A). It is a suprasegmental feature of speech that allows a sound to be extended over several sounds (B, C). Though not easily demonstrated in written language, prosody allows a speaker to switch codes given the context, purpose, and audience.

98. **A.**

A writer, unable to use gestures and facial expressions, must make use of myriad rhetorical devices to appeal to pathos. Thus, it is easier for a speaker to elicit emotion than a writer. Writers must develop irony and ambiguity through use of explicit devices and figurative language. Writers use punctuation, italics, boldface type, font, ellipses, and other means to indicate statement, emphasis, questioning, imperative, and exclamation.

99. **D.**

Editing is concerned with accuracy of language conventions of spelling, grammar, and punctuation.

100. **A.**

The sentence should read: *Agnes **peeled** the vegetables while her mother prepared the tossed salad. Peal* means to ring or make a ringing sound. *Peel* means to cut away the skin.

HOW THE OPEN-RESPONSE ITEMS WILL BE SCORED

Two or more qualified educators will read your open-response responses, using scoring scales and standardized procedures that have been approved by the Massachusetts Department of Education. They will use scoring scales that describe varying levels of performance when they judge the overall effectiveness of each of your responses.

They will be looking to see that you demonstrate an understanding of the content of the Field and will score your work on the extent to which you achieve the purpose of the assignment, and your answers are appropriate and accurate in the application of subject matter knowledge, provide high-quality and relevant supporting evidence, and demonstrate a soundness of argument and understanding of the subject area.

Performance Characteristics Used by Scorers

Scorers use the following performance characteristics to guide them in considering your responses to the open-response items.

Characteristics Definitions

Purpose The extent to which your response achieves the purpose of the assignment.

Subject Matter Knowledge Accuracy and appropriateness in your application of subject matter knowledge

Support The quality and relevance of your supporting details

Rationale The soundness of your argument and the degree of your understanding of the subject matter

Open-response questions will earn from a high of 4 to a low of 1. The following describes what you need to do to earn the highest score.

4	**The "4" response reflects a thorough knowledge and understanding of the subject matter.** • You fully achieve the purpose of the assignment. • You show substantial, accurate, and appropriate application of subject matter knowledge. • Your supporting evidence is sound; with high-quality, relevant examples. • Your response reflects an ably reasoned, comprehensive understanding of the topic.
3	**The "3" response reflects an adequate knowledge and understanding of the subject matter.** • You largely achieve the purpose of the assignment. • You have a generally accurate and appropriate application of subject matter knowledge. • Your supporting evidence is adequate; with some acceptable, relevant examples. • Your response reflects an adequately reasoned understanding of the topic.
2	**The "2" response reflects a limited knowledge and understanding of the subject matter.** • You have partially achieved the purpose of the assignment. • You have a limited, possibly inaccurate or inappropriate application of subject matter knowledge. • Your supporting evidence is limited; and have few relevant examples. • Your response reflects a limited, poorly reasoned understanding of the topic.
1	**The "1" response reflects a weak knowledge and understanding of the subject matter.** • You have not achieved the purpose of the assignment. • You show little or no appropriate or accurate application of subject matter knowledge. • Your supporting evidence, if present, is weak; you have few or no relevant examples. • Your response reflects little or no reasoning about or understanding of the topic.

Your response to an open-response item would be designated "unscorable" if it is unrelated to the assigned topic, is illegible and can't be read, not in the appropriate language, is too short insufficient to score, or merely repeats the assignment.

If you have not answered an open-response item, it will be designated "blank."

OPEN-RESPONSE QUESTION #1

Sample Response that would receive a top score of 4 points:

Cavafy uses the analogy of an ordinary person's life to the journey home of the Greek hero Odysseus in Homer's <u>Odyssey</u> in order to encourage readers to give value to the pursuit, rather than to the end. To assure people that they do not necessarily have to face malice and terror, such as Odysseus did with the monstrous Cyclops, the cannibal Lestrygonians, and vengeful Poseidon, the persona claims that this will not happen if they maintain an elevated spirit. Although he draws the analogy to a journey largely free of amusement and gratification, the persona advocates avoiding strife, and rather focusing on absorbing the sensual pleasures the world has to offer us. He portrays experiences in Mediterranean ports that Odysseus might have had if he had not been embroiled in confrontations with malicious, angry, or jealous monsters, gods, and sorceresses. Contradicting the lesson in Homer's epic, the persona states that Ithaca, the goal of the journey, should be valued only as the cause of the journey in the first place.

It is at the end of the poem that the most powerful unspoken allusion appears: Penelope. Whereas the persona paints an appealing portrait of a lifestyle in the first five verse paragraphs, in the last one, when he continues to extol the journey over the destination, the reader cannot help but imagine Odysseus's wife, Penelope, who endured many hardships, and was forced to exercise an inhuman amount of faith and patience, as she waited many years for her husband to return. The persona says of Ithaca (implying Penelope): "She has nothing more to give you./And if you find her poor, Ithaca has not deceived you." It is the persona's gently shocking yet powerful way of devaluing intimacy, and praising beauty, experience, and wisdom as more worthy pursuits in life.

Index

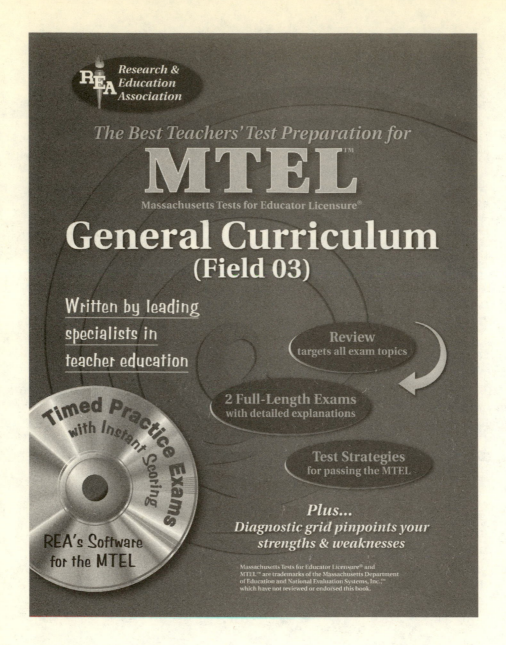

Available at your local bookstore or order directly from us by sending in coupon below.

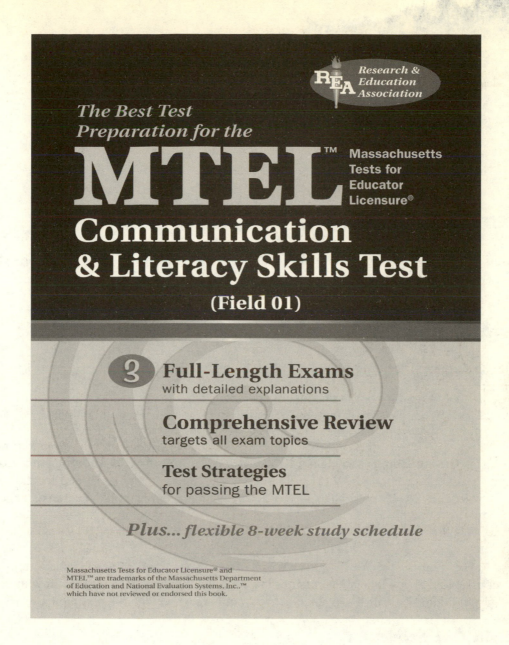

Installing REA's TestWare®

SYSTEM REQUIREMENTS

Pentium 75 MHz (300 MHz recommended) or a higher or compatible processor; Microsoft Windows 98 or later; 64 MB available RAM; Internet Explorer 5.5 or higher.

INSTALLATION

1. Insert the MTEL English (07) CD-ROM into the CD-ROM drive.

2. If the installation doesn't begin automatically, from the Start Menu choose the RUN command. When the RUN dialog box appears, type d:\setup (where d is the letter of your CD-ROM drive) at the prompt and click OK.

3. The installation process will begin. A dialog box proposing the directory "C:\Program Files\REA\MTEL_English\" will appear. If the name and location are suitable, click OK. If you wish to specify a different name or location, type it in and click OK.

4. Start the MTEL English TestWare® application by double-clicking on the icon.

REA's MTEL English TestWare® is **EASY** to **LEARN AND USE**. To achieve maximum benefits, we recommend that you take a few minutes to go through the on-screen tutorial on your computer. The "screen buttons" are also explained here to familiarize you with the program.

TECHNICAL SUPPORT

REA's TestWare® is backed by customer and technical support. For questions about **installation or operation of your software**, contact us at:

> **Research & Education Association**
> **Phone: (732) 819-8880 (9 a.m. to 5 p.m. ET, Monday–Friday)**
> **Fax: (732) 819-8808**
> **Website: *www.rea.com***
> **E-mail: info@rea.com**

Note to Windows XP Users: In order for the TestWare® to function properly, please install and run the application under the same computer administrator-level user account. Installing the TestWare® as one user and running it as another could cause file-access path conflicts.